INTERNATIONAL INTELLECTUAL PROPERTY AND
THE COMMON LAW WORLD

International Intellectual Property and the Common Law World

Edited by
CHARLES E. F. RICKETT
and
GRAEME W. AUSTIN
The University of Auckland, New Zealand

·HART·
PUBLISHING
OXFORD – PORTLAND OREGON
2000

Hart Publishing
Oxford and Portland, Oregon

Published in North America (US and Canada) by
Hart Publishing c/o
International Specialized Book Services
5804 NE Hassalo Street
Portland, Oregon
97213-3644
USA

Distributed in the Netherlands, Belgium and Luxembourg by
Intersentia, Churchillaan 108
B2900 Schoten
Antwerpen
Belgium

Hart Publishing Ltd is a specialist legal publisher based in Oxford, England.
To order further copies of this book or to request a list of other
publications please write to:

Hart Publishing Ltd, Salter's Boatyard,
Folly Bridge, Abingdon Road, Oxford OX1 4LB
Telephone: +44 (0)1865 245533 or Fax: +44 (0)1865 794882
e-mail: mail@hartpub.co.uk
www.hartpub.co.uk

British Library Cataloguing in Publication Data
Data Available
ISBN 1 84113–179–2 (paper)

Typeset by Hope Services (Abingdon) Ltd.
Printed in Great Britain on acid-free paper
by Biddles Ltd, Guildford and King's Lynn.

Preface

In July 1999 the Research Centre for Business Law at The University of Auckland convened a two-day conference to examine a range of topics under the title of the present book. The Conference attracted a strong field of international experts, and resulted in the presentation of a range of papers of very high quality. Those papers, reworked by their authors after the Conference, form the contents of this volume.

We, and the Research Centre, are very grateful to the essayists. Each essayist approached their task with enthusiasm, skill and scholarship. The volume is testimony to the intellectual capacity, foresight and experience of some of the common law world's leading intellectual property lawyers. It also contains considerable material of interest for those who work in this exciting, challenging and important area. As Justice Gummow says in his introductory chapter, "[t]here is a need to increase an awareness in all branches of the profession, both of the basics of the subject and of its immediate 'cutting edge'". Our conviction is that this collection will aid that task.

We express our gratitude also to Richard Hart for his willingness to undertake this volume's publication, and for his understanding and patience. Further, we are indebted to Rachel Carnachan, generously sponsored by Chapman Tripp Sheffield Young, for her invaluable research assistance in the preparation of this volume.

The Research Centre for Business Law, in convening an international conference of the quality witnessed to by the contents of this book, depends in large measure upon the willingness of sponsors to be involved. The July 1999 Conference was most generously supported by a number of organisations. First, the primary sponsor was the merchant banking firm of Fay, Richwhite & Co. This was the third of the Centre's conferences to be sponsored by Fay, Richwhite, and the Centre once again expresses its sincere appreciation. Secondly, the New Zealand Law Foundation supported the attendance of several law students from the various New Zealand law schools. Thirdly, the Ministry of Commerce, which is the government department responsible for administering New Zealand's intellectual property law statutes, generously sponsored a session. Fourthly, but by no means least, many of New Zealand's national law firms sponsored sessions and provided speakers to comment on the main papers. These firms were A.J. Park & Son, Baldwin Shelston Waters, Bell Gully, Buddle Findlay, Chapman Tripp, James & Wells, Rudd Watts & Stone, and Simpson Grierson. The financial commitment of these organisations made possible the Conference which generated this volume of papers. The authors of those papers also benefited from the lively contributions of participants at the Conference, which was as it should be.

CHARLES E F RICKETT
GRAEME W AUSTIN

The University of Auckland
Auckland Anniversary Day
31 January 2000

Contents

Contributors

The Hon Justice W.M.C. Gummow, AC, Justice of the High Court of Australia

Marci A. Hamilton, Distinguished Visiting Professor of Law, Emory University School of Law

Brian Fitzgerald, Associate Professor and Head of the School of Law, Southern Cross University

Louise Longdin, Senior Lecturer in Commercial Law, The University of Auckland

Graeme W. Austin, Senior Solicitor, Chapman Tripp, New Zealand

Sam Ricketson, Sir Keith Aicken Professor of Law, Monash University

John Robinson Thomas, Associate Professor of Law, George Washington University

John Smillie, Professor of Law, University of Otago

The Hon Sir Nicholas Pumfrey, Judge of the Chancery Division of the High Court of England and Wales

John N. Adams, Professor of Intellectual Property, University of Sheffield

Susy Frankel, Senior Lecturer in Law, Victoria University of Wellington

Ian Eagles, Professor of Commercial Law, The University of Auckland

Table of Cases

1

International Intellectual Property Law and the Common Law World— Introduction

THE HON JUSTICE W.M.C. GUMMOW

It is always a pleasure to speak and to write about intellectual property. I found it such, and so, I think, by and large, did the students during the 20 years or so over which I taught a course in the subject. For some reason, never clearly apparent, intellectual property intrigued even the slothful student. It is a subject which engages the imagination.

Part of the appeal of the subject is the opportunity it provides for stumbling upon the unexpected. In her paper, which is Chapter 4, dealing with copyright infringement and the on-line service provider, Louise Longdin points to the tendency in the common law countries to tuck the works they protect by copyright "into idiosyncratic legislative nooks and crannies". The history of the copyright protection in the United Kingdom for "Peter Pan" is an example. Thirty years ago, dealings in that copyright produced the litigation between the Board of Governors of the Hospital for Sick Children and Walt Disney Productions, Inc.[1] Special protection is now made for the rights of the Hospital for Sick Children of Great Ormond Street, London, by section 301 of and Schedule 6 to the Copyright, Designs and Patents Act 1988 (UK). This is so notwithstanding the expiration of copyright in the work in 1987, 50 years after the death of Sir James Barrie. How was this legislative nook and cranny created? The answer has been given as follows by Lord Wyatt of Weedon.[2] In the entry for his journal for Thursday, 10 March 1988, there appears the following:

> In the Lords this afternoon a very English little debate on an amendment of Jim Callaghan's.[3] To make the copyright of Peter Pan extend indefinitely, it having run out at the end of 1987, for the benefit of the Great Ormond Street Children's Hospital who have been receiving the royalties up till now. Callaghan is a nice man at heart and his wife[4] has something to do with the Hospital.

---

[1] [1968] Ch 52.
[2] *The Journals of Woodrow Wyatt* (S. Curtis ed) (London, Macmillan, 1998), i, 513.
[3] Lord Callaghan, the former Prime Minister.
[4] Lady Callaghan was Chairman of the Board of Governors of the Hospital.

The scope and potential of the subject of intellectual property is made the more attractive by its international dimension. That point is emphasised in the papers in this collection. They represent the efforts of lawyers who come from across the common law world. Those involved in the subject, whether as teachers, practitioners or judges, have a lot in common. But there are differences to which one should not be blind.

At least to an outside observer, the United Kingdom, by its membership of the European Union, is a party to what appears to be a nascent federal system. That the word "federal" is discouraged by some political circles in the United Kingdom is attributed largely, one might think, to a misunderstanding as to its meaning in federations such as the United States, Canada and Australia. In Britain, "federalism" and, in particular, the phrase "a federal Europe" appear to suggest a concentration of power in supranational institutions. The more accurate use of "federalism" is to identify a system for the distribution of legislative, executive and judicial power between the political entities making up the federal structure.

As I have indicated, the United States, Canada and Australia undoubtedly have a federal system. Intellectual property legislation is federal, enacted by federal legislatures with specific and limited heads of power. For example, in Australia, the question has arisen whether the Plant Variety Rights Act 1987 (Cth) and the Plant Breeder's Rights Act 1994 (Cth) are to be supported as laws with respect to "patents of inventions" within the meaning of section 51(xviii) of the Constitution, which confers legislative power on the Commonwealth Parliament with respect to "[c]opyrights, patents of inventions and designs, and trademarks". This question is presently under reservation in the High Court.[5] Article I, section 8, clause 8 of the United States Constitution empowers the Congress to legislate "[t]o promote the Progress of Science and useful Arts, by securing for limited Times to . . . Inventors the exclusive Right to their respective . . . Discoveries". The validity of the United States plant variety legislation appears to have been assumed, the litigation turning upon issues of construction. In what must have been one of his last significant judgments, in *Imazio Nursery, Inc.* v. *Dania Greenhouses*,[6] Judge Rich explained that the present United States plant patent legislation had matured from legislative proposals first before the Congress more a century ago.[7] In their essays, which appear respectively as Chapters 7 and 8, John Thomas and John Smillie discuss the current state in the United States, New Zealand and Australia of what they rightly identify as the traditional debate whether there can be a valid claim for a method of medical treatment. In Australia, at least, the debate has turned upon the construction of particular legislation reflecting the terms of the Jacobean statute. However, I suspect that in the United States and Australia there is lurking,

---

[5] *The Grain Pool of Western Australia* v. *The Commonwealth of Australia*, judgment has now been delivered and is reported (2000) 170 ALR 111. The statutes were held valid.

[6] 69 F 3d 1560 (Fed. Cir. 1995).

[7] *Ibid.*, 1562–3.

beneath the questions of interpretation, constitutional issues as to the scope of the relevant legislative power.

A significant issue in federal systems is the place of the economic torts (and confidential information in contractual rights, including those involved in franchising arrangements), which often are significant elements in intellectual property disputes. In Australia and the United States, but not in Canada, these "common law" aspects are drawn into the federal courts. However, in an important respect, the law in Australia differs from that in the United States. In Australia, as in the United Kingdom and New Zealand—a fundamental point in Susy Frankel's essay (Chapter 11)—the common law does not entertain actions for "unfair competition". Rather, various balances between competing claims and policies are struck in particular causes of action, or left to legislative regimes.

Other problems may arise in federal systems. There has been little, if any, consideration in Australia[8] of the "pre-emption" doctrine. This United States doctrine fixes upon federal statutes to restrict development in the several States of their common law respecting unfair competition.[9] Again, as Marci Hamilton points out in Chapter 2, when dealing with database protection, the power of the Congress to stretch the reach of the copyright law is constrained by the First Amendment. The same may be true of "anti-dilution" legislation which has the effect of conferring property rights in words, symbols and images which have worked their way into the popular culture, thrust there, as Judge Kozinski has put it, "by well-orchestrated campaigns intended to burn them into our collective consciousness".[10] Even in Australia, where there is no equivalent of the First Amendment, the federal power to legislate with respect to trade marks has been construed by the High Court in *Davis* v. *The Commonwealth*[11] as not permitting the registration as trade marks of common words and expressions which have no capacity to distinguish the activities of the registered proprietor or those promoted by it.

Such considerations do not appear in a constitutional setting in other jurisdictions, but as is exemplified by Sam Ricketson's treatment of trade mark dilution (Chapter 6), fundamental and conflicting questions of policy arise at the legislative level and, given legislative indeterminacy, for the courts in deciding particular cases. Part of the difficulty in this field is in locating any clear and authoritative determination of what is involved in the notion of "dilution". Nevertheless, the points made by Marci Hamilton in her paper have a general importance for the whole subject. Perhaps, in the past, the courts too readily have attempted to skim across complicated surfaces by the use of such adages as "taking a free ride" and "reaping without sowing".

---

[8] See *Perre* v. *Apand Pty. Ltd* (1999) 73 ALJR 1190, 1223–4.

[9] There is an incisive discussion of principle in the dissenting judgment of Judge Kozinski in *White* v. *Samsung Electronics America, Inc.*, 989 F 2d 1512, 1517–9 (9th Cir. 1993).

[10] "Trademarks Unplugged" (1993) 68 *NY Univ L Rev* 960, 975.

[11] (1988) 166 CLR 79, 96–7.

The exclusive rights (to avoid the perhaps perjorative term "monopoly") given by statute under the various intellectual property regimes provide the occasion for what anti-trust and competition lawyers would stigmatise as abuse of market power and engagement in other offensive activities. The proper accommodation between the strong interests and values involved will be a matter for continuing controversy. I doubt if intellectual property can or should be kept safe from competition lawyers. In that regard, Chapter 12, provided by Ian Eagles, is a cautionary reminder of what can happen as judges and legislators create new rights and appear to push outwards the limits of intellectual property protection. There may be cause for apprehension in the author's spectre of a well-funded army of intellectual property lobbyists who are "conjured into being by the market's discovery that these shadowy intangibles have become the mainsprings of investment and profit in any modern economy worthy of the name". A striking case in point is the conflict presently seen in Australia between those seeking legislative expansion of copyright protection in respect of new forms of technological use, and the educational institutions, who complain of the resultant pressure upon their limited funding to provide information needed for the pursuit of their scholastic tasks.

Ian Eagles also makes the valuable point that, whilst both intellectual property law and competition law have as one of their ultimate goals the pursuit of alleged economic efficiency, this has not always been the only goal of anti-trust law. He points out that the development in the United States of anti-trust legislation just a century ago had populist as well as economic roots and that it is to the former that the law periodically tries to return.

The impact of requirements emanating from the European Union upon the intellectual property statute law of the United Kingdom has been enormous. One recent example is the "anti-dilution" provision in section 10 of the Trade Marks Act 1994 (UK).[12] Another, referred to by Marci Hamilton in Chapter 2, is the implemention by the United Kingdom[13] of the European Union's Database Directive of 1996. Hamilton perceives the European initiative as the product of the efforts of database lobbyists who acted with an eye to building up a momentum from Europe which would carry forward into legislation by the United States Congress.

One consequence of the United Kingdom's membership of the European Union is that the days are gone when, for Australians, the patents legislation of 1949 in the United Kingdom and of 1952 in Australia had a fairly close affinity, as did the respective trade mark legislation of 1938 and 1955. We in Australia more or less have had to make our own way since the changes made to the Designs Act 1906 (Cth) by the Designs Act 1967 (Cth) and the Designs Act 1968

[12] See H. Carty, "Dilution and Passing Off: Cause for Concern" (1996) 112 *LQR* 632, 657–60; T. Martino, *Trade Mark Dilution* (Oxford, OUP, 1996), chap. 12.
[13] The Copyright and Rights in Databases Regulations 1997, SI No 3032 of 1997. See also D. Vaver, "Copyright in Europe: The Good, The Bad and The Harmonised" (1999) 10 *AIPJ* 185, 187–8.

(Cth). The distance which now obtains between the legislation of the two countries is further emphasised by the discussion in Chapter 9, provided by Sir Nicholas Pumfrey, of the protection of designs in the United Kingdom under the Copyright, Designs and Patents Act 1988 (UK). Further, as the author emphasises, the recent Community harmonisation directive[14] turns upon yet another definition of "design".

The essays of Graeme Austin (Chapter 5) and of John Adams (Chapter10) deal with issues of jurisdiction in choice of law in intellectual property disputes. This is a matter of first importance. The traditional view respecting the territorial nature of intellectual property rights influenced the judgments in the High Court of Australia in *Potter* v. *The Broken Hill Pty. Co Ltd.*[15] It was of great significance in applying the "double actionability" rule associated with the decision in *Phillips* v. *Eyre*,[16] notwithstanding that that case was concerned with common law actions in tort, not the enforcement of statutory regimes with respect to patents for inventions. The doctrinal questions involved were to an extent considered by Fullagar J in a threats case, *Norbert Steinhardt and Son Ltd.* v. *Meth.*[17] Recently, in *Pearce* v. *Ove Arup Partnership Ltd.*,[18] the English Court of Appeal held that the English courts had jurisdiction to entertain an action for infringement of copyright subsisting under Dutch law. This appears to have been by virtue of Articles 2 and 6 of the Brussels Convention. It also was said that, if the alleged facts had occurred in England, the English courts would have given a remedy. It may be that this decision is to be understood against the background of what I have described earlier as the nascent federalism which is developing from the structure of the European Union.

Developments in technology cut across the national character of intellectual property rights and the limited reach in national courts. Two decisions, one of the Supreme Court of New South Wales and one of the New Zealand High Court, make the point. In *Macquarie Bank Ltd.* v. *Berg*,[19] Simpson J dismissed an *ex parte* application for an interlocutory injunction restraining the further publication on an Internet site of material allegedly defamatory of the plaintiffs. The application proceeded on the footing that the defendant was not then to be found in New South Wales and that any acts done by him resulting in publication of the material in that State were done from outside the State, probably from the United States of America. The order sought was limited to publication or dissemination within New South Wales but, her Honour pointed out, such a limitation would be ineffective. There appeared to be no means by which material, once published on the Internet, could be excluded from transmission to or receipt in any geographical area.

---

[14] Design Directive 98/71/EC.
[15] (1906) 3 CLR 479.
[16] (1870) LR 6 QB 1.
[17] (1961) 105 CLR 440.
[18] [1999] 1 All ER 769.
[19] [1999] NSWSC 526 (2 June 1999).

On the other hand, in *New Zealand Post Ltd.* v. *Leng*,[20] Williams J granted an interlocutory mandatory injunction requiring the defendant, a New Zealand resident, forthwith to delete from any Internet service or site any domain name over which he had the power of amendment the words "NZ Post" or any similar name.[21] His Honour referred to cases in the United States[22] and the United Kingdom[23] dealing with similar issues respecting the Internet.

Developments in technology have a significant impact upon the body of law which may be identified as intellectual property. In Australia, the Circuit Layouts Act 1989 (Cth) provides a new species of intellectual property, bringing with it new questions of overlap with other legislative regimes.[24] It is too late now to do the same for computer programs. But to push subject-matter which is both functional and ephemeral into formulations of literary work continues to present considerable problems of statutory interpretation. A recent example is the litigation which reached the High Court of Australia in *Data Access Corporation* v. *Powerflex Services Pty. Ltd.*[25]

The papers in this collection include a treatment of sales, licences and consumer protection as regards computer software. Brian Fitzgerald's paper (Chapter 3) indicates that this is a subject of some importance. And it attracts great controversy. It is a matter of interest that in April 1999 the National Conference of Commissioners on Uniform State Laws in the American Law Institute reversed a proposal to promulgate Article 2B of the Uniform Commercial Code which would deal with legal rules for computer information transactions. What now is proposed is the adoption by the several States of a Uniform Computer Information Transaction Act. The course of events in the United States demonstrates the conflicting and powerful economic interests that are in play in this area.

Intellectual property law, statutory and decisional, moves fast. When I ceased teaching the subject, few of the prescribed cases had been on the list when I had begun teaching it 20 years before. Such is the economic importance of the issues that arise that more disputes are reaching the ultimate courts of appeal. There is a need to increase an awareness in all branches of the profession, both of the basics of the subject and of its immediate "cutting edge". A reader with this in mind has much profit to derive from studying the papers reproduced in the chapters that follow.

---

[20] [1999] 3 NZLR 219.
[21] *Ibid.*, 232 (see order 2).
[22] *Panavision International, LP* v. *Toeppen*, 141 F 3d 1316 (9th Cir. 1998).
[23] *British Telecommunications plc v. One in a Million Ltd* [1999] FSR 1 (CA).
[24] *Avel Pty. Ltd* v. *Wells* (1992) 36 FCR 340.
[25] (1999) 73 ALJR 1435.

Part 1

Intellectual Property and the Information Society

One of the foundation stones of the information society, the law of copyright turns creative endeavour into vendible products. Each of the Chapters in this Part explores some of the key questions that the law of copyright seeks to answer: which materials of culture should become property?; who should own them?; and what should the incidents of this property be?

In the common law tradition, copyright's principal purpose is considered to be its incentive function. Societies seek to encourage creativity by rewarding it with property rights. Societies are not, it is assumed, peopled with Johnsonian "blockheads" who would be content to write for free.

Conceived of in this way, a copyright system requires societies to engage with a series of difficult policy decisions aimed at ensuring that potential authors are provided with sufficient encouragement to create without overly burdening others who may wish to make use of copyright works. Every decision about the characteristics of copyright law is also a decision about the nature and scope of the "public domain", the counterpoint to copyright protection.

As the technological context and societal values change, societies must struggle to ensure that there is an appropriate balance between copyright and the public domain. Each of the Chapters in this Part is concerned with this issue. Focussing on the issue of database protection, Marci Hamilton asks whether data, key building blocks for creative endeavour, ought to become property. Brian Fitzgerald's and Louise Longdin's Chapters engage with the changing technological context. Fitzgerald considers whether the values of the copyright system, particularly those that protect the public domain, ought to continue to inform the shape of information policy in an era of increasing privatisation of the materials of culture. Focusing on the position of on-line service providers, Longdin engages the issue of who should be liable for the potentially massive copyright infringement facilitated by the Internet. One of the many issues distilled by the Internet is that of determining which nation's laws ought to govern copyright infringement, now that copyright materials may be made to flow across domestic borders at the click of a mouse. This is the subject of Graeme Austin's Chapter, which discusses some of the private international law issues that the Internet distills.

2

Database Protection and the Circuitous Route Around the United States Constitution

I INTRODUCTION

The database industry, or the information collection industry, always has been with us. The Ten Commandments themselves are a collection of information. More recently, there have been telephone books, mailing lists and subscriber lists. But never before has there been a self-identified, well-heeled database industry seeking legal protection for its investment.

The difference, of course, is the computer. The computer has made it possible to gather, store, and disseminate vast amounts of information in small amounts of time through relatively little expenditure of human capital. Computers also have made it significantly easier to copy such collections in little time and with little effort. As collections of information have proliferated and become more sophisticated and the recipients have been able to connect to such information through their own computers, data collection has been transformed into a respectable and profitable database industry.[1]

* This chapter is based on a speech delivered at the 1999 Fay, Richwhite Conference, *International Intellectual Property and the Common Law World*, Auckland, New Zealand, 15 July 1999. Thanks go to Professor Charles Rickett of The University of Auckland for inviting me to participate and to the attendees of that conference for their insightful feedback. Thanks go also to Rochelle Dreyfuss for her helpful comments, and to Jennifer Davis, Doug Landon, Willard Knox, and Arti Tandon, Benjamin N. Cardozo School of Law, for their first-rate research assistance.

[1] See L. Jacobson, "Dueling Over Data", *Nat'l J*, 10 January 1998, at 64 ("Warren Publishing joined the Coalition Against Database Piracy ('CADP'), a group of information sellers that wants stronger laws protecting database collection, which the industry says is worth at least $28 billion worldwide and growing at a pace of about 4 per cent a year"): see also J.F. Hayden, "Copyright Protection of Computer Databases After *Feist*" (1991) 5 *Harv J L & Tech* 215, 215: "[t]he increased sophistication of computer databases has made them invaluable tools for a range of uses. At the same time unprecedented advances in computer technology have helped to spur growth in the computer information industry. As computers have become more powerful, they have also become more affordable. As a result, systems previously found only in research labs are now standard fixtures in offices and homes. Increased accessibility has created vast numbers of users demanding additional products and services, and this has been a further push for expansion in the computer information industry as a whole. Databases now assume vital importance in virtually every segment of the

There are always two ramifications when a new industry appears on the horizon: (i) it can now afford the costs of lobbying for government protection, and (ii) it can justify such protection on the ground of its contribution to the economy. Both of these factors have played into the push for database legislation around the world. The industry has turned to legislatures around the world to protect its investment from free riders and others.

There is another economic factor that has contributed to the drive to create database legal protection. That is the increasing presence of multinational corporations. No longer do we have domestic intellectual property industries pushing for protection only in their home countries, a state of affairs that dominated as recently as a decade ago. The information era, combined with the growing global economy, has encouraged the creation of multinational corporations that naturally look to various legislative bodies around the world simultaneously. The database industry, though largely based in the United States,[2] lobbied for database legislation first in the European Union, and succeeded.[3] Such a move was legally well-informed, because the United States Constitution places formidable barriers in the way of database protection.

In section II, I describe the state of the law on database protection in the United States that made the US a less desirable location to initiate database legislation in the first instance. In section III, I describe the European Union's Database Directive, its counterpart in Britain and a database proposal by the World Intellectual Property Organisation, which operates to harmonise intellectual property law. In section IV, I describe proposed database legislation in the United States. In section V, I discuss how the United States Constitution, including the enumerated powers doctrine and the First Amendment, are likely to shape whatever database protection eventually is provided in the United States and around the world.

---

economy." See also Brief of the Information Industry Ass'n and ADAPSO, The Computer and Software Services Industry Ass'n, Inc. As Amici Curiae In Support Of Neither Party at n.17, *Feist Publications, Inc.* v. *Rural Telephone Service Co.*, 499 US 340 (1991) (No 89–1909): "[a] recent federal government survey reports revenues of the electronic information service industry are expected to grow about 20 percent during 1990 to $9 billion. Revenues are expected to reach $19.2 billion over the next four years. U.S. Department of Commerce, 1990 Industrial Outlook, 29–3 (1990)."

[2] See *Hearing on HR 354, the Collections of Information Antipiracy Act Before the House Judiciary Subcomm. on the Courts and Intellectual Property*, 106th Cong. (1999) (testimony of Marilyn Winokur, Executive Vice President of Micromedex, on behalf of Micromedex and the Coalition Against Database Piracy) (stating that "the United States is the world leader in the creation and distribution of informational databases" and that "U.S. databases provide the world with information on everything from antidotes to poison, to prescription drugs, to the keys to building safer cars, to comprehensive compilations of patents and related information"), available in 1999 WL 156183 (FDCH); see also *Report of the Register of Copyrights, US Copyright Office, Report on Legal Protection for Databases* (1997), 19–28 (discussing database industry practices).

[3] See Directive 96/9/EC of the European Parliament and of the Council of 11 March 1996 on the Legal Protection of Databases [1996] OJ L77 20.

II DATABASE PROTECTION IN THE UNITED STATES

Aspects of databases have been eligible for protection on a variety of legal theories in the United States. First, the selection and arrangement of the data are eligible for copyright protection if they are original.[4] Secondly, various State laws provide protection against unfair competition or common law misappropriation.[5] Thirdly, a database creator can employ contracts to create protection.[6] Fourthly, there is self-help. Technological fences can be built around the database to keep out interlopers.[7] The Digital Millennium Copyright Act proscribes manufacturing or selling devices that would circumvent such self-help measures.[8]

Despite these legal protections for collections of information, facts, except those covered by trade secret agreements,[9] have belonged to the public domain. In a landmark constitutional and copyright decision in 1991, the United States Supreme Court determined that copyright protection for databases may extend to original arrangement and selection of information but may not extend to the information itself. That decision is the now-famous *Feist Publications, Inc.* v. *Rural Telephone Service Co.*[10] The Court reasoned that the Copyright Clause

---

[4] See Copyright Act 1976, 17 USC § 103 (1994) (discussing protection of compilations); *ibid.*, § 101 (defining "compilation" as a "work formed by the collection and assembling of preexisting materials or of data that are selected, coordinated, or arranged in such a way that the resulting work as a whole constitutes an original work of authorship").

[5] See *International News Serv.* v. *Associated Press*, 248 US 215 (1918).

[6] See *ProCD, Inc.* v. *Zeidenberg*, 86 F 3d 1447, 1453–5 (7th Cir. 1996); *National Car Rental Sys., Inc.* v. *Computer Assoc's. Int'l, Inc.*, 991 F 2d 426, 433 (8th Cir. 1993); *Bennett* v. *Computer Assocs. Int'l, Inc.*, 932 SW 2d 197 (Tex. 1996); *Ross* v. *Briggs & Morgan*, 540 NW 2d 843 (Minn. 1995); *State* v. *Corcoran*, 522 NW 2d 226 (Wis. 1994).

[7] See P. Wayner, *Digital Copyright Protection* (Boston, Mass., AP Professional, 1997) (discussing "some techniques that can make life more complicated for copyright infringers" because "there is no absolute way to prevent people from copying the digital versions of your text, your music, your movie, or your data"). Such mechanisms include encryption, which requires special software to display the information on the screen, and tagging, which allows for illicit copies to be returned to their original owners because of an embedded identification "tag". See *ibid.*, 1–2. CD-ROMs, text boxes, special tape decks, satellite television, and cable television are means of distributing encrypted data in an inexpensive fashion but only to those who have the "unlocking key". See *ibid.*, 2–3. See also S. Schutt, *Understanding Network Management Strategies and Solutions* (Blue Ridge Summit, Pa., BbWindcresta/McGraw-Hill, 1993), 56–8 (discussing the public-key encryption system known as the Data Encryption Standard (DES) developed by IBM and the National Institute of Standards and Technology (NIST), the private-key encryption system known as the Kerberos system developed at MIT, the message authentication code (MAC), callback modems, and the US Government's use of C2 security and DES encryption chips).

[8] See Digital Millennium Copyright Act 1998, 17 USC § 1201(a)(2) (stating that "[n]o person shall manufacture, import, offer to the public, provide or otherwise traffic in any technology, product, service, device, component, or part thereof, that—(A) is primarily designed or produced for the purpose of circumventing a technological measure that effectively controls access to a work protected under this title").

[9] See *Bonito Boats, Inc.* v. *Thunder Craft Boats, Inc.*, 489 US 141, 154–7 (1989); W. Patry, "The Enumerated Powers Doctrine and Intellectual Property: An Imminent Constitutional Collision" (1999) 67 *Geo Wash L Rev* 359, 394.

[10] 499 US 340 (1991).

of the United States Constitution *prohibits* Congress from creating property rights in information.[11]

A The *Feist* Decision

The *Feist* decision's constitutional parameters were unexpected in the United States copyright community.[12] To that point, Congress and copyright practitioners were accustomed to thinking of copyright as a legal universe circumscribed exclusively by the federal Copyright Acts.[13] To answer the question posed in the case—whether the white pages in a telephone book are copyrightable—the Court could have limited its decision to one interpreting the Copyright Act of 1976.[14] The Court, however, reached out to decide the case on constitutional grounds.

To understand the *Feist* decision, it is necessary to provide a brief explanation of the Constitution's structure and Congress's powers. Under the Constitution, Congress is limited to the exercise of its enumerated powers in Article I and various amendments to the Constitution.[15] Thus, if Congress is to have any power over information, it must be located in a particular power listed in the Constitution. The Copyright Clause states:[16]

> The Congress shall have power . . . to promote the progress of science and useful arts, by securing for limited times to authors and inventors the exclusive right to their respective writings and discoveries.

Speaking unanimously, the United States Supreme Court made it clear in *Feist* that the Copyright Clause gives Congress the power to grant copyright in original works of authorship but *prohibits* Congress from creating property rights in data and information. The Court read the Copyright Clause to mean that only works of "originality" are eligible for copyright protection.[17] Because data and information do not exhibit a mark of originality, they are categorically excluded from copyright protection.[18]

---

[11] US Constitution, Art. 1, § 8, cl. 8; see *Feist Publications, Inc.* v. *Rural Telephone Service Co.*, 499 US 340, 349–50, 358 (1991).

[12] See generally M.A. Hamilton, "Justice O'Connor's Intellectual Property Opinions: Currents and Crosscurrents" (1991) 13 *Women's Rights L Rep* 71.

[13] See Copyright Act 1976, 17 USC §§ 101–803 (1994); Copyright Act 1909, Pub L No 349, 35 Stat 1075 (repealed 1976).

[14] 17 USC § 101 (1994).

[15] See US Constitution, Art. 1, amendments I; XIII, § 2; XIV, § 5; XV, § 2; XVI (taxes); XIX; XX §§ 3, 4; XXIII; XXIV ("Congress shall have power to enforce [these] article[s] by appropriate legislation"); see also *Printz* v. *United States*, 521 US 898, 919 (1997) (stating that the Constitution conferred upon Congress "not all governmental powers, but only discrete, enumerated ones").

[16] US Constitution, Art. 1, § 8, cl. 8.

[17] See *Feist Publications, Inc.* v. *Rural Telephone Service Co.*, 499 US 340 (1991).

[18] *Ibid.*, 344–8; see also *Harper & Row, Publishers, Inc.* v. *Nation Enterprises*, 471 US 539, 556 (1985) ("[n]o author may copyright his ideas or the facts he narrates").

According to *Feist*, the mere act of independent creation of a work, a fact, or an idea is not sufficient to justify copyright protection under the Copyright Clause. The Court made clear in *Feist* that the "*sine qua non* of copyright is originality" and that the "originality" requirement is a two-part test:[19]

> To qualify for copyright protection, a work must be original to the author. *Harper &
> Row*, [471 U.S.] at 547–549. Original, as the term is used in copyright, means only that
> the work was independently created by the author (as opposed to copied from other
> works), *and* that it possesses at least some minimal degree of creativity.

The Court's reasoning rests on the belief that data, facts and ideas are "building blocks" necessary for the creation of new works.[20] When combined with those original works that have entered the public domain, authors and scientists have the raw materials to achieve the constitutional goal set by the Copyright Clause, to "promote the progress of science and useful arts" through the production of new works.[21] The Court thus tethered the Copyright Clause to the end of engendering a market place in expression and presumed that the raw materials for expression need to remain free.[22]

In sum, the Court interpreted the Copyright Clause to permit copyright in only those works which are original and to prohibit copyright in that which lacks originality. The two requirements mutually presuppose each other. If Congress were to attempt to provide property protection for information under the Copyright Clause, it would violate the Clause's prohibition on such protection.[23] It may also violate the First Amendment.[24]

B Data Protection versus Data Availability

While there had been lower courts that recognised protection for databases on the theory of "sweat-of-the-brow", in other words, protection afforded because

---

[19] *Ibid.*, 345 (emphasis added).

[20] See, for example, *Sheldon* v. *Metro-Goldwyn Pictures Corp.*, 81 F 2d 49, 54 (2nd Cir. 1936); see also R.A. Gorman, "Fact or Fancy? The Implications for Copyright" (1982) 29 J *Copyright Soc'y* 566; L.A. Kurtz, "Speaking to the Ghost: Idea and Expression in Copyright" (1992) 47 U *Miami L Rev* 1221.

[21] See *Harper & Row, Publishers, Inc.* v. *Nation Enterprises*, 471 US 539, 548 (1985) ("copyright does not prevent subsequent users from copying from a prior author's work those constituent elements that are not original . . . [including] works, facts, or materials in the public domain").

[22] Other elements of the Copyright Clause contribute to the generation of a vital market place of expression of well. The Clause limits protection for copyrightable works to "limited times". The *Feist* decision, combined with the time limit on exclusive control, ensures a plentiful public domain from which new works will emerge and contribute to the "uninhibited, robust, and wide-open" market place of expression that is guarded by the First Amendment.

[23] The same reasoning, in the patent context, was employed in *Bonito Boats, Inc.* v. *Thunder Craft Boats, Inc.*, 489 US 141, 156–7 (1989) where the Court held that a State could not provide patent-like protection supplementing federal patent law, because the law, by indicating that which was to be protected, also implicitly indicated that which could not be protected and must be free.

[24] See nn. 102 and 118–21 below and accompanying text.

of the effort expended in assembling and maintaining the database,[25] the *Feist* Court explicitly rejected the notion that the Copyright Clause could protect mere effort.[26] Rather, the United States copyright system is product-centred. If the product is original, it is protected. If not, no amount of labour or investment behind it will justify copyright protection.[27]

Before the appearance of the database industry, there was a widespread assumption in the United States that facts and ideas were generally available for all to use. Newspapers were caches of information that could be mined by anyone for any purpose. Unless protected under contract, any information coming one's way was "fair game" for the recipient to use. Theories of free speech and copyright law were built on the presupposition that the "building blocks" of expression were available to all. Scientists had a right to mine whatever information was available. Librarians were charged with collecting information and disseminating it as widely as possible. Bits of history, information, facts and data were naturally born into the public domain.

As the earlier listing of database legal protection should have made clear, this vision of an endless stream of available information is somewhat unrealistic.[28] There were some legal restrictions that created barriers to information dissemination and use even before the database industry grew to its current status. But those protections were on the margins; they did not significantly or noticeably restrict access to the vast majority of useful information. By planting the background assumption that information must be available in a free society into its interpretation of Congress's powers under the Copyright Clause, the Supreme Court set high hurdles to enacting constitutional extra-copyright database legislation. Such legislation cannot unduly burden information availability, cannot assign a property right in such information, and cannot impede the development of the market place of expression. In short, it must be pro-competitive and narrowly tailored.

Thus, database protection in the United States started from two potentially conflicting positions: a nascent set of regulations to protect databases and an assumption that there is a positive social good in making information available. The database industry—including the news industry, the computer software

---

[25] The following courts adopted the "sweat-of-the-brow" standard: *Illinois Bell Tel. Co* v. *Haines & Co.*, 905 F 2d 1081, 1085 (7th Cir. 1990); *Hutchinson Tel. Co* v. *Fronteer Directory Co*, 770 F 2d 128, 131 (8th Cir. 1985); *Leon* v. *Pacific Tel. & Telegraph Co.*, 91 F 2d 484 (9th Cir. 1937); *Jeweler's Circular Publ'g Co.* v. *Keystone Publ'g Co*, 281 F 83 (2nd Cir. 1922). See also J. Ginsburg, "No 'Sweat'? Copyright and Other Protection of Works of Information After *Feist* v. *Rural Telephone*" (1992) 92 *Colum L Rev* 338; J Ginsburg, "Creation and Commercial Value: Copyright Protection of Works of Information" (1990) 90 *Colum L Rev* 1865, 1880–1.

[26] See *Feist Publications, Inc.* v. *Rural Telephone Service Co*, 499 US 340 359–60 (1991) (discussing that the purpose of the revisions in the Copyright Act 1976, was to ensure that "sweat-of-the-brow" alone was not sufficient to create copyright protection).

[27] See generally, M.A. Hamilton, "The Historical and Philosophical Origins of the Copyright Clause" (forthcoming) *Cardozo Occasional Papers* (1999) No. 4.

[28] See nn.1–2 above and accompanying text.

industry and the stock price information industry[29]—has consciously pursued expansion of the former. Following them, in heated disagreement, have been groups including scientists, librarians and constitutional law scholars seeking to protect the latter.[30] The database industry understood its needs before the opposition was organised. As a result, database legislation was prompted by the industry and the early versions primarily reflected its priorities. As the debate over database protection matures, however, the view from the other side is being injected slowly. In the end, the debate at both the international and national levels is over where to draw the line between producers and users of databases. As usual, the devil is in the details.

III THE EUROPEAN UNION DATABASE DIRECTIVE, THE UNITED KINGDOM
DATABASE IMPLEMENTATION, AND THE 1996 WIPO PROPOSAL

Database protection for aspects beyond the original selection and analysis of the data was born in the European Union in 1996.[31] The UK followed suit soon thereafter.[32] The World Intellectual Property Organisation, which attempts to harmonise intellectual property laws, also expressed interest in the issue at about the same time.[33]

[29] Computer software creators look upon database protection as an opportunity to gain proprietary control over not only the computer programs they sell but also the information that is loaded onto those programs.

[30] See *Hearing on HR 354, the Collections of Information Antipiracy Act Before the House Judiciary Subcomm. on the Courts and Intellectual Property*, 106th Cong. (1999) (testimony of Joshua Lederberg, President-emeritus, Rockefeller University, on behalf of the National Academy of Sciences, National Academy of Engineers, Institute of Medicine, and American Association for the Advancement of Sciences; Charles Phelps, Provost, University of Rochester, on behalf of the Association of American Universities, American Council on Education, and National Association of State Universities and Land-Grant Colleges; James G. Neal, Dean, University Libraries, Johns Hopkins University, on behalf of the American Association of Law Libraries, American Library Association, Association of Research Libraries, Medical Library Association, and Special Libraries Association. See also Letter from Marci A. Hamilton, Professor of Law, Director, Intellectual Property Law Program, Benjamin N. Cardozo School of Law, to Honorable Orrin G. Hatch, Chairman, Committee on the Judiciary, United States Senate (4 September 1998) (stating that the Collections of Information Antipiracy Act (HR 2281, Title V) violates the United States Constitution) (available at <http://www.marcihamilton.com/ip/hatchdatabase.html>); *Consumer and Investor Access to Information Act of 1999: Hearing on HR 1858 Before the Subcomm. on Telecommunications, Trade, and Consumer Protection of the House Comm. on Commerce*, 106th Cong (1999) (statement of Andrew J. Pincus, General Counsel, US Dept. of Commerce) (available at <http://www.uspto.gov/web/offices/ dcom/olia/hr1858.htm>).

[31] Directive 96/9/EC of the European Parliament and of the Council of 11 March 1996 on the Legal Protection of Databases [1996] OJ L77/20 (hereafter "Database Directive").

[32] The Copyright and Rights in Databases Regulations 1997, SI 1997, No 3032.

[33] Basic Proposal for the Substantive Provisions of the Treaty on Intellectual Property in Respect of Databases, CRNR/DC/6, World Intellectual Property Organisation (WIPO) Preamble (30 August 1996).

A The European Union Database Directive

Database law first appeared in the European Union's Database Directive of 1996.[34] The Directive was enacted in response to complaints about free-riding and was shaped by the United States' Supreme Court's *Feist* parameters.

The Directive, like United States law, draws a line between copyright protection for databases and other protection. Like US law, the Directive limits copyright protection to the "selection or arrangement of [database] contents" resulting from "the author's own intellectual creation".[35] Also consistent with US law, the copyright protection of databases under the Directive does not "extend to their contents".[36]

The Directive does not leave database protection at copyright law, however. In its most important provisions, it institutes a system of *sui generis* database protection. Before moving to the details of the EU's database protection, I will focus briefly on the fact that the protection is termed *sui generis*. There are two important ramifications.

First, by making the protection *sui generis*, the Directive avoids the *Feist*-inspired debate over whether copyright should extend to facts or effort. The tension between information availability and database rights addressed through constitutional reasoning in *Feist*, exists at the heart of copyright regimes in other countries as well. The denomination *sui generis* also permits the EU members to enact legislation without having to delve into the theoretical bases and justifications of their individual copyright laws. The label is a sidestep, an important sidestep, around a set of thorny issues.

Secondly, there is an important legal result accruing from placing database protection outside the copyright parameter. Because the protection is not intellectual property protection, the Directive arguably is not controlled by the international intellectual property treaties. The Berne Convention requires national treatment: if a country provides intellectual property protection to its citizens, it must provide at least as strong protection for other nationals owning intellectual property products within its borders.[37] The EU's *sui generis* protection—

---

[34] See generally Database Directive, n. 31 above.

[35] *Ibid.*, Art. 3(1).

[36] *Ibid.*, Art. 3(2); see also M. Nimmer and P. Geller, *International Copyright Law and Practice* (New York, Matthew Bender, 1998) (discussing implementation of database provisions in foreign countries' laws).

[37] *Ibid.* The Universal Copyright Convention provides for national treatment by stating that "works of nationals of any Contracting State shall enjoy in each other Contracting State the same protection as that other State accords" to "works of its own nationals". See Universal Copyright Convention, 6 September 1952, 6 UST 2731, TIAS No 3324, 735 UNTS 368, revised 24 July 1971, Paris Text, Art. II, 25 UST 1341, TIAS No 7868. The Berne Convention also contains a provision providing protection to: "(a) authors who are nationals of one of the countries of the Union, for their works, whether published or not; (b) authors who are not nationals of one of the countries of the Union, for their work first published in one of those countries, or simultaneously in a country outside the Union and in a country of the Union": see Berne Convention for the Protection of Literary and Artistic Works, 9 September 1886, revised Paris, 24 July 1971, Art. 3(1), 25 UST 1341,

because it is not intellectual property protection—arguably is not governed by the Berne Convention's national treatment requirement. Therefore, the EU has attempted to enact database protection that treats foreign nationals less well than nationals. Under the Database Directive, the EU countries need not provide protection to those owning databases within their borders if their home country does not provide database protection.[38]

(i) Definition and Eligibility

Under the Directive, a "database" is a collection of "works, data, or other materials".[39] To receive protection, the database maker must prove two elements: substantial investment and substantial extraction or use by the second comer. First, a database "maker" is eligible for protection if he or she has made a "substantial investment in either the obtaining, verification or presentation of the contents" judged "qualitatively and/or quantitatively".[40] In other words, effort or monetary investment justifies protection. This is clearly a response to the *Feist* Court's rejection of effort as a sufficient basis for copyright protection of databases. Secondly, if the maker has made such a substantial investment, he may prevent extraction or use of the whole or a substantial part, "evaluated qualitatively and/or quantitatively".[41] Database makers, therefore may prohibit the use of only a portion of the database. The interpretation of "substantial part" will determine the extent to which the EU Directive will pave the way for the protection of bare or raw information.

(ii) User Liabilities and Rights

One who takes a "substantial part" of the database may be liable under the *sui generis* database protection.[42] All those using the database are not liable under the Directive. One may take "insubstantial parts" and may do whatever one wishes with the database unless the use conflicts "with normal exploitation" of the database or "unreasonably prejudice[s] the legitimate interests of the maker".[43] In laymen's terms, the database user may not harm the *business*

TIAS No 7868, 828 UNTS 221. Additionally, the WIPO Copyright Treaty has adopted a provision stating that "Contracting Parties shall apply *mutatis mutandis* the provisions of Arts. 2 to 6 of the Berne Convention in respect of the protection provided in this Treaty": see WIPO Copyright Treaty, adopted by the Diplomatic Conference on 20 December 1996, at Art. 3, reprinted in M.A. Leaffer (ed.), *International Treaties on Intellectual Property* (2nd edn., Washington, DC, Bureau of National Affairs, 1997).

[38] See Database Directive, n.31 above, Art. 11 (stating that the right shall apply to any "database whose makers or rightholders are nationals of a Member State or who have their habitual residence in the territory of the Community").

[39] *Ibid.*, Art. 1(2).

[40] *Ibid.*, Art. 7(1).

[41] *Ibid.*

[42] *Ibid.*, Arts. 7 and 8.

[43] *Ibid.*, Art. 8(1) and (2).

interests of the database maker. Beyond those interests, however, the user should have significant latitude. The scope of the user's rights will depend on the expansiveness of the Member States' interpretation of the database maker's business interests.

(iii) Term

The Database Directive sets a term limitation of 15 years from the January immediately following creation of the database.[44] By altering the database through additions, deletions, or alterations, however, the term limitation can be mooted. Whenever substantial changes are made, the resulting database is a *new* database for purposes of the term limit and the 15-year clock begins to tick anew.[45] Thus, any database that is regularly updated may well be eligible for perpetual protection.

B The United Kingdom's Implementation of the Database Directive

The UK implemented the Database Directive in 1997.[46] In line with the Directive, the UK distinguishes between copyright protection for database selection and arrangement of information and a "database right".[47] Mirroring US copyright law, and the Directive, copyright protection is accorded a database under the UK implementation statute if the "selection and arrangement" of the database are original.[48] In the spirit of US law and the Directive's general principles, the UK database right also permits use of a copyrighted database for the "purposes of research or private study".[49] Research or study "for a commercial purpose", though, is not protected against a copyright infringement suit by the database owner.[50] In addition, the UK database "right"—enacted pursuant to the Directive's *sui generis* database protection provisions—attaches to a database even if the database is not original.[51]

(i) Definition and Eligibility

The UK followed the Directive's definition of "database" verbatim.[52] It also has adopted the eligibility language from the Database Directive. The right subsists

[44] See Database Directive, n.31 above, Art. 10 (2).

[45] *Ibid.*, Art. 10 (3).

[46] The Copyright and Rights in Databases Regulations 1997, SI 1997, No 3032 (herein "SI 1997/303").

[47] *Ibid.*

[48] *Ibid.* Amendment of the Copyright, Designs and Patents Act 1988, s. 3A(2); see also Explanatory Note, para. 3.

[49] *Ibid.*, amendment at s. 8(2).

[50] *Ibid.*, amendment at s. 8(3).

[51] *Ibid.*, explanatory Note, para. 5.

[52] Compare SI 1997/3032, n. 46 above, s. 6 (defining "database" as a "collection of independent works, data, or other materials") with Database Directive, n. 31 above, Art. 1(2) (same).

in a database if there has been a "substantial investment" in "obtaining, verifying or presenting" the contents of the database.[53] The UK implementation does not, however, adopt the "qualitatively and/or quantitatively" modifiers of substantial investment. Thus, it leaves to the courts the determination of what is meant by "substantial".

(ii) User Liabilities and Rights

Like the Directive, the UK database right makes those who use all or a "substantial part" of a database liable.[54] There are some specific exceptions. Users not liable include researchers and teachers using the database for a noncommercial purpose.[55] The UK also added an interesting provision, which is essentially an innocent infringer's right: if it is not possible to identify the database's maker or it would be reasonable to conclude the term of protection has expired, the user is immune from liability.[56]

(iii) Term

The implementation borrows the term of protection prescribed in the Directive: 15 years.[57] It does not, unlike the Directive, state that additions transform an existing database into a new database for purposes of calculating the term.

C The 1996 WIPO Proposal: A First Step Toward Harmonisation

After the Database Directive was issued, WIPO held a meeting in December 1996 that addressed, among other items, the international harmonisation of database protection. No final agreement was reached on databases at that meeting, but a Basic Proposal was issued by the Committee of Experts.

The Proposal begins by emphasising the need to "strike a balance" between the database industry producers and the users of information.[58] It also draws a distinction between copyright protection for databases and other protection. Like the Database Directive, the WIPO Proposal distinguishes between databases demonstrating originality in selection and arrangement and those that are not original. It would provide protection for the original elements of the former

---

[53] See *Ibid.*, s. 13(1); Explanatory Note, para. 6(b).
[54] *Ibid.*, s. 16(1) and (2).
[55] *Ibid.*, s. 20.
[56] *Ibid.*, s. 21.
[57] *Ibid.*, s. 30; Explanatory Note, para. 6(e).
[58] See Basic Proposal for the Substantive Provisions of the Treaty on Intellectual Property in Respect of Databases, CRNR/DC/6, World Intellectual Property Organisation (WIPO), Preamble (30 August 1996) (herein "WIPO Proposal").

under copyright law, and for all other aspects of a database under a separate regime.[59]

(i) Definition and Eligibility

The WIPO definition of "database" is identical to the EU/UK definition, though the explanatory notes expand well beyond the original formulation.[60] According to the notes, a "database" includes "collections of literary, musical or audiovisual works or any other kind of works, or collections of other materials such as texts, sounds, images, numbers, facts, or data representing any other matter or substance [including] expressions of folklore".[61] Following the EU's lead, the WIPO Basic Proposal would provide database protection to those who have made a "substantial investment" in the formation of the database.[62]

(ii) User Liabilities and Rights

Database users are prohibited from extracting all or a substantial part of a database.[63] The WIPO Proposal leaves particular exceptions to this liability to the Member States adopting the treaty.[64] In the notes, however, the Proposal adopts the language of the EU Directive, stating that exceptions are appropriate only when they do not "conflict with normal exploitation of the database" or "unreasonably impair or prejudice the legitimate interests" of the database owner.[65]

(iii) Term

The WIPO Proposal does not set a definite term limit on database rights. The notes discuss the fact that the EU Directive chose a 15-year term and 1996 proposed US legislation proposed a 25-year term.[66] The WIPO Proposal leaves this issue to the Diplomatic Conference, and includes two alternatives: 15 years or 25 years.[67] The WIPO Proposal also adopts the EU Directive's device of permitting existing databases to become new databases through the introduction of new information, thereby opening the door to perpetual protection.[68]

---

[59] WIPO Proposal, n. 58 above, notes on Art. 1(1.04); Notes on Art. 2(2.07); cf. Art. 12 (stating that rights therein "shall be without prejudice to any other rights . . . in respect of copyright", among others).

[60] Compare *ibid.*, Art. 2 (defining "database" as a "collection of independent works, data, or other materials") with Database Directive, n. 31 above, Art. 1(2), and SI 1997/3032, n. 46 above, s. 6.

[61] See WIPO Proposal, n. 58 above, Art. 2.

[62] *Ibid.*, Art. 1(1); Notes on Art. 1(1.12).

[63] *Ibid.*, Art. 2(ii).

[64] *Ibid.*, Art. 5(1).

[65] *Ibid.*, Notes on Art. 5(5.01). Compare Database Directive, n. 31 above, Art. 8.2.

[66] *Ibid.*, Notes on Art. 1 (1.10).

[67] *Ibid.*, Art. 8; Notes on Art. 8 (8.03).

[68] *Ibid.*, Art. 8(3); Notes on Art. 8 (8.06).

D Summary

The EU, UK and WIPO database approaches share some interesting character-istics.[69] First, each takes as a given the United States Constitution's requirement announced in *Feist* that copyright in databases may extend only to original selection and arrangement of the information and not to the information itself.[70] This appears to be an attempt to avoid outright rejection of such a regime by the United States. Thus, the United States—and in this case the United States Constitution—appears to be the 800-pound gorilla in the intellectual property arena. But it is a gorilla intended to be circumvented.[71] The EU has led the enactment of such legislation. By enacting a Directive that does not provide for national treatment, it has challenged the US to follow suit or to fall behind in the market place. Thus, there is significant incentive for the US to find con-stitutional routes to such protection.

Secondly, each awards extra-copyright database rights only to those who make a "substantial investment" in the database, which means that the *raison d'être* for such protection is to reward effort. In other words, this appears to be a rather direct response to *Feist's* rejection of "sweat-of-the-brow" as a justifi-cation for copyright protection. It is an attempt to "fix" the situation for those who have invested in database creation. It is not a guaranteed reward. There is no entitlement to monetary or other return. Rather, it is a reward that makes it possible for the database producer to enter the market and attract customers with some assurance that others cannot free ride on his efforts.

Thirdly, each institutes a lengthy term of protection that is likely to be dis-proportionate to the needs of the industry. The vast majority of databases are time-sensitive.[72] The terms of protection proposed to date are shorter than the copyright term to be sure, but they are quite lengthy—15 to 25 years—in light of the fleeting market demand for many collections of information. The lengthy terms proposed have made it absolutely necessary to identify and accommodate important categories of fair users. The terms tip the scale so far in the direction of the producers that non-commercial, fair users need significant and explicit protections.

[69] Neither Australia nor New Zealand has enacted extra copyright protection for databases to date.

[70] See *Feist Publications, Inc.* v. *Rural Telephone Service Co*, 499 US 340, 344–8 (1991).

[71] See P. Samuelson, "The Copyright Grab", *Wired,* March 1997.

[72] See <http://www.newshare.com> (discussing service of providing time-sensitive information to publishers, broadcasters, and entrepreneurs from database); <http://www.complianceintl.com> (discussing possession of database that allows company to serve as an electronic provider of time-sensitive regulatory information); <http://www.mn-news.com> (using time-sensitive database to distribute newspapers and magazines).

IV   PROPOSED UNITED STATES DATABASE LEGISLATION

In May 1996, the first database protection bill in the United States was introduced in Congress.[73] It defined "database" as "a collection, assembly or compilation, in any form or medium now or later known or developed, of works, data or other materials, arranged in a systematic or methodical way".[74] The term was 25 years, ten years longer than the EU Directive.[75] That bill did not make it out of the Committee. At this stage, few beyond the database industry in the United States understood the impact of such legislation and therefore few objected, and the legislation was drafted heavily in their favour.

Since then, the proposals for database protection before Congress have proliferated. During the spring of 1999, Senator Orrin Hatch took the highly unusual step of entering three different legislative database proposals into the Senate record. Two were drafted by interest groups while the third was drafted as a middle ground by Senate staffers. He did not endorse any one, but stressed the necessity of curbing "database piracy".[76]

At the same time that the Senate has three proposals, the House of Representatives has two very different proposals. Representative Howard Coble has introduced HR 354, The Collections of Information Antipiracy Act of 1999,[77] and Representative Bliley has introduced HR 1858, The Consumer and Investor Access to Information Act of 1999.[78] The names alone indicate how disparate their approaches are. Because they mark the current ends of the spectrum of proposals before Congress right now, I will focus on them to describe the situation in the United States.

A   The Collections of Information Antipiracy Bill

The Collections of Information Antipiracy bill is pro-industry. The Act would protect not only the database owner's chosen market, but also any potential market.

---

[73] Database Investment and Intellectual Property Antipiracy Act of 1996, HR 3531, 104th Cong (1996) (herein "Database Investment bill").

[74] *Ibid.*, § 2.

[75] Compare WIPO Proposal, n. 58 above, Art. 10 (stating that the term of protection "shall expire fifteen years" from "the date of completion of the making of the database") with Database Investment bill, n. 73 above, § 6 (stating that the database shall remain protected "for a period of twenty-five years").

[76] See Database Piracy Legislation, 145 Cong Rec S31601 (19 January 1999) (statement of Senator Orrin Hatch), available in 1999 WL 21166 (Cong Rec).

[77] See Collections of Information Antipiracy Act, HR 354, 106th Cong (1999) (herein "Antipiracy bill").

[78] See Consumer and Investor Access to Information Act, HR 1858, 106th Cong (1999) (herein "Consumer Access bill").

(i) Definition and Eligibility

The Antipiracy bill would cover a wide variety of information, including "facts, data, works of authorship, or any other intangible material capable of being collected and organized in a systematic way".[79] To be eligible for protection, a database creator must have invested "substantial or other resources" in the creation of the database.[80]

(ii) User Liabilities and Rights

The Antipiracy bill takes a pro-industry approach that accords database producers protection against interference with their actual *and* potential markets.[81] A user is liable to the database owner if he causes "harm to the actual or potential market" of the database, if he offers or intends to offer the product containing a substantial portion of the original database, and if the actual or intended sale is "in commerce".[82] Moreover, the owner need not show that he has plans or even the means to enter the "potential" market but only that it is a market "commonly exploited by persons offering similar products or services incorporating collections of information".[83] Through indirection, it also permits a database owner to claim that a substantial portion of the database has been taken by showing that only two items of information were taken. "Individual" items of information are not substantial, but any other taking apparently including as few as two pieces of information may be.[84] This is a much more producer-friendly approach than the EU, UK or WIPO approach and one more likely to cross United States constitutional boundaries.

The Antipiracy bill excludes "certain nonprofit education, scientific, or research uses" from liability as long as such uses do not harm "directly the actual market".[85] There is also provision for "individual act[s] . . . done for the purpose of illustration, explanation, example, comment, criticism, teaching, research, or analysis, in an amount appropriate and customary for that purpose . . . if it is reasonable under the circumstances".[86] Users in this category get this preference if their work is for non-profit purposes, if the person using the database is acting in "good faith", if the new database or work generated is significantly different from the database, *and* if the user is not in the same "field or business" as the database maker.[87] There is also protection for news reporting, including "news gathering, dissemination, and comment".[88]

---

[79] See Antipiracy bill, n. 77 above, § 1401(2).
[80] *Ibid.*, § 1402.
[81] *Ibid.*
[82] *Ibid.*
[83] *Ibid.*, §§ 1401(3) and 1402.
[84] *Ibid.*, § 1403(b).
[85] *Ibid.*, § 1403(a)(1).
[86] *Ibid.*, § 1403(2)(A).
[87] *Ibid.*, § 1403(2)(A)(i)–(iv).
[88] *Ibid.*, § 1403(e).

(iii) Term

The Antipiracy bill does not set a term limit *per se*, but rather sets a "limitation" on when actions can be maintained under the Act. "No criminal or civil action shall be maintained . . . for the extraction or use of all or a substantial part of a collection of information that occurs more than 15 years after the portion of the collection that is extracted or used was first offered for sale or otherwise in commerce."[89] The bill tries to avoid the perpetuation of protection problem raised in the EU and WIPO provisions, however, by stating that no portion of a database that is taken more than 15 years after *that* portion was offered in commerce may be protected.[90]

B The Consumer Access Bill

The Consumer Access bill is markedly less aggressive than the Antipiracy bill in serving the industry's interests. Oddly enough, however, it institutes no time limit on such protection.

(i) Eligibility

The Consumer Access bill would be considerably friendlier to the information user and less friendly to the database producer than the Antipiracy bill. Like most database protection formulations, the database maker must have made a substantial investment to be eligible for protection.[91] The information that would be protected under the Consumer Access bill includes "facts, data, or any other intangible material" but it excludes "works of authorship".[92] This is a significant exclusion, because it precludes database legislation from removing copyrighted works of authorship from the public domain.

(ii) User Liabilities and Rights

User liabilities are considerably narrower under the Consumer Access bill than any other proposal to date. A user is prohibited from duplicating, selling or distributing another's database if he is distributing the copy "in commerce in competition" with the original database.[93] The bill defines "in competition" as the displacement of "substantial sales or licenses of the database of which it is a duplicate" and as a significant threat to the "opportunity to recover a return on

---

[89] See Antipiracy bill, n. 77 above, § 1408(c).

[90] *Ibid.*

[91] See Consumer Access bill, n. 78 above, § 101(1).

[92] *Ibid.*, § 103 (defining "information" as "facts, data, or any other intangible material capable of being collected and organized in a systematic way, with the exception of works of authorship").

[93] *Ibid.*, § 102.

the investment".[94] There is no talk of a "potential" market, as in the Antipiracy bill. Moreover, there must be proof both that substantial sales or licences have been displaced *and* that the duplicate has negated the opportunity to obtain a return on the investment. This is a significantly higher hurdle to enjoining users than the EU, UK, or WIPO provisions.

The Consumer Access bill also provides more explicit exceptions from the bill's liability than other versions. News reporting, law enforcement, scientific, research, and educational uses are excluded from the reach of the bill.[95]

(iii) Term

Despite its generally information user friendly approach, the Consumer Access bill turns away from users by failing to set a term of limitation on database protection. All databases, whether new or established, can be protected against commercial competitors for an infinite term.

The Antipiracy bill and the Consumer Access bill contain a reporting requirement, which reflects the tentativeness with which the United States is approaching such legislation. They call for a report by the Federal Trade Commission to Congress within 36 months of enactment to ascertain the state of the database market, including the availability of databases and information, the extent of competition between producers, and the amount of investment in the industry.[96] This may be the single most important aspect of the bill given that the economic case is yet to be made proving that such legislation is necessary or good for the market.

C Summary

The database industry has taken a blanket approach to obtaining protection. It has made proposals in the EU, its member countries and the United States. In an interesting nod to the US Constitution, each starts from the framework laid out in *Feist* and proceeds from there. Yet, most defy the spirit of *Feist*, which would keep facts available to ensure a healthy market place of expression. The proliferation of proposals portends some database protection at some level once the political arena has worked its way through the competing demands. The most significant hurdle the pending Congressional proposals face is the United States Constitution.

---

[94] *Ibid.*, § 101(5).
[95] *Ibid.*, § 103. Like most other database proposals, the Access bill also permits independent gathering of the same information already collected in an existing database.
[96] *Ibid.*, § 108.

V   HOW THE UNITED STATES CONSTITUTION LIMITS DATABASE PROTECTION IN
THE UNITED STATES

The US Constitution imposes a number of hurdles to database legislation. The most significant barriers will arise from the enumerated powers doctrine and various doctrines under the First Amendment.

A The Copyright Clause and the First Amendment

Without debate, the framers of the United States Constitution included in the original Constitution the Copyright Clause among the list of Congress's enumerated powers.[97] At the same time they did not include a bill of rights.[98] Even though the Copyright Clause permits authors to suppress the speech of others when that speech copies the authors' expression and, even though the constitution contained no explicit rights of the people, the framers were hopeful that they had crafted a document that would battle tyranny and thereby further liberty.[99] They assumed that by giving power over written works to authors (rather than the more potentially powerful publishers) and by limiting the powers of Congress and not including a power over speech or the press, that a market place of expression might grow. These are fundamental constitutional principles.

As a matter of history, then, the Copyright Clause precedes the First Amendment, and, as a matter of legal theory, it must be taken into account to understand how and why the Constitution, taken as a whole, protects and promotes speech. The Copyright Clause structures the market place of expression that is presupposed by the First Amendment, which limits the government's interference with it. But for the Copyright Clause's fostering of a market place of expressive products, there would be no real value in the First Amendment's limitations of the government's interference with that market. The Copyright Clause directs Congress, when it enacts the copyright law, to do so in the public good, which is best served when the market is diverse, of high quality and great quantity.

Those theories of freedom of expression that do not take the Copyright Clause into account—and that would include many in the United States—rest on an incomplete constitutional foundation. Both the Copyright Clause and the First Amendment are best understood within the larger framework of the

---

[97] US Constitution, Art. I, § 8, cl. 8.

[98] See J. Madison, *The Debates in the Federal Convention of 1787 Which Framed the Constitution of the United States of America* (G. Hunt and J.B. Scott eds, Buffalo, N.Y., Prometheus Books, 1987), 557 (herein "Madison, Debates") (motion to include Bill of Rights rejected).

[99] See J. Madison, *Notes of Debates in the Federal Convention of 1787* (Athens, Ohio UP, 1966), 627 (Letter to Congress).

Constitution, which divides power within the United States to ensure that no single social entity receives a concentration of power that would permit that entity to tyrannise the people.[100]

The Copyright Clause is the First Amendment's partner in the preservation of liberty in three ways. First, United States copyright law, which is based on capitalist economic theory having its roots in the Protestant ethos, structures the market place of expression by commodifying the creative product. The product is philosophically distinct from the producer and is not measured according to the value of the producer. This particular point was driven home by the *Feist* decision, which held that only the qualities of the product determine copyrightability.[101] Under the Supreme Court's reading of the Copyright Clause, it is irrelevant whether the creator laboured, invested or sacrificed for the product. All that matters is whether the product is original.[102] It is the quality of the product that justifies the right to sue copiers, not the quality or identity of the creator.

This construct encourages creative activity by any and all, encourages distribution to the masses, results in a proliferation of meanings, and fosters a diversity of viewpoints. By distinguishing the identity of the producer from the product and attaching rights only to works that satisfy certain criteria, United States copyright law also engenders an egalitarian attitude toward creators and a critical attitude toward works, both of which are essential to creating a free market place in creative works.

Under the *Feist* vision of the constitutional structure underlying copyright law, all citizens may be authors, and therefore demand for the building blocks to make new works is intense. In a system where few are likely to be authors, fewer building blocks might be acceptable. But under a system that identifies every individual, from child to adult, as a potential author, there must be many building blocks to avoid repetition and frustration and to foster a diverse market. Thus, the *Feist* reading of the Copyright Clause presupposes the necessity of a diverse and rich public domain of facts and works of authorship that have exceeded their copyright term.

Database legislation that takes facts and information out of the public domain and grants proprietary rights over them violates the Copyright Clause and the First Amendment by removing the underpinnings necessary for the construction of a diverse, high-quality, high-quantity market place of expression. On the spectrum of US proposals, the Consumer Access bill (except for its

---

[100] See US Constitution, Arts. I, II and III. See also Madison, *Debates*, n. 60 above, 639 ("the impropriety of delegating such extensive trust to one body of men is evident") (quoting letter from George Washington, to President of Congress (17 September 1787)). For discussion of the US Constitution's means of separating power within the society, see M.A. Hamilton, "Power, the Establishment Clause, and Vouchers" (1999) 31 *Conn L Rev* 807; M.A. Hamilton, "The People: The Least Accountable Branch" (1997) 4 *Uni Chic L Sch Roundtable* 1; M.A. Hamilton, "The Constitution's Pragmatic Balance of Power Between Church and State", *Nexus: J Opinion*, Fall 1997, 33.

[101] See *Feist Publications, Inc.* v. *Rural Telephone Service Co*, 499 US 340, 345–7 (1991).

[102] *Ibid.*, 349–53.

perpetual term of protection) is much more in line with the spirit of the Copyright Clause and the First Amendment than any of the other proposals to date.

The question that will be asked in the United States courts about any federal database legislation is whether the legislation is an attempt to create copyright-like rights in data. The more similar the legislation is to copyright protection, the more likely it will be found to be an inappropriate enactment pursuant to the Copyright Clause. Misappropriation legislation may be permissible under another of Congress's powers, but simply naming such legislation "misappropriation" will not be enough. The legislation must not create *property* rights in data and information.[103] Admittedly, the line between misappropriation and property rights is not clear-cut at this time, but the Supreme Court's decisions in *INS*[104] and *Feist* will serve as the two ends of the spectrum, respectively. The US courts are likely to have little patience with pretextual constitutionality.[105] With the Copyright Clause foreclosed, the question is which power might serve.

B The Commerce Clause and Database Legislation

Those defending federal database legislation in the United States argue that it can be passed pursuant to Congress's power under the Commerce Clause, Article 1, § 8, cl. 3, of the Constitution. They concede, as they must, that *Feist* precludes Congress from enacting database protection under the Copyright Clause, but argue that the Commerce Clause opens another avenue.[106]

There was a time in United States constitutional jurisprudence when the Commerce Clause was thought to be a catch-all for any and all of Congress's schemes. The Supreme Court did not place meaningful limits on the exercise of Congress's Commerce power. In recent years, however, the Court has been building a series of fences around federal congressional power to protect the States against overreaching.[107] Thus, any database legislation passed pursuant to the Commerce Clause will face some significant hurdles.

---

[103] See Letter from Marci A. Hamilton, Professor of Law, Director, Intellectual Property Law Program, Benjamin N. Cardozo School of Law, to Honorable Orrin G. Hatch, Chairman, Committee on the Judiciary, US Senate (4 September 1998) (available at <http://www.marcihamilton.com.html>).

[104] *International News Serv.* v. *Associated Press*, 248 US 215 (1918).

[105] See *Arcara* v. *Cloud Books*, 478 US 697, 708 (1986) (O'Connor J concurring).

[106] See *Hearing on HR 354, the Collections of Information Antipiracy Act Before the House Judiciary Subcomm on the Courts and Intellectual Property*, 106th Cong (1999) (testimony of Marilyn Winokur, Executive Vice President of Micromedex, on behalf of Micromedex and the Coalition Against Database Piracy), available in 1999 WL 156183 (FDCH); *Supplemental Statement on HR 2652: The Collections of Information Antipiracy Act*, 105th Cong (1998) (statement of Jane C. Ginsburg, Professor of Law, Columbia University School of Law), available in 1998 WL 62976 (FDCH); J.C. Ginsburg, "Copyright, Common Law, and *Sui Generis* Protection of Databases in the United States and Abroad" (1997) 66 *U Cinn L Rev* 151.

[107] See *Alden* v. *Maine*, 527 US 706 (1999); *College Savings Bank* v. *Florida Prepaid Post-secondary Educ. Expense Bd.*, 527 US 666 (1999); *Florida Prepaid Postsecondary Educ. Expense Bd.* v. *College Savings Bank*, 527 US 627 (1999); *Printz* v. *United States*, 521 US 898 (1997); *Seminole Tribe of Florida* v. *Florida*, 517 US 44 (1996); *United States* v. *Lopez*, 514 US 549 (1995).

The Commerce Clause, by its terms, gives Congress power over *inter*state commerce, not *intra*state commerce. The Court recently held that Congress must have proof that the activity being regulated "substantially affects" interstate commerce. It is not enough if the activity being regulated only creates a *de minimis* impact on interstate commerce.[108] The size and multinational quality of the database industry makes it clear that Congress would have power over most database issues under this aspect of the Commerce Clause.

As discussed above, though, the Congress cannot use the Commerce Clause as a pretext for creating database legislation that would violate the Copyright Clause. To be on the safe side, therefore, the legislation must be directed at commerce, in this instance, commerce in databases, not a means of investing individuals with property rights in information. The safest route would be for the Congress to enact a species of unfair competition legislation. The decision in *Feist* opens the door for such legislation, stating that "[p]rotection for the fruits of [data] research . . . may in certain circumstances be available under a theory of unfair competition".[109] The question raised by this statement is: what "circumstances" would justify protection of information? From the Court's reading of the Copyright Clause and the First Amendment, the circumstances must be exceedingly narrow.

The Court has held that information could be protected for very short periods of time (24 hours) in certain, narrow circumstances, such as news reporting.[110] The guiding constitutional principle is that information should be as free as possible. In other words, any law impeding the flow of information must be narrowly tailored to an existing market evil.

The Antipiracy bill is likely to be in trouble on this reading, because neither is it narrowly tailored nor does it rest on a factual base that indicates there is a definite market evil in need of federal legislative action. It permits individuals to horde information for up to 15 years, and it rests on no fact-finding by Congress that would indicate the necessity for such an invasion of the market place of ideas. Indeed, the absence of fact-finding regarding the database industry, its economic base, its growth and the conditions for further growth is quite striking in the congressional record. There is a generalised sense that "pirates" should not be able to "steal" databases that others have invested in, but no economic analysis of any substance.[111]

It is informative to compare the *reference* to unfair competition in the Court's unanimous patent law decision in *Feist* with the *discussion* of unfair competition law in the Court's unanimous decision in *Bonito Boats*, both of which were

---

[108] See *United States v. Lopez*, 514 US 549, 564 (1995).

[109] *Feist Publications, Inc. v. Rural Telephone Service Co.*, 499 US 340, 354 (1991).

[110] See *International News Serv. v. Associated Press*, 248 US 215, 241 (1918).

[111] Of course, this is not peculiar to database legislation. Congress is capable of passing a mind-boggling array of laws on the basis of extremely little information. When constitutional rights are at stake, though, the Supreme Court has required some evidence of the necessity for such legislation. See, for example, *City of Boerne v. Flores*, 521 US 507 (1997); *City of Richmond v. JA Croson*, 488 US 469 (1989).

written by Justice Sandra Day O'Connor. In *Bonito Boats*, the Court stated that unfair competition law is concerned "with protecting *consumers* from confusion as to source. While that concern may result in the creation of 'quasi-property rights' in communicative symbols, the focus is on the protection of consumers, not the protection of producers as an incentive to product innovation".[112] The Antipiracy bill does not fare well under this reasoning, because it is not a narrowly drafted unfair competition law intended to protect consumers, but rather is on its face an attempt to protect producers who have invested in databases.

In addition, competition law is not supposed to provide a tool for some competitors to wield against others, but rather a means of furthering competition between them.[113] The record remains open on the question whether database protection in general is pro- or anti-competitive. If such legislation is passed, the courts will be placed in the difficult position of having to guess whether it is pro- or anti-competitive.

One of the crucial means of tailoring database legislation is by limiting the term of protection. The *INS* case permitted one news organisation to stop another news organisation from using its gathered information for 24 hours.[114] The leap from *INS*, which is the only decision of its kind in the United States Supreme Court, to the 15-year term in the EU, UK, WIPO and the Antipiracy bill is enormous.[115] The leap from *INS* to the Consumer Access bill's infinite term is, well, infinite.

Commerce Clause doctrine also raises other hurdles. The Court recently made clear in a series of cases interpreting the Eleventh Amendment that Congress may not employ the Commerce Clause to enact a private right of action against a State.[116] Thus, Congress could not provide relief for database owners against the States or their officers acting in their official capacity.[117] With State universities and public libraries being large data consumers, this is a significant limitation.

In sum, the Copyright Clause is forbidden territory for protecting information and the Commerce Clause offers limited options.[118] Even if database

---

[112] See *Bonito Boats, Inc.* v. *Thunder Craft Boats, Inc.*, 489 US 141, 157 (1989).

[113] See *Manufacturing Research Corp.* v. *Greenleetool Co.*, 693 F 2d 1037, 1043 (11th Cir. 1982); *Northwest Power Prods., Inc.* v. *Omark Indus., Inc.*, 576 F 2d 83, 89 (5th Cir. 1978).

[114] See *International News Serv.* v. *Associated Press*, 248 US 215, 231 (1918).

[115] See nn. 38, 51, 60 and 61 above, and accompanying text.

[116] See generally *Alden* v. *Maine*, 527 US 706 (1999); *College Savings Bank* v. *Florida Prepaid Postsecondary Educ. Expense Bd.*, 527 US 666 (1999); *Florida Prepaid Postsecondary Educ. Expense Bd.* v. *College Savings Bank*, 527 US 627 (1999).

[117] *Ibid.*

[118] See Patry, n. 9 above. There may also be an argument that database legislation could be enacted pursuant to the so-called "foreign affairs power". See, for example, M. Lao, "Federalizing Trade Secrets Law in an Information Economy" (1998) 59 *Ohio St L J* 1633, 1682–4 (discussing foreign affairs power with respect to trade secrets law). On this theory, Congress would have power to enact database legislation on the basis of international treaties covering the topic signed by the President and approved by a 2/3 vote of the Senate. If such a treaty were self-executing, the treaty language automatically would become the law of the United States; if it were not, Congress could

legislation could pass muster as a permissible enactment under the Commerce Clause, the First Amendment may still serve as a limitation on the reach of such legislation.

C First Amendment Doctrine and Database Legislation

While database legislation is, in general, viewpoint neutral, it is aimed at a particular type of content—facts and information. It is legislation that builds fences around building blocks necessary to create a market place of expression and ideas. It impacts on crucial elements of the market place of speech, including research, commentary, news reporting and creative works. As such, it may well be subject to strict scrutiny under First Amendment doctrine.[119] As a result, a content producer defending the database bill in court would have to prove that the Congress had a compelling interest in passing the bill and that it narrowly tailored the bill to fit its goal.[120] In other words, the means (the provisions of the bill) must fit tightly with the end intended to be achieved. On the current state of the record in Congress, this will be a nearly intolerable burden to bear. The Congress has not demonstrated that there is a compelling need for database protection. Aside from the fact that the EU now has protection that does not provide for national treatment, there is precious little evidence that such legislation is crucial to the industry or in the interests of the United States polity. Nor have any of the proposals' proponents demonstrated that its measures are closely tailored to the particular evil at which they are aimed. The debate has been premised on presupposition rather than fact.

Even if the Supreme Court were not to invalidate database legislation altogether under a First Amendment theory, it might use the values of the First Amendment to narrow the interpretation of an ambiguous database statute. United States constitutional theory provides that courts are to read ambiguous statutes in a way that ensures that they do not violate the Constitution.[121] The meanings of the new terms introduced by the database bills, including "actual or potential market", "substantial investment" and especially "substantial part"

enact a law pursuant to the treaty. This path is not free from hurdles. The treaty power does not permit treaties to violate constitutional prohibitions, such as the First Amendment, and the jury is out on the question of the extent to which federalism concerns may limit the impact of such treaties on the states. See M. Halberstam and M.A. Hamilton, "RFRA Through the Treaty Power? A Response to Professor Neuman" (forthcoming 2000).

[119] See *Young* v. *American Mini Theaters, Inc.*, 427 US 50, 61 (1976) (discussing "the free dissemination of ideas"); *Miller* v. *California*, 413 US 15, 34–5 (1973) (quoting *Roth* v. *United States*, 354 US 476, 484 (1957)) (discussing the "unfettered interchange of ideas"); *Stanley* v. *Georgia*, 394 US 557, 564 (1969) (stating the "right to receive information and ideas . . . is fundamental to our free society").

[120] See *New York* v. *Ferber*, 458 US 747 (1982); *Widmar* v. *Vincent*, 454 US 263 (1981).

[121] See *NLRB* v. *Catholic Bishop of Chicago*, 440 US 490, 500 (1979) ("an Act of Congress ought not to be construed to violate the Constitution if any other possible construction remains available").

could be interpreted narrowly and in favour of the user in order to avoid First Amendment strictures.

First Amendment doctrine would also offer the possibility of challenging database legislation under a "void for vagueness" theory. A database statute that is so vague as to discourage the use of information may exert a chilling effect on freedom of speech. In such a case, the Court would invalidate the vague and severable provisions of the statute.[122] The Antipiracy bill, with its narrow exceptions and its expansive scope that includes prohibitions on use of data even when the database maker has neither the intent or means to enter a certain market, certainly raises this possibility. Once the Supreme Court declares a statute unconstitutional on vagueness grounds, Congress will then have a second opportunity to pass a clearer statute.

D Summary and Conclusion

The introduction of US constitutional principles into the database debate moves the focus away from the industries and their needs to a larger picture of the polity's needs. If it is not too late, such a focus can be quite helpful. From a US constitutional perspective, the outcome to fear is worldwide protection of databases and the concomitant creation of a sense of entitlement for database producers before anyone else joins the discussion. The race to regulate databases is a wise political move on the part of database producers, but potentially detrimental to the interests of all those who have taken the availability of information for granted for decades, if not centuries.

Under the US Constitution, the key problem in most database proposals to date is their intent to cover not just the database as a whole but rather much smaller segments of data. By defining a "significant" portion of a database as anything more than one piece of information, such legislation sets itself up for the charge that it is not protecting databases and the competitiveness of the database industry but rather data itself. Therein lies the resistance of the Copyright Clause and the First Amendment to such legislation.

Database legislation that is limited to protecting data*bases* rather than data would pose less significant constitutional hurdles than the current proposals in the United States. It would also speak to the problem of free-riding on database investment without providing a windfall for database producers. Data*base* legislation would not rob later creators of the building blocks of information contained, but rather would protect against those commercial free riders who attempt to profit on the database product as a whole. It would appear that the current debate over such legislation has been skewed by the overreaching of the database industry, which has urged Congress to enact legislation that goes far

---

[122] See *Kolender* v. *Lawson*, 461 US 352 (1983); *Smith* v. *Goguen*, 415 US 566, 572–3 (1974); *Gooding* v. *Wilson*, 405 US 518 (1972); *Connally* v. *General Constr. Co.*, 269 US 385, 391 (1926).

beyond forbidding free riders and pirates from taking database products to providing a right in the vast majority of the information contained within the database.

Thus, the appellation "database legislation" is in fact a misnomer. All existing legislation and proposals to date are in fact "data" legislation. If the US Constitution is to be taken into account, the line between protecting databases and data in such legislation must be drawn closer to the protection of data*bases* than the protection of the data.

VI CONCLUSION

The United States Congress feels pressured to pass database legislation because the European Union already has such legislation coupled with a provision that eschews national treatment.[123] The perceived unfairness of the current legal situation has galvanised Congress to act and database lobbyists to push. This may be the first clear instance of a new and clever path to getting around the troublesome United States Constitution's barriers: start in the European Union. Having set the agenda, however, it will be interesting to observe whether the EU's Database Directive will maintain centre stage on this issue as the United States attempts to find its way to a version of database protection that can coexist peacefully with the Constitution. Once the Constitution speaks, through the United States Supreme Court, the locus of database protection is likely to change from legislation that protects the vast majority of data in a database to legislation that protects databases. As United States constitutional contours become more apparent, the database industry that succeeded in the EU may well shift course by endorsing whatever the US Constitution permits once the Court speaks, for the purpose of securing predictability and stability. Thus, having started with *Feist*, international database law may well gravitate toward the United States Supreme Court's second data decision.

---

[123] See n. 38 and accompanying text.

3

Commodifying and Transacting Informational Products Through Contractual Licences: The Challenge for Informational Constitutionalism

BRIAN FITZGERALD*

I INTRODUCTION

We are now fully immersed in the information age, an epoch wherein digitised information has become a key economic resource.[1] The immediate role for law is to fathom, consider and construct the parameters of informational or digital property. While traditional intellectual property doctrines, such as copyright and patent, still play a major role in defining informational property, it is the rise of the contractual licence (in contrast to the sale of goods) that has sparked the imagination in relation to commodifying informational property.[2]

The contractual licence acts as an elliptical distribution mechanism, granting the licensee rights of user but never divesting the licensor of ultimate ownership. The licence and the product merge, leading people to say the licence is the product.[3] This can be contrasted with the distribution of a tangible book in which rights of ownership in the tangible chattel pass to the purchaser while the copyright owner retains control over the intellectual property. In the case of intangible informational products, there are many cases where there is no transfer of ownership in any item, but simply a licence to use the intellectual property. As

* I would like to thank Andrew Christie, Gail Evans and Anne Fitzgerald for their assistance.

[1] See further B. Fitzgerald, "Imagining the Digital Environment" (paper presented at Australian Intellectual Property Conference, 5 March 1999); B. Fitzgerald, "Conceptualising the Digital Environment: The Death of a Historical Understanding of Production and Distribution" (paper presented at Digital Distribution and Music Revolution mp3 Summit, Queensland Parliament House, 7 July 1999); L. Thurow, "Needed: A New System of Intellectual Property Rights" (1997) *Harv Bus Rev* 95, 96.

[2] See "Symposium: Intellectual Property and Contract Law for the Information Age: The Impact of Article 2B of the Uniform Commercial Code on the Future of Information and Commerce" (1999) 87 *Calif L Rev* 1; R. Nimmer, "Images and Contract Law—What Law Applies to Transactions in Information?" (1999) 36 *Hous L Rev* 1.

[3] R.W. Gomulkiewicz, "The License is the Product: Comments on the Promise of Article 2B for Software and Information Licensing" (1998) 13 *Berk Tech LJ* 891.

we are now capable of distributing property in an intangible form, which in turn can be easily copied and further distributed, the information industry has moved to a distribution system based on licensing rather than sale.

The contractual licence will either rely on the preliminary commodification process undertaken by (the statutory regimes of) copyright or patent law and use this as the basis of the licence, or it will itself commodify the information and construct property through the private legislative ordering of the contractual licence.[4] In so doing, the contractual licence will either complete or fully effectuate commodification in the process of distribution.

The contractual licence can be seen to be a commodifying and distributive mechanism. This is a most powerful mechanism, especially in the information age. We are challenged to understand and respond to the rise of this new process and to infuse it with a principled basis of operation.[5]

In this chapter, I seek to present an overview of some of the key issues that have arisen in relation to the contractual licence, focussing on the debate that has emerged from the promulgation of Article 2B of the American Uniform Commercial Code, now to become the Uniform Computer Information Transactions Act (hereafter "UCITA"),[6] a statute purporting to provide structure and guidance to the process of commodifying and distributing informational products through contractual licences.

Computer software which acts as the customising agent of information technology is one of the most prominent informational products in our market at this point in time. Software has become so integral to our daily lives that I am minded to conceptualise it as a form of discourse which in turn informs my understanding of how the law might regulate software.[7] Throughout this chapter I will simply use the term "informational product", which includes software and other informational products.

I seek in this chapter to explain:

(a) The context for information transactions which is the information society;
(b) The rationale of the UCITA;
(c) What a licence is;
(d) How a licence is created;

---

[4] On closer analysis, the underlying basis of this second instance of commodification is arguably the common law principle of unjust enrichment which acts to protect the value added to information: B. Fitzgerald and L. Gamertsfelder, "Protecting Informational Products Through Unjust Enrichment Law" [1998] *EIPR* 244; D. Dobbs, *Law of Remedies: Damages, Equity and Restitution* (2nd edn., St Paul, Minn., West Publishing, 1993), chaps. 4–7.

[5] Along with technology, the contractual licence is seen as the saviour of copyright in the digital age. It is an enforcement methodology.

[6] On 29 July 1999, the National Conference of Commissioners on Uniform State Laws (hereafter "NCCUSL") voted to promulgate UCITA by a vote of 43–6, with 2 States abstaining. The States voting against the bill were Alaska, Iowa, Minnesota, Nebraska, North Carolina and Utah. For further commentary, see <http://www.badsoftware.com>. UCITA has been adopted as law in the States of Maryland and Virginia and is under close consideration in a number of other states: see <http://www.ucitaonline.com/whathap.html>.

[7] B. Fitzgerald, "Software as Discourse? A Constitutionalism for the Information Society" (1999) 24 *Alternative L J* 144.

(e) The legitimate scope of a licence, in the context of free speech, fair use, open competition and reverse engineering; and

(f) Informational constitutionalism, being the principles that will mediate power in the information society.

II WHAT IS THE INFORMATION SOCIETY?

The information age has been upon us for some time, at the very least since the American Vice President Al Gore advised us that we had embarked on the information superhighway. This has been the story of the decade of the 1990s. With each new day, we are exposed to some new information technology that can make things easier, faster, more functional and even more fun. I can now talk, mail, shop and even experience various types of (virtual) reality through information technology. In the future I can see myself voting, consuming, relaxing, taking medical and legal advice and so on with the aid of information technology. All of this is adding up to something known as the "information society", a product of the information age, where information technology and the consequent supply of information become the underpinning structure of social and economic life. They dictate how we live, how we work, how money is made,[8] and so on. It is a society where information has become a key resource that drives the economy. In an advanced information society, information plays a significant role in structuring social existence, the way we live. Many people are suggesting that this is the next big challenge of information technology, the structuring of our social existence through virtual reality and other technological extensions of life[9] and living.[10] While the information society may promise

---

[8] Thurow, n. 1 above, 96: "[w]ith the advent of the information revolution—or the third industrial revolution (call it what you will)—skills and knowledge have become the only source of sustainable long-term competitive advantage. Intellectual property lies at the centre of the modern company's economic success or failure. . . . What used to be tertiary after raw materials and capital in determining economic success is now primary. Major companies such as Microsoft own nothing of value except knowledge. Fighting to defend and extend the domain of their intellectual property is how they play the economic game. With this reality comes the need for more differentiated systems of determining who owns what, better protection for whatever is owned, and faster systems of dispute resolution. Bill Gates is the perfect symbol of the new centrality of intellectual property. For more than a century, the world's wealthiest human being has been associated with oil—starting with John D. Rockerfeller in the late nineteenth century and ending with the Sultan of Brunei in the late twentieth century. But today, for the first time in history, the world's wealthiest person is a knowledge worker." See further L. Thurow, *Building Wealth: New Rules for Individuals Companies and Countries in the Knowledge-Based Economy* (New York, Harper Collins, 1999).

[9] B.F. Fitzgerald, "Life in Cyberspace: A Simulating Experience" (1997) 3 *Computer and Telecommunications L Rev* 136; S. Turkle, *Life on the Screen: Identity in the Age of the Internet* (New York, Simon and Schuster, 1995).

[10] *Towards an Australian Strategy for the Information Economy:* a preliminary statement of the government's policy approach and a basis for business and community consultation, July 1998, <http://www.noie.gov.au>: "[i]n Australia, and in many places around the world, students now use computers at home and school to research projects; governments supply information and services online, so that citizens needn't leave home to lodge forms or get the help they want; farmers access

to enhance social and economic well-being, it also threatens those very things. Issues relating to privacy will be prominent, as will concerns about the disparity between the information rich and the information poor, and the appearance of a new imperialism.[11]

Professor Frank Webster explains the information society in terms of five categories: technological, economic, occupational, spatial and cultural. Across these areas, Webster explains how information has informed economics, the way we work and the way we live. While the information revolution has brought significant changes across these categories, Webster is still wary in his conclusion of pronouncing that we have entered the information age or the information society.[12] I tend to disagree, believing that social and economic change has and will continue to be profound due to the information revolution, allowing us to acknowledge a fundamental shift from industrial to informational existence.

A The Information Society is a Post-Industrial and International Society

In the information society, (digitised) information is an important and highly valued commodity that becomes dominant in the market. The intangibility of product information and markets by internet; people do banking—borrowing, transferring and investing money—electronically; businesses offer their goods and services for sale on websites, and consumers make purchases by browsing virtual shops and sending orders and payment over the net; friends and family members keep in touch with each other over long distances, by sending email messages; businesses exchange documents instantly and without paper; students do university degrees and professional training online; people interested in films, books, hobbies—anything—can meet like-minded people from around the world in chat rooms to share their interest."

[11] See further G. Hearn, T. Mandeville and D. Anthony, *The Communication Superhighway: Social and Economic Change in the Digital Age* (Sydney, Allen and Unwin, 1998), chap. 2 (notions of "technological determinism" versus "social constructivisim"); T. Jordan, *Cyberpower:The Culture and Politics of Cyberspace and the Internet* (London, Routledge, 1999); S. Turkle, *The Second Self: Computers and the Human Spirit* (New York, Simon and Schuster, 1984); J. Wajcman, *Feminism Confronts Technology* (Cambridge, Mass., Polity Press, 1991); F. Block, *Post-industrial Possibilities: A Critique of Economic Discourse* (Los Angeles, Cal., UCLA Press, 1990); N. Garnham, "Communication Technology and Policy" in M. Gurevitch and M.R. Levy (eds.), *Mass Communications Review Yearbook* (Beverly Hills, Cal., Sage, 1985), 285 (considering the pervasive nature of the information society and its never-ending expansion into the more private and less commercial spheres of life).

[12] "What is clear is that we ought to be sceptical of suggestions that we have undergone a sea change in social relationships. Features of capitalist continuity are too insistently evident for this: the primacy of market criteria, commodity production, wage labour, private ownership and corporate organisation continues, establishing links with even the distant past. Nonetheless, it is surely indisputable that, over the post-war period, we can observe some significant shifts in orientation, some novel forms of work organisation, some changes in occupational patterns and the like": F. Webster, *Theories of Information Society* (London, Routledge, 1995), 6–29. See also A. Giddens, *The Consequences of Modernity* (Stanford, Cal., Stanford UP, 1990). Compare Hearn, Mandeville and Anthony, n. 11 above, chap. 1; and the notion of the "long-wave" theory of economic advancement (electronic-photonic information age): P. Hall and P. Preston, *The Carrier Wave: The New Information Technology and the Geography of Information 1846–2003* (London, Unwin Hyman, 1988); G. Dosi *et al.*, *Technical Change and Economic Theory* (London, Pinter Publishers, 1998); D. Bell, "The Social Framework of the Information Society" in T. Forester (ed.), *The*

(digitised) information brings change to the nature of economic transactions and economic management. This is contrasted with the industrial society where tangible goods are/were the focus of exchange.

Webster explores this issue through the example of the nationalistic mass production model of the Ford Motor Corporation giving way to globalisation and the transnational corporation, wherein information has been pivotal in the development of the post Ford information society. The Ford economic model is defined by Webster as one of mass production and consumption carried on by industrial workers within the boundaries of the nation state. According to Webster, globalisation, which in large part has been generated by information-based industries, such as banking and finance, has led to a demise of the Ford economic model, and to a situation where flexibility of production and consumption inform a transnational society. For Webster, information has facilitated this move to a post industrial information-based society and is pivotal to its continued functioning. From this analysis, one is presented with a view that society has moved into a new epoch or age, the information age, and that it will be one that extends beyond national boundaries and is much more international or transnational in nature.[13]

The following quotation from the American Vice President Al Gore tells us much the same thing:[14]

> We are on the verge of a revolution that is just as profound as the change in the economy that came with the industrial revolution. Soon electronic networks will allow people to transcend the barriers of time and distance and take advantage of global markets and business opportunities not even imaginable today, opening up a new world of economic possibility and progress.

In short, the fundamental premises of the new society include the notion that information is currency, that there is an intangible delivery of products, and that there is a non-territorial and decentralised nature to the way we do business. Time, space and physicality are reconceptualised.

We stand on a precipice overlooking one of the most significant shifts in the distribution of commodities within our market, wondering just how the physicality that we now experience, and take so much for granted, will transform into intangibility. Some things are easy to conceptualise as going digital. The creative arts and associated products that we now enjoy and that can be delivered as audio or visual commodities are things that we can conceptualise as turning into intangibility. The potential exists more broadly, though, to move our social, cultural and economic existence from a physical base to an intangible base.

The revolution currently under way in the music industry is an example that (while easy to conceptualise for some) gives insight into the potential

Microelectronics Revolution (Cambridge, Mass., MIT Press, 1980), 506; I. Lloyd, *Information Technology Law* (2nd edn., London, Butterworths, 1997), pp. xxxv–xxvii and chap. 1; M. Castells, *Information Age: Economy Culture and Society (Volumes 1–3)* (Oxford, Blackwell, 1996).

[13] Webster, *ibid.*, 135ff.
[14] <http://www.iitf.nist/elecomm/ecomm.htm>.

intangibility of distribution. Although it has been developing over the last few years, the mp3 format that is now used to allow the free and easy copying of digital quality music from the Internet onto a digital CD player, downloaded also from the Internet, highlights how the distribution chain has gone digital.[15] In this instance, we are seeing the delivery of digital player and digital CD through digital means. We have already seen the delivery of software and other recreational items across the Internet. More and more will change. This is just the start of the greatest revolution in the distribution of commodities that we have ever seen.[16] And this movement to digital distribution will be based on the dissemination of digitised information.

Central to the operation of the information society and the expansion of electronic business (e-commerce) is the Internet, an international communication network which transcends territoriality (states), physicality and time. It presents us with a most sophisticated form of internationalised intangible distribution. The Internet is itself in large part the revolution, as it presents us with communication pathways we could not have envisaged not so long ago.

In summary, we need to posit some of these key elements of the information society and note their significance, as they are fundamental to the topic under consideration.

B Key Elements of the Information Society

The key elements of the information society can be listed as follows:[17]

—Information is a core resource. This challenges us to understand the process of commodification of information. Law (along with the market, and increasingly with technology) seeks to commodify information, by drawing the boundaries of the digital estate, e.g. copyright law.

—Information is intangible, thus allowing ease of copying and rapid international movement, and eschewing notions of time and space.

—The information society is non-territorial. Much human endeavour has been to dominate territory. Since 1648, Western civilisation has moved towards the nation state, defined by sovereignty and jurisdiction over bounded territory, or territorial blocks. The information society undermines that concept. This is a major problem for regulation.

—The information society is characterised by rapid, cheap and easy communication (including copying). This impacts upon the commodification process.

---

[15] See further: <http://www.mp3.com>.

[16] mp3 is a microcosm of the digital distribution architecture that promises to emerge. It represents the link between product and consumer—distribution architecture—which other (especially entertainment) information commodities (beyond music) will inevitably embrace.

[17] See D. Tapscott, *The Digital Economy: Promise and Peril in the Age of Networked Intelligence* (New York, McGraw-Hill, 1996).

How does one commodify or fence information if the fences are too easily removed?

—The information society is truly global, and the market is much larger and cheaper to enter.

—The information society is decentralised, which raises questions over a command or centralised model of distribution.

—The information society is personalised, which raises issues of customisation, where products are made to "fit or order", in contrast to the standardised mass market production line of the industrial era.

—The information society is marked by convergence. The notion that digitisation has led to the convergence of core communication networks raises issues of access and monopolies.

—Digitization and computer technology are central features of the information society. These underpin the other core elements, putting in focus issues concerning the power of any one entity to control codes and technology and thereby exert undue influence over communicators in general.

The advent of the information society demands that the basic laws governing commercial transactions are founded on an appreciation of the dynamic of transacting intangible commodities across the world in rapid time.

III THE COMMODIFICATION AND DISTRIBUTION PROCESS:
THE CONTRACTUAL LICENCE

Information is commodified through a combination of intellectual property law and general common law, such as contract and unjust enrichment,[18] which we can call information law. Information law is integral to the constitutionalism (the regulation of power) of information society.[19] The commodification process seeks to fence off and package the digital estate, which otherwise has no physical boundary.[20] Once commodified, information can be bought and sold in the market place. Law plays an integral role in defining the structure of the informational commodity. In this sense, information law acts like *infrastructure* in the digital economy and environment.

[18] Fitzgerald and Gamertsfelder, n. 4 above.

[19] Fitzgerald, n. 7 above. The definition of power belongs to Michel Foucault: "[w]hat I mean is this: in a society such as ours, but basically in any society, there are manifold relations of power which permeate, characterise and constitute the social body, and these relations of power cannot themselves be established, consolidated nor implemented without the production, accumulation, circulation and functioning of a discourse.": M. Foucault, *Power/Knowledge* (C. Gordon (ed.), Brighton, Harvester Press, 1980), 93.

[20] E. Mackaay, "The Economics of Emergent Property Rights on the Internet" in P. Bernt Hugenholtz (ed.), *The Future of Copyright in the Digital Environment* (The Hague, Kluwer, 1996), 13.

To the fore in the issue of commodification is the notion that information needs to be freely available to ensure social and cultural prosperity.[21] Law seeks to facilitate this need through mediating principles, such as fair dealing or fair use in copyright law, which serve to balance private commodification against public use.

In the digital world, the essential transaction is the licensing of information commodities, not the sale or transfer of a tangible product. The value of the commodity is the information, and the right to control and exploit it. In this regard, the rights that are assigned in conjunction with the licence, set out as terms of the contract, are crucial, as they define the "product" which the licensee receives. The more restrictions that are placed on the licensee's use of the software or other information, the less is its value, and the greater is the value retained by the licensor, thus allowing use of the same information in future transactions. UCITA is an attempt to provide guidelines for the appropriate scope of software and information licensing.[22]

A UCITA: Background and Overview

UCITA seeks to regulate and facilitate contractual licences by providing rules for the formation and performance of information transactions. It applies to "computer information transactions" as defined in section 102,[23] including commercial agreements to create, modify, transfer or distribute:

---

[21] J.P. Barlow, *Selling Wine Without Bottles: The Economy of Mind on the Global Net* (<http://www.eff.org/barlow>): "[t]he riddle is this: if our property can be infinitely reproduced and instantaneously distributed all over the planet without cost, without our knowledge, without its even leaving our possession, how can we protect it? How are we going to get paid for the work we do with our minds? And, if we can't get paid, what will assure the continued creation and distribution of such work? . . . The future forms and protections of intellectual property are densely obscured from the entrance to the Virtual Age. Nevertheless, I can make (or reiterate) a few flat statements which I earnestly believe won't look too silly in fifty years. In the absence of the old containers, almost everything we think we know about intellectual property is wrong. We are going to have to unlearn it. We are going to have to look at information as though we'd never seen the stuff before. The protections which we will develop will rely far more on ethics and technology than on law. Encryption will be the technical basis for most intellectual property protection. (And should, for this and other reasons, be made more widely available.) The economy of the future will be based on relationship rather than possession. It will be continuous rather than sequential." See futher M. Hamilton, chap. 2 of this vol.; M. Hamilton, "Appropiation Art and the Imminent Decline in Authorial Control Over Copyrighted Works" (1994) 42 *J of the Copyright Soc of the USA* 93; Y. Benkler, "Free as the Air to Common Use: First Amendment Constraints on Enclosure of the Public Domain" (1999) 74 N Y *Univ L Rev* 354; R. Dreyfuss, "We Are Symbols and Inhabit Symbols, So Should We Be Paying Rent? Deconstructing the Lanham Act and Rights of Publicity" (1996) 20 *Colum.–VLA J L & A* 123.

[22] This chapter is focussed on the creation and legitimacy of contractual licences and does not give any detailed examination of terms and warranties that may be implied into such licences through UCITA. On these issues, see G. Evans and B. Fitzgerald, "UCC Draft Art 2B: The Ascendancy of Freedom of Contract in the Digital Millennium?" (1998) 21 *UNSWLJ* 404.

[23] S. 102 provides: " '[c]omputer information transaction' means an agreement and the performance of that agreement to create, modify, transfer, or license computer information or

(a) computer software;
(b) multimedia interactive products;
(c) computer data and databases; and
(d) Internet and on-line information.

The important point to note from this is that UCITA covers information transactions and not just transactions concerning software.

There are five key themes that underpin UCITA. These are:

(a) the paradigm transaction is a licence of computer information, rather than a sale of goods;
(b) innovation and competitiveness have come from small entrepreneurial companies as well as larger companies;
(c) computer information transactions engage fundamental free speech issues;
(d) a commercial law statute should support freedom of contract and the interpretation of agreements in light of the practical commercial context; and
(e) a substantive framework for Internet contracting is needed to facilitate commerce in computer information.

In essence, UCITA creates a new form of sale of goods regime for digital products, such as software and other informational products. This is necessary, as the transactional process of licensing of software is not adequately covered by existing sale of goods legislation, which finds it hard to classify software. For example, in the case law software is sometimes classified as a good and sometimes as a service, leading one commentator to label software the digital chameleon.[24]

Under UCITA, a good is not "computer information", nor is computer information a good. The commentary[25] explains that there is meant to be no overlap

---

informational rights in computer information." As the commentary explains: "[t]his term refers to transactions where the primary focus of the transaction includes the computer information. It does not cover information that is merely incidental to a transaction. On the other hand, the term is not limited to cases where the computer information is the single primary purpose of the deal. In many cases, aspects of a transaction focus on computer information, while other aspects focus on goods or other contractual subject matter. As indicated in Section 103(b), where there is a blend of goods and computer information, this Act will apply to the computer information, while Article 2 or 2A of the Uniform Commercial Code will apply to the goods. The mere fact that information related to a transaction is sent or recorded in digital form is not sufficient to be within this definition. The creating, modifying or obtaining the computer information itself must be a primary purpose of the agreement. Thus, a contract for airplane transportation is not a transaction within this Act simply because the ticket is in digital form. The subject matter is not the computer information, but the service—air transportation from one location to another. The term does not apply to the many cases in which a person provides information to another person for purposes of another transaction such as making an employment or loan application."

   [24] I thank Baden Appleyard for this conceptualisation. See further *Toby Constructions Products Pty. Ltd.* v. *Computa Bar (Sales) Pty. Ltd.* [1983] 2 NSWLR 48; *Caslec Industries Pty. Ltd.* v. *Windhover Data Systems Pty. Ltd.*, unreported, Federal Court of Australia, 13 August 1992, Gummow J; *St Albans City Council* v. *International Computer Ltd.* [1997] FSR 351; *Advent Systems Ltd.* v. *Unisys Corp.*, 925 F 2d 670 (3rd Cir. 1991): Evans and Fitzgerald, n. 22 above.

   [25] Commentary of the NCCUSL Drafting Committee on UCITA is available at <http://www.law.upenn.edu/bll/ulc/ucita/citaam99.htm>.

between goods-based statutes and UCITA, and that if goods and computer information are involved in a transaction, goods-based rules apply to the goods, while UCITA applies to the computer information.[26] There are two exceptions to this "gravamen of the action"-styled rule:[27]

> because computer information may be transferred on tangible media, which may be goods, there is a question about what law applies to the plastic diskette or other media. When the media is the carrier of computer information, it is within this Act. This Act applies to goods that are a copy, documentation, or packaging of the computer information. These are incidents of the transfer of computer information. This Act covers both the software and the media on which the software is copied or documented.
>
> Second, in some cases, computer information is so embedded in and sold or leased as part of goods that the computer information is merely incidental to the goods. These cases are a narrow exception to the gravaman of the action test under this Act with respect to goods.

The complex interrelationship between information and goods promises to cause some difficult interpretive issues. However, the clear intent of UCITA is encouraging.[28] The commentary gives the example of a modern television set, which may be controlled by a computer program, and suggests that the sale of an ordinary television is not within the scope of UCITA. Likewise, many motor vehicles are reliant on software, but the sale of the vehicle is not covered by UCITA, although upstream development or supply contracts for the computer program would be within UCITA.

---

[26] "SECTION 103. SCOPE; EXCLUSIONS
(a) This [Act] applies to computer information transactions.
(b) Except as otherwise provided in subsection (d) and Section 104, if a computer information transaction includes subject matter other than computer information, the following rules apply:
(1) If a transaction includes computer information and goods, this [Act] applies to the computer information and informational rights in it. However, if a copy of a computer program is contained in and sold or leased as part of other goods, this [Act] applies to the copy and the computer program only if:
(A) the other goods are a computer or computer peripheral; or
(B) giving the buyer or lessee of the goods access to or use of the program is ordinarily a material purpose of transactions in goods of the type sold or leased.
(2) In all cases not involving goods, this [Act] applies only to the computer information or informational rights in it, unless the computer information and information rights are, or access to them is, the primary subject matter, in which case this [Act] applies to the entire transaction.
(c) To the extent of a conflict between this [Act] and [Article 9 of the Uniform Commercial Code], [Article 9] governs. . . ."

[27] See commentary to UCITA.

[28] In the most recent draft of UCITA, dated 15 October 1999 (see <http://www.law.upenn. edu/bll/ulc/ulc_frame.htm>), a revised version of s. 104 provides rules whereby in mixed (goods/information) transactions parties can "opt in or out" of the UCITA regime for the whole of the transaction. I thank Paul Shupack for bringing this to my attention.

B What is a Contractual Licence?

Licenses are contracts which define user rights in relation to information products.[29] Two forms of licence known to consumers are the shrink-wrap and click-wrap licence. "Shrink-wrap licences" are normally used where the software is sold in a store with wrapping around the software product, so that the licence is usually disclosed only after opening the package. "Click-wrap licences" are normally used in an on-line environment such as the Internet, and involve the acceptance of the terms and conditions of a software licence by clicking on a button before first using a program. The decision in *ProCD, Inc.* v. *Zeidenberg*[30] held that shrink-wrap, and arguably click-wrap, licences are enforceable in the United States.

Typical licence terms might:

(a) include detailed rights of user of information/software;
(b) preclude commercial use of a database/software;
(c) limit a right to access/rental;
(d) limit use to a specific computer;
(e) limit use to internal operations of the licensee;
(f) prevent distribution of information/software;
(g) require distribution in a defined package of software and hardware; and
(h) preclude modification of the computer information or reverse engineering.

The commentary on UCITA, citing *DSC* v. *Pulse Communications, Inc.*,[31] explains that the question whether a licence is created does not depend on the extent to which the contract transfers title of a copy of the software, as title to a copy is distinct from questions about the extent to which use of the information is controlled by a licence.

One of the claims in the *DSC* case hinged on the application of section 117 of the American Copyright Act 1976. Section 117 provides that "an owner of a copy of a computer program" may make a copy of the program if this is necessary to use it. The question at issue was whether Pulsecom could defend a claim of contributory infringement by showing that the alleged primary infringers, the Regional Bell Operating Companies (RBOCs), were protected by section 117, which required them to show the RBOCs were the "owners of the copy of the software" as opposed to owners of the copyright in the software. The Court said

---

[29] Somewhat contentiously the commentary explains that "the term thus does not include an unrestricted sale of a copy; sales lack express contractual restrictions on use. Similarly, a 'copyright notice' which merely informs the buyer of the rights and restrictions associated with a first sale under copyright law does not change a sale of a copy into a license. To be a license, the contract must control the rights. A license exists if a *contract* grants greater privileges than a first sale, restricts privileges that might otherwise exist, or deals with issues that are not attributes of a first sale."

[30] 86 F 3d 1447 (7th Cir. 1996).

[31] 170 F 3d 1354 (Fed. Cir. 1999). See further R. Nimmer, *The Law of Computer Technology* (3rd edn., St Paul, Minn., West Group, 1997), 1–143–1–144; compare *MAI Systems Corporation* v. *Peak Computer, Inc.*, 991 F 2d 511 (9th Cir. 1993), cert. dismissed, 510 US 1033 (1994).

that the RBOCs' licence did not give them ownership of the copyright and, as the restrictions on use of the copy were very severe, the licence did not give them ownership of the copy.[32] The Court noted that section 117 had, in draft, read "rightful possesors of a computer program" but had been changed to "owner" in the final enactment. Therefore, it remains unclear in American law when the user of software under a licence will be said to be the owner of a copy of the software.[33]

In this regard, it is also important to mention section 109 of the Copyright Act 1976, which codifies what is called the first sale doctrine, which normally means that the tangible embodiment of the copyright but not the intellectual property can be unconditionally disposed of by the purchaser, the copyright owner having exclusive control over the first sale of the item. Section 109 also provides that, unless authorised by the copyright owner of computer software, the end user cannot for commercial gain rent, lease or lend a copy of the computer software. Does that mean they can undertake the even more commercially sensitive act of selling a copy if they own one? Does that mean that the first sale doctrine does apply to a copy of a program?[34] *Microsoft Corporation* v. *Harmony Computers & Electronics Inc.*[35] suggests not, but this case confuses ownership of the copyright with ownership of the copy of the program. Section 109 talks only about "disposing of" (through rental, lease or lending), and one wonders whether drafters of the section did not appreciate that a copy can be sold. Recall

---

[32] *DSC* v. *Pulse Communications, Inc.*, 170 F 3d 1354, 1360–2 (Fed. Cir. 1999).

[33] For further debate on the issue of ownership of copies, see D. Nimmer, E. Brown and G.N. Frischling, "The Metamorphosis of Contract into Expand" (1999) 87 *Calif L Rev* 17, 32–40, arguing that in many cases there will be a "sale" of a copy; M.A. Lemley, "Beyond Pre-emption: The Law and Policy of Intellectual Property Licensing" (1999) 87 *Calif L Rev* 111, 128–31. Nimmer *et al.* suggest that where end users "acquire full dominion" over the tangible object, i.e. where the "licensor" of the software "release[d] from their control", "actually sold or otherwise permanently disposed of those physical goods", the transferee is the owner of the physical media, with rights under the first sale provisions. They make the interesting argument that, where software is digitally delivered (as opposed to purchase of a physical medium including the software), there should still be a "first sale" of a "copy", because, if Internet distribution does not constitute sale of a "copy" then presumably the recipient of the (non-)copy may send further (non-)copies to other recipients, which would not be an infringement, since there would be no distribution of "copies". Hence, they reject as "implausible" the view that Internet distribution does not result in distribution of a copy. I thank Mark Lemley and Jay Dougherty for discussion of this issue.

[34] The Court in *DSC* v. *Pulse Communications, Inc.*, 170 F 3d 1354 (Fed. Cir. 1999), impliedly supports this where it says (at 1361): "[e]ach of the DSC–RBOC agreements limits the contracting RBOC's right to transfer copies of the POTS–DI software or to disclose the details of the software to third parties. For example, the DSC–Ameritech agreement provides that Ameritech shall 'not provide, disclose or make the Software or any portions or aspects thereof available to any person except its employees on a "need to know" basis without the prior written consent of [DSC]. . . .' Such a restriction is plainly at odds with the section 109 right to transfer owned copies of software to third parties." The Court explicitly recognised the application of the first sale doctrine to software, where it held Pulsecom not liable for direct copyright infringement of software purchased on the open market free of any licence conditions (at 1363). See further Lemley, n. 33 above, 131. In many standard form software licences the licensee is allowed to sell the copy of the software only along with the machine (not by itself), and the purchaser must agree to be bound by the terms of the licence.

[35] 864 F Supp. 208 (EDNY 1994).

that "owner" in section 117 originally read "rightful possessor".[36] The question remains whether the first sale doctrine does have a role to play in the area of software licensing. If the first sale doctrine does apply, then the ability to control exploitation of the digital product is significantly reduced.

UCITA deals specifically with "mass-market licenses", which are described as small dollar value, routine and anonymous transactions involving information that is directed to the general public in cases where the transaction occurs in a retail market available to and used by the general public. A mass-market licence is normally a consumer contract and not an ordinary commercial transaction between businesses using ordinary commercial methods of acquiring or transferring commercial information. The commentary explains that a mass-market transaction is characterised by (a) the *market* in which the transaction occurs, (b) the *terms* of the transaction, and (c) the *nature* of the information involved:

The market is a retail market where information is made available in pre-packaged form under generally similar terms to the general public as a whole and in which the general public, including consumers, is a frequent participant. The prototypical retail market is a department store, grocery store, gas station, shopping center, or the like. These locations are open to, and in fact attract, the general public as a whole. In a retail market, the majority of the transactions also involve relatively small quantities, non-negotiated terms, and transactions to an end user rather than a purchaser who plans to resell the acquired product. The products are available to anyone who enters the retail location and can pay the stated price.

The terms of the transaction will normally involve information aimed at the general public as a whole, including consumers. This does not include information products for a business or professional audience, a subgroup of the general public, members of an organization, or persons with a separate relationship to the information provider. . . . The transactions covered are purchases of true mass-market information and do not include specialty software for business or professional uses, information for specially targeted limited audiences, commercial software distributed in non-retail transactions, or professional use software. Generally, this is inconsistent with substantial customization of the information for a particular end user. Customization that is routine in mass markets or that is done by the licensee after acquiring the information does not take the information, and therefore the transaction, outside the concept of a mass-market transaction.

The nature of the transaction is that it will be with an end user. An end user licensee is one that generally intends to use the information or the informational rights in its own internal business or personal affairs. . . . However, the definition, by excluding on-line transactions not involving a consumer establishes an important principle. In the new transactional environment of on-line commerce, it is important not to regulate

---

[36] While Australian law does not contain a statutory first sale doctrine (see J. McKeough and A. Stewart, *Intellectual Property in Australia* (2nd edn., Sydney, Butterworths, 1997), 132; *Pacific Film Laboratories Pty. Ltd.* v. *FCT* (1970) 121 CLR 154), recent amendments to the Australian Copyright Act along the lines of s. 117 of the American Copyright Act refer to the "owner or licensee of a copy" of a program: Copyright Amendment (Computer Programs) Act 1999 (Cth).

transactions beyond consumer issues. This gives commerce room to develop while preserving consumer interests.

C The Creation of Mass-market Licences: *ProCD, Inc.* v. *Zeidenberg*

Courts in the United States have recently recognised the validity of (the creation process of) mass-market software licences in the form of shrink-wrap and click-wrap licences.[37] Prior to *ProCD, Inc.* v. *Zeidenberg*,[38] most courts refused to enforce shrink-wrap licences because consumers had not meaningfully assented to the terms of the licence.[39] They regarded a contract of sale as having taken place at the time the consumer tendered payment and the store rang up the sale. The licence inside the box was held to be no more than a proposal to vary the contract or change the nature of the transaction to which the consumer had not separately agreed.[40]

Similarly, at first instance the District Court in *ProCD* held that consumers do not have adequate notice, since the terms of the licence are printed inside the box rather than on the outside. The mere reference to the terms at the time of initial contract formation was not considered to present buyers with an adequate opportunity to decide whether they are acceptable. In that case, ProCD sought to enforce a shrink-wrap licence attached to its database, entitled SelectPhone, a compilation of telephone directories on CD-ROM disks which the defendant purchased in a retail store. Printed on the outside of the package was a notice that use of the CD-ROMs was restricted by the terms of an enclosed licence. This licence contained both in the user's manual found inside the product's packaging and encoded on the CD-ROM disks themselves, restricted use to non-commercial purposes. In violation of this licence, the defendant sold the information contained on the CD-ROMs to third parties.

---

[37] The following material is taken from Evans and Fitzgerald, n. 22 above.

[38] 86 F 3d 1447 (7th Cir. 1997); see also *Hill* v. *Gateway 2000, Inc.*, 105 F 3d 1147 (7th Cir. 1997), where the Seventh Circuit held that a plaintiff's purchase of a computer was governed by contract terms shipped to her along with the computer. Endorsing the decision of the Seventh Circuit in *ProCD*, the District Court for the Northern District of California in *Hotmail Corporation* v. *Van Money Pie, Inc.*, 47 USPQ 2d 1020 (ND Cal. 1998), in respect of click-wrap licences, recently held that defendants were bound by Terms of Service posted on a Website as a result of their act of clicking on a button "I agree".

[39] Nevertheless, it appears to be open to the court to validate shrink-wrap licences under existing law: see UCC Art. 2–204, which states that a "contract for the sale of goods may be made in any manner sufficient to show agreement, including conduct by both parties which recognises the existence of a contract". Similarly, §19 of the *Restatement (Second) of Contracts* provides that "[t]he manifestation of assent may be made wholly or partly by written or spoken words or by other action or by failure to act". In fact, this rationale was used by the Seventh Circuit in support of its decision in *ProCD*.

[40] In *Vault Corp.* v. *Quaid Software Ltd.*, 847 F 2d 255 (5th Cir. 1988), the Court refused to enforce a Louisiana statute purporting to validate shrink-wrap licences in so far as the licence terms interfered with consumer rights under Federal copyright law.

In determining the enforceability of the shrink-wrap licence, the District Court treated the sale of software as a sale of goods under the Uniform Commercial Code, rather than as a "licence". Judge Barbara Crabb relied on section 2–209 of Article 2, which requires the express consent of a party to any proposed contractual modifications. Under Article 2, the shrink-wrap licence was not binding on the buyers because they did not have the opportunity to object to the proposed user agreement or even review it before purchase and they did not assent to the terms explicitly after they learned of them. Furthermore, the terms of the software user agreement were not presented to the defendants at the time of sale. The sole reference to the user agreement was a disclosure in small print at the bottom of the package, stating that the defendants were subject to the terms and conditions of the enclosed licence agreement. The District Court's construction of the transaction as a sale meant that restrictions on consumer use as well as attempts to limit warranties and liabilities in the shrink-wrap licence were not enforceable.

However, the Court of Appeals for the Seventh Circuit reversed the decision.[41] It held that shrink-wrap licences are enforceable unless their terms are objectionable on grounds applicable to contracts in general, e.g. if they violate a rule of positive law, or are unconscionable. In upholding the shrink-wrap agreement, the Court determined that ProCD had made an offer to license its product which was accepted by Zeidenberg's conduct in choosing to use the software, after he was afforded an opportunity to read the terms of the licence. By so using the software, the defendant was bound by the terms of the licence. In enforcing the shrink-wrap licence restriction, the Court would permit only home use of the information. Judge Frank Easterbrook took the view that ProCD would be unable to recoup its considerable investment in compiling, double-checking, formatting, and updating the telephone directory data if users could just up-load the data onto their personal websites.

Judge Easterbrook's analysis of the facts in *ProCD* is characterised by neo-classical economic and contract theory in which the focus of decision-making is the efficient operation of the market.[42] Neo-classical economic analysis[43] appears to offer practical and policy advantages in so far as it lends the law a seemingly greater coherence. It provides a coherent interpretation of the effects of a particular measure, in this case the appropriation of ProCD's database, on the information industry and its consumers, and on its income. The point of departure for the economic analysis is the model of the perfectly competitive

---

[41] *ProCD, Inc.* v. *Zeidenberg*, 86 F 3d 1447 (7th Cir. 1997).

[42] According to this viewpoint there is an external logic, which does not exist in the law itself, but in the concept of "economic efficiency": see F. Easterbrook, "Foreword: The Court and the Economic System" (1984) 98 *Harv L Rev* 4.

[43] Neo-classical economics treats the individual as the basic unit of analysis. It assumes that individuals act rationally to maximise their own self-interest: R.A. Posner, *The Economic Analysis of Law* (3rd edn., Boston, Mass., Little Brown, 1986), 4–16.

market,[44] and the role of prices in achieving such a market. In *ProCD*, the question of how the market works and how it values the information commodity was critical in deciding the ultimate distribution of resources in this case. The decision was based on the rationale that upholding the shrink-wrap licence allowed the plaintiff to exercise price arbitrage, price discrimination being a process which not only benefited ProCD, by facilitating the recovery of its investment, but also benefited consumers through lower prices.[45]

D Creating Layered Contractual Licences under UCITA

A general theme of UCITA is to promote freedom of contract, and one of the ways it does this is to facilitate flexible information transactions. In particular UCITA encourages the acceptance of the notion of layered (and open: section 305) information contracting whereby the notification of terms of the contract can be supplied after the act of distribution to the consumer. Sections 112, 208 and 209 set out the basis on which a software licence can be validated even though the terms of the contract may not be disclosed to the consumer until first use of the product, which is usually after the act of purchase. In essence, these sections give legislative force to the *ProCD* decision.

Under section 112, a person can manifest assent to a contractual term through signature or other conduct.[46] Appropriate notice of contractual terms must be given before assent will be found.[47] As the commentary explains, determining

---

[44] The market is defined as "a decentralised mechanism for allocating resources": see C. Veljanovski, *The New Law and Economics* (Oxford, Centre for Socio-Legal Studies, 1982), 19–20.

[45] *ProCD, Inc.* v. *Zeidenberg*, 86 F 3d 1447 (7th Cir. 1997). On the interrelationship of supply, demand and price, see Veljanovski, *ibid.*, 31–44.

[46] "SECTION 112. MANIFESTING ASSENT; OPPORTUNITY TO REVIEW.

(a) A person manifests assent to a record or term if the person, acting with knowledge of, or after having an opportunity to review the record or term or a copy of it:

(1) authenticates the record or term to adopt or accept it;

(2) intentionally engages in conduct or makes statements with reason to know that the other party or its electronic agent may infer from the conduct or statement that the person assents to the record or term.

(b) An electronic agent manifests assent to a record or term if, after having an opportunity to review, the electronic agent:

(1) authenticates the record; or

(2) engages in operations that the circumstances clearly indicate constitute acceptance."

[47] S. 112:

"(e) With respect to an opportunity to review, the following rules apply:

(1) A person has an opportunity to review a record or term only if the record or term is made available in a manner so that a reasonable person ought to have had it called to the person's attention and permit review.

(2) An electronic agent has an opportunity to review a record or term only if the record or term is made available in manner that would enable a reasonably configured electronic agent to react to the record or term.

(3) If a record or term is available for review only after a person becomes obligated to pay or begins its performance, the person has an opportunity to review only if:

(A) it had a right to a return if it rejected the record;   *cont.*

whether a person manifested assent to a record or term entails analysis of three issues:

First, the person must have had knowledge of the record or term or an opportunity to review it before assenting. This is implicit, but not stated in the *Restatement*. Opportunity to review requires that the record be available in a manner that ought to call it to the attention of a reasonable person.

Second, given an opportunity to review, the person must do something that assents to the terms. The person may authenticate the record or term, express assent, or engage in conduct with reason to know that in the circumstances the conduct indicates assent. *Restatement (Second) of Contracts* § 19. Conduct manifests assent if the party intentionally acted with knowledge or reason to know that the other party would infer assent from its actions or words.

Third, the conduct or authentication must be attributable to the person. General agency law and Section 213 provide standards for attribution.

In expanding on the issue of assent, the commentary refers to two scenarios. Scenario One involves a registration screen for America Online which prominently states: "[p]lease read the license. It contains important terms about your use and our obligations with respect to the information. Click here to review the **License**. If you agree to the license, indicate this by clicking the 'I agree' button. If you do not agree, click 'I decline'." The on-screen buttons are clearly identified. The bold text is a hypertext link which, if selected, promptly displays the licence. The commentary suggests that a party that indicates "I agree" manifests assent to the licence and adopts its terms.

Scenario Two relates to the first computer screen of an on-line stock-quotation service and requires that the potential licensee enter a name, address and credit card number. After entering the information and striking the "enter" key, the licensee has access to the data and receives a monthly bill. In the centre of the screen, amidst other language in small print, is the statement: **"Terms and conditions of service; disclaimers"** indicating a hyperlink to the terms. The customer's attention is not drawn to this sentence, nor is the customer asked to react to it. The commentary explains that, even though entering a name and identification, coupled with using the service, is assent to a contract, there is no assent to the "terms of service" and disclaimers since there is no act indicating assent to the record containing the terms. It adds that a court would determine the contract terms on other grounds, including the default rules of UCITA and usage of trade.

(B) the record proposed a modification of contract;

(C) the record provided particulars of performance under Section 305; or

(D) in a case not involving a mass-market license, the parties at the time of contracting had reason to know that a record or terms would not be presented at or before the initial use or access to the information or informational rights.

(4) The right to a return under paragraph (3) may arise by law or by agreement.

(f) The provisions of this section may be modified by an agreement setting out standards applicable to future transactions between the parties."

Sections 208[48] and 209[49] of UCITA deal with the notion of adopting terms of a contract and further introduce the notion of layered contracting. Section 208 states the basic principles about when and how terms of a record are adopted, while expressly recognising that commercial deals often involve layered contracting and rejecting the idea that a contract and all its terms must be formed at a single point in time. The section permits layered contracting where the parties have reason to believe that terms will be proposed at some later time, acknowledging that many commercial transactions involve a rolling or layering process. The commentary explains:

> While some courts seem to hold that an initial agreement per se concludes the contracting as a single event notwithstanding ordinary practice and expectations that terms will follow, other courts recognize layered contract formation and term definition, correctly viewing contracting as a process, rather than a single event. ProCD, Inc. v. Zeidenberg, 86 F.3d 1447 (7th Cir. 1996). This section, along with the contract formation principles, explicitly accepts the layering principle and provides a standard for distinguishing when the intent or expectation is to conclude the contract at the initial

[48] "SECTION 208. ADOPTING TERMS OF RECORDS.

(a) Except as otherwise provided in Section 209, a party adopts the terms of a record, including a standard form, if the party agrees to the record, by manifesting assent or otherwise.

(b) The terms of a record may be adopted as the terms of the contract after beginning performance or use under the agreement, if the parties had reason to know that their agreement would be represented in whole or in part by a later record to be agreed on and there would be no opportunity to review the record or a copy of it before performance or use began. If the parties fail to agree to terms and did not intend to form a contract unless they agreed, Section 202(e) applies.

(c) If a party adopts the terms of a record, the terms become part of the contract without regard to the party's knowledge or understanding of individual terms in the record, except for a term that is unenforceable because it fails to satisfy another requirement of this [Act]."

[49] "SECTION 209. MASS-MARKET LICENSE.

(a) A party adopts the terms of a mass-market license for purposes of Section 208 only if the party agrees to the license, by manifesting assent or otherwise, before or during the party's initial performance or use of or access to the information. A term is not part of the license if:

(1) the term is unconscionable under Section 111 or is unenforceable under Section 105(a) or (b); or

(2) subject to Section 301, the term conflicts with terms to which the parties to the license expressly agreed.

(b) If a licensee does not have an opportunity to review a mass-market license or a copy of it before becoming obligated to pay and does not agree, by manifesting assent or otherwise, to the license after having that opportunity, the licensee is entitled to a return under Section 112 and, in addition, to:

(1) reimbursement of any reasonable expenses incurred in complying with the licensor's instructions for return or destruction of the computer information or, in the absence of instructions, incurred for return postage or similar reasonable expense in returning it; and

(2) compensation for any reasonable and foreseeable costs of restoring the licensee's information processing system to reverse changes in the system caused by the installation, if:

(A) the installation occurs because information must be installed to enable review of the license; and

(B) the installation alters the system or information in it but does not restore the system or information upon removal of the installed information because of rejection of the license.

(c) In a mass-market transaction, if the licensor does not have an opportunity to review a record with proposed terms before the licensor delivers or becomes obligated to deliver the information, and if the licensor does not agree, by manifesting assent or otherwise, to those terms after having that opportunity, the licensor is entitled to a return."

point as contrasted to an expectation that terms will be provided for later agreement. In information commerce, the circumstances often indicate that initial general assent assumes that terms will be developed or presented later to fill out the details of the transaction. Such circumstances include customary practices in software licensing, but also will include use of electronic agents by licensees. For example, a business or a consumer may instruct its electronic agent to search the Internet for car dealers willing to meet pre-set terms and offer prices within a pre-set range. While the business or consumer will expect to stand on the terms accepted by the dealer, both it and the dealer expect more details to be added to the contract, such as warranty, maintenance, and other standard provisions, without having to consider all such terms in the first interaction of the automated contracting system.

The section clarifies that contract terms can be proposed and agreed to as part of completing the initial contract even though proposed after the beginning of performance by one or both parties. Such terms are treated as part of the initial contracting process if at the time of initial agreement, the parties had reason to know and, thus, expected that this would occur and that terms of a record to be agreed would provide elaboration of their contract. If, instead, the parties considered their deal to be closed at the outset, then subsequently proposed terms from either party are treated as a proposed modification of the agreement, effective only under concepts applicable to such modifications. The third alternative, of course, is that the initial agreement leaves terms open and allows one party to specify what those terms are at some later date. The act of specifying the terms is, in effect, merely a performance of the contract.

As the commentary also explains, in many cases where assent is sought after the person paid or delivered, or became obliged to pay or deliver, the manifestation of assent is not effective unless the person has a right to a return if they choose to refuse the license.[50]

Section 209 deals with mass-market licences, including consumer contracts. It defines the circumstances under which a party's assent to a mass-market licence adopts the terms of that record and places limitations on the effectiveness of mass-market licences. The section is meant to be read in connection with sections 208 and 112.

The commentary explains that a party adopts the terms of a record only if it agrees to the record by manifesting assent or otherwise. A party cannot manifest assent unless it had an opportunity to review the record before that assent occurs. This means that the record must be available for review and be called to the person's attention in a manner such that a reasonable person ought to have noticed it. A manifestation of assent requires conduct or statements indicating assent, and that the person has reason to know that, in the circumstances, this will be the case.

Adopting the terms of a record for purposes of section 209 occurs pursuant to section 208. The commentary explains that if the terms of the record are proposed for assent by a party only after it commences performance of the

---

[50] See also s. 112(e). The commentary provides that the return obligation applies in mass-market contracts and in other contracts if the expectation is that the terms will be provided at or before the first use of the information.

agreement, the terms become effective under these sections only if the party (e.g. the licensee) had reason to know that terms would be proposed after the initial agreement. The commentary continues that, even if reason to know exists, this section requires that the terms be presented not later than the initial use of the information and that, if the mass-market licence was not made available before the initial agreement, the party is given a right to a return should it refuse the licence.

Section 209(b) assures the licensee of an opportunity to review and an effective choice to accept or reject a licence presented after initial payment. It creates a return right that places the end user in a situation whereby it can exercise a meaningful choice regarding licences presented after initial agreement. The commentary explains:

> This return right also does not arise if there was an opportunity to review the license before making the initial agreement. In subsection (b) the exposure to potential liability for expenses of reinstating the system after review creates an incentive for licensors to make the license or a copy available for review before the initial obligation is created. Subsection (b) does not apply to transactions involving software obtained online if the software provider makes available and obtains assent to the license as part of the ordering process. On the other hand, in a mail order transaction, if the license is first received along with the copy of the information that was ordered, subsection (b) applies. The return right under this section includes, but differs from the return right in Section 112(e). The return in Section 209 is cost free in that the end user receives reimbursement for reasonable costs of return and, in a case where installation of the information was required to review the license and caused adverse changes in the end user's system, to reasonable costs in returning the system to its initial condition. The fact that this section states an affirmative right in the mass market to a cost free refund does not affect whether under other law outside of this Act, a similar right might exist in other contexts.

The advent of the layered contract questions fundamental principles of notice that have long been seen as sacrosanct in the law of contract. The success or failure of this new approach in the information market will depend largely on its ability adequately to satisfy the needs of mass-market consumers.

IV THE LEGITIMATE SCOPE OF A LICENCE: THE RECONCILIATION PRINCIPLE

One of the major issues for debate in relation to Article 2B was the extent to which a contractual licence could override established principles of copyright law (such as fair use) and competition law. In the USA, the ability of State common law or statute to override copyright law is resolved by the extent to which the Federal legislation pre-empts the State law. A similar principle known as the doctrine of inconsistency operates in Australia pursuant to section 109 of the Constitution.

Section 105(a) and (b) of UCITA govern the extent to which contract can override other established information property fundamentals.[51] In essence, this is a question of how to reconcile freedom of contract with the public domain interest. UCITA seeks to facilitate freedom of contract in that it provides default or gap filling rules used when the parties do not agree to the contrary. It seeks to balance such an approach against public interest through section 105.[52]

The commentary explains these provisions in the following way:

The transition from print to digital media has created new demands for information. Because digital information is so easily copied, increased attention has been focused on the formulation of rights in information in order to encourage its creation and on the development of contracting methods that enable effective development and efficient marketing of information assets. Here, as in other parts of the economy, the fundamental policy of contract law is to enforce contractual agreements. At the same time, there remains a fundamental public interest in assuring that information in the public domain is free for all to use from the public domain and to provide for access to information for public purposes such as education, research, and fair comment. While the new digital environment increases the risk of unfair copying, the enforcement of contracts that permit owners to limit the use of information and the development of technological self-help measures have given the owner of information

---

[51] "SECTION 105 RELATION TO FEDERAL LAW; FUNDAMENTAL PUBLIC POLICY; TRANSACTIONS SUBJECT TO OTHER STATE LAW:

(a) A provision of this [Act] which is pre-empted by federal law is unenforceable to the extent of the pre-emption.

(b) If a term of a contract violates a fundamental public policy, the court may refuse to enforce the contract, may enforce the remainder of the contract without the impermissible term, or so limit the application of the impermissible term as to avoid any result contrary to public policy, in each case, to the extent that the interest in enforcement is clearly outweighed by a public policy against enforcement of the term.

(c) Except as otherwise provided in subsection (d), if this [Act] conflicts with a consumer protection statute or administrative rule of this State in effect on the effective date of this Act, the conflicting statute or rule governs.

(d) If the law of this State in effect on the effective date of this [Act] applies to a transaction governed by this [Act], the following rules apply:

(1) A requirement that a term, waiver, notice, or disclaimer be in a writing is satisfied by a record.

(2) A requirement that a writing or a term be signed is satisfied by an authentication.

(3) A requirement that a term be conspicuous or the like is satisfied by a term that is conspicuous in accordance with this [Act].

(4) A requirement of consent or agreement to a term is satisfied by an action that manifests assent to a term in accordance with this [Act].

(e) Failure to comply with a law or policy referred to in this section has only the effect specified in the law or policy.

[52] UCITA does not alter substantive provisions of State consumer protection statutes. As the commentary explains: "this recognises the role of independent and divergent state consumer protection statutes in the fifty States. In addition, UCITA contains a number of consumer protection rules for consumer contracts within UCITA or under the more general reference to mass-market licenses, a category that includes all consumer contracts. These rules augment existing consumer protection statutes and the existing protections control to the extent of any conflict. The consumer-related rules include: 109 (choice of law); 217 (electronic error); 211 (limit on mass-market license; right to return); 303 (limit on no-oral modification clause); 304 (limit on modification of continuing contract); 406 (warranty disclaimer); 409 (third-party beneficiary); 704 (perfect tender); 803 (exclusion of personal injury claim); 811 (limitation on agreement to specific performance remedy)."

considerable means of enforcing exclusivity in the information they produce or collect. This is true not only against those in contractual privity with the owner, but also in some contexts against the world-at-large.

The effort to balance the rights of owners of information against the claims of those who want access is very complex and has been the subject of considerable controversy and negotiation at both the federal level and internationally. The extent to which the resolution of these issues at the federal level ought to pre-empt state law is beyond the scope of this Act, the central purpose of which is to facilitate private transactions in information. Moreover, it is clear that limitations on the information rights of owners that may be imposed in a copyright regime where rights are conferred that bind third parties, may be inappropriate in a contractual setting where courts should be reluctant to set aside terms of a contract. Subsections (a) and (b) draw the balance between fundamental interests in contract freedom and fundamental public policies such as those regarding innovation, competition, and free expression.

Subsection (a) restates the normal rule that if a Federal law invalidates a State contract law or contract term in a particular setting, Federal law prevails. The commentary explains that while subsection (a) refers to pre-emptive Federal rules, other doctrines grounded in the First Amendment, copyright misuse and other Federal law may limit enforcement of some contract terms in some cases. The view of the commentary is that no general pre-emption of contracting arises under copyright or patent law.[53]

Subsection (b) confirms the legal principle that, in certain cases, terms may be unenforceable because they violate a fundamental public policy that clearly overrides the policy favouring enforcement of private transactions as between the parties. As the commentary explains, this principle is recognised under American common law and in the *Restatement (Second) of Contracts* § 178 and following, and is a supplementary legal principle incorporated under section 114.

The commentary further argues that fundamental State policies are most commonly stated by the legislature and, in the absence of legislative action, courts should be reluctant to override a contract term. It explains that in evaluating a claim that a term violates this subsection, courts should consider a variety of factors, including:

(a) the extent to which enforcement or invalidation of the term will adversely affect the interests of each party to the transaction, or the public;

(b) the interest in protecting expectations arising from the contract;

(c) the purpose of the challenged term;

(d) the extent to which enforcement or invalidation will adversely affect other fundamental public interests;

(e) the strength and consistency of judicial decisions applying similar policies in similar contexts;

---

[53] See further *National Car Rental Sys., Inc.* v. *Computer Assoc's Int'l, Inc.*, 991 F 2d 426 (8th Cir. 1993); *ProCD, Inc.* v. *Zeidenberg*, 86 F 3d 1447 (7th Cir. 1996). For critical analysis of this view, see Nimmer, Brown and Frischling, n. 33 above; and Lemley, n. 33 above.

(f) the nature of any express legislative or regulatory policies; and

(g) the values of certainty of enforcement and uniformity in interpreting contractual provisions.

The commentary further explains that the public policies most likely to be applicable to transactions within this Act are those relating to innovation, competition, and fair comment. It goes on to say:

> Innovation policy recognizes the need for a balance between conferring property interests in information in order to create incentives for creation and the importance of a rich public domain upon which most innovation ultimately depends. Competition policy prevents unreasonable restraints on publicly available information in order to protect competition. Rights of free expression may include the right of persons to comment, whether positively or negatively, on the character or quality of information in the marketplace.
>
> Striking the appropriate balance depends on a variety of contextual factors that can only be assessed on a case-by-case basis with an eye to national policies.
>
> A term or contract that results from an agreement between commercial parties should be presumed to be valid and a heavy burden of proof should be imposed on the party seeking to escape the terms of the agreement under subsection (b). This Act and general contract law recognizes the commercial necessity of also enforcing mass-market transactions that involve the use of standard form agreements. The terms of such forms may not be available to the licensee prior to the payment of the price and typically are not subject to affirmative negotiations. In such circumstances, courts must be more vigilant in assuring that limitations on use of the informational subject matter of the license are not invalid under fundamental public policy.
>
> Even in mass-market transactions, however, limitations in a license for software or other information such as terms that prohibit the licensee from making multiple copies, or that prohibit the licensee or others from using the information for commercial purposes, or that limit the number of users authorized to access the information, or that prohibit the modification of software or informational content without the licensor's permission are typically enforceable. *See, e.g., Storm Impact, Inc.* v. *Software of the Month Club*, 1998 WL 456572 (N.D. Ill. 1998) ("no commercial use" restriction in an on-line contract). On the other hand, terms in a mass-market license that prohibit persons from observing the visible operations or visible characteristics of software and using the observations to develop non-infringing commercial products, that prohibit quotation of limited material for education or criticism purposes, or that preclude a non-profit library licensee from making an archival copy would ordinarily be invalid in the absence of a showing of significant commercial need.

The commenatry explains that under the general principle enunciated in subsection (b), courts also may look to Federal copyright and patent laws for guidance on what types of limitations on the rights of owners of information ordinarily seem appropriate, recognising, however, that private parties generally have sound commercial reasons for contracting for limitations on use, and that enforcing private ordering arrangements in itself reflects a fundamental public policy enacted throughout the Uniform Commercial Code and the common law.

As UCITA confirms, key legal areas to be considered in the reconciliation of freedom of contract with public use and innovation, include fair use/fair dealing (e.g. reverse engineering) and competition law. In relation to free speech, the requirement of "state action" will be a complex issue.[54]

A Fair Use: Reverse Engineering and De-compilation of Software

In order to develop complementary and improved software products, software developers often need to reverse engineer industry standard software in an attempt to make software that can be interoperable (conversant) with the industry standard. In many cases, in order to reverse engineer software one needs to copy (and in some cases "borrow" parts of) the software, which is technically an infringement of the copyright owner's exclusive rights over reproduction. In the US, the courts[55] have employed fair use doctrine[56] to mediate this issue, while in Australia the government has enacted a (part) legislative solution through amendment to the Copyright Act.[57] Fair use defines the appropriate balance between a monopoly right given as an incentive for innovation and the public interest in the free flow of information for a variety of cultural reasons.[58] In Australia, the Copyright Law Review Committee[59] has recommended the adoption of a more broad-based fair use right similar to the US model in place of the narrower and more specific fair dealing exceptions: see, e.g. sections 40, 41 and 42 of the Copyright Act 1968 (Cth). The fate of reverse engineering for interoperabilty

[54] *Shelley* v. *Kraemer*, 334 US 1 (1948); *Flagg Brothers, Inc.* v. *Brooks*, 436 US 185 (1978); L. Tribe, *American Constitutional Law* (2nd edn., New York, Foundation Press, 1988), 1711 ff.

[55] *Sega Enterprises Ltd.* v. *Accolade, Inc.*, 977 F 2d 1510 (9th Cir. 1992); *Computer Associates International, Inc.* v. *Altai, Inc.*, 982 F 2d 693 (2nd Cir. 1992). See also Digital Millennium Copyright Act 1998 (USA), s. 1201(f); European Software Directive 91/250 [1991] OJ L122/42, Art. 6.

[56] Copyright Act 1976 (USA), s. 107; B. Fitzgerald, "Underlying Rationales of Fair Use: Simplifying the Copyright Act" (1998) 2 *Southern Cross Univ L Rev* 153. On reverse engineering and de-compilation generally, see A. Fitzgerald and C. Cifuentes, "Interoperability and Computer Software Protection in Australia" (1998) 4 *Computer and Telecommunications L Rev* 271; C. Cifuentes and A. Fitzgerald, "Reverse Engineering of Computer Programs: Comments on the Copyright Law Review Committee's Final Report on Computer Software Protection" (1995) 6 *J of Law and Information Science* 241.

[57] Attorney General D. Williams and Senator R. Alston, "Copyright Changes to Help Australian Software Industry", 23 February 1999 (<http://www.dcita.gov.au>); see Copyright Act 1968 (Cth), ss. 47D-F, introduced by the Copyright Amendment (Computer Programs) Act 1999 (these provisions condition, and arguably reduce, the scope of the legality of reverse engineering for inter-operability, on the consent of the owner or licensee of the copy of the program used to make the reproduction or adaptation: s. 47D; cf Digital Millennium Copyright Act 1998 (USA), s. 1201(f). On 30 September 1999, the High Court of Australia handed down its decision in *Data Access Corporation* v. *Powerflex Services Pty. Ltd.* (1999) 73 ALJR 1435, which suggested that the legality of reverse engineering for inter-operability purposes under the copyright law as it stood before the recent amendments was to be narrowly defined.

[58] Fitzgerald, n. 56 above.

[59] Copyright Law Review Committee, *Report on the Simplification of the Copyright Act 1968 Part 1 Exceptions to the Exclusive Rights of Copyright Owners* (1998) <http://www.agps.gov.au/clrc/>.

purposes under copyright law will depend on how the amended legislation operates and whether a broad-based fair use exception is introduced into Australian law.

The question remains as to the extent to which reverse engineering rights can be contractually prohibited.[60] The degree to which reverse engineering can survive the contractual licence is seen by many software developers as being of the utmost significance. The commentary, while not being definitive, suggests that contractually prohibiting reverse engineering will in some cases fall foul of section 105(b) of UCITA. In Australia, the Copyright Act 1968(Cth), as amended by the Copyright Amendment (Computer Programs) Act 1999 (Cth), provides, in section 47H, that an agreement that has the effect of limiting sections 47D–47F (which permit reverse engineering for certain purposes on certain conditions) is of no effect. However, as sections 47D–47F are conditioned on the activities being undertaken by or on behalf of the owner or licensee of a copy of the program and the copy of the software not being an infringing copy, there may be scope for arguing that the software manufacturer still has the capacity to license the product on terms that do not permit reverse engineering, thereby defeating sections 47D–47F and circumventing section 47H.

In the US, the facilitation of reverse engineering (at least until the Digital Millennium Copyright Act 1998) was seen as being part of the fair use doctrine. The degree to which a contractual licence can override fair use is a broader question that has caused immense concern among leading US copyright scholars.[61]

B Competition Law

In an ideal world competition law will act to balance the monopolies copyright, patent and contract create in relation to software and other information products. It will act to define the scope of the grant of intellectual property rights. Originally the approach in the European Union was that dealings within the scope of the intellectual property rights granted by the relevant intellectual property law were immune from competition law, while other dealings were subject to competition law. The continuation of such an approach has been questioned in a decision that looks primarily at the anti-competitive effect of intellectual property rights, i.e. the scope of the grant as defined by intellectual property and competition law.[62]

[60] It is interesting to note that under the European Software Directive (Council Directive of 14 May 1991 on the legal protection of computer programs [1991] OJ L122/42), contractual prohibition of reverse engineering for interoperability purposes is not allowed: Arts. 6(1) and 9(1).

[61] P. Samuelson and K. Opsahl, "Licensing Information in the Global Information Market: Freedom of Contract Meets Public Policy" [1999] *EIPR* 387.

[62] See further *Radio Telefis Eireann and Independent Television Publications Ltd.* v. *European Commission and Magill* [1995] 4 CMLR 718; Arts. 81 and 82 EC (ex Arts. 85 and 86) (European Union); G. Morgan and A. Wilson, "Restrictions on the Transfer of Software" (1996) 3 *CTLR* 82; Art. 40 TRIPS; I.A. Stamatoudi, "The Hidden Agenda in *Magill* and Its Impact on New Technologies" (1998) 1 *J of World IP* 153; I Govaere, *The Use and Abuse of Intellectual Property Rights in the EC* (London, Sweet and Maxwell, 1996).

The appropriate interplay between competition law and intellectual property law is of utmost importance to the construction of a digital identity, and is currently being played out in the *United States* v. *Microsoft Corp.* case.[63] In Australia, much focus has been placed on section 51(3) of the Trade Practices Act 1974 (Cth), which exempts certain intellectual property rights from the full application of the Act. Section 51(3) was set for reform in accordance with the Draft Report[64] published by the National Competition Council.[65] The proposal was to remove the licensing intellectual property rights from the section 51(3) exemption, which would have made competition lawyers even more eager to look at the monopolies created through intellectual property legislation; and more particularly, the monopolies imposed by a contractual licence of intellectual property such as software. However, the Final Report has recommended against removing the licensing of intellectual property rights from the section 51(3) exemption,[66] although another government inquiry on the interplay of intellectual property and competition law is currently being undertaken by the Australian Intellectual Property and Competition Review Committee.[67]

In 1995 the US Department of Justice and the Federal Trade Commission issued the *Antitrust Guidelines for the Licensing of Intellectual Property*, which govern the interaction of intellectual property and competition law. The guidelines contain three main principles:

(a) for the purpose of antitrust analysis, the Agencies (the Department of Justice and the Federal Trade Commission) regard intellectual property as being essentially comparable to any other form of property;
(b) the Agencies do not presume that intellectual property creates market power in the antitrust context; and
(c) the Agencies recognise that intellectual property licensing allows firms to combine complementary factors of production and is generally pro-competitive.

These guidelines, along with the European approach and the call for reform in Australia, are a good indication that competition law will act to inform the

---

[63] See <http://www.microsoft.com>. For the findings of fact delivered by Judge Jackson on 5 November 1999, see <http://www.usdoj.gov/atr/cases/f3800/msjudgex.thm>. Judge Jackson has since concluded in *United States* v. *Microsoft Corp.*, 87 F Supp. 2d 30 (DDC 2000) that Microsoft violated antitrust law (sections 1 and 2 of the Sherman Act and Section 1 of the Clayton Act) in the Internet browser software market. The nature of the remedy to be awarded in this case is currently being considered by Judge Jackson. On the notion of copyright misuse, which at this point is seen as being distinct from general competition law, see *Alcatel USA, Inc.* v. *DGI Technologies, Inc.*, 166 F 3d 772 (5th Cir. 1999); *Lasercomb America* v. *Reynolds*, 911 F 2d 970 (4th Cir. 1990); *Practice Management Info. Corp.* v. *American Medical Ass'n*, 121 F 3d 516 (9th Cir. 1997); Lemley, n. 33 above, 151–9.

[64] Draft Report, "Review of Sections 51(2) and 51(3) of the Trade Practices Act 1974", 93–132 (<http://www.ncc.gov.au/nationalcompet/section%2051%20review/section%2051.htm>).

[65] See <http://www.ncc.gov.au>.

[66] Final Report, "Review of Sections 51(2) and 51(3) of the Trade Practices Act 1974", <http://www.ncc.gov.au/nationalcompet/section%2051%20review/NCC%20TPA.pdf>.

[67] See further details at <http://ipcr.gov.au/ipcr/.>.

scope of intellectual property rights in the future, and this will have a significant impact upon the legitimate scope of contractual licences of information products.

I have argued elsewhere that the fair use doctrine takes its shape from principles of economic utilitarianism, competition (anti-trust) law, free speech and personal use.[68] In my view, the integration of these principles with UCITA through section 105 is vitally important to the acceptance and success of UCITA.

V   THE NEW CONSTITUTIONALISM: THE NEW TECHNOLOGIES AND INFORMATIONAL COMMODIFICATION

Traditionally, constitutionalism (which means the regulation of power) has focused on the regulation of governmental power. That was before the Internet and the digital environment. Now that information has become so integral to our daily lives, and to the construction of our social and cultural being, issues concerning the allocation and distribution of informational rights need to be conceptualised in terms of constitutionalism—the constitutionalism (regulation of power) of the information society.

One of the primary issues for consideration in defining the constitutionalism of the information society concerns the commodification of information.[69] The contractual licence which has emerged as the primary method of distributing (and enforcing rights in) informational products plays an important role in the commodification process. As we become more reliant on the digital environment for basic communicative architecture, it is imperative that we ensure the commodification of digital information facilitates the public domain and open competition.

The issue of how we should reconcile freedom of contract with fair use and open competition is at root a question of information constitutionalism. When we make those choices about the degree to which contract and its private ordering[70] can override public interest safeguards, we are making important decisions about the regulation of power and the allocation of communicative resources within our society. This in turn will impact upon the construction of our social and cultural being.

I conceptualise software as a form of discourse (like speech), that acts to construct our identity in the digital environment. Software is an integral part of the digital architecture, which we so frequently use to communicate with others. The choices we make in the legal regulation of software will impact upon the way we look in the digital environment.

---

[68] Fitzgerald, n. 56 above.

[69] The great Internet riddle is how to package the digital estate.

[70] On this notion, see J.H. Reichman and J.A. Franklin, "Privately Legislated Intellectual Property Rights: Reconciling Freedom of Contract with Public Good Uses of Information" (1999) 147 *U Penn L Rev* 875.

Likewise, the choices we make over the scope of contractual licences will impact upon the way in which we can further use information and the scope of our existence. In the depths of the contractual freedom facilitated by UCITA exists an important question concerning the digital construction of identity and the consequent regulation of power relations within our society. The principles of open competition, free speech and public domain which stand in the face of freedom of contract are the key to a transactional justice that will inform a constitutionalism (principles that mediate power relations) for the information society.[71]

VI CONCLUSION

It seems inevitable that information laws like UCITA will enter our jurisprudence. However, debate over the scope and dimension of such laws involves fundamental questions concerning the structures of the information society, and it is important that we conceptualise these issues against this broader backdrop. In short, in the process of commodifying information we are engaging with basic issues of constitutionalism.

UCITA, in its attempt to move the law towards an understanding of the digital environment, is to be applauded. However, fear of an unprincipled overgrowth of contract in the digital environment challenges us to respond to the freedom of contract rhetoric of UCITA, with arguments in support of fair use and competition. The resolution of this commodification and distribution issue will be extremely important to the way in which we conceptualise, interact with and continue to build the digital environment.

Just a parting thought. If the digital distribution of music through mp3 technology[72] is any indication (and I believe it is), we are entering upon an era of massive digital distribution of informational entertainment products primarily through the contractual licence. With this in mind, we should be vigilant at the outset in ensuring that the information licence is structured so as to prosper our social and cultural as well as material existence.

---

[71] See further Y. Benkler, "Free as the Air to Common Use: First Amendment Constraints on Enclosure of the Public Domain" (1999) 74 *N Y Univ L Rev* 354, 429–40; C. McManis, "The Privatisation (or Shrink-Wrapping) of American Copyright Law" (1999) 87 *Calif L Rev* 173; D. McGowan, "Free Contracting, Fair Competition and Draft Art 2B: Some Reflections on Federal Competition Policy, Information Transactions and 'Aggressive Neutrality'" (1998) 13 *Berk Tech L J* 1173; M. Madison, "Legal-ware: Contract and Copyright in the Digital Age" (1998) 67 *Fordham L Rev* 1025; G. Lunney, "Protecting Digital Works: Copyright or Contract?" <http://www.tulane.edu/journal/jtip>; J. Boyle, *Shamans, Software, Spleens* (Cambridge, Mass., Harvard UP, 1996); D. Lange, "Recognising The Public Domain" (1981) 44 *Law and Contemporary Problems* 147; cf. R. Nimmer, "Breaking Barriers: The Relationship Between Contract and Intellectual Property Law" (1998) 13 *Berk Tech L J* 827.

[72] On mp3 and legal issues, see <http://www.mp3.com> and <http://cyber.harvard.edu>.

4

Shall We Shoot a Messenger Now and Then? Copyright Infringement and the On-line Service Provider

LOUISE LONGDIN

I INTRODUCTION

It is well known, to technophiles and technophobes alike, that the global on-line environment known as the Internet is the defining characteristic of today's information society. The Internet's infrastructure[1] has been derived from two "root systems", the first developed essentially by and for the public and academic sectors. The second sprang up to support the burgeoning use of Internet services, in particular the World Wide Web[2] and email, and now sustains a considerable volume of commercial as well as non-commercial traffic. The advent of the Internet and the convergence of telecommunications networks and digital technologies[3] allow millions of users to disseminate easily, cheaply, simultaneously and irrevocably, not only their own original expressions, but those of others. In this hyper-connected world where all kinds of information (be it text, sound, music, film, graphics or photographic) can be compressed into a digital stream of ones and zeros and then transmitted, uploaded, downloaded, manipulated or linked to a site in any jurisdiction, copyright owners have become anxious to staunch what they perceive to be the steady haemorrhaging, digit by digit, of their intellectual property into cyberspace. There is also a

[1] The global infrastructure is a matrix of interconnected regional and local computer systems and networks. Software technology allows data to be transmitted between many geographically disparate computer terminals, irrespective of their make, type or operating system, as long as all linked computer systems use public standard Internet protocol specifications.

[2] Often conflated into the Internet itself, the World Wide Web is simply one of several services available on the Internet. Other Internet services include email, telnet and file transfer. In essence, the Web is a worldwide database comprised of millions of linked web pages which store independently contributed information. For a succinct history of the development of the Internet and the World Wide Web, see European Network for Communication and Information Perspectives, *Intellectual Property Rights: The Development of Information Infrastructures for the Information Society* (ENCIP Working Paper Series, 1996), 25 ff.

[3] Convergence technology enables pictures and sounds to be transmitted together as digital, compressed data in one transmission vehicle. Thus, on-line communication and web casting are results of the convergence of the traditional communication media: broadcasting and telecommunications.

growing awareness among authors that new technologies threaten to trivialise their newly won moral rights, if only because the intrinsic worth of copyrighted works to which they are attached may no longer be as visible in this new medium.[4]

My aim in this chapter is to examine the position and predicament of on-line service providers faced by claims for copyright or moral rights infringement carried out not only by themselves during the process of electronic data transmission but also by the digital and pixel pirates who happen to be their users or subscribers. In exploring the nature and scope of provider liability, the chapter assesses not only the legitimacy of general pleas of messenger immunity (a custom with a long historical pedigree in the hard copy world) but also the notion that where there are different types of intermediary, there can exist different types of copyright liability as well as different kinds of remedy.[5] The chapter identifies the three main groups of interdependent stakeholders in digital networked environments and explores the tension that has arisen between these groups and the distorting flow-on effect it is likely to have on traditional international copyright standards. The shape any new standards will take depends by and large on how this tension is resolved.

While it is appreciated that on-line service providers can attract copyright liability only where there is an infringement under the applicable national law,[6] it is left to another contributor to this volume to venture into the murky waters of choice of law and jurisdiction.[7] This chapter also refrains from even attempting any systematic comparative treatment of copyright law. Particular substantive issues in particular jurisdictions are selected where they highlight a given approach to provider liability or where they can indicate possible legislative parameters for those jurisdictions motivated to do something about the problem.

Some peripheral analysis of the liability of on-line go-betweens under defamation principles is undertaken where this usefully provides a window on their liability under copyright doctrine. While some countries may be inching towards a single horizontal liability standard for on-line service providers, regardless of the nature of the substantive law involved,[8] any definitive exploration of this wider trend remains outside the parameters of this chapter.

---

[4] Y. Gendreau, "Digital Technology and Copyright: Can Moral Rights Survive the Disappearance of the Hard Copy?" (1995) 6 *Ent L Rev* 214.

[5] This was one of the conclusions of the six country, transnational study which resulted in the IMPRIMATUR Report, *Liability for On-Line Intermediaries* (Amsterdam, Institute for Information Law, 1997). See also S. Loughnan, "Service Provider Liability for User Copyright Infringement on the Internet" (1997) 8 *AIPJ* 18; and F. Macmillan and M. Blakeney, "Internet and Communication Carriers' Copyright Liability" [1998] *EIPR* 52.

[6] Indeed, the whole edifice of copyright law rests on the vindication of rights in the place in which they were infringed.

[7] For an expanded treatment of these issues, see G. Austin, chap. 9 of this volume.

[8] E.g., B. Fitzgerald, "Internet Service Provider Liability" in A. Fitzgerald, B. Fitzgerald, P. Cook and C. Cifuentes (eds.), *Going Digital: Legal Issues for Electronic Commerce, Multimedia and the Internet* (Australia, Prospect Intelligence Report, 1998), 153, argues there is a desperate need for a

II CYBERSPACE STAKEHOLDERS

Copyright doctrine serves two ends. On the one hand, it encourages original or innovative expression by prohibiting free riders from copying such expression and provides for authors to be recognised and remunerated for their works or products once disseminated. On the other, it contrives (through the only firm judge-made informing principle in copyright law) to foster the free dissemination of ideas (while protecting the way in which they are expressed) and thereby to encourage cultural, social and economic development. There has always been a tension between these two principles, a tension which new technologies have sometimes exacerbated. In the 1970s the invention of photocopying led to easy proliferation of copies and necessitated a recasting of international copyright standards to cater for the process of reprography. Now digital networked communication systems, which have spawned a myriad of new opportunities and new risks, have much more seriously disrupted the balance struck in copyright law between the two traditional groups of stakeholders in the off-line environment: the proprietors and the users of copyright material. The new information revolution has also seen the emergence of a new player, one with an equally strong vested interest in the outcome of the copyright liability debate. This new player is the on-line service provider. This chapter addresses in turn the main concerns of each stakeholder and examines both the legitimate and the self-serving arguments by which they seek to advance their cause.

A Copyright Proprietors: Fears and Responses

Copyright owners' oldest and most fundamental right is to authorise reproduction of a literary or artistic work in any manner or form.[9] Applied literally in a digital networked environment, exclusive governance of *reproduction* means that a copyright owner can control each and every time her work is transmitted and appears in the volatile memory of a computer, for each such event involves

"reasoned framework for assessing internet service provider liability across many areas of law and society: pornography, copyright, defamation and negligence". While the IMPRIMATUR Report, n. 5 above, 68 and 80, suggests that there is an emerging international trend for the parameters of liability under defamation and copyright to converge, R. Julia-Barcelo, "Liability for On-Line Intermediaries: A European Perspective" [1998] *EIPR* 453, 458–9, asserts that any such trend would discombobulate copyright owners who adhere strongly to the notion that the law of copyright has certain unique characteristics which necessitate a different legal and technological treatment. In their view, were a uniform liability regime to be imposed on on-line service providers for third party infringement of any type of substantive law, such a regime might set the threshold for exemption too low.

[9] Berne Convention for the Protection of Literary and Artistic Works 1886, Art. 9(1) (herein "Berne Convention"). This instrument, together with its subsequent revisions, sets out for its adherents minimum standards governing the works in which copyright will subsist and the various economic rights to be exclusively reserved to owners: see further, text accompanying nn. 55–64 below.

reproduction of that work. Thus, copyright proprietors, through an auspicious combination of technological change and linguistic fortuity, can be said to have been delivered an unexpected windfall,[10] albeit one whose full enjoyment can be seriously hindered by thorny jurisdictional issues.

Copyright owners worry that such state of the art digital technologies as high velocity scanners and optical character recognition software have the potential to allow free riders to gobble up digitised copyright material and then disseminate an indeterminate number of perfect whole copies. Performers and copyright owners in the music industry similarly look askance at the facility with which phonograms and performances fixed in phonograms can be made available on the Internet without authorisation.

The widespread use of new digital technologies also facilitates infringement of authors' moral rights,[11] as an ever growing number of Internet service users are able to acquire and use software to morph visual images (both still and moving) and sounds (which can include voice and music) and to disseminate quickly and widely the possibly distorted result. The ease with which the content of websites can be framed by,[12] and linked to,[13] other website users is equally alarming in owners' eyes. Mindful of the serious threat that digital networked communication poses to traditional copyright markets, copyright owners have sought to increase protection for their works in digitised form on four main fronts.

(i) Technology to the Rescue

First, on the basis that "the answer to the machine lies in the machine",[14] copyright owners are looking to digital technology for a solution.[15] Encrypted data, digital envelopes, watermarks, software metering mechanisms and copyright management information[16] attached to electronic copies of works are all assist-

---

[10] J. Litman, "New Copyright Paradigms", <http://www.mscn.com/-litman/paradigm.htm>.

[11] See text accompanying nn. 65–72 below.

[12] The use of frames to subdivide web pages allows the designer of site X to copy material from site Y and then display Y's material wholly or partly in a frame on X's own site. Framing, thus, may give rise to both moral rights and copyright concerns, not only because it can mislead users of a web site as to the creator of its content, but because it can also be used to juxtapose material from several unrelated sources as part of a display. For a fuller treatment of copyright implications of the practice, see D. Cendali, C. Forssander and R. Turiello, "An Overview of Intellectual Property Issues Relating to the Internet" (1999) 89 *The Trademark Rep* 485, 526–9.

[13] Linking is a popular tool commonly used on the World Wide Web. It allows items of information to be associated with one another by means of cross references or links which may appear on screen as a line of underlined "hypertext" or as an icon. The copyright implications of linking are discussed below in the text accompanying nn. 47–9 below.

[14] C. Clark, "The Answer to the Machine Lies in the Machine" in B. Hugenholtz (ed.), *The Future of Copyright in a Digital Environment* (The Hague, Kluwer Law International, 1996), 139.

[15] It is commonly held that copyright can no longer be effective by itself and requires technology to make it enforceable on the Internet: see Loughnan, n. 5 above, 30.

[16] Art. 11 of the World Intellectual Property Organisation Copyright Treaty 1996 (herein "WCT") requires contracting parties to prohibit measures intended to circumvent technological protection and ban the deliberate tinkering with or removal of intellectual property rights management

ing copyright owners to control access to, and uses of, their works to a much greater extent than is possible in the analogue world.[17] Moreover, technological identification and protection mechanisms are becoming increasingly effective, not only at tracking on-line consumption patterns of protected material by individual users and product tampering, but also at tracing the dissemination of putatively infringing material to a particular computer terminal, if not to the actual user.

(ii) Differential Pricing

Internet and click-wrap licensing technology now makes it increasingly possible for copyright owners to charge for all conceivable uses of their works.[18] Authors can opt to release their works solely on-line and offer potential users a smorgasbord of choices for a range of fees; so much for a timed browse, so much to copy and incorporate all or part of the author's work as part of the user's own, and so much to include the work in a news item, digital library or archive. It has even been suggested that copyright owners could feasibly charge a fee (no doubt a high one) for the right to criticise or parody their on-line works[19] (should they be able to bring themselves to overlook the affront to their dignity).

(iii) Expanding the Scope of Exclusive Rights

Rights owners have also sought to expand the rights which attach to copyright ownership.[20] Particularly important is the extension of the right of authorising

information which may be represented by numbers and codes. Under Art. 12(2) of the WCT, "rights management information" is information attached to a copy of a work or appearing in connection with the communication of a work to the public which identifies the author of the work, and sets out terms and conditions of its use. States must provide adequate and effective legal remedies against persons who remove or alter rights management information themselves or who distribute a work, communicate it to the public, or import it for distribution knowing that rights management information has been altered or removed. (Adopted by the Diplomatic Conference in Geneva, 20 December 1996, the WCT acts as a special agreement under the Berne Convention and came into effect on 19 September 1997, after 30 instruments of ratification or accession were deposited with the Director General of WIPO. Even if a party to the WCT is not bound by the Berne Convention, it must still comply with the substantive provisions of the Convention's 1971 Paris Revision.)

[17] E.g., the United States provides an encryption research exemption intended to advance the state of knowledge relating to encryption technology and the development of encryption products. See 17 USC §1201 (g) (1998) (Digital Millennium Copyright Act 1998).

[18] T. Heide, "The Berne Three Step Test and the Proposed Copyright Directive" [1999] *EIPR* 105, 106.

[19] *Ibid.*, 108.

[20] Proponents of an expanded copyright can call here on Chicago school law and economics which tends to regard copyright as serving far more than the creation and dissemination of new expression: see N.W. Netanel, "Copyright and a Democratic Civil Society" (1996) 106 *Yale L J* 283, 286. Since proponents of the school are wont to treat works as investment opportunities, they are apt to regard copyright as the gateway through which such investment is marshalled: see W.J. Gordon, "Assertive Modesty: An Economics of Intangibles" (1994) 94 *Colum L Rev* 2579, 2579 n.1, where she contends that copyright law is by and large "a mode of converting mental labor into a 'vendible commodity'". Put simply, Chicago school proponents would have copyright subject to wide proprietary rights extending to all envisaged uses.

communication to the public[21] in the World Intellectual Property Organisation Copyright Treaty (herein WCT). Article 8 thereof provides:

> [A]uthors of literary and artistic works shall enjoy the exclusive right of *authorising any communication* to the public of their works, by wire or wireless means, *including the making available to the public of their works in such a way that members of the public may access these works from a place and at a time individually chosen by them.*[22]

The provision envisages the making available of all kinds of digitised material by a variety of distribution channels (cable, satellite, telephone lines or packaged media such as CD-ROMs and CDs) and exploitation via computers, television sets and other electronic platforms. In the Internet context, the right applies where end users dictate *when* they surf for material, rather than the person who is responsible for putting the material on-line.[23] Article 8 has been interpreted, in strong support of copyright owners' interests, to mean that if, at any point of a transmission or at the end of a transmission, a work is communicated to the public, including through display on a screen, each and every such communication to the public requires the authorisation of the author.[24] On another view, equally gratifying to copyright owners, the act of connecting a file server containing a work to a publicly accessible network will amount to an exercise of the right, even where subscribers to the network do no more than browse the work, that is, do not download it, and where the actor does not send it to anyone in particular.[25] Both interpretations appear to support the notion that the exercise of the right does not require the making or distribution of copies of a work.[26]

With its effect of both expanding and future proofing copyright protection in relation to the provision of on-line technology neutral services, the new expanded exclusive right of authorising communication to the public has been

---

[21] Art. 11bis of the Berne Convention. Art. 8 of the WCT, which expanded this right, has been aptly likened to liquid concrete flowing into and filling the cracks in Art. 11, while displacing none of the existing stratum. See C. Creswell, "Copyright Protection Enters the Digital Age: The New WIPO Treaties on Copyright & On Performances and Sound Recordings" (1997) 15 *Copyright Rep* 4, 5. The most substantial crack filled by Art. 8 was the lack in Art. 11bis of a right of communication to the public extending to wire transmission of text and images.

[22] Emphasis added. Under the WIPO Performers and Phonograms Treaty 1996 (herein WPPT), producers of phonograms and performers whose performances are recorded in phonograms are also granted a counterpart right to make their works available on-line to unrelated persons who may have individual access from different places and at different times to the publicly accessible site. See Arts. 7, 10 and 14.

[23] Art. 8 deals with point-to-point transmissions to members of the public rather than simultaneous single point to multi-point transmissions: see M.J. Davison, "Australian Proposals for Copyright Reform: Some Unresolved Issues and Lessons from America" (1999) 1 *Digital Tech L J* <http://wwwlaw.murdock.edu.au/dtlj/articles/vol1–1/davison.html>, para. 5.

[24] European Commission, Explanatory Memorandum to Art. 3 of the *Draft Proposal for a Directive on the Harmonisation of Certain Aspects of Copyright and Related Rights in the Information Society*, COM(97)628, 10 December 1997.

[25] Creswell, n. 21 above, 5.

[26] D.L. Hayes, "Advanced Copyright Issues on the Internet" (1998) 7 *Texas Intell Prop L J* 1, 41.

described as a strong contender for the title of principal right in the digital environment competing with the right of reproduction, the cornerstone of copyright in the traditional hard copy world.[27] It strikes me, however, that, in relation to digital exploitation of works, reproduction has been somehow reconceptualised *as* communication.

The acquisition of the new right (ostensibly under the ægis of clarification of copyright doctrine to suit digital networked environments) can be viewed as a victory for copyright proprietors,[28] a significant annexation of territory previously in no man's land. (Article 6 of the WCT also represents a victory for copyright owners, albeit one of less significance, for while it certainly broadens the exclusive right of distribution,[29] the Agreed Statement[30] concerning the Treaty provision would restrict distribution to fixed copies which can be put into circulation as tangible objects.)

(iv) Chasing the Deep Pockets

Copyright proprietors whose rights have been infringed in a digital networked environment have one last strategy left to deploy, chasing the often amply funded and easily identifiable on-line service provider.[31] In this scenario, copyright owners can disregard primary infringers of no real substance, and shape up for a serious fight with their on-line service provider(s). However, the downside for copyright owners is that some deep pocketed on-line service providers' superior capacity to bankroll damages can also allow them to fight back strenuously via expensive lawyers' and lobbyists' fees. Understandably, then, copyright owners would like to change the rules in their favour by portraying themselves as weak and defenceless victims. Given their victories on the

---

[27] Heide, n. 18 above, 108.

[28] Litman, n. 10 above. The victory has occurred, moreover, in the face of the preamble to the WCT which expressly upholds the dual role of copyright, avowing that contracting states recognise "the profound impact of the development and convergence of information and communication technologies on the creation and use of literary and artistic works"; and "the need to maintain a balance between the rights of authors and the larger public interest, particularly education, research and access to information".

[29] From cinematographic works under Art. 14(1) of the Berne Convention to other works.

[30] In the context of a Diplomatic Conference, Agreed Statements are mechanisms commonly deployed to explain the text and nuances of treaty articles. They may supply some of the history and background against which particularly difficult treaty provisions were eventually adopted or set out reservations about their application. The Agreed Statement to Art. 6 of the WCT describes the exclusive right of distribution as the copyright owner's right of authorising the making available to the public of the original and copies of their copyright material through sale or other transfer of ownership. However, what is "original" and what are "copies" refer only to fixed copies which can be circulated as tangible objects. Thus, distribution in intangible form, such as digital material on the Internet will actually fall under the right of authorising communication to the public: see Australian Copyright Law Review Committee, *Simplification of the Copyright Act 1968, Part 2, Categorisation of Subject Matter and Exclusive Rights and Other Issues* (Canberra, February 1999), 31.

[31] See S. Pomeroy, "Promoting the Progress of Science and the Useful Arts in the Digital Domain: Copyright, Computer Bulletin Board, and Liability for Infringement by Others" (1996) 45 *Emory L J* 1035, 1072.

technological and legal fronts, such portrayal would seem to be overdone. Far from crumbling, the walls of Fortress Copyright are actually getting higher. It is by no means obvious that copyright owners should be allowed to take hostages as well, no matter how deep their pockets.

B End Users and Public Interest Proponents

It is now time to look at matters from the other side of the fence. The Berne Convention sets up a three step test which permits the "reproduction of artistic and literary works in special cases provided that the reproduction does not conflict with a normal exploitation of the work and does not unreasonably prejudice the legitimate interests of the author".[32] Some common law countries, most notably the United Kingdom, Australia, New Zealand and Singapore, have opted to meet this test by providing for an array of specific exemptions allowing limited copying for the purposes of private use or study, education, research, archival creation, news reporting, criticism and review, none of which is particularly directed at the use of works in digital networked environments. By contrast, the United States largely meets public interest objectives through its broad fair use exemption which has now been extended, in certain specific circumstances, to accommodate the avoidable reality of the digital age that one must often have first to copy the whole of a work in order fairly to use a part of it.

Serious concern has been expressed over the cultural, political, educational and economic ramifications of elevating property rights over public access to opinions, ideas and other information.[33] Leaving aside the views of those extremist hackers and "cyberians", who believe that all information should be free to all people at all times, many Internet users and public interest proponents (who may well also be copyright owners themselves) would agree that copyright law can no longer remain tethered to the pre-digital, pre-convergence era where notions of copying still heavily rely on differentiation between broadcasting (radio or satellite communications), telecommunications, recording, entertainment and publishing services. They too are seeking new standards for communication in cyberspace on the ground that its original hallmark, the free untempered exchange of information and ideas, is jeopardised if, as foreshadowed above and discussed below, they can access information only either by technically infringing copyright or under some form of licence or authorisation.

Forceful arguments have been put that the traditional exceptions for fair use which apply in the hard copy environment should be carried over to the on-line

---

[32] Art. 9(2).
[33] E.g., see Netanel, n. 20 above; Litman, n. 10 above; and J. Waldron, "From Authors to Copiers: Individual Rights and Social Values in Intellectual Property" (1993) 68 *Chicago-Kent L Rev* 841.

world.[34] Some public interest proponents go further, contending that it should not be an infringement of copyright merely to engage, in a digital environment, in the time honoured activity of browsing, that is, listening to, viewing or reading works for short periods without specific authorisation.[35]

C On-line Intermediaries

Our third category, the on-line service providers, forms a bewilderingly diverse group. They do not (and indeed cannot) display the neat dichotomy of opposed interests which characterised our previous two categories. Their functions and fears are correspondingly more difficult to isolate and describe. At the risk of considerable technological over-simplification and truncation of commercial reality, I will try to do both.

(i) A Provider Taxonomy

Many service providers play an active role in copying, adapting and selecting material before making it available on-line. Others, however, play a much more passive part in the electronic data transmission process. There is a trend among judges, legislators and commentators to distinguish the various kinds of digital communications facilitators and their access regimes for liability allocation purposes. The real debate is about where to draw the lines and how bright the lines are once they are drawn.

In dealing with the issue of go-betweens' tortious or copyright liability for third party digital transmissions, commentators and judges have turned to various functional (and sometimes fanciful)[36] analogies drawn from the hard copy world to help them describe what various types of intermediaries actually do, have the power to do, or are responsible for. Even where a particular analogy or

---

[34] Particularly trenchant criticism can be found in J. Boyle, "A Theory of Law and Information: Copyright, Spleens, Blackmail and Insider Trading" (1992) 80 *Cal L Rev* 1413, 1467–9 and Netanel, n. 20 above, at 287–9. It is, moreover, one commentator's perception that the traditional user exemptions have been eroded by the broadening of the three step test in Art. 9(2) of the Berne Convention (to increase authorial rights of "normal exploitation") during the course of the test's transplantation into several recent legislative proposals and international initiatives intended to tailor and harmonise new exceptions for digital networked environments: see Heide, n. 18 above.

[35] J. Litman, "The Exclusive Right to Read" (1994) 13 *Cardozo Arts & Ent L J* 29; N. Elkin-Koren, "Copyright Law and Social Dialogue on the Information Superhighway: The case Against Copyright Liability of Bulletin Board Operators" (1995) 13 *Cardozo Arts & Ent L J* 345, 385; J. Jannuska, "The Great Canadian 'Cache' Grab: Rethinking Browsing as Copyright Infringement", <http://catalw.com/logic/docs/jj-browse.html>; cf D. Nimmer, "Brains and Other Paraphernalia of the Digital Age" (1996) 10 *Harv J L & Tech* 1, 9–12.

[36] D.R. Johnson and K. Marks, "Mapping Electronic Data Communications onto Existing Legal Metaphors: Should We Let Our Conscience (And Our Contracts) Be Our Guide?" (1993) 38 *Vill L Rev* 487, 498, suggest that computer networks may be regarded as "transporters of information" and, as a corollary, that on-line service provision may be compared, functionally speaking, to the interstate trucking industry.

metaphor is adopted as a guide to determining the copyright liability of an on-line player, it would be simplistic to confine that player to wearing just one label. Technology allows operational malleability[37] and providers can play more than one role or can fit (or semi-fit) several functional metaphors from one moment in time to another. (As will be seen, for example, a systems operator could be functioning as a common carrier, broadcaster, or publisher simultaneously, or in quick succession,[38] and a university could function as an Internet access provider as well as a cable service programme provider.) Rather than embrace the notion of hybrid models to sort and classify providers, it is my preference to use functional analogies or metaphors for what they are, guidelines only, and not straitjackets.

In the rough taxonomy provided below, allocation to categories does not depend on ascribed status, but rather on actual role, based on an analysis of function(s) performed or physical facilities owned or operated. Classification also hinges on the extent to which providers know or are aware of infringing content. As discussed later in the chapter, liability regimes (whether already devised or presently being fashioned) tend to focus largely on a provider's role and state of knowledge.

(a) Common Carriers or Mere Conduits

These are the on-line intermediaries, most akin to the common messenger in the analogue world, on whose shoulders, it is argued, liability should rest either lightly, or not at all, on the grounds that they know nothing of the content they carry. The sub-group comprises all those communications carriers and network operators who provide and maintain the telephone lines, fibre-optic cables, switches, routers and microwave links essential for data transmission on the Internet. It is this physical network infrastructure to which other on-line service providers must have access not only themselves to engage in activities on the Internet, but also to connect their own subscribers to the World Wide Web, email, "chat rooms" and newsgroups.

(b) Internet Access Providers

As the nomenclature suggests, all Internet access providers provide their sub-scribers with access to the Internet, including email. Many sell bandwidth to users, and host on their own servers user-created web sites which may incorpo-rate all kinds of digitised copyrighted material. In order to decrease network traffic and browsing time for users, providers often store or cache in the random access memory (RAM) of their own servers copies of web pages which their users may wish to revisit. Internet access service providers can also operate their own web sites, selecting and providing access to extensive material, some of

---

[37] D.R. Johnson and K. Marks, n. 36 above, 498.
[38] Pomeroy, n. 31 above, 1041.

which may be subject to copyright. Some such entities assert copyright in compilations of users' works and parts of works which they post on their services on the ground that they have added value by providing the means of transmission.[39]

(c) On-line Hosts

Many on-line intermediaries do not provide Internet access at all, but typically rent space from an Internet access provider in order to provide access to content put on-line wholly or partly by third parties but communicated within their systems. These on-line hosts include bulletin board operators, systems operators (sysops),[40] companies which maintain intranets and extranets for their employees[41] and educational institutions operating distance learning programmes. The exchange of material between a web page host's various users can involve news groups or chat rooms and may or may not occur in real time. The role of computer bulletin board operators has been variously likened to that played by common carriers, publishers and broadcasters.[42] Furthermore, when systems operators such as universities allow wide dissemination of information by allowing users to search their databases and extract material, they are acting like libraries and booksellers.

(d) Information Location Tool Providers

This group comprises providers who refer and link users to on-line sites by using information location tools such as directories, indexes, references, pointers and hypertext links.

(e) Cyber-café Proprietors

At its most expansive, the term on-line service provider could conceivably include the proliferating number of cyber-café proprietors who furnish the physical apparatus and opportunity for users to link into cyberspace. Arguably, they maintain premises for public entertainment where infringing performances of works can take place on computer screen displays depending on whether café customers can be viewed as a collective public or, despite their closely hunched

---

[39] E.g., the terms of service between two of the largest on-line service providers in the world, America Online and Compuserve, and their respective users assert that the service provider has compilation copyright (including moral rights in America Online's case) in any content users may submit to the provider for display in "public areas" such as message boards or information services.

[40] A sysop controls the terms of access to, and the content of, an electronic bulletin board. Where a bulletin board is large, covering hundreds of topics, there may well be several sysops dealing with discrete areas of subject matter.

[41] Intranets are corporate or institutional islands of information which may be connected to the Internet across a firewall which denies access to the public. Extranets also utilise standard Internet protocol technology and firewalls but the firewall is configured to allow some linking of known sites.

[42] D.J. Loundy, "E-Law: Legal Issues Affecting Computer Information Systems and Systems Operator Liability" (1993) 3 *Alb L J Sci & Tech* 79, 88–9; T.A. Cutera, "Computer Networks, Libel and the First Amendment" (1992) 11 *Computer L J* 555, 556; Pomeroy, n. 31 above, 1040–1.

proximity to each other, as isolated individuals locked into their separate pursuits on the Internet.

(ii) Vulnerability and Vetting

(a) Assailable On-line Practices

Providers face being often unwittingly, and always unwillingly, caught in the cross-fire between users and copyright owners. Some common on-line services, such as caching and the provision of information location tools, primarily provided to or for the benefit of users, expose providers to liability for infringement on their own account. Attempts can also be made to saddle them with liability for multiple users who upload or download protected works without the copyright owner's authorisation. Three matters need attention.

First, the practice of proxy caching,[43] designed to reduce network congestion and transmission time, presents serious problems for providers. After the United States decision *MAI Systems Corporation* v. *Peak Computer, Inc.*,[44] it cannot be ignored that even short term caching involves the making of copies. In that case, it was held that the unauthorised copying of a computer program into a computer's RAM, in the course of turning on and running the computer for maintenance purposes, amounted to reproduction of the program. Since copies of cached works can be further transmitted, displayed on users' screens or performed from a provider's proxy server to members of the public, caching can also infringe copyright owners' traditional rights of public performance or public display (as well their new rights under the WIPO Treaties).

The second matter is the linking of one web site with another. Not only does this raise trade mark and tortious concerns (especially where the link implies a relationship between sites), but it can also expose providers to copyright liability. On one view, the ubiquitous link is an innocuous tool, the practice no different from placing references in other people's work.[45] On another view, links are potentially pernicious[46] because they can be used to conjure up infringing content. It was on this ground that particular web site links were identified and

---

[43] Caching can be of the local or proxy type. Local caching of web pages recently visited by a user usually occurs on the end user's computer in RAM and/or the hard drive. If the user revisits the web page, it will be retrieved from the local cache rather than from the original site using the network again. Proxy caching occurs on the provider's server rather than the end user's computer. Thus, large on-line service providers with many users may store a web page visited by user A on their own servers for a period of time just in case user B subsequently wants to access the same page. Retrieval from the provider's proxy server is faster for B than from the original source server. See Hayes, n. 26 above, 64.

[44] 991 F 2d 511 (9th Cir. 1993), cert. dismissed, 510 US 1033 (1994). Similar reasoning prevailed in *Triad Systems Corp.* v. *Southeastern Express Co.*, 6 F 3d 1330, 1335 (9th Cir. 1995).

[45] M. O'Rourke, "Fencing Cyberspace: Drawing Borders in a Virtual World" (1998) 82 *Minn L Rev*, <http://www.dlib.org/dlib/april98/04orourke.html>, para. 9.

[46] See Hayes, n. 26 above, 85–6.

challenged in *The Shetland Times* v. *Wills*[47] and *Christian Dior/Fashion TV Paris, World Media Live, SECM et W2M.*[48]

Thirdly, on-line go-betweens can face claims that they are acting like *publishers* when they disseminate content prepared by third parties. This analogy is often invoked in defamation actions and its purpose, especially as deployed in the United States, is to drop the liability threshold for publisher/providers below that obtaining for mere distributor/providers.[49]

(b) Pressure to Monitor Content

Providers can be expected to challenge any suggestion (usually lobbied for vigourously by copyright owners) that since many of them are better placed than anyone to monitor technically the content of digital transmissions, they should legally be required to do so.[50] Monitoring would certainly increase the time and expense involved in digital transmission (factors which are by no means inconsiderable) but providers can also conjure up other compelling reasons why they should resist legislative or judicial pressure to assume the onus of routinely vetting users' digital transmissions for infringing items.

First and pragmatically, real problems exist with the present scope of monitoring or packet sniffing technology. Certainly it may catch obscene or objectionable material by detecting the transmission of particular key words, terms or expressions, but it is of dubious effectiveness in tracking defamatory statements or breaches of copyright or moral rights where much can depend on nuance and the juxtaposition of material. Where the courts still struggle to

[47] [1997] EMLR 277. The interlocutory nature of this proceeding before the Scottish Court of Session meant that the question whether links may be infringing in themselves was unfortunately never directly addressed. Hyper linking (without confusion of source) was found non-infringing in itself in *Ticketmaster Corp.* v. *Tickets.com*, US District Court, CD Cal., 27 March 2000.

[48] The Tribunal de Grande Instance de Paris issued an injunction ordering the delinking of specified sites against the producers and service providers of a commercial web site after finding trade mark infringement (22 February 1999): see <http://www.legalis.net/legalnet/judicaire/decisions/ord> for the judgment.

[49] As discussed in the text accompanying n. 112 below, publisher/service providers must usually meet a higher standard because, unlike mere distributors (whose state of knowledge must be proven), they are presumed to have knowledge of actionable conduct. The publisher analogy tends to disintegrate unless providers are found to have exercised some editorial control over the material they disseminate, to have implemented monitoring of user-postings or to have access to technology to control user access. See Pomeroy, n. 31 above, for an extended analysis of United States treatment of the distributor/publisher distinction in relation to on-line service providers.

[50] The Information Infrastructure Task Force, *Intellectual Property and the National Information Infrastructure, The Report of the Working Group on Intellectual Property Rights* (Washington D.C., 1995), 117, concluded that: "[o]n-line service providers . . . are in the position to know the identity and activities of their subscribers and to stop unlawful activities. And, although indemnification from their subscribers may not reimburse them to the full extent of their liability and other measures may add to the cost of their doing business, they are still in a better position to prevent or stop infringement than the copyright owner. Between these two relatively innocent parties, the best policy is to hold the service provider liable." Cf IMPRIMATUR Report, n. 5 above, 78, which states that although copyright owners are exerting pressure to monitor on those on-line intermediaries who are in a position technically to monitor, this does not mean that that law should necessarily follow where technology leads and impose a legal requirement to monitor on those intermediaries.

construe what amounts to substantial copying of a work or to apply the idea/expression dichotomy, it would be amazing if a software algorithm could make such subtle distinctions.[51] Secondly, copyright owners requiring (and presumably paying for) technological monitoring are likely to prefer an overkill rather than an underkill approach and would probably submit for tracing a wide raft of key expressions as the purported protectable core of their work. It can be seen that a global gridlock could readily arise where too many digital transmissions were being sniffed, too often on behalf of too many copyright owners in too many jurisdictions. Some sites operated by on-line service providers would become congested monitoring hubs to be avoided by the technologically discerning.

Moreover, detection of infringement (or rather putative infringement) is still likely to be *ex post facto*, given the speed and sheer volume of digital traffic. Unless monitoring conferred *ex post* immunity, it would be pointless to require it *ex ante*. Lastly, in the increasing number of jurisdictions which now regulate privacy, attempts by on-line service providers to monitor their users' digital transmissions can fall foul of privacy legislation or administrative codes of practice, and/or be in breach of the emergent common law tort of privacy. Unless authorised by users, monitoring could in some circumstances constitute interference with communications and bring providers into conflict with criminal legislation governing such interference.[52]

III   THE PARAMETERS OF LIABILITY

A   The Rights of Copyright Owners and Authors

As long ago as 1625 it was observed that:[53]

> [M]any . . . moderne booksellers are but needless excrements, or rather vermine . . . since they . . . publish bookes, contrived, altered and mangled at their own pleasures, without consent of the writers . . . change the name sometymes, both of the booke and author (after they have been ymprinted).

Were he alive and productive today, the maker of this lament could well be describing the kind of havoc that can be played with electronic versions of authors' works when access to word processing and morphing technologies is

---

[51]   Pomeroy, n. 31 above, 1086.

[52]   E.g., the Crimes Act 1963 (NZ), Part IXA, s. 216; the Telecommunications (Interception) Act 1979 (Cth), s. 7(1); and the Computer Misuse Act 1993 (Singapore), s. 6, all criminalise unauthorised interception of electronic communications. In the United States, the Cable Communications Policy Act 1994 (47 USC § 551) protects cable system subscribers' privacy and the Electronic Communications Privacy Act 1986 (18 USC § 2511(3)) prohibits anyone providing an electronic communication service to the public from intentionally divulging the contents of any communication while in transmission on that service to anyone but the intended recipient.

[53]   One George Wither quoted in G. Davies, *Copyright and the Public Interest*, IIC Studies in Industrial Property and Copyright Law, Vol. 14, (VCH, Weinheim, 1994), 17–8.

easily procured and purportedly even 7-year-olds are able to cut, paste and send information in digital form.

(i) Protected Subject Matter

Provided they meet the minimum standards of the Berne Convention, treaty adherents are free to fill in finer details of implementation and can also extend protection beyond Berne limits. Different nations protect different works in different ways. Thus, although both civil and common law Berne adherents have gone well beyond the protection of traditional literary and artistic works and have proceeded by itemising extended categories of protected subject matter,[54] the civilians list to a much lesser extent. Different common law countries tuck the works they protect by copyright into idiosyncratic legislative nooks and crannies,[55] while the civilians contain their lists within a framework of overarching principle.[56] The lack of any theoretical unifier in common law copyright regimes means that some material can fall through the cracks and fail to receive any protection at all. On other occasions, works are protected under multiple heads with sometimes conflicting indicia of liability to confuse (or intimidate) potential infringers. We see that in some jurisdictions (subject of course to fixation requirements) a web page can contemporaneously enjoy protection as a "compilation" (a subcategory of literary work),[57] an artistic work,[58] a film[59] or even a cable programme.[60]

[54] As an example of the common law approach, New Zealand, here a fairly dedicated follower of United Kingdom legislative fashion, protects the following as original works: literary, dramatic, musical or artistic works; sound recordings; films; broadcasts; cable programmes; and typographical arrangements of published editions: see Copyright Act 1994 (NZ), s. 14.

[55] Thus, "audiovisual works" are protected in the United States, but not as such in the United Kingdom and New Zealand. Furthermore, proposed Australian copyright reforms envisage the creation of two protected categories only, original creations and derivative productions: see Australian Copyright Law Review Committee, *Simplification of the Copyright Act 1968, Part 2, Categorisation of Subject Matter and Exclusive Rights and Other Issues* (February 1999).

[56] E.g., the French Law on the Intellectual Property Code 1992, Art. L112–1, states broadly that it protects the rights of authors in "all works of the mind whatever their kind, form of expression or merit", before proceeding to provide some specific examples of protected works. It does not then branch into refined definitions, as tends to be the norm in common law countries.

[57] Indeed, in New Zealand, e.g., the across the board copyright threshold of originality is set so low and the statutory definition of "compilation" is couched so widely that web pages compiled of works or parts of works or just digital data will readily qualify for protection, a protection, moreover, which may be perpetual should web pages be constantly updated. See L. Longdin, "Computerised Compilations: A Cautionary Tale from New Zealand" [1997] *IJILT* 249, 268.

[58] In the United Kingdom and New Zealand, the absence of any æsthetic test allows any web page displaying photographs or graphic works (comprising maps, graphs, diagrams, charts or plans) to qualify readily for protection as an artistic work.

[59] One possibility which has been strengthened recently by courts in several jurisdictions is that the moving visual displays demonstrating the computer graphics component of video games may be protected as "films": see *Nintendo Co. Ltd.* v. *Golden China TV-Game Centre* (1993) 28 IPR 313 (Supreme Court of South Africa); *Sega Enterprises* v. *Galaxy Electronics* (1996) 35 IPR 161 (in which the Federal Court of Australia held that a computer game is a "cinematographic film" under the definition in the Australian legislation, a definition much narrower than its United Kingdom and New Zealand counterpart because it also includes sounds embodied in a soundtrack associated with

(ii) Economic Rights

The boundaries and precise definition of economic rights vary considerably from country to country, largely according to the version of the Berne Convention to which the country in question adheres,[61] and depending on whether it has adopted either or both of the two 1996 WIPO Treaties. If we take the common United Kingdom/New Zealand approach as a common law exemplar, copyright proprietors (who may well not be the actual authors or creators of copyrighted works) have been given a grab bag of economic rights allowing them to restrict the performance of certain acts in relation to certain protected categories of subject matter.[62] Thus, owners of copyright in *all* types of protected work are given the exclusive right to copy them and issue copies to the public. They can also perform a literary, dramatic or musical work in public; show or play in public, a sound recording, film, broadcast or cable programme; broadcast or include most kinds of work in a cable programme service; and adapt a literary, dramatic or musical work. Last, but by no means least, copyright owners can authorise the commission of any of the foregoing acts.[63]

(iii) Authors' Moral Rights

Implementation of Art 6[bis] of the Berne Convention in common law countries[64] secures moral rights for writers, musicians, dramatists, artists, designers and film directors.[65] In some common law jurisdictions, such as the United Kingdom

visual images); and *John Richardson Computers Ltd.* v. *Flanders* [1993] FSR 497, 499 (where Ferris J observed, albeit hypothetically, that a computer screen display, while not entitled to be protected as a "literary work" in itself—because it is the product of a program not the program *per se*—may also be entitled to separate copyright protection as a "film" as well as possibly an "artistic work" in the form of a photograph or a reproduction of a drawing).

[60] In *The Shetland Times* v. *Wills* [1997] EMLR 277, it was conceded for interlocutory purposes that the *The Shetland Times'* web site which displayed articles and photographs extracted from the hard copy newspaper it published was *prima facie* a cable programme service. Although Lord Hamilton in the Court of Session did not deal directly with the point, it can be extrapolated from his finding that the information sent to readers from the web site could be a "cable programme" subject to copyright.

[61] Signatories to the Agreement on Trade-Related Aspects of Intellectual Property Rights including Trade in Counterfeit Goods 1993 (TRIPS) who are not Berne Convention members are nevertheless required to adhere to the provisions of the Berne Convention (Paris Revision, 1971).

[62] Cf France, as a civil law exemplar, which confines itself to two broad and open ended economic rights, the right of reproduction and the right of performance: see Law on the Intellectual Property Code 1992, Arts. L122–1 to L122–3.

[63] Copyright, Designs and Patents Act 1988 (UK), s. 16: Copyright Act 1994 (NZ), s. 16.

[64] Canada, in 1931, was the first common law jurisdiction to make a positive legislative response to Art. 6[bis] probably because of its familiarity with the French civilian concept of *droits moreaux* via the law of Quebec. While the United States has a limited form of protection for visual arts (see text accompanying nn. 69–70 below), Australia is expected to provide for moral rights once the long-standing debate over waiver provisions is resolved. See *AGD E-news on Copyright*, No 2, July 1998 at <http://law.gov.au/publications/copyright_news/frameset.html>.

[65] The concept was first inserted into the Berne Convention in 1928. Its scope was extended in Brussels (1948), when it became binding on signatories, and again in Stockholm (1967). The WPPT

and New Zealand, moral rights are treated more as obligations[66] owed to their owners than as exploitable property in the hands of their owners. Since they have not been forced into a proprietary mould, there is no bundle of exclusive rights against the whole world, no emphasis on the right to reproduce, transmit or otherwise make available to the public. The focus rather rests on presentation, exhibition and display in any medium.

Depending on whether one is adopting a civil or a common law perspective, there are either two or three distinct moral rights. First, there is the right to be identified as author or director (*right of paternity*),[67] and, secondly, the right not to have one's work subjected to derogatory treatment (*right of integrity*). The United Kingdom and New Zealand have created a third express moral right, the right to prevent a work from being wrongly attributed to oneself (*false attribution right*).[68] In these two jurisdictions, moral rights generally apply across the board to all kinds of works with two pointed exceptions. The paternity right and the right of integrity are denied authors of "computer programs" and "computer generated works" on the ground that such works are too depersonalised to register the stamp of the authorial self. The false attribution right does, however, apply to both these kinds of works, and its exercise is becoming increasingly important to the creators of misattributed copyright in digital works which produce sophisticated and highly sought after animated and special effects. There is yet one further, *ersatz* moral right, provided for in the United Kingdom and New Zealand statutes, a limited right of privacy for those who commission photographs and films (*commissioner's right to privacy*).

Under the common United Kingdom/New Zealand position, paternity rights and privacy rights apply to any *substantial* part of the work. By contrast, the integrity and false attribution rights can be invoked in relation to *any* part of a work. Generally speaking, it is only the work's true creator who has standing to claim the rights of paternity, integrity and the false attribution. (The privacy right for films and photographs belongs to the person who commissions them.) Deemed authorship confers no moral rights. In the case of films, the moral rights are vested in the director, thus side-stepping for this narrow purpose any debate about where true ownership resides.

---

now also grants moral rights to performers in recognition of the fact that a performance too can be digitally manipulated and misattributed to the wrong performer.

[66] Generally speaking, the right of paternity imposes a positive obligation to do something on those who handle or deal with a copyrighted work, whereas the right of integrity and the right not to have one's work falsely attributed are negative obligations imposed on all the world in relation to works.

[67] This right in common law jurisdictions is largely congruent with its civilian counterparts. However, in some jurisdictions, such as the United Kingdom and New Zealand, the paternity right cannot be infringed unless it is first asserted. The right may be asserted generally or in relation to particular prescribed circumstances.

[68] Where this right exists in civil law countries, it is usually treated as an offshoot of the right of paternity (as in France), or as part of the law of privacy (as in Germany), or of defamation. In the United Kingdom and New Zealand, the right's duration is only 20 years.

In contrast to the United Kingdom and New Zealand, the United States[69] limits moral rights protection to visual and graphic artists in respect of "one-off" or "limited" editions of their work.[70] What happens to properly authorised copies or reproductions thereafter is deliberately placed beyond the reach of moral rights protection. On-line service providers appear to have little to fear from moral rights breaches by users unless the protected "one off" or "limited" edition is created on-line in the first place.

B Modes of Infringement

Many common law jurisdictions, of which the United Kingdom and New Zealand can be regarded as typical, make an explicit distinction between primary and secondary infringement of copyright owners' economic rights, between those who themselves engage in the infringing activity and those who are held accountable for the infringing action of another. In other countries, such as the United States, the distinction is implicit. The approach in that jurisdiction has been to graft onto copyright doctrine notions of vicarious and contributory liability which have their roots in tort doctrine and other areas of law.[71] Looking across jurisdictions, the concept of secondary liability generally requires some degree of fault or contribution on the part of the infringer and is predicated on the notion that there is a primary infringer. Liability, even where injunctive relief is sought by a copyright owner, is normally imposed only where persons know or have reason to believe copyright infringement has occurred.

(i) Primary Infringement of Economic Rights

Primary liability is strict in the United Kingdom and New Zealand, and infringement takes place if and when a restricted act is carried out. An infringer's

---

[69] Via State and Federal statutes such as the Visual Artists Rights Act 1990 (17 USC § 106A1 13(d)).

[70] Statutory protection, thus, extends only to paintings, drawings, prints or sculptures which exist only in single copies or limited editions of 200 or less, and which have been personalised in some way by the artist. Single copies of photographs produced specifically for exhibition are also protected, while anything made "for hire" is excluded. "Made for hire" is a term of art which covers a work specially ordered or commissioned for use as a contribution to a collective work or as part of a motion picture or other audio visual work. More significantly, "work for hire" includes works produced by employees within the scope of their employment.

[71] In the United States, secondary infringement in copyright (and defamation) law may rest on either the notion of vicarious or contributory liability. Vicarious liability may exist where a provider's right and ability to supervise coalesce with an obvious and direct financial interest in the exploitation of the copyrighted materials. Lack of knowledge that the primary actor is infringing is not a defence under these circumstances. (See M.B. Nimmer and D. Nimmer, *Nimmer on Copyright: A Treatise on the Law of Literary, Musical and Artistic Property and the Protection of Ideas* (New York, Matthew Bender, 1976), para. 12.70.) Contributory liability may exist where a provider *substantially participates* in the infringement. The contribution of technology or services may be construed as contributory if they constitute the means to infringe. To be regarded as contributorily liable, a provider would have to have actual knowledge or a reason to know of the infringing nature of the activities of the primary infringer (Nimmer and Nimmer, *ibid.*, para. 12.75).

mental state, though totally irrelevant to liability, can have an impact on the remedy awarded. Thus, if providers do not know, and have no reason to believe, copyright existed in a transmitted work, they are susceptible to injunctive relief and to an account of profits, but not to damages. Where they have derived benefit from the infringement or have acted in a particularly flagrant way, they can be liable for additional damages.[72] A similar situation relating to direct infringement obtains in the United States. There, where intermediaries themselves perform any act reserved exclusively for a copyright holder, however technical in nature, they can face absolute liability. Again, intent is irrelevant to the availability of injunctions[73] or damages.[74]

The remainder of this section proceeds to analyse the more significant and troublesome ways in which on-line go-betweens can be found directly liable for breaches of copyright owners' economic rights. (I cannot and do not hope, however, to plot here each and every possible forensic turn in every jurisdiction.)

(a) On-line Copying

Under the broadly similar United Kingdom/New Zealand statutory formulae,[75] virtually any form of storage of a work in digital form without the licence of the copyright owner can constitute primary infringement.[76] This situation is of obvious concern to users of digital networked systems who need to download information simply in order to browse it. It is of equal concern to on-line intermediaries such as communications carriers or network operators, because it exposes them to liability for primary infringement on the ground that they make temporary or incidental cache copies of works as they are transmitted over the Internet.[77] Indeed, it has been estimated that the transmission of a video on demand from a database in Germany to a home computer in Portugal will imply at least a hundred ephemeral acts of storage.[78]

The process of on-line transmission of information from sender A to recipient B requires A's computer's transmission control protocol mechanism to

---

[72] Copyright, Designs and Patents Act 1988(UK), s. 97; Copyright Act 1994 (NZ), s. 121.

[73] See 17 USC § 502 (Copyright Act 1976 (US)), though a court may deny an interim injunction if a provider lacks intent: see Nimmer and Nimmer, n. 30 above, para. 14.106.

[74] 17 USC § 504, (Copyright Act 1976 (US)). Copyright owners can choose whether they demand actual damages and profits or statutory damages (fault on the part of the provider may be reflected in the quantum awarded here).

[75] Under the Copyright, Designs and Patents Act 1988 (UK), s. 17(2); and the Copyright Act 1994 (NZ), s. 2; the test for copying means in relation to any description of work, reproducing or recording the work in any material form; and includes, in relation to a literary, musical or artistic work, storing the work in any medium including "by electronic means" in the United Kingdom and "by any means" in New Zealand.

[76] The United Kingdom statute dissolves any doubt on this issue, expressly stating that copying includes transient copies: Copyright, Designs and Patents Act 1988 (UK), s. 17(6).

[77] See *MAI Systems Corporation* v. *Peak Computer, Inc.*, 991 F 2d 511 (9th Cir. 1993), cert. dismissed, 510 US 1033 (1994). The language used in both the 1996 WIPO Treaties reflects a lack of consensus over whether the strict *MAI* approach would be internationally harmonised.

[78] European Commission, Explanatory Memorandum to Art. 5(1), para. 3, of the *Draft Proposal for a Directive on the Harmonisation of Certain Aspects of Copyright and Related Rights in the Information Society*, COM(97)628, 10 December 1997.

divide the information into "packets" or "bits" of a predetermined size for its journey through various interconnected computers or "routers". Some commentators remain sceptical that transmission of these packets of information through an intermediary's network could ever amount to copying, on the ground that it is difficult to characterise this very fleeting moment as a form of "storage".[79] Such an approach is congruent with the House of Lords' decision in *R. v. Gold and Schifreen*.[80] Notwithstanding that this was not a civil copyright action, but a criminal one involving forgery and counterfeiting, their Lordships found that the process by which a number and a password were held momentarily in the control centre of a computer before being expunged irretrievably was not a process of a lasting and continuous nature to which the words "recorded or stored" could properly be applied. In their view, these words connoted the preservation of information for an appreciable time with the object of subsequent retrieval.[81] Longer term caching practices, however, undeniably expose on-line service providers themselves to claims of primary infringement.

Although copyright is a strict liability statute in the United States, courts there have been loathe to find providers *directly* liable for third party infringement on the grounds of technical infringement alone. *Playboy Enterprises* v. *Frena*[82] was one case where the court not only looked for, but found, something more to trigger a finding of direct liability. The court was swayed by evidence of direct involvement on the part of a computer bulletin board operator, who had allowed not only the public display of unauthorised copies of pictures (copyrighted by Playboy) but had also permitted its subscribers to download infringing copies into their own computer systems. It was indeed the absence of any such volitional act on the part of another bulletin board operator in *Religious Technology Center* v. *Netcom On-Line Communication Services, Inc.*[83] that led the court there to distinguish *MAI* and to refuse to find the provider directly liable for technical infringement.

---

[79] Hayes, n. 26 above, 6; and T. Aplin, "Internet Service Provider Liability for Moral Rights Infringement in Australia" (1999) 1 *Digital Tech LJ*, (<http://wwwlaw.murdoch.edu.au/dtlj/articles/vol1–1/aplin.html>), para. 23. The Information Infrastructure Task Force, n. 50 above, 27, also suggests that interim or partial copies of works created during transmission in RAM in interim node computers may not constitute "fixed" copies on the ground that a live transmission, while it may result in a fixation, is not a fixation in itself.

[80] [1988] 2 WLR 984, 990–1.

[81] There is yet another technological reason to doubt that simple routing of data through intermediaries' networks may inevitably involve copying the whole or a substantial part of a work. While the several packets relating to A's communication all have the same destination, namely B's address, they do not necessarily travel from A to B together. Indeed they may pass automatically through a series of completely different computers or routers to be reunited and reassembled into the original communication by B's transmission protocol mechanism.

[82] 839 F Supp. 1552 (M D Fla. 1993).

[83] 907 F Supp. 1361 (ND Cal. 1995).

(b) Issuing Copies to the Public

Copyright owners in many common law jurisdictions have the exclusive right to put into circulation copies of works not previously circulated. This allows them to enjoy what is often dubbed the "right of first sale" which leaves second hand sales or distributions outside the control of the copyright holder.[84] The first sale defence in the United States is subject to statute and express exhaustion of rights principles. By contrast, in the United Kingdom and New Zealand, it has been inferred from legislative silence. Article 8 of the WCT has not sought to do away with this defence.[85] Thus, on one view, on-line purchasers could be conceptualised as having benefited from a species of "distribution", and be free to disseminate limitless "second hand" copies of copies of copies of copies unregulated across the Internet.[86] On another view, any felt need to conceptualise what second hand digital copies might be (and how many, if any, copies a first purchaser can make) can simply be bypassed by finding that a user does not infringe copyright at all if she only receives and re-transmits the copy electronically because such transient transmission does not amount to copying.[87] It strikes me, however, that if a work remains in the memory of the first purchaser's computer long enough to be able to amount to receipt of the first issue of the copy, arguably by the same token, it can also remain there long enough to be said to have been copied before it is passed on electronically by the user.

(c) Infringement by Inclusion in Cable Programme Service

Copyright owners in the United Kingdom and New Zealand have an exclusive right to include their works in a cable programme service, a right which presently falls short of transmission over the Internet. Persons including a work in a cable programme service can also have copyright in the transmitted product if it can be classified as a "cable programme", defined as "any item included in a cable programme service". Thus, not each and every transmission by cable is protected as a cable programme; one must first look to the nature of the transmission to see whether it qualifies as a "cable programme service". Under the New Zealand/United Kingdom statutory formula[88] such service consists "wholly or mainly in sending visual images, sounds and other information by means of a telecommunications system other than by wireless communication".

---

[84] Rentals of works to the public are another matter and have generally been treated differently since copyright owners were given rental rights in 1993 by GATT/TRIPS.

[85] Both the WCT and WPPT preserve the freedom of contracting parties to determine the conditions under which the exclusive distribution right will be exhausted. Contracting parties can, thus, opt for either national or international exhaustion of rights after first sale and decide whether or not it lies in their interest to allow parallel importation of digital copies of works.

[86] See Nimmer and Nimmer, n. 30 above, para. 8.12[B].

[87] H.L. MacQueen, "Copyright and the Internet" in L. Edwards and C. Waelde (eds.), *The Law of the Internet: Regulating Cyberspace* (Oxford, Hart Publishing, 1997), 67, 81–2, posits that there would be no infringement under the United Kingdom statute if passing on were done electronically because it would not amount to even transient copying.

[88] Copyright, Designs and Patents Act 1988 (UK), s. 7; Copyright Act 1994 (NZ), s. 4(1).

Information transmitted must be able to be received at two or more places, whether or not simultaneously, in response to demand by different users or be for presentation to members of the public.[89] Expressly excluded from being categorised as cable programme services are interactive communication systems, such as telecommunication systems which are treated as essentially two-way private or domestic communications between users and providers.

Generally speaking, then, a copyright owner's right to include her work in a cable programme service[90] covers transmission through electronic networks, excluding the whole or part of interactive services where users are able to add to or modify content sent through the system.[91] Where mixed services with genuinely interactive elements exist, these elements can be quarantined and excluded leaving any elements which communicate information to users to be treated as part of the cable programme service.[92] For example, suppose a director of a university distance learning programme sends the same common body of learning materials subject to copyright to all its on-line student subscribers, the sending of the material will be a cable programme service while each individual student's on-line return of a completed assignment will be excluded as will be the service provider's return of marks and comments tailored to the individual students concerned.

Some on-line service providers are clearly in the business of providing the physical infrastructure for "cable programme services". In the example above, it is possible for there to be two possible "cable programme service" providers and hence two putative infringers, i.e. the director of the distance learning programme and the cable system operator who actually provides the transmission infrastructure and transmits or retransmits the content. No statutory distinction exists between the selector of infringing content for the home page or common source web site and the infrastructure provider who transmits or retransmits the infringing content to the individual users of the programme since, traditionally, they were one and the same.[93] Thus, both players are exposed to primary liability, the on-line service provider despite the fact that it may have no knowledge

---

[89] "To the public" is generally not defined in common law copyright statutes but has been construed by the High Court of Australia in *Telstra* v. *Australian Performing Arts Association* (1997) 146 ALR 649, 657, 694 as incorporating the notion of the copyright holder's public, or more precisely, according to Kirby J (at 692), as " the group which the copyright owner would contemplate as its public for the performance of its work". Moreover, in the views of Dawson and Gaudron JJ (at 658), single point-to-point transmissions were to the public. They also noted that "to the public" is a broader concept than that of "in public" (a concept relevant to the right to show or perform a work in public: see n. 100 below) since the latter makes clear that the place where the relevant communication occurs is irrelevant.

[90] Copyright Act 1994 (NZ), s. 16(1)(f); Copyright, Designs and Patents Act 1988 (UK), ss. 16(1)(d) and 20.

[91] IMPRIMATUR Report, n. 5 above, 4–5.

[92] In *The Shetland Times* v. *Wills* [1997] EMLR 277, Lord Hamilton was prepared to sever the interactive part of a web site (which comprised an invitation for users to send in comments or suggestions by email) in order to find that the operation of the rest of the *prima facie* infringing web site was a cable programme service.

[93] IMPRIMATUR Report, n. 5 above, 5.

or control over the content being transmitted.[94] (A way out, however, may exist for service and access providers under rather enigmatic provisions, which exclude from the definition of a "cable programme service",[95] "services which are, or to the extent that they are, run for persons providing broadcasting or cable programme services or providing programmes for such services". If this provision, one of a raft of exceptions dealing with services that are not truly aimed at the public, can be extended to the infrastructure provider and transmitter, these entities would not be construed as providing a "cable programme service" and would, accordingly, not be liable primarily for copyright infringement by web site operators "including" works in cable programmes.)

(d) Broadcasting

Under the very similar United Kingdom/New Zealand position, while a broadcast is a copyright work in its own right,[96] broadcasting is also a restricted act in relation to literary, artistic, dramatic and musical works, sound recordings or films, broadcasts or cable programmes. Although the statutory provisions differ slightly in format, both jurisdictions essentially define a broadcast as meaning a transmission of visual images, sounds and other information, whether or not encrypted, of a programme by wireless communication, where the transmission is capable of being lawfully received in, or presented to, members of the public in the same jurisdiction or elsewhere.

On-line service providers who transmit infringing content selected by others by wireless means are not forced to bear such a heavy risk of infringement as cable service programme providers. The former, unlike the latter, are not plagued by the lack of a statutory distinction between content provider and content distributor. Where broadcasters have "no responsibility to any extent"

---

[94] This was the conclusion reached by the High Court of Australia in *Telstra* v. *Australian Performing Arts Association* (1997) 146 ALR 649, in relation to one of the fact situations in that case which involved callers hearing music on hold after making a call on a conventional fixed line telephone to a Telstra subscriber who, if busy, had the call diverted to a common music on hold facility operated by Telstra. For details of all fact situations (which involved transmissions of music on hold from several different sources to callers on both fixed line and mobile telephones) and findings of the High Court, see MacMillan and Blakeney, n. 5 above, and Aplin, n. 79 above. In the United Kingdom and New Zealand, any telecommunications carrier, relying on a system which conveys visual images, sounds or other information by electronic means, who transmits copyrighted music on hold or in an answerphone message, played by one of its subscribers to any member of the public who might care to call up that user, would also be directly infringing copyright in the music (if the transmission was unauthorised). Again, in these two jurisdictions it could be a simple matter of finding that the carrier had technically included the work in a cable programme service. For example, in *The Shetland Times* v. *Wills* [1997] EMLR 277, Lord Hamilton was quite prepared to find a *prima facie* case of copyright infringement based on the United Kingdom provisions governing cable service programme providers, although the infrastructure provider was not actually a defender in that case.

[95] Copyright, Designs and Patents Act 1988 (UK), s. 7(2)(e); Copyright Act 1994 (NZ), s. 4(2)(e).

[96] The author of a broadcast is the "maker" of the broadcast, or where a broadcast relays another broadcast by reception and immediate transmission, the person making that other broadcast. Copyright Act 1994 (NZ), s. 5(2)(c); Copyright, Designs and Patents Act 1988 (UK), s. 9(1)(b).

over a broadcast's contents, they are not held primarily liable for infringement.[97]

(e) Showing, Playing or Performing Works in Public

Browsing the Internet can implicate the right of public performance and/or public showing in the United Kingdom and New Zealand, which both define performances to include "any mode of visual or acoustic presentation of artistic, musical, dramatic or literary works, including presentation of the work by means of a broadcast, film or cable programme".[98] Since several common law courts have been prepared to find that computer screen and video game displays are "films",[99] there is no reason why the display of a web site on a screen cannot be construed as a performance or display of a work provided it can be said to occur *in public*. It is this last requirement which may present a hurdle to finding providers liable for infringement, but the mere fact that recipients of transmitted displays are geographically or temporally dispersed would not preclude a finding that the performance is in public.[100]

Some on-line intermediaries can draw comfort from the New Zealand copyright statute, which provides that they will not be showing, playing or performing a work in public if they simply retransmit visual sounds or images. Nor, under the United Kingdom counterpart provision, are providers by whom visual images and sounds are sent carrying out this particular restricted act.[101]

(ii)   Secondary Infringement of Economic Rights

In both the United Kingdom and New Zealand, the copyright statutes' secondary infringement provisions are designed to catch persons who deal with infringing copies, provide the means of making infringing copies, or permit or enable infringing performances to take place. Formulated in the hard copy age, these provisions tend to emphasise possessing, knowingly distributing or exhibiting in public infringing copies which are "articles".[102] Thus, where digital copies do

---

[97] Copyright, Designs and Patents Act 1988 (UK), s. 6(3)(a); Copyright Act 1994 (NZ), s. 3(2)(a). Under Australian copyright legislation, by contrast, communications carriers can, in certain circumstances, be construed as broadcasters. This was the finding of the majority in the High Court of Australia in *Telstra* v. *Australian Performing Arts Association* (1997) 146 ALR 649, in relation to a raft of fact situations where callers on mobile phones were put on music on hold.

[98] Copyright, Designs and Patents Act 1988 (UK), s. 19; Copyright Act 1994 (NZ), s. 2.

[99] See n. 59 above.

[100] For an extended analysis of case law and issues involved in the interpretation of "in public", see *Copinger and Skone Jones on Copyright* (14th edn., London, Sweet & Maxwell, 1999), paras. 7–125-7–13. The authors emphasise that the chief guide to the question should be common sense. Also useful is the test promulgated in *Australian Performing Rights Association Ltd.* v. *Commonwealth Bank of Australia* (1992) 25 IPR 157, 171, which rests on whether the persons forming the audience are bound together by a domestic or private tie or by some aspect of their public life. See also Hayes, n. 26 above, 62.

[101] Copyright, Designs and Patents Act 1988 (UK), s. 19(4); Copyright Act 1994 (NZ), s. 32(4).

[102] Thus, in the United Kingdom, the legislative provisions prohibiting parallel importing do not apply to intangible digital material transmitted over the Internet. (In New Zealand, since the

not exist in tangible form (a highly common occurrence), they cannot readily cover the conduct of on-line service providers, although if they do, the latter should not be any worse off than hard copy dealers or distributors.[103] The secondary infringement provisions most likely to catch go-betweens (such as cyber-café proprietors) are those which prohibit knowingly permitting an infringing performance of a literary, dramatic or musical work in a place of public entertainment or knowingly providing the apparatus (such as a computer terminal and display screen) for an infringing performance.

Both the United Kingdom and New Zealand copyright statutes also expressly impose secondary liability on those providers who act as telecommunications carriers or network operators (but specifically not broadcasters or cable service programme providers), where they transmit a work by means of a telecommunications system knowing, or having reason to know, that infringing facsimiles will be received either in the home jurisdiction or elsewhere.[104] Under such circumstances, the person faxing the work is likely to be found to have directly infringed copyright by copying the work before, or during the course of, the transmission.

(iii) Knowledge and Belief

Taking the United Kingdom and New Zealand as our model once again, when a secondary infringement claim is brought against a provider, it must be established that the entity in question knew or had reason to believe it was distributing infringing material. While on-line intermediaries owe no general duty to be vigilant, they can be found liable if shown to have had actual or constructive knowledge of the act of infringement. For actual knowledge, the question is one of fact. Where a provider deliberately puts its head in the sand to avoid having to rectify an infringing situation, actual knowledge cannot be construed from such struthious conduct. On the other hand, providers cannot be said to have actual knowledge merely because they are aware, as all must be, that the material they transmit will, from time to time, contain infringing copies. Such knowledge cannot usefully (from a copyright holder's point of view) be ascribed to any specific transmission to, or from, any specific user. Thus, constructive knowledge can be attributed to providers only where they have reason to believe they are distributing infringing material at any one time. The test is an objective one involving a concept of knowledge derived from facts from which a reasonable

Copyright (Removal of Prohibition on Parallel Importing) Amendment Act 1998, parallel importation of articles (if non-infringing in the country where "made") is no longer a secondary infringement.)

[103] C. Gringas, *The Laws of the Internet* (London, Butterworths, 1997), 199, asserts that the presence of an infringing work on a hard drive could, at a stretch, be construed as "possessing". Accordingly, an on-line service provider could be said to "possessing", "exposing" or "distributing" the work when it hosts a user's web site, although it would only be secondarily liable for infringement if it knew or should have known that the work was an infringing copy.

[104] Copyright, Designs and Patents Act 1988 (UK), s. 24(2); Copyright Act 1994 (NZ), s. 37(2).

provider would arrive at the relevant belief.[105] It also seems to follow that there must be a period of time during which the go-between can evaluate the facts and form a reasonable belief.[106] To fix a provider with knowledge the instant it receives notice would scarcely accord with tests of reasonableness in any jurisdiction. Arguably, where the conduct of on-line go-betweens is being assessed for fault, they should be treated at least as tolerantly as fleamarket proprietors who physically own the stalls which sellers lease to set out their wares and who are fully aware that some trader, sometime, somewhere in the fleamarket is likely to offer infringing copies for sale.

(iv) Authorisation and Contributory Infringement

On-line service providers are susceptible to claims of infringement where it can be said they have authorised others to infringe copyright. English courts have found the term "authorise" to equate to "sanction, approve or countenance",[107] but not to the extent that it means to condone.[108] Authorisation under the Anglo-American tradition generally requires the authoriser to have the capacity to exert some control over the person who actually infringes or over access to the apparatus or facilities which the authorisee uses to infringe. Entities which set up facilities to provide or facilitate Internet access are therefore at some risk in relation to this form of liability. However, merely making available the means for on-line infringement is not tantamount to authorising infringment, provided that the means can also be used for non-infringing purposes. This is so even if providers know that the means will inevitably be used to infringe copyright.[109] Whether providers have some degree of actual or apparent right to control their users' conduct is thus crucial.[110] Where those who provide Internet and on-line facilities do not, at the outset, apprise users of the existence of copyright and moral rights and strongly advise them against breach when they upload or download material, they can be found to be implicit authorisers of their users' infringements. This, in essence, was the message delivered by *University of New South Wales* v. *Moorhouse*.[111] In that case, a university library's photocopying facilities were used to make infringing copies of a book. The facility provider was found to have authorised its user's breach of copyright because its notice

---

[105] *Copinger and Skone Jones on Copyright*, n. 100 above, para. 8–11.

[106] *Ibid.*

[107] *Falcon* v. *Famous Players Film Co.* [1926] 2 KB 474.

[108] *Amstrad Computer Electronics plc* v. *British Phonographic Industry Ltd.* [1986] FSR 159, 207 (CA); *CBS Songs Ltd.* v. *Amstrad plc* [1988] AC 1013, 1055 (HL). In the latter case, manufacturers of double-headed audio tape decks were found not to have implicitly authorised their customers' copyright infringements, despite the fact that their product facilitated infringement and they knew infringement was likely to occur. The pivotal factors were that the means to infringe could be used for perfectly legitimate as well as infringing purposes and the suppliers had explicitly warned users against copyright infringement.

[109] *Ibid.*

[110] *Ibid.*

[111] (1975) 133 CLR 1.

beside the photocopy machine was an inadequate warning. From a policy perspective, one wonders about such *pro forma* strictures which would confine liability to those few ignorant or badly advised providers who never learned properly to recite the magic incantation "Don't Infringe" to their users. The nostrum makes little sense in the analogue world and makes even less in a digital environment. While service providers such as universities can control the use of terminals, they have virtually no control over the content users can upload or download. (In *Moorhouse*, the university controlled not only the photocopying machines but also the book copied.) It is, furthermore, easier in a digital networked environment for users readily to bypass warning notices and not to be part of any direct contractual nexus with an on-line service provider.

The concept of contributory infringement can be viewed as roughly equivalent to authorisation of infringement. A small body of United States jurisprudence has been built around the issue of contributory liability by on-line service providers for third party infringement. In *Religious Technology Center* v. *Netcom On-Line Communication Services, Inc.,*[112] the leading case, Whyte J was clearly concerned by the spectre of cascading chains of liability for on-line go-betweens when he observed that "where the infringing subscriber is clearly liable for the same act, it does not make sense to adopt a rule that could lead to the liability of countless parties whose role in the infringement is nothing more than setting up and operating a system that is necessary for the functioning of the Internet".[113] He proceeded to note that where a provider's system is used merely as an automatic pass through for infringing material created by a third party, there is a requirement of some element of causation or volition (which we would call foreseeability or policy-based causation) on the part of a provider before it can be found contributorily liable.

Using similar reasoning, the court found bulletin board operators had substantially participated in user infringement in *Sega Enterprises* v. *MAPHIA*[114] and *Sega Enterprises* v. *Sabella*.[115] The providers were held contributorily liable on causative grounds, not only because they had solicited unauthorised uploading of video games on to their own servers, but also because they had facilitated the downloading of infringing copies. It was irrelevant to each finding that the service provider in question might not have known exactly when or what games would be uploaded or downloaded by what users.

In looking for causation or volition, at least one United States court has been prepared to find these elements present where providers have failed to respond adequately to notices of infringement from copyright owners. The outcome of the decision in *Religious Technology Center* v. *Netcom On-Line Communications Services, Inc.*[116] turned on a judicial evaluation of provider response. In

[112] 907 F Supp. 1361 (N D Cal. 1995).
[113] *Ibid.*, at 1370.
[114] 857 F Supp. 679 (N D Cal. 1995).
[115] US Dist. Lexis 20470 (N D Cal. 1996).
[116] 907 F Supp. 1361 (N D Cal. 1995).

that case, a former member of the Church of Scientology posted on an electronic bulletin board, without authorisation, both the published and unpublished works of Hubbard, the founder of the Church of Scientology. Netcom failed to remove material from its network system after being advised of the putative infringement by the copyright owner. Whyte J refrained from finding contributory liability on the part of the provider, because the copyright owner had not proved the likelihood of ownership of the copyright. As his Honour observed:[117]

> Where [an on-line service provider] cannot reasonably verify a claim of infringement, either because of a fair use defence, the lack of copyright notices on the copies, or the copyright holder's failure to provide the necessary documentation to show there is a likely infringement, the [service provider's] lack of knowledge will be found reasonable and there will be no liability for contributory infringement for allowing the continued distribution of the works on its system.

Thus, once put on notice, providers can be compelled to make a considered judgement about whether a complainant's claim of infringement is reasonable regardless of what sort of a position they are in to do this. Clearly, it would not be reasonable for an intermediary in a jurisdiction such as the United Kingdom and New Zealand, where works are not required to be accompanied by copyright notices, to ignore a claim of infringement simply because a copyright notice is absent from the works to which the claim relates. The United States case of *Leibovitz* v. *Paramount*[118] demonstrates just how difficult it may be for providers faced with digitally morphed material to make up their minds, in the face of a copyright owner's claim of infringement, about what activity can legitimately amount to a user's right to fair use or to parody a work. (In that case, infringement was found not to exist when the head of actor Leslie Neilson was superimposed upon the body of a naked and pregnant Demi Moore as depicted in a well publicised magazine cover photograph.)

In a defamation context, where those who repeat, republish or retransmit defamatory material can under some circumstances be subject to liability as though they themselves were the original publishers, courts in the United States have determined that the extent to which providers attempt to control or regulate the content of a bulletin board can be crucial to their liability for user defamation. This issue was addressed directly in *Cubby, Inc.* v. *Compuserve, Inc.*[119] In that case, Compuserve provided access for subscribers using their own personal computers to an on-line general information service featuring about 150 special interest fora. The "Journalism Forum" was one of these and was independently managed under contract by one company under a separate con-

---

[117] 907 F Supp. 1361, 1374 (ND Cal. 1995). Whyte J also looked for, but did not find, vicarious liability on the part on the on-line service provider, largely on the ground that while it might have had the right and ability to control its subscribers' activities, it did not derive any direct financial benefit from their infringing activities.

[118] 137 F 3d 109 (2nd Cir. 1998).

[119] 776 F Supp. 135 (SDNY 1991).

tract with another company which published the allegedly defamatory material in an on-line newsletter. Since the provider had no editorial control over the newsletter's contents (the newsletter was made available immediately to subscribers) and could not be proved to have had knowledge of the defamatory comments, it was found to be a news distributor ("an electronic for profit library") rather than a publisher. As such, it was found neither directly nor contributorily liable for defamation because, as the court observed, it had no more editorial control over a publication than a public library, bookshop or news stand and it would be no more feasible for it to examine every publication it carries than it would be for any other distributor to do so.[120]

Another American defamation case which twisted and turned on the publisher versus distributor distinction was *Stratton Oakmont, Inc.* v. *Prodigy Services Co.*[121] The question in that case was whether a bulletin board operator could be held liable for the content of messages posted by users. The court found that it had expressly held itself out as a family oriented network, making it widely known that it deployed an automatic software screening program for monitoring and editing purposes. Thus, unlike Compuserve in *Cubby*, the provider actually made concrete decisions about content, albeit at one remove, through its agents, the board leaders. Ironically, since it had attempted monitoring and editorial control in relation to obscene and offensive matter, the provider was found by the court, for its pains, to be a publisher of defamatory material and vicariously liable for its board leaders' failure to detect and remove it. Another instructive feature of the case was that the court headed off the providers' attempt to exit from future problems by clever drafting. It completely disregarded "talismanic language" in the contract between the provider and the board leaders, which expressly sought to provide that their relationship was *not* one of agency. Providers immediately perceived that *Stratton* created a very strong disincentive against monitoring pro-activity. Its approach was seen as highly likely to hobble expansion of the Internet, inhibit the free flow of information and interactive content on-line, as well as greatly diminish the diversity of on-line service providers.[122] The so-called "Good Samaritan" defence,[123] promptly enacted by the United States to overturn *Stratton,* now ensures that no providers or users of interactive computer services shall be liable for blocking illegal content or making available the technical means to restrict access to illegal content[124] (with no requirement that the block be reasonably imposed). It also ensures that "no provider or user of an interactive telecommunications service shall be treated as the publisher or speaker of any information that it transmits where this information has been provided by another information

---

[120] *Ibid.*, 140. Nor was Compuserve found vicariously liable through agency, because there was no direct contractual nexus between it and the publisher of the defamatory content who communicated with and billed all its members separately.

[121] 23 Media L Rep (BNA) 1794 (NYSC 1995).

[122] K. Siver, "Good Samaritans in Cyberspace" (1997) 23 *Rutgers Comp & Tech L J* 1, 19.

[123] Telecommunications Act 1996 (US), s. 230(c)(1).

[124] Telecommunications Act 1996 (US), s. 230(c)(2).

provider".[125] These defence provisions, however, have been deliberately couched to deny immunity to on-line service providers in relation to copyright infringement claims. [126]

(v) Moral Rights Infringement in Digital Networked Environments

Just as on-line service providers can be held primarily or secondarily liable for breaches of copyright proper perpetrated by their users, so too can they be susceptible to claims in relation to their abuse of authors' moral rights. As discussed above, digital works can be readily scanned, uploaded, altered or combined with other works. Framing technology, moreover, allows any identifying names and copyright information to be cropped off material before it is electronically redistributed. It also can facilitate derogatory treatment of works allowing as it does for material to be presented in a different context from which its author originally intended and in a manner beyond her control.[127] An illustrator, for example, could find her graphics on-line, not only unacknowledged but digitally morphed to enable a scurrilous advertisement to be emblazoned across them and accompanied by a hypertext link to decidedly dubious lyrics.

In the civilian way of looking at things authors are the sole and best judges of whether the integrity of their work has been infringed. In those jurisdictions, authors are entitled to insist on having their works presented or played to the public in a manner of their choosing. By contrast, the mere mutilation, distortion or other derogatory treatment of a work without more does not infringe its integrity under the United Kingdom and New Zealand copyright statutes, which set out in some detail the circumstances in which the right can be said to be infringed. These circumstances all require, *after* the derogatory treatment has occurred, that some public act be performed in relation to the work in question. Public acts include "commercial publication" defined as "making the work available to the public by means of an electronic retrieval system",[128] broadcasting and including a derogatory treatment of the work in a cable programme service. There is a need to demonstrate actual rather than potential harm to honour and reputation under both statutes.[129] Thus, no liability exists for private acts of digital vandalism which remain invisible to the public.

Both the United Kingdom and New Zealand statutes create categories of liable persons in relation to the rights of integrity and paternity. In relation to the right of integrity, those of particular importance in the context of on-line

---

[125] An on-line service provider is not liable for third party content, even where it knows of the defamatory content and delays in removing it: see *Zeran* v. *America Online*, 129 F 3d 327 (4th Cir. 1997), in which the defence was first successfully invoked. The defence was also successfully run in *Blumenthal* v. *Drudge & AOL*, 922 F Supp. 44 (DDC 1998).

[126] Telecommunications Act 1996 (US), s. 230(d)(2) and (4).

[127] M. de Swart, "Keeping Your Site Nice: Unfair Practices on the World Wide Web" (1997) 8 *AIPJ* 181, 187.

[128] Copyright, Designs and Patents Act 1988 (UK), s. 175(2); Copyright Act 1994 (NZ), s. 11.

[129] Copyright, Designs and Patents Act 1988 (UK), s. 80(1); Copyright Act 1994 (NZ), s. 98(1)(b).

service provider liability are persons who actually carry out the derogatory treatment, persons who are responsible for the derogation becoming public by broadcasting it, including it in a cable service programme or putting it into an electronic retrieval system, and persons who distribute an infringing copy otherwise than in the course of business so as to affect prejudicially the honour or reputation of the author or director. Since Internet service providers are highly likely to be engaged from time to time in the transmission of work subject to derogatory treatment at the hands of their users, they are likely to be liable persons. While neither statute speaks explicitly in terms of primary and secondary infringement, such a distinction is clearly implicit. For those who commit the act of derogation itself, or expose it to the public once done, liability is absolute and the motives or intentions of the putative infringer irrelevant.

In relation to the right of attribution, there is also a detailed catalogue of infringing acts similar to those found in the statutes' integrity right and paternity right provisions. There is one significant departure from the general model, however. The knowledge requirement extends to cover most forms of primary infringement as well. Proof that the alleged infringer knew, or had reason to believe, that the attribution or representation complained of is false is required whenever the infringing act consists of issuing to the public copies of the work, in or on which the false attribution or misrepresentation is found,[130] and broadcasting or including in a cable programme a film or literary, dramatic or musical work together with the misattribution or misstatement.[131]

An author's right of attribution can be infringed by any treatment of a web site or material on that web site which fails properly to identify and acknowledge the authorship of that work. Similarly, where the site is repackaged by means of framing technology, the author's right not to have authorship of work misattributed can be infringed.[132]

As with the integrity right, those who authorise others to commit an act of misattribution or misappropriation are themselves liable as infringers.[133] In such cases, fault presumably need only attach to the authoriser, not the authorisee. As also in the case of economic right infringement, where an on-line service provider fails reasonably to verify a claim of moral rights abuse by an author, when it is in a position to do something about redressing the situation, it can be held liable under the *Netcom* principle discussed above.

---

[130] Copyright Act 1994 (NZ), ss. 102(3)(a) and 103(3). Under the United Kingdom statute, liability is absolute in such cases: Copyright, Designs and Patents Act (UK) 1988, s. 84(2).

[131] *Ibid.*

[132] de Swart, n. 127 above, 187.

[133] Copyright Act 1994 (NZ), ss. 102(7), 103(7), and 104(6).

IV DIVERGENCE AND CONVERGENCE IN THE TREATMENT OF ON-LINE
INTERMEDIARIES

Commentators and legislators now largely agree that Internet access or service providers are conceptually distinguishable from those communications carriers and network operators who merely provide and maintain the infrastructure (telephone wires, cables, satellite or microwave links) for electronic data transmissions. The distinction is based on the assumption that Internet service providers have a greater ability to monitor their systems and remove infringing material.[134] As well as taking the gate money, they can act as bouncers, screening and imposing contractual conditions on would be sub-operators or end users in the on-line environment. They are also thought to be better placed to monitor user generated content.

A useful starting point in allocating liability or immunity is Aplin's[135] analysis of types of activity. Her continuum ranges from "simple access" to "value added access". At one end, there are those who merely connect subscribers to network facilities and allow them to download and upload information via that connection. (They equate to common carriers or mere conduits.) At the other end, "value added access" occurs where the provider stores material in a file system, makes it available to the public via a web server and transmits it on request.[136] The United States has now statutorily formulated a comparable active/passive polarisation of service provider activity. It is instructive to draw upon both these notions, which do not rely on the normal or predominant status of would-be defendants but instead allocate liability according to where in the spectrum their services fall at any given moment in time (that is to say, liability depends on what they do, not what they are). I would prefer to build on this functional, but bipolar, spectrum by dividing it into three sub-spectra on the basis that, if we are to construct workable rules rather than open discretions, lines have to be drawn somewhere. The classification adopted below has both functional and temporal dimensions. It also recognises that technological malleability allows on-line service providers to attract liability under different heads on different occasions.

A The Technical Infringers: Carriers, Conduits and Cachers

If any on-line intermediaries are able to invoke messenger immunity, it should be those who act as mere conduits for data transmission, for theirs is a true content passivity. Here, communications carriers could readily be likened to the

---

[134] Loughnan, n. 5 above, 20; Macmillan and Blakeney, n. 5 above, 52; IMPRIMATUR Report, n. 5 above, 2.

[135] See n. 79 above.

[136] *Ibid.*, para. 32.

post offices and couriers of the off-line world, none of whom is generally sad-
dled with liability in relation to either the nature or content of the tangible items
they transport or deliver. The post office analogy becomes more debatable,
however, when applied to claims for exemption by those access providers who
host chat groups or allow real-time conferencing between two or more users.
Equally debatable is the position of other access providers who allow users to
transmit information to other users by email, or link information from one site
with information from another. A more appropriate comparison would be with
those who rent stadiums and concert halls for performers.

To hold true conduits liable would effectively impose on them a positive
obligation to vet the copyright status of every item to be delivered. This is not
just a problem for carriers. Such scrutiny would lead to significant loss of delivery time and privacy, not only of recipients and senders themselves, but also of
any third parties alluded to in intercepted communications. Either the economic
viability of the service provider industry would be at risk, or the cost of the service would have to increase. Such scrutiny would also have implications for
freedom of expression.[137]

At the 1996 WIPO Diplomatic Conference, there was considerable disagreement over the issue whether an express exemption from liability was necessary
for on-line service providers (especially carriers) in the light of the new right to
authorise communication to the public. An Agreed Statement to Article 8 of the
WCT was adopted by the Conference, to the effect that the "mere provision of
physical facilities for enabling or making a communication" did not amount to
an exercise of that right within the meaning of the WCT or the Berne
Convention. There was no elaboration on what acts would be exempted under
the banner of "mere provision of physical facilities". The phrase could be interpreted to apply not only to the obvious categories of communications carriers
and network owner/operators but also to cyber-café proprietors and universities who supply users with terminals and Internet access. The Agreed Statement,
it should be noted, is expressly limited to the new exclusive right of communication to the public. It does not extend to the right to reproduce a work. Even
greater controversy dogged the question[138] whether an infrastructure or physical facilities provider should be exempt for making cache copies on its servers
and for temporary copies made during transmission (that is, when it is not
"communicating to the public"). In an attempt to resolve the problem, an
Agreed Statement was adopted in relation to the right of reproduction which
still leaves open the question whether temporary copies in RAM fall within
the copyright owners' right of reproduction.[139] Despite this uncertainty, some

---

[137] H. Perritt Jr., "Tort Liability, The First Amendment and Equal Access to Electronic
Networks" (1992) 5 *Harv J L & Tech* 65, 135–6.

[138] The controversy revolved around the right of reproduction contained in the proposed Art. 7
of the WCT. That Art. was eventually dropped entirely from the adopted version of the Treaty.

[139] The Agreed Statement concerning Art. 1(4) provides: "[t]he reproduction right, as set out in
[Art. 9 of Berne] and the exceptions permitted thereunder, fully apply in the digital environment, in
particular to the use of works in digital form. It is understood that the storage of a protected work

jurisdictions have proceeded (or are proceeding) to exempt some (but not all) go-betweens for their part in both the transmission, routing and caching of infringing works uploaded or downloaded by third parties.

(i) Caching Exemptions

As we have seen, the *MAI* decision demonstrated to providers that, by engaging in even short term caching, they could be technically liable as primary (or in United States terms "direct") infringers.[140] The United States has now acted to head off such liability by creating exemptions for incidental acts of reproduction in the Digital Millennium Copyright Act 1998. Thus, it exempts from direct liability and claims for monetary damages, on-line service providers who cache information in their systems on behalf of their users.[141] The exemption operates differently according to whether the caching is merely temporary (as for real time transmissions) or of longer duration. To qualify for the temporary caching exemption, providers[142] must not have themselves posted infringing material, but simply have stored it unmodified until requested by a user. Where infringing material is stored for longer periods, the exemption applies only where providers (i) have no actual knowledge of infringing content; (ii) know of no facts or circumstances "from which infringing activity is apparent"; or (iii) act quickly to remove or block off the material once the provider "obtains such knowledge or awareness". Providers, moreover, must derive no "directly attributable" financial benefit from situations where they have the right and ability to control infringing activity and must remove or disable infringing material upon receipt of written notice. While the Digital Millennium Copyright Act also creates two other exemptions to overturn *MAI,* these are narrow and still do not protect Internet users downloading or browsing copyright material.[143]

Australian legislative initiatives are wider, setting up temporary copying exemptions in order to communicate. No infringement would exist in the making by any person of a temporary reproduction of a work, adaptation of a work or an audiovisual item as part of the technical process of making or receiving a communication.[144] Europe too, has taken similar initiatives in its *Amended Proposal for*

in digital form in an electronic medium constitutes a reproduction within the meaning of [Art. 9 of Berne]."

[140] 991 F 2d 511 (9th Cir. 1993), cert. dismissed, 510 US 1033 (1994).

[141] 17 USC, §512 (b) (1998).

[142] For the purposes of this particular exemption, a service provider is defined in 17 USC §512 (k)(B) (1998) as "a provider of online services or network access, or the operator of facilities therefor, and includes an entity described in subparagraph (A)". The latter entity is another category of service provider (a mere conduit or passive carrier), defined in 17 USC §512 (k)(A) as "offering the transmission, routing or providing of connections for digital online communications, between or among points specified by a user, of material of the user's choosing, without modification to the content of the material as sent or received".

[143] One exception permits the making of random access copies of programs during the course of computer hardware maintenance: see 17 USC § 117 (1998). The other accommodates the reality of webcasting allowing Internet broadcasters to create ephemeral copies: see 17 USC § 112 (1998).

[144] Copyright Amendment (Digital Agenda) Bill 1999, cls. 45 and 94 propose the insertion of new ss. 43A and 111A in the Copyright Act 1968 (Cth).

a Directive on the Harmonisation of Certain Aspects of Copyright and Related Rights in the Information Society, by proposing that temporary acts of reproduction (both on-line and off-line) which are (i) integral to a technological process made for the sole purpose of enabling use of a work and (ii) have no separate economic significance, should fall outside the scope of the reproduction right.[145] On its face, the exemption would cover only incidental or transient copies made during the otherwise legal use of protected material. The European Commission's Explanatory Memorandum to an earlier, virtually identical proposal appears to suggest that the basis for judging legal use could either be a licence or legal exception. The Memorandum also stipulates that the Berne "three step test" must be met in order to ensure a fair balance of rights and user interests.[146]

(ii) Exemption for Mere Transmissions of User Posted Material

The United States now exempts (from monetary damages at least, and under some circumstances from injunctive relief as well) service providers[147] who merely transmit user-posted material, such as email, provided *all* of the following conditions are met:[148]

(a) The infringing material must have been put on-line by or at the direction of a person other than the service provider.
(b) The transmission, routing, and storage of the infringing material must be "carried out through an automatic technical process without selection of the material by the service provider".
(c) The service provider must not select the recipients of the infringing material, except as an automatic response to the sender's request.
(d) The provider must not maintain any copy of the transmission which is readily accessible to anyone other than the recipient.
(e) The provider must not modify the content of the infringing transmission in any way.

Thus, immunity follows not status, but function. On-line service providers cannot simply don a communications carrier, router or network operator hat when it suits them. Their liability depends entirely on their acts or omissions relating to a particular infringing data transmission.

---

[145] European Parliament and Council Amended Proposal for a Directive on the Harmonisation of Certain Aspects of Copyright and Related Rights in the Information Society, COM(1999)250 final, Art. 5(1).

[146] European Commission, Explanatory Memorandum to Art. 5 of the Draft Proposal of December 1997: see <http://www.raekoeve.de/ecdraft.htm>. See also text accompanying n. 32 above.

[147] The only type of service provider who can enjoy this exemption is defined in 17 USC § 512(k)(1)(A) (1998). The definition is set out in n. 142 above.

[148] 17 USC § 512(a) (1998).

The framers of the Australian Copyright Amendment (Digital Agenda) Bill 1999[149] have proposed a less generous immunity regime for what they call "carriers and carriage service providers". Such entities would not be liable for having authorised any infringement of copyright in a work or audiovisual item *merely because* they provided the facilities used by a person to do something the right to do which is included in the copyright. They would remain subject to a statutory test for authorisation.[150] The European Commission Amended Proposal features no specific provisions concerning the liability of carriers for user posted material, although, as will be seen herein, the exemption it does contain for temporary technical acts of reproduction does offer strong comfort for service providers in general and this group in particular.

(iii) Exemptions for Linkers

The United States is the first common law jurisdiction to exempt information tool providers from monetary (but not injunctive) remedies where they have referred or linked users to an on-line location containing infringing material, provided that they (i) do not have actual or constructive knowledge of the infringement, (ii) do not receive any benefit directly attributable to the infringing activity, and (iii) respond expeditiously to remove the reference or link upon notification of claimed infringement (such notice must be reasonably sufficient to enable the service provider to locate the link or reference).[151]

B Content Providers and Compilers

Clustered towards the other end of the active/passive spectrum are those responsible for actively selecting and manipulating content in networked digital environments. They are undeniably, in Aplin's parlance, "value adders".[152] Under the copyright law of most jurisdictions they will be primary or direct infringers, to the extent that they themselves (or their agents or employees) supply or manipulate content.[153] Other obvious "value adders" are educational institutions operating interactive distance learning programmes which (through their academic staff) commonly put on-line large quantities of material to students and researchers. The United States appears poised to exempt non-profit educa-

---

[149] Cls. 42 and 95 would insert new ss. 39B and 112E into the Copyright Act 1968 (Cth).

[150] See text accompanying n. 159 below.

[151] 17 USC § 512(k) (1998).

[152] Aplin, n. 79 above, para. 4.

[153] According to M. Schaeffer, C. Rasch and T. Braun, "Liability of On-Line Service and Access Providers for Copyright Infringing Third Party Contents" [1999] *EIPR* 208, this principle is now expressly embodied in s. 5 of the German Teleservices Act 1997, where providers who make their own content available in a network may be found primarily liable according to the rules contained in general legal provisions. This imposition of liability was principally intended to cover on-line offers of offensive material, but appears to cover copyright infringement, at least in this particular context.

tional institutions running such programmes.[154] Equally problematic is the position of on-line libraries and archives. (Again, the United States has already provided a very limited exemption from liability for this group.[155])

One group of value adders who will never be singled out for limited liability of any kind are the Internet access providers who host their own web sites and those who assert (and would probably strenuously defend) their own copyright in compilations of users' works and parts of works which they have posted on their services. Such rights to works posted on or transmitted by on-line services can be acquired by a service contract or can simply be asserted by unilateral claim. Clearly, these providers cannot claim copyright ownership of on-line compilations and still expect to insulate themselves from copyright or moral rights liability in relation to the content of their works.

C The In-betweens

Once the conscious content providers and the mere conduits are lopped off the spectrum, it becomes exceedingly problematic to find the appropriate treatment for the remaining bloc of value adders. In many cases, these providers will play an active, even aggressive, role in making available content prepared, manipulated and morphed by others (the nearest off-line analogy is publishers and editors). They can also have some say in choosing recipients of material and exercise control over their users. They range in size from giants such as America Online to tiny one-person enterprises. For reasons already discussed, the "let liability lie where it falls under ordinary domestic copyright legislation" approach is not appropriate. Different nations and different interest groups have therefore sought to offer a wide variety of *nostra* for treating this varied group. Implicit in a particular jurisdiction's approach to the problem of allocating liability will be its own perceived national interests with all the attendant choice of law and jurisdictional problems that this can bring. It is for this very reason, however, that in the long term even the most self-absorbed of jurisdictions can eventually be brought to accept that a protocol for international harmonisation of liability and remedies would be in its own best interest. That dawning is still some way off, however, if only because of the upheaval it is likely to cause in each country's wider copyright liability policies in the short term. In working towards this position longer term, it is suggested that something more than the mere provision of on-line services should be required to found liability for third party

[154] 17 USC § 402 (1998) requires the United States Register of Copyrights to make recommendations to Congress on how to promote distance education through digital technologies, including interactive digital networks, while maintaining an appropriate balance between the needs of users and the rights of copyright owners. Such recommendations are to follow consultation with representatives of copyright owners and non-profit education institutions, libraries and archives, but pointedly not user representatives.

[155] 17 USC, §403 (1998) provides a very narrow exemption for ephemeral recordings made by these entities.

infringement in the despatialised realm of the Internet. I will now explore what that something more might be.

(i) Financial Benefit Factor

Whether a provider receives a financial benefit directly attributable to a particular act of infringement carried out by a third party may well be crucial to its liability. In the United States, financial benefit has always been a factor in finding vicarious liability in defamation and copyright cases.[156] Under the Digital Millennium Copyright Act 1998, as seen above, financial interest is enough to disqualify even a mere conduit or network operator from that statute's limitation of liability provisions. Financial benefit need not be obvious or direct. It must amount, however, to more than what the provider in question received in *Marobie v. National Association of Fire Equipment Distributors.*[157] In that case, the owner of an infringing website paid his on-line service provider a flat fee every three months irrespective of how many hits the site received or what was accessed. That was not enough to convince the court that the provider received a financial benefit from the infringing material. An on-line service provider could be said to derive indirectly a financial benefit where it actively sponsors, endorses or advertises infringing material put on-line by a third party. (Another way of dealing with this would be to treat such participatory or affirmatory conduct as authorisation of acts carried out by the primary infringer.)

(ii) Failure to Monitor or Take Down

As explained earlier, many copyright owners would have even this in-between bloc proactively pre-vet user communications for potentially infringing items, rather than leave the question of infringement to a forensic lottery. For them, even the time between an infringement notification and the granting of an interlocutory injunction is too long. Copyright owners would prefer to avoid what to an outside eye might seem to be a minimal risk. From the copyright owners' perspective, an injunction is a less than optimal remedy, because once infringing material is put on-line it can be disseminated to an indefinite number of users at an indefinite number of locations at a speed which even the most fast track of interlocutory procedures cannot possibly hope to match. Were such a viewpoint to become legislative reality it would have a dramatic effect on the structure and viability of the on-line service industry. While the giant on-line service providers presumably have (if they want, or will have if regulation so requires) ready access to state of the art monitoring technology (with all its warts), plus the services of bevies of copyright lawyers for the complex decisions required, many thousands of on-line service provider pygmies would find a monitoring require-

---

[156] *Religious Technology Center* v. *Netcom On-Line Communications Services, Inc.,* 907 F Supp. 1361 (N D Cal. 1995).
[157] 983 F Supp. 1167 (ND Ill 1997).

ment virtually impossible to satisfy and would presumably drop out of the market completely or be absorbed by their larger brethren. Neither outcome bodes well for the health of the competitive process. Market-driven concentration is one thing, regulation-driven mergers quite another.

For the reasons given above, a positive obligation to monitor would be unwise. This is not to say that on-line intermediaries should not be subject to injunctive restraint should they fail to remove or block access to material within a reasonable time of being notified of an infringement. Any injunction imposed should of course be technically feasible and economically reasonable, something that most countries' adjectival law is already flexible enough to achieve. If more precision is thought to be necessary, one could emulate the framers of the American Digital Millennium Copyright Act 1998 by requiring written notification by copyright owners. Such notification must identify both the infringing material and the copyrighted work. To guard against wrongful third party attempts to subvert the process, the notification must be accompanied by a signed statement that the notifiers are authorised to act on behalf of the copyright owner.[158] In the event that disputes arise (as they inevitably must), United States legislation exempts on-line service providers from liability to their users if they delete or disable the allegedly infringing material in good faith. One difficulty with the American approach is that it provides no compensatory regime where the notified infringement turns out to be no infringement at all. (However, misrepresentation of material facts may subject copyright owners to claims for damages and legal fees.) No doubt, jurisdictions which, like the United States, are net exporters of copyright works, are likely to find this template attractive. I would prefer to see the problem dealt with by something like the present undertaking as to damages.

(iii) Liability Dependent on Authorisation

Many common law jurisdictions now expect copyright owners to assume some of the onus of protecting their works but any argument that owners should be pro-active and encrypt works put on-line still does not address the very real problem that many works at risk of infringement include those created in the traditional media and put on-line unbeknowst to copyright owners. Once infringing (or putatively infringing) material is detected on-line, the person best placed to remove it is usually the on-line service provider. Authorisation or contributory liability can be inferred from a provider's failure to remove infringing material of which it has received notice, in which case the focus for determining authorisation may rest more on the on-line service provider's post- rather than pre-transmission conduct. Alternatively, authorisation criteria could take into

[158] 17 USC § 512(c)(3) (1998). To qualify for liability limitation, on-line service providers must have designated an agent to receive notifications of claimed infringement by making contact information available via their services and including it on their web sites in a location accessible to the public and the US Copyright Office.

account the totality of the relationship between primary infringer and provider. The three-limbed test set out in the Australian Copyright Amendment (Digital Agenda) Bill 1999 would do just that. Under this proposal, matters which courts would be required to take into consideration include:[159]

(a) the extent (if any) of the provider's power to prevent the carrying out of the infringement;
(b) the nature of the relationship between the provider and the infringer; and
(c) whether the provider took reasonable steps to prevent or avoid the infringement, including whether the provider complied with any relevant industry codes of practice. (Here there would presumably have to be at least *prima facie* evidence of infringement before service providers have to assume the burden of taking reasonable care).

(iv) Innocent Dissemination Defence

Another possible way out of the impasse would be to provide for an innocent dissemination defence, similar to that available in some common law defamation regimes for distributors, booksellers and libraries. In order for a provider to be cast as an innocent disseminator of defamatory material, it must show it was merely a conduit for the passage of words and not responsible for the meaning or nuances they contain. The United Kingdom has now codified the defence for, *inter alia*, "operators of, or access providers to, communications systems over which the statement complained of is transmitted by a person over whom they have no effective control".[160] A provider must prove that it:

(a) was not the author, editor or publisher of the statement complained of; and
(b) took reasonable care in relation to its publication; and
(c) did not, and had no reason to, believe that whatever part it had in the publication caused or contributed to the publication of a defamatory statement.

In my view, the innocent dissemination defence is a liability benchmark suitable for transposing into the language of copyright. The onus could be placed on providers to demonstrate that they:

(a) were not the primary infringer; and
(b) took reasonable care in relation to the transmission; and
(c) neither knew nor ought to have known that the transmission was likely to contain infringing material.

This hypothetical statutory gauntlet would still not solve the "to control or not to control" conundrum for providers. On the one hand, if providers do monitor or issue copyright warning notices to users and yet still let through infringing material, they could be found to have acted negligently both in terms of the statutory defence and for wider tort purposes. On the other hand, if they

---

[159] Cl. 87 would insert a new s. 101 (1A) in the Copyright Act 1968 (Cth).
[160] See Defamation Act 1996 (UK), s. 3(e).

do not attempt to control what their users do at all, they could be said not to have taken reasonable care. Some commentators have suggested that the key to solving the conundrum could lie in self-regulatory codes, which require providers to take positive steps not only to educate users about copyright and moral rights infringement, but also to ensure or at least facilitate user compliance via service provider/user contractual terms. [161]

(v) Returning Primary Infringers to the Front Line

As seen above, the very nature of the on-line medium means that as soon as infringing material enters a digital networked environment there is a cascading effect on liability. In focusing on problems relating to intermediaries' liability for third party infringement, one should never lose sight of the fact that, first and foremost, copyright owners' litigious instincts should be directed towards the primary infringer. To this end, it is important to be able to identify the chain of responsibility so that liability can be attributed to those who actually create infringing material. One writer has toyed with the notion that on-line service providers, particularly bulletin board operators, should not permit anonymous use by subscribers in order to facilitate the tracing of direct infringers.[162] (Anonymity is, of course, what attracts many would-be posters of material to bulletin boards in the first place).[163] Even if an identification system were as cautious and as structured as that used for secret Swiss bank accounts, it could never be foolproof because user validation will remain a problem as long as the purported user is not necessarily the person who actually logs on. What appears to be a more likely scenario for the future is the widespread implementation of technological tracking systems which can at least locate the physical computer terminal from which infringing material is disseminated.

V CONCLUSION

This chapter has focused on the plight of on-line service providers who find themselves used as lightning conductors in the stormy clashes between copyright owners and users. In so doing, it confirms that copyright paradigms which remain tightly tailored to old technology specific media must be coherently recalibrated for digital networked environments. On the international stage, the recasting that has thus far taken place has occurred largely at the behest, and to the advantage, of copyright owners. There is an urgent need for new principles and an enforcement regime which is fair, practical and efficient for all three

---

[161] Fitzgerald, n. 8 above, 163.

[162] Pomeroy, n. 31 above, 1084.

[163] Cutera, n. 42 above, 557; E. Schlachter, "Cyberspace, the Free Market and the Free Marketplace of Ideas: Recognising Legal Differences in Computer Bulletin Board Functions" (1993) 16 *Hastings Comm & Ent L J* 89, 91.

groups of stakeholders: copyright owners, Internet users and on-line service providers.

It is completely unjustifiable in any jurisdiction to continue to hold *all* on-line service providers technically liable for third party infringement, irrespective of their ability to prevent or put a stop to infringement. It is neither pragmatically possible, nor fair to either users or providers, to force the law to gallop ahead of the algorithms, and to require providers to implement technological mechanisms for monitoring content. No amount of *ex ante* monitoring or pre-vetting control would allow providers to know definitely when infringing content was entering or exiting their systems. There are not only serious privacy concerns at issue here for users. Their existing fair use exemptions could far too readily be pre-empted by on-line service providers who are forced onto the liability defensive.

While passive carriers, routers and cachers in some common law jurisdictions have (or at least have had proposed for them) limited exemption from liability, there is no such tidy reprieve in sight for those providers who do take an active part in putting on-line material prepared and manipulated by others. Their treatment should follow the principle that they are only liable if they have knowledge of, or a vested financial interest in, infringing third party content, and where taking it down or blocking its use within a reasonable time is a reasonable technical option open to them. This general approach can be achieved through legal mechanisms (such as an innocent dissemination defence or authorisation criteria) which comport with ordinary tortious standards of reasonableness. (The question whether monetary damages are available against the provider, as well as injunctive relief, should normally turn on the conduct of the provider in the post-notice of infringement period. The question whether putatively infringing material should become *prima facie* infringing material is after all a question which publishers have to address in the hard copy world.)

Finally, in seeking new legal solutions to copyright problems created or exacerbated by new communication technologies, it must not be overlooked that those very same technologies can also be deployed to provide solutions for copyright owners. Encryption measures are capable of achieving highly effective protection for on-line content providers who may or may not also be copyright owners. The upside for both copyright owners and on-line services providers could be that opportunity for user infringement simply diminishes. The downside for users, if technology is used increasingly to freeze copyrighted expression, is that they may be cut off from facts and ideas and deprived of the fair use of works and information which still remains their due even in a digital world.

5

Copyright Across (and Within) Domestic Borders

GRAEME W. AUSTIN

In principle the law of copyright is strictly territorial in its application.[1]

A purely territorial approach will not help us confront the reality of the twenty-first century.[2]

I INTRODUCTION

Among the issues that occupied the Legal Realists was whether institutions such as property and contractual rights are "pre-legal", or whether they depend on the state for their existence and protection. The Realists sought to show that property and contract "necessarily requir[e] the state to determine the character of relations among its citizens in the market place",[3] echoing a conclusion reached by Jeremy Bentham over a century earlier.[4] Controversy over the state's role in the regulation of property rights—the interrelationship between *imperium* and *dominium*—has never abated, of course.[5] The new challenges for copyright law posed by digitisation and the Internet are the latest context in which the tension between private property and state regulation is to be played out.

At the public international law level, the "upward harmonisation" agenda[6] means that, on the global scene, there is more, and more uniform, copyright law

---

[1] *Abkco Music & Records, Inc.* v. *Music Collection International Ltd.* [1995] RPC 657, 660 (*per* Hoffmann LJ).

[2] P. Geller, "Intellectual Property in the Global Market Place: Impact of TRIPS Dispute Settlements" (1995) 29 *Int'l Lawyer* 99.

[3] J. Singer, "Legal Realism Now" (1988) 76 *Cal L Rev* 465, 482.

[4] J. Bentham, *Theory of Legislation* (London, Paternoster Library, 1896) vi, 111 ("[t]here is no such thing as natural property, . . . it is entirely the work of law").

[5] See generally, M. Cohen, "Property and Sovereignty" (1927) 13 *Cornell LQ* 8; J. McLean, "Property as Power and Resistance" in J. McLean (ed.), *Property and the Constitution* (Oxford, Hart, 1999), chap. 1.

[6] See K. Aoki, "Considering Multiple and Overlapping Sovereignties: Liberalism, Libertarianism, National Sovereignty, 'Global' Intellectual Property, and the Internet" (1998) 5 *Ind J Global Leg Stud* 443, 443.

than ever before, a development given fresh momentum by the integration of most of the substantive Articles of the Berne Convention[7] in the World Trade Organisation regime through the Agreement on Trade Related Aspects of Intellectual Property Rights (hereafter "TRIPS Agreement").[8] The latest initiatives, the two 1996 World Intellectual Property Organisation treaties, the WIPO Copyright Treaty[9] and the Performances and Phonograms Treaty,[10] have made significant additions to the copyright and neighbouring rights armoury. All states parties to these treaties are now required to enact legislation that provides copyright owners with a new right in the bundle of rights comprising a copyright that is tailored for the Internet: in addition to having the right to copy, perform or distribute publicly, copyright owners also have the right "to communicate a work to the public".[11] The treaties also require states parties to give legal force to controls on access to copyright materials[12] and to the integrity of copyright management information.[13]

Private international law issues have been largely ignored in public international instruments touching on copyright. This is a significant gap: private international law is likely to be one of the battlegrounds in which the contest over the continued viability of the regulation of copyright by the domestic state is fought. The 1996 WIPO Treaties are, for instance, silent on the issue of where copyright owners' new rights are to be localised. The Berne Convention itself addresses tantalisingly few private international law questions.[14] The major choice of law provision in the Berne Convention, Article 5(2), is notoriously ambiguous.[15] The rule that the applicable law is that of "the place where protection is claimed" has been interpreted in decidedly contradictory ways. Some commentators regard the provision to demand application of the law of the forum, or even the law that provides most effective protection of the copyright work.[16] Others see it as reinforcing a strictly territorial view: the applicable law

---

[7] Berne Convention for the Protection of Literary and Artistic Works (1971 text), 1161 UNTS 3.

[8] Agreement on Trade Related Aspects of Intellectual Property Rights, 15 April 1994, (1994) 33 ILM 81.

[9] WIPO Copyright Treaty, 20 December 1996, (1997) 36 ILM 65.

[10] WIPO Performances and Phonographs Treaty, 20 December 1996, CRNR/DC/95.

[11] See, e.g., WIPO Copyright Treaty, Art. 8.

[12] See, e.g., WIPO Copyright Treaty, Art. 11.

[13] See, e.g., WIPO Copyright Treaty, Art. 12.

[14] One private international law issue is dealt with specifically in the Berne Convention. Art. 14bis(2)(a) provides that "[o]wnership of copyright in a cinematographic work shall be a matter for legislation in the country where protection is claimed". In *Itar-Tass Russian News Agency* v. *Russian Kurier, Inc.*, 153 F 3d 82 (2nd Cir. 1998), the court did not treat this principle as being of general application. Instead, it held that, generally, copyright ownership was to be determined under the law of the territory with the closest relationship with the property and the parties. See further, Section III below.

[15] See generally J. Ginsburg, "The Private International Law of Copyright in an Era of Technological Change" (1998) 273 *Recueil des Cours* 238, 322 (discussing a variety of possible interpretations of Art. 5(2)).

[16] P. Geller, "Conflicts of Laws in Cyberspace: Rethinking International Copyright in a Digitally Networked World" (1996) 20 *Colum-VLA J L & Arts* 571, 595.

is that of the place *for which* protection is claimed,[17] implying, for instance, that where a work is copied without authorisation in New Zealand, New Zealand's copyright law applies. Likewise, Australian law applies to copying within Australia. The latter construction is consistent with a territorial approach to the international copyright regime. The territoriality of copyright means that there is no domestically enforceable international law of copyright. Instead, a copyright owner's rights are divided into geopolitical zones: an international copyright actually means a vast collection of territorially-confined domestic rights: a New Zealand copyright, an Australian copyright, a South African copyright, and so on.

Until recently in the copyright field, private international law issues have arisen relatively infrequently. In the era of digitisation and the Internet, however, in which works may cross almost all international borders almost instantly, interest in this aspect of copyright law has intensified.[18] Some scholars consider that digitisation and the Internet have so profoundly changed the environment within which copyright industries must operate that equally profound changes to copyright's legal context should be anticipated. Leading copyright scholar, Professor Jane C. Ginsburg, commented recently, "if authors and their works are no longer territorially tethered, can changes in the fundamental legal conceptions of existing regimes for the protection of authors be far behind?"[19]

The principal change that Professor Ginsburg and other scholars advocate is a loosening of copyright from its territorial confines.[20] Instead of comprising a mosaic of distinct, territorially-confined copyrights, an international copyright regime tailored to the era of digitisation and the Internet would allow a copyright owner to assert a different governing law in cases of cross-border copyright infringement. For copyright infringements effected via the Internet, this might mean that the law of the place of the upload to the digital network applies to all infringements, wherever they occurred.[21] Alternatively, the law of the place of the defendant's domicile might govern. The aim of such approaches is

[17] C. Bradley, "Territorial Intellectual Property Rights in an Age of Globalism" (1997) 37 *Va J Int'l L* 505, 549.

[18] Raymond Nimmer was one of the first modern commentators to anticipate the importance of private international law issues in the cyberspace context: R. Nimmer, "Licensing on the Global Information Infrastructure: Disharmony in Cyberspace" (1995) 16 *Nw J of Int'l L & Bus* 224.

[19] J. Ginsburg, "The Cyberian Captivity of Copyright: Territoriality and Authors' Rights in a Networked World" (1999) 15 *Santa Clara Computer & High Tech L J* 347, 348–9.

[20] See generally J. Ginsburg, "Ownership of Electronic Rights and the Private International Law of Copyright" (1998) 22 *Colum-VLA J L & Arts* 165, 168.

[21] J. Ginsburg, "Putting Cars on the Information Superhighway: Authors, Exploiters, and Copyright in Cyberspace" (1996) 95 *Colum L Rev* 1466, 1498. This approach borrows from the European Commission Cable and Satellite Directive of 1993, which, in Art. 3(b), localises the act of communication to the public not in the receiving countries, but "solely in the Member State where, under the control and responsibility of the broadcasting organisation, the programme-carrying signals are introduced into an uninterrupted chain of communication". Council Directive 93/83 of 27 September 1993 on the co-ordination of certain rules concerning copyright and rights related to copyright applicable to satellite broadcasting and cable retransmissions [1993] OJ L248/15.

more efficient enforcement of copyright infringements,[22] and the development of a more efficient global licensing regime. Courts, licensees and licensors alike are likely to find an international copyright regime that has moved "beyond territoriality"[23] easier to cope with than a system that, at least potentially,[24] requires adjudicators and parties to copyright transactions to engage with a multiplicity of applicable laws.[25]

There has been a vigorous debate in periodical literature about *which* of the variety of candidates for a governing law should be applied in a copyright infringement action in which a defendant has engaged in unauthorised activity that infringes a copyright owner's rights in a number of territories.[26] In this chapter, I do not engage with this debate. Instead, this chapter focuses on some of the possible implications for copyright law that might flow from a departure from copyright's territoriality premise. As Brian Fitzgerald's chapter in this volume attests, it is commonly thought that "[t]he information society is non-territorial".[27] The non-territorial character of the information society needs to be understood partly as brute reality. Cross-border transmission of digitised informational products and other cultural materials serves to constitute the borderless-ness of the information society. But conclusions about the non-territorial character of the *legal* regulation of the information society are also partly normative; they reflect, and, in future years will continue to reflect, social policy choices about the role of the domestic state in the regulation of domestic information policy.

I believe that non-territorial approaches to copyright law would precipitate a potentially profound change in the nature of copyright law, one that should not necessarily be regarded as positive. An important corollary of loosening copyright from its territoriality premise is a loosening of the connection between the domestic state and the regulation of copyright. If copyright law is a key component of domestic information policy, the diminution of the role of domestic states in its regulation should be of concern.[28] Before the "fundamental legal conceptions" underlying the regulation of copyright at private international law are radically changed, some further reflection on the territorial character of copyright may be useful.

---

[22] See A. Reindl, "Choosing Law in Cyberspace: Copyright Conflicts on Global Networks" (1998) 19 *Mich J Int'l L* 799, 825 (commenting that "[e]nforcement concerns undoubtedly have . . . the most prominent influence on choice of law analysis").

[23] A phrase borrowed from Professor Geller: P. Geller, "The Universal Electronic Archive: Issues in International Copyright" (1994) 25 *IIC* 54, 55.

[24] Alternative approaches to territoriality that have been put forward include: the law of the place of upload, the law of the author's residence, the law of the defendant's residence or place of business. These are discussed extensively in Ginsburg, n. 15 above.

[25] Reindl, n. 22 above, 808.

[26] This debate is exhaustively discussed in Reindl, *ibid.*

[27] B. Fitzgerald, chap. 3 of this volume, 40.

[28] I develop this point in further detail in G. Austin, "Social Policy Choice and Choice of Law for Copyright Infringement in Cyberspace" (forthcoming) (2000) 79(3) *Oregon L Rev.*

II TERRITORIALITY IN ANGLO-AMERICAN COPYRIGHT JURISPRUDENCE

English case law has typically adopted a strictly territorial approach to cross-border copyright infringement. Until recently, the territorial perspective had such force that it was assumed that a domestic court had no jurisdiction over the infringement of copyright in a foreign territory.[29] Infringement of foreign intellectual property rights was treated in much the same manner as infringement of rights in foreign land.[30] For a domestic court to exercise jurisdiction was characterised as offending principles of comity.[31] In *Pearce* v. *Ove Arup Partnership Ltd.*,[32] a recent decision involving an allegation of infringement of copyright in the Netherlands, the English Court of Appeal has now retreated from the rigid jurisdictional prohibition, holding that there is no *per se* prohibition against the exercise of jurisdiction over infringement of foreign copyrights, at least where the validity or existence of the foreign rights is not at issue.[33] Whether this decision is regarded by Commonwealth courts as being of general application or limited to the European Union context will be a key point to watch in the emerging private international law of copyright infringement.

In straightforward cases of copyright infringement occurring within other territories, there has been relatively little discussion of choice of law questions. Indeed, it appears to have been uniformly assumed that the relevant law is that of the territory where the rights were alleged to have been infringed. In *Tyburn Productions Ltd.* v. *Conan Doyle*,[34] for instance, a 1990 English decision, the plaintiffs sought, in effect, a declaration of non-infringement of the US copyrights in the detective fiction of Sir Arthur Conan Doyle. The declaratory plaintiffs were screenwriters who had developed and wished to have produced and distributed screenplays for a television film featuring the famous detective Sherlock Holmes and his sidekick Dr Watson. The relevant copyrights were owned by an English resident, Lady Bromet, Conan Doyle's only surviving child. Presumably because personal jurisdiction over Lady Bromet could not be secured in an American forum, the plaintiffs sought a declaration from the English court that she had "no rights in the characters Sherlock Holmes and Dr Watson under the copyright, unfair competition or trade mark laws of the United States of America"[35] such as would entitle her to prevent distribution of the film in the United States. The court declined the application, accepting the

---

[29] See generally G. Austin, "The Infringement of Foreign Intellectual Property Rights" 113 *LQR* 321.

[30] The common law principles with respect to disputes involving foreign land rights were affirmed in *British South Africa Co.* v. *Companhia de Moçambique* [1893] AC 602, and *Hesperides Hotels Ltd.* v. *Muftizade* [1979] AC 508.

[31] *Potter* v. *The Broken Hill Pty. Ltd.* (1906) 3 CLR 478 (HCA).

[32] [1999] 1 All ER 769.

[33] *Ibid.*, 799.

[34] [1990] RPC 185.

[35] *Ibid.*, 188 *per* Vinelott J.

submission that the jurisdictional prohibition against adjudicating with respect to foreign intellectual property rights applied equally to patents, trade marks and copyrights.[36] The court also noted that, even if it had ruled on the scope of the US copyrights, there was no evidence that its decision would be treated as binding by a US forum. Hence, it would be "an exercise in futility to allow th[e] claims".[37] For present purposes, what is significant about the *Tyburn Productions* decision is that the application focussed exclusively on the parties' rights under US copyright law. No issue as to the application of any other law was raised. Had the English court entertained the plaintiff's case, it presumably would have focussed on whether the creation of the screenplay infringed Lady Bromet's right to prepare derivative works, a right accorded to authors under section 106(2) of the US Copyright Act 1976.[38] The broadcasting of the films on American television would have implicated her right, under section 106(4), "to perform the copyrighted work publicly". In addition, the English Court would presumably have been required to engage with US doctrine involving infringement of copyright in fictional characters.[39]

In *Pearce* v. *Ove Arup Partnership Ltd.*, there was again no question about which nation's copyright laws were involved. Although the plaintiff had drafted the architectural plans in London, the construction of the building in The Netherlands was alleged to have infringed the plaintiff's rights under Dutch copyright law. Similarly in *Abkco Music & Records Inc.* v. *Music Collection International Ltd*,[40] authorisation of exploitation of copyright materials in the United Kingdom was considered to involve UK copyright law only, even though the act of authorisation occurred offshore. In *Abkco Music*, the English Court of Appeal took the opportunity to emphasise that "the law of copyright is strictly territorial in its application".[41] In the New Zealand case of *Atkinson Footwear Ltd.* v. *Hodgskin International Services Ltd.*,[42] the unauthorised importation of footwear into Australia was considered to implicate only Australian intellectual property rights.

---

[36] [1990] RPC 185, 192.

[37] *Ibid.*, 196 *per* Vinelott J. In *Pearce* v. *Ove Arup Partnership Ltd.* [1999] 1 All ER 769, 799, the English Court of Appeal emphasised this aspect of Vinelott J's decision, noting that *Tyburn Productions* should not be regarded as standing for a rigid jurisdictional prohibition against the exercise of jurisdiction by a domestic court over foreign copyright infringement.

[38] 17 USC §§ 101 ff.

[39] The leading analysis in US copyright law is that of Judge Learned Hand in *Nichols* v. *Universal Pictures Corp.*, 45 F 2d 119, 121 (2nd Cir. 1930): "[i]f Twelfth Night were copyrighted, it is quite possible that a second comer might so closely imitate Sir Toby Belch or Malvolio as to infringe, but it would not be enough that for one of his characters he cast a riotous knight who kept wassail to the discomfort of the household, or a vain and foppish steward who became amorous of his mistress. These would be no more than Shakespeare's 'ideas' in the play, as little capable of monopoly as Einstein's Doctrine of relativity, or Darwin's theory of the Origin of Species. It follows that the less developed the characters, the less they can be copyrighted; that is the penalty an author must bear for marking them too indistinctly."

[40] [1995] RPC 657.

[41] *Ibid.*, 660.

[42] (1994) 31 IPR 186.

United States copyright cases that have involved infringements in foreign territories disclose a more diverse approach. Some cases adhere to the territoriality premise.[43] In a recent decision from within the Second Circuit, for instance, the court recognised that infringement of copyright in a game-show format by an Italian television company raised issues under Italian copyright law. Declining the defendant's application to dismiss the proceedings on *forum non conveniens* grounds, the Court opined: "[t]here is no reason to believe that this Court will be unable to apply Italian copyright law as necessary".[44] A number of other district and circuit courts have recognised that a US court may ascertain and apply foreign copyright laws.[45] The general approach of these courts reflects the view that a defendant's unauthorised activities in different territories may breach different rights under different territorially-confined laws. A useful illustration, again from within the Second Circuit, is *Psihoyos* v. *Liberation, Inc.*,[46] which involved unauthorised copying of a photograph in Austria, followed by its unauthorised distribution in the United States. With respect to the making of the unauthorised reproductions, the District Court for the Southern District of New York noted that no infringement of rights under the US copyright statute had occurred.[47] The US Act was held to apply, however, to the subsequent unauthorised distributions within the United States.[48]

In other decisions, a loosening of copyright from its territorial confines may be detected. Predictably, this has occurred most clearly in the context of copyright ownership: international licensing of copyright materials invariably cuts across principles associated with territoriality. In *Itar-Tass Russian News Agency* v. *Russian Kurier, Inc.*,[49] the first US appellate decision to consider the issue of choice of law for copyright ownership, the Second Circuit held that different laws might apply to questions of ownership of copyrights and their infringement. The case involved newspaper articles that had been first published in major Russian newspapers that were distributed mainly in Russia. The defendant had copied and distributed the articles without authorisation in the New York area. At issue was a threshold question concerning the standing of the Russian publishers to sue. The Court considered that this required it to decide whether Russian or US work-for-hire principles applied to determine who owned the copyrights. On the private international law questions, the Court concluded: "[w]ith respect to the Russian plaintiffs, Russian law determines the ownership and essential nature of the copyrights alleged to have been infringed

---

[43] The territoriality of US copyright was underlined recently by Justice Ginsburg in a concurring opinion in *Quality King Distributors, Inc.* v. *L'Anza Research International, Inc.*, (1997) 523 US 135.

[44] *World Film Services, Inc.* v. *RAI Radiotelevisione Italiana SpA*, US Dist. Lexis 985 (SDNY 1999), 26.

[45] See, e.g., *London Film Prods. Ltd.* v. *Intercontinental Communications*, 580 F Supp. 398 (SDNY 1984); *Boosey & Hawkes* v. *Disney*, 145 F 3d 481 (2nd Cir. 1998).

[46] US Dist. Lexis 5777 (SDNY 1997).

[47] *Ibid.*, 5 n. 2.

[48] *Ibid.*, 6.

[49] 153 F 3d 82 (2nd Cir. 1998).

and . . . United States law determines whether those copyrights have been infringed in the United States and, if so, what remedies are available".[50] The Court's decision on the latter point reflected a territorial approach: the governing law was that of the place of the infringement. With respect to the issue of ownership, however, the Court followed the approach of the *Restatement (Second) of the Conflict of Laws*[51] holding that the law "with the most significant relationship to the property and the parties governed".[52] The significant point from the decision is that different laws might govern ownership and copying. In cases involving unauthorised distribution of copyright works in a number of territories, *one* nation's copyright laws would govern the ownership of copyright, even though infringement issues might be determined by a variety of different domestic copyright laws.

Even in the infringement context, recent US case law discloses a willingness to localise foreign infringements within one territory, typically the United States. In *National Football League* v. *Primetime 24 Joint Venture*, the National Football League ("NFL") alleged that the defendant, Primetime 24, had captured over-the-air broadcast signals in the United States and then retransmitted them to satellites for retransmission abroad, including to viewers in Canada. The NFL alleged infringement of its rights under the US copyright statute to perform its copyright work publicly. Noting that it is "axiomatic that the copyright laws of the United States do not apply extraterritorially", Primetime 24 argued that the plaintiff had failed to state a proper claim, on the basis that all the actions complained of took place outside the United States. The District Court for the Southern District of New York disagreed, holding that the uploading to the satellite within the United States infringed the right of public performance under section 106(4) of the US Copyright Act, "even though it takes one or more further steps for the work to reach the public".[53]

It is interesting to compare the *Primetime 24* approach with that adopted in *Psihoyos* v. *Liberation, Inc.* In the latter case, it appeared to follow that, because the copying and distribution may be regarded as discrete acts, different domestic copyright laws might apply if the different acts occurred in different territories. In *Primetime 24*, however, because unauthorised "broadcasting" appeared to be a single action, it may have been easier to localise the infringements in one territory.[54] Hence the case was regarded as implicating only the plaintiffs' US rights. An alternative, more traditionally territorial approach to this problem might be to consider that the infringement of the public distribution right is complete only when the broadcast reaches the relevant public. A territorial approach would apply US law to any unauthorised copying of the works that

---

[50] 153 F 3d 82, 84 (2nd Cir. 1998).

[51] (American Law Institute, St Paul, Minn., 1971).

[52] 153 F 3d 82, 90 (2nd Cir. 1998) (internal quotation omitted).

[53] US Dist. Lexis 163181 (SDNY 1999), 6.

[54] See also *On Command Video Corp.* v. *Columbia Pictures Industries*, 777 F Supp. 787 (ND Cal. 1991), which adopted a similar approach in the domestic context.

was involved in preparing the work for broadcast in the United States, but Canadian law would apply to the broadcasting of the work *to* the (Canadian) public.[55]

The *Primetime 24* decision is probably most significant for what it discloses about judicial attitudes toward the extraterritorial application of US copyright law. Under the defendant's "strictly territorial" theory, the court observed, "anyone in a foreign nation (irrespective of whether that nation is a signatory to any of the international copyright conventions or, in practice, enforces its copyright laws against its own nationals or itself at the instance of Americans) can reach into the United States, capture the first transmission of signals from the United States, and retransmit those signals for public viewing within its borders without liability under the United States Copyright Act to the holder of the United States copyright".[56] It is telling that these sentiments were expressed in a case where the applicable foreign law was Canadian. Though there are differences between US and Canadian copyright principles, Canada is hardly copyright's Barbary Coast.[57] Departure from the territoriality premise is portrayed as a results-driven strategy that maintains the potency of US copyrights in an era in which technology allows copyright works to be easily transmitted across international borders.

The approach in *Primetime 24* is also consistent with an important strand of copyright theory that has now been adopted within both the Second[58] and Ninth[59] Circuits. Under this approach, a US court may award a plaintiff the profits that the defendant derived from unauthorised distribution of a work abroad, where at least one infringing copy of the work had been made within US borders. Significantly, damages may extend to encompass the defendant's unauthorised activities in foreign territories even without proof of the content of the laws of the territories in which the activities took place.[60] In support of its analysis, the *Primetime 24* court cited with approval an important article by Professor Ginsburg,[61] in which she argued that this theory might be extended, allowing US copyright law to apply to infringements abroad, even where no

---

[55] This appears to have been the view adopted by the Ninth Circuit in *Allarcom Pay Television, Ltd.* v. *General Instrument Corp.*, 69 F 3d 381 (9th Cir. 1995) (holding that broadcasts sourced in the United States, but received in Canada, did not implicate US federal copyright laws).

[56] US Dist. Lexis 163181 (SDNY 1999), 8.

[57] Cf. *Curb* v. *MCA Records, Inc.*, 898 F Supp. 568, 595 (MD Tenn. 1995), in which the Court observed: "[p]iracy has changed since the Barbary days. Today, the raider need not grab the bounty with his own hands; he need only transmit his go-ahead by wire or telefax to start the presses in a distant land."

[58] See *Sheldon* v. *Metro-Goldwyn Pictures Corp.*, 106 F 2d 45, 52 (2nd Cir. 1939); *Update Art, Inc.* v. *Modiin Publ'g Ltd.*, 843 F 2d 67, 73 (2nd Cir. 1988).

[59] See *Los Angeles News Service* v. *Reuters Television International Ltd.*, 149 F 3d 987 (9th Cir. 1998).

[60] Elsewhere I have discussed some of the problems of a doctrinal character with this approach. See G. W. Austin, "Domestic Laws and Foreign Rights: Choice of Law in Transnational Copyright Infringement Litigation" (1999) *Colum-VLA J L & Arts* 1.

[61] J. Ginsburg, "Comment, 'Extraterritoriality and Multiterritoriality in Copyright Infringement'" (1997) 37 *Va J Int'l L* 587.

infringing copy had been made within the United States. Professor Ginsburg argued that US law might apply, for instance, where the United States was the place where the defendant planned and implemented the foreign infringements. The *Primetime 24* court appears to endorse Professor Ginsburg's view that more effective enforcement of copyright owners' rights is likely to follow from these extraterritorial strategies.

III EXTRATERRITORIALITY, COPYRIGHT AND THE NATION STATE

Departure from the territoriality premise tacitly promotes a perspective on the nature of copyright that has more in common with natural rights justifications for the copyright system than the utilitarian perspectives that are more familiar in the Anglo-American tradition.[62] The natural rights justification for copyright recognises the close connection between authors and their works and rewards creative endeavour with property rights. Natural rights rationales downplay the connection between copyright and the regulatory state. A copyright is not viewed as a grant of rights by the state; rather, copyrights flow naturally from an author's creative endeavours.

In developing natural rights rationales for copyrights, many intellectual property theorists have found John Locke's[63] analysis of the basis for property entitlements particularly attractive.[64] Authors seem to exemplify the labourer who adds labour to things in the state of nature in order to create something new. In the copyright context, the state of nature includes ideas, facts and human experience. Because of the seemingly endless scope of the "intellectual commons" authors also appear to comply with Locke's requirement in the famous proviso, that "enough and as good" be left for others. Significantly, Locke explains the origins of property in terms of a unilateral act: the decision to mix labour with something previously held in common does not seem to require any pre-existing law or bureaucratic structure.[65]

In a variety of more contemporary discourses and legal developments touching on copyright the connection between copyright and the regulatory state is coming to seem more attenuated. One of the aims of the Clinton administration's 1995 Information Infrastructure Task Force Report,[66] for instance, seems to have been to make copyright law seem more "natural", and to depend less on

---

[62] For extensive discussion of the various philosophical bases of intellectual property rights, see J. Hughes, "The Philosophy of Intellectual Property" (1988) 77 *Geo LJ* 287.

[63] J. Locke, *Two Treatises of Government* (Peter Lawslett (ed.), 2nd edn., Cambridge, CUP, 1967), Book II, chap. V.

[64] See, e.g., W. Gordon, "A Property Right in Self Expression: Equality and Individualism in the Natural Law of Intellectual Property" (1993) 102 *Yale LJ* 1533.

[65] M. Robertson, "Liberal, Democratic, and Socialist Approaches to the Public Dimension of Private Property" in McLean, n. 5 above, chap. 12.

[66] B. Lehman, Chair, Information Infrastructure Task Force, Intellectual Property and the National Information Infrastructure (Wahington, DC, US Patent & Trademark Office, 1995).

bureaucratic state action and regulation for existence and protection. The Task Force wanted people to understand copyright principles in much the same way as they understand what theft of tangible goods is all about. The Task Force authors wanted to get to people early, recommending that copyright principles be introduced into national civics curricula at all educational levels. Core copyright concepts ought to be introduced at the elementary school level, the Task Force submitted, because children "can relate to the underlying notions of property—what is 'mine' versus what is 'not mine', just as they do for a jacket ball and a pencil".[67] The idea appears to be that copyright should come to seem as natural as property rights in tangible objects.

Rhetorically, there is also much in common between the loosening of the connection between the state's regulation of copyright, and the familiar complaint that "the United States has become increasingly vulnerable to piracy, expropriation, and otherwise inadequate protection of its intellectual property in certain foreign countries".[68] Such statements seem to overlook the territorial reality that international copyright is a creature of individual nation states. Instead, the statement seems to imply that creative effort by US authors provides entitlements to property rights that spread across the globe.

Of course, as every common lawyer knows, the institution of property is not "natural" at all; property is a complex system that regulates relationships between people within individual societies. It follows that the explanatory force of the labour theory of property entitlements can only ever be partial: it neither explains why people join together in society to protect their property nor accounts for the terms upon which they do so.[69] Copyrights and other intellectual property rights seem peculiarly artificial species of property, however. Copyright inhibits individual action in ways that have few parallels for tangible property. Making another copy of the program embedded on one's own CD-ROM seems intuitively quite different from snatching away someone's ball or pencil. Moreover, as will be discussed in further detail below, copyright is, at least in the Anglo-American system, a complex system of checks and balances designed to ensure that the system as a whole continues to serve the public good.

The development of private international law theories that seek to loosen the connection between copyright and the nation state also have much in common with the shift towards the privatisation of copyright regulation through the institution of contract. As Brian Fitzgerald discusses in Chapter 3 of this volume, the Seventh Circuit's decision in *ProCD, Inc.* v. *Zeidenberg*[70] has added new impetus to this development. Judge Easterbrook held that a contract restricting commercial use of data that would not be protected by copyright law

---

[67] *Ibid.*, 205.
[68] M. Leaffer, "Protecting United States Intellectual Property Abroad: Toward a New Multilateralism" (1991) 76 *Iowa L Rev* 273.
[69] See generally, C.M. Rose, *Property and Persuasion: Essays on the History, Theory and Rhetoric of Ownership* (Boulder, Col., Westview Press, 1994).
[70] 86 F 3d 1447 (7th Cir. 1996).

was not pre-empted by the Federal copyright statute.[71] "A simple two-party contract" is not, in Judge Easterbrook's view, "equivalent to any of the exclusive rights within the general scope of copyright" and "therefore may be enforced".[72] According to this perspective on the relationship between contract and copyright, parties are free to enter into private arrangements with respect to informational materials, even though such arrangements might be quite inconsistent with the various policies and checks and balances that comprise the copyright system. Indeed, as Marci Hamilton discusses in Chapter 2 of this volume, the prohibition against the propertisation of raw data articulated by Justice O'Connor in *Feist Publications, Inc.* v. *Rural Telephone Service Co.*[73] is just such a policy: in the Supreme Court's view, because facts are among the building blocks of creative expression they should remain in the public domain. A related development is the addition of a new Chapter 12 to the US copyright statute, which enacts prohibitions on circumventing access control measures that purveyors of copyright materials might impose on their use.[74] Once again, such controls may allow copyright owners to cut across the copyright regime; contractual restrictions on access to copyright works, combined with technological anti-circumvention devices, may also prohibit access to aspects of works—such as ideas, data or material whose copyrights have expired—that would not be protected by federal copyright law. As Brian Fitzgerald discusses,[75] the privatisation of copyright issues is likely to be given an added boost by the enactment of the Uniform Computer Information Transactions Act, which will result in the contractual licence becoming the primary vehicle for the distribution of key informational products.[76]

The privatisation of copyright issues through the combination of contract and technologies that impose access restrictions on informational materials is consistent with the view that, while it may be the state's business to secure property rights, so as to maximise exchange efficiency, it is *not* the state's role to temper these rights in order to serve broader public policy agenda.[77] Private arrangements—effected largely beyond the purview of the regulatory state—are considered manifestly superior to legislative or regulatory intervention. In the copyright context, these ideas make doctrines such as fair use, moral rights, and

[71] For a detailed discussion of federal preemption in the context of contractual restrictions on the use of copyright materials, see M. Lemley, "Beyond Preemption: The Law and Policy of Intellectual Property Licensing" (1999) 87 *Calif L Rev* 111.

[72] *ProCD, Inc.* v. *Zeidenberg*, 86 F 3d 1447, 1455 (7th Cir. 1996).

[73] 499 US 340 (1991).

[74] As Professor Ginsburg discusses, the wording of the new provisions, which restrict access to the copyright "work", rather than to "copies", gets around any restrictions over the copyright owner's subsequent control over individual copies imposed by the "first sale" doctrine articulated in § 109(a) of the US Copyright Act 1976. See generally Jane C. Ginsburg, "Copyright Legislation for the Digital Millennium" (1999) 23 *Colum-VLA J L & Arts* 137.

[75] B. Fitzgerald, chap. 3 of this volume.

[76] The most recent draft of UCITA, dated 15 October 1999, is available at <http://www.law.upenn.edu/bll/ulc/ulc_frame.htm>.

[77] For the classic statement of these views, see R. Coase, "The Problem of Social Cost" [1960] *J of L & Econ* 26.

compulsory licensing—doctrines that are associated with broader perceptions of the public good—seem particularly suspect.

Departure from the territoriality of domestic copyright law is also likely to make individual nation states less relevant in the regulation of copyright within their respective territories. If one nation's laws are to determine what may be copied, distributed publicly, performed—perhaps even read—in other territories it is obvious that the latter are likely to have less control over the regulation of informational and other cultural materials within their respective borders.

The privatisation of the regulation of copyright has recently come under rigorous critical scrutiny. In an important recent article, Julie Cohen comments: "[t]hat copyright owners have discovered a way to reconfigure transactions that currently generate significant uncompensated benefits in order to capture those benefits for themselves says nothing about whether the result will be efficient from a societal perspective".[78] In general terms, this strand of critique calls for recognition of the fact that copyright law does more than accord rights to authors: in the Anglo-American tradition, copyright law is a product of a myriad of social policy choices relating to how best to fashion information policy. The market place may not be the best arbiter of these choices.

In the private international law context, however, there has been less scrutiny of the diminishment of state control over the regulation of copyright.[79] A comprehensive critique of these developments is beyond the scope of this chapter. It would involve, first, a detailed doctrinal analysis of extraterritorial approaches to copyright infringement.[80] Secondly, an empirically-based analysis of the risks to copyright owners posed by cross-border digital transmission of copyright materials would be needed, one that also considered the degree to which extraterritorial approaches to choice of law for copyright infringement would provide meaningful solutions.[81]

Scrutiny of new choice of law proposals also requires us to engage with the issue of the relevance of the domestic state to the regulation of copyright. A deeper appreciation of the role of the state in the regulation of copyright may assist us in answering the more normative question concerning the kind of role the domestic state ought to have in the regulation of copyright. Some of these concerns are discussed in the following section of this chapter.

---

[78] J. Cohen, "*Lochner* in Cyberspace: The New Economic Orthodoxy of Rights Management" (1998) 97 *Mich L Rev* 462, 541.

[79] An important exception is Bradley, n. 17 above.

[80] I make an attempt at providing some doctrinally-based scrutiny of new choice of law theories in Austin, n. 60 above. See also Bradley, n. 17 above.

[81] Compare, e.g., *Playboy Enterprises* v. *Chuckkelmerry Publishing, Inc,.* 939 F Supp. 1032 (SDNY 1996). In this trade mark dispute, the court required the owner of the foreign website to deploy technical mechanisms to block the site to US websurfers. The court reasoned that requiring the site to shut down entirely would be an overreaching exercise of its jurisdiction.

IV COPYRIGHT AND DOMESTIC INFORMATION POLICY

Copyright contributes most obviously to the shape of domestic information policy by encouraging authors to create new works, and entrepreneurs to invest in their dissemination. Whereas the patent system encourages the production of efficient information, manifest in inventions or other new methods of manufacture, copyright law's incentive scheme ensures that members of society have access to an abundance of informational materials, some of it useful, some not. In so doing, copyright helps to generate a "pluralism of opinion, experience, vision and utterance".[82] To achieve this end, legislatures sometimes expand the scope of copyright owners' rights to ensure that these rights keep pace with new methods of exploitation and that the incentive scheme remains meaningful.

The public good served by copyright is a product of the specific character and scope of the rights accorded. These are determined to a large extent by specific limitations that legislatures impose on copyright owner's rights. The "fair use" (or "fair dealing") doctrine is the most obvious of these; but the scope of authors' rights is also a product of more detailed limitations and defences that allow copyright works to be used for certain socially desirable purposes, such as research, criticism, review and education. Limitations on copyright owners' rights are not insignificant or irritating adjuncts to the system; they provide the necessary scope for second-comers to create new works, and also enable other socially desirable activities to continue. As Julie Cohen puts it, decisions about how to shape domestic copyright laws reflect "first order social welfare choices about the sort of information society we want to have".[83] Within utilitarian perspectives on copyright law, it is axiomatic that private rights are accorded for the public benefit,[84] and the private rights that are accorded are of a decidedly public character.

The upward harmonisation agenda means that the shape of domestic copyright laws will increasingly be determined by public international law obligations. However, it is significant that, in a number of contexts, public international law instruments defer to domestic legislatures. In the context of limitations on copyright owners' rights, for instance, public international law instruments tend to impose generally worded obligations on states parties.[85] Many of the details of limitations on copyright owners' rights are to be worked

[82] D. Ladd, "The Harm of the Concept of Harm in Copyright" (1983) 30 *J Copyright Soc* 421.

[83] Cohen, n. 78 above, 464.

[84] This perspective dominates in US Supreme Court copyright jurisprudence. See, e.g., *Sony Corp. of America* v. *Universal City Studios, Inc.*, 464 US 417 (1984): "[t]he Monopoly privileges that Congress may authorize are neither unlimited nor primarily designed to provide a special private benefit. Rather, the limited grant is a means by which an important public purpose may be achieved".

[85] See, e.g., WIPO Copyright Treaty, Art. 10: "Contracting Parties may, in their national legislation, provide for limitations of or exceptions to the rights granted to authors of literary and artistic works under this Treaty in certain special cases that do not conflict with a normal exploitation of the work and do not unreasonably prejudice the legitimate interests of the author."

out within domestic contexts. Similarly, public international law instruments may be silent on key questions. The protection of computer programs is an example. Though Article 10 of the TRIPS Agreement specifies that "[c]omputer programs, whether in source or object code, shall be protected as literary works under the Berne Convention (1971)", it does not specify the level of protection required for non-literal aspects of computer programs. In recent cases, there has been some disagreement between English and American courts about the scope of such protection,[86] a difference of opinion which may reflect differing views about the appropriate level of competition in domestic software development sectors.

Domestic legislatures can and do make changes to copyright laws that reflect policy conclusions about how best to shape domestic information policy. Indigenous people's challenges to intellectual property regimes provide an example of a critically important context in which unique domestic policy choices will need to be made about the shape of domestic laws.[87] Most attention has so far been given to issues relating to patents and plant breeders' rights.[88] Though they have perhaps attracted rather less attention, broadly analogous issues also arise in the copyright context. Colonised nations are not only a source for tangible resources: they have also provided a rich source for new designs, craft techniques and performance styles.[89] Often, little compensation for the use of these materials of culture has flowed back to the societies whose cultural works, sometimes developed over centuries, provided the inspiration.[90] Western copyright law accommodates the issues that arise in this context only with difficulty, and often not at all. The highly individualised focus of Western copyright law, requiring, for example, the identification of individual authors, may be difficult to reconcile with creative processes that occur within tribal contexts. Also, the limited duration of copyright protection may sit awkwardly in the context of non-Western notions of time and spirituality.[91]

It is too soon to anticipate how indigenous peoples' challenges to the shape of domestic intellectual property regimes will be accommodated. Various ideas

---

[86] Compare *Computer Associates International, Inc.* v. *Altai, Inc.*, 982 F 2d 693 (2nd Cir. 1992) with *Ibcos Computers Ltd.* v. *Barklays Mercantile Highland Finance Ltd.* [1994] FSR 275.

[87] This is not to suggest that international law developments are irrelevant to indigenous peoples' challenges to domestic intellectual property regimes. See generally, M. Blakeney, "Claims by Aboriginal and Torres Straight Islander Peoples to Cultural Expressions and Traditional Knowledge", Conference Paper presented at the 12th Annual Conference of the Intellectual Property Society of Australia and New Zealand, Auckland, 30 August 1998 (on file with editors); C. Iorns, "The Draft Declaration on the Rights of Indigenous Peoples" (1993) 64 *ALB* 4.

[88] See generally R.J. Coombe, "Intellectual Property, Human Rights and Sovereignty: New Dilemmas in International Law Posed by the Recognition of Indigenous Knowledge and the Conservation of Biodiversity" (1998) *Indiana J of Global L Stud* 59.

[89] See e.g., E.J. Coppins, "Pakeha Citation of Maori Motifs, Symbols and Imagery" (unpublished paper on file with The University of Auckland Davis Law Library, 1997).

[90] See generally Coppins, *ibid.* (detailing numerous instances of unauthorized commercial exploitation of artistic work by Maori).

[91] See K. Puri, "Cultural Ownership and Intellectual Property Rights Post-*Mabo*: Putting Ideas into Action" (1995) 9 *IPJ* 293, 308.

have been mooted, such as establishing consultative processes with indigenous peoples, precluding certain cultural artifacts to the subject of intellectual property rights, and vesting certain materials of culture in tribal groups.[92] What is relatively clear, however, is that the domestic contexts in which these challenges will be addressed are likely to be very different. In New Zealand, the legal background against which the challenges of Maori are likely to be addressed is dominated by the Treaty of Waitangi, a treaty signed by the Crown and some 500 Maori leaders in 1840. Amongst its provisions is a guarantee to Maori of *"te tino rangatiratanga"* or "full chieftainship" over *"taonga"*, a word that broadly translates as "treasured possessions", a concept that encompasses both tangible and intangible treasures. Its relevance to the intellectual property will be obvious. In other nations, other concepts are likely to be relevant to the challenges of indigenous peoples in the intellectual property law context, such as the fiduciary obligations of the executive towards indigenous peoples, or the doctrine of aboriginal title. Within the decolonisation agenda, it should not be anticipated that accommodation of indigenous peoples' interests and rights in domestic intellectual property laws will be approached in the same manner or lead to the same kinds of results.

Another illustration of important social policy choices being reflected in domestic intellectual property law is the 1997 decision by the New Zealand government to remove parallel importation restrictions on copyrighted goods.[93] The New Zealand government considered that the changes would result in net welfare gains for the domestic citizenry,[94] notwithstanding any fears about the threats to consumer welfare posed by freer markets for foreign manufactured goods.[95] The New Zealand response to grey market goods is quite different from that adopted in other nations. In US copyright law, for instance, the Supreme Court has emphasised that the first sale doctrine protects only against the *re*-importation of copyright goods that were manufactured in the United States and initially exported to a foreign territory.[96] United States copyright owners' rights to prevent the importing of material first manufactured abroad remains intact. The differences in approach reflect different conclusions about how domestic copyright laws should be fashioned in order to serve the public good.[97]

---

[92] A variety of strategies is discussed in Blakeney, n. 87 above.

[93] Copyright (Removal of Prohibition on Parallel Importing) Amendment Act 1998. Prior to promoting the reforms, the New Zealand government commissioned a report on the economic implications of removing the ban on parallel importing. See NZ Institute of Economic Research, *Parallel Importing: A Theoretical and Empirical Investigation*, 1997 Report to the Ministry of Commerce (<http://www.moc.govt.nz/cae/parallel/index.html>).

[94] See, e.g., Hon. John Luxton, MP, *Imported Goods and Plant at World Best Prices*, Ministerial Press Release, 14 May 1998 (<http://www.executive.govt.nz/budget98/news/parallel.htm>).

[95] The latter point may be particularly important in New Zealand, where the removal of parallel importation restrictions applies to a wider range of goods. Also significant is that copyright law itself protects a wider range of goods, including goods that are mainly or even exclusively functional. See further D. Vaver, "Copyright in the Commercial World" [1974] *NZ Recent Law* 20.

[96] See *Quality King Distributors, Inc.* v. *L'Anza Research International, Inc.*, 523 US 135 (1997).

[97] See Luxton, n. 94 above.

Extraterritorial approaches to the international regulation of copyright may jeopardise the ability of policy choices reflected in domestic copyright laws to remain meaningful in the states that enacted them. Moreover, these approaches go further than the public international law regime has gone in achieving international standardisation of copyright law norms.[98] As we have seen, the public international law regime includes areas which dictate the shape of domestic copyright laws in addition to contexts in which public international law instruments permit domestic nations to develop copyright laws in ways that suit domestic circumstances. Because copyright laws touch on fundamental areas of human endeavour,[99] some pause might be warranted before we endorse choice of law strategies that would reduce even further the control of domestic nations over the shape of the copyright laws that are to apply within their borders.

V CONCLUSION

In the current era of privatisation of copyright—in which content providers rely increasingly on contracts and technological controls on access to copyright materials—the relevance of concerns about the role of the domestic state in the regulation of copyright may seem doubtful. Anticipating the enactment of UCITA, and bolstered by decisions such as *ProCD, Inc.* v. *Zeidenberg* and the new legal sanctions given to anti-circumvention devices, content providers may simply opt out of the copyright regime, deciding instead to rely on private law protections, supported by shrink-wrap or click-wrap licences and the like. Content providers are likely to continue to set in place contractual terms that attempt simply to override any possible restrictions on their rights that might be imposed by particular domestic copyright regimes. To be concerned about extraterritorial application of *copyright* laws may now be like worrying overly about damage to the door of the stable from which content providers have already decided to bolt.

However, this objection does not account for the possibility that untrammeled contractual freedom in the area of information policy may prove intolerable. Indeed, this has been acknowledged already in some contexts. Consistently with the European Council Directive on the Legal Protection of Computer Programs,[100] section 50B(4) of the United Kingdom Copyright, Designs and Patents Act 1988 voids conditions in agreements which seek to limit the ability of authorised users of computer programs to decompile the program in order to create an independent program to be operated with it. Encouraging interoperability

[98] This argument is elaborated extensively in Bradley, n. 17 above.

[99] See generally J. Waldron, "From Authors to Copiers: Individual Rights and Social Values in Intellectual Property" (1993) 68 *Chicago-Kent L Rev* 841.

[100] Council Directive 91/250/EEC (14 May 1991) on the legal protection of computer programs [1991] OJ L122/42, Arts. 6 and 9.

is a sufficiently important public policy in the European Union context that it overrides inconsistent private arrangements.[101]

Somewhat sanguinely, Judge Easterbrook commented in *ProCD, Inc.* v. *Zeidenberg* that "[c]ontracts . . . generally affect only their parties; strangers may do as they please, so contracts do not create 'exclusive rights'".[102] To this, the obvious objection is that lots of contracts might have an equivalent effect. If every click-wrap licence were to prohibit all fair use of the work that is accessed, for instance, this would very likely inhibit the free flow of information in society and jeopardise future creative endeavour. Contrary to Judge Easterbrook's analysis, dissemination of information may be regarded as too important to leave to the market place alone to regulate.

In a difficult decision involving the respective rights of academic publishers and researchers in a commercial institution, the Court of Appeals for the Second Circuit referred to the "delicate balances established by the Copyright Act".[103] Copyright law's checks and balances have developed over hundreds of years, and reflect countless policy decisions about how best to fashion both copyright's creativity incentives and the character and scope of the public domain. Many of these decisions have been made, and are likely to continue to be made, with domestic circumstances in mind. The aim of these decisions is, or should be, to ensure that copyright law continues to serve the public good. Even in the cyberspace era, the notion of "the public" located in particular nation states remains a coherent idea. What recent private international law thinking puts at issue is whether information policy should continue to have the opportunity to be forged with domestic circumstances in mind.

Those concerned about the ability of domestic states to make meaningful policy decisions about the future shape of domestic copyright law have thus far focussed mainly on public international law and the law of contract. In this context, it seems, rigorous policy scrutiny of private international law developments should also be placed on the copyright policy agenda.

---

[101] For discussion of interoperability under Australian law, see B. Fitzgerald, chap. 3 of this volume (section IV).

[102] 86 F 3d 1447, 1454 (7th Cir. 1996).

[103] *American Geophysical Union* v. *Texaco*, 60 F 3d 913 (2nd Cir. 1995).

Part 2

Developments in Industrial Property

If wealth in modern economies is increasingly associated with intangible property, it seems to follow that more intangible property will lead to greater wealth. It should thus be of little surprise that traditional intellectual property rights are under increasing pressure to expand. The first three Chapters in this Part concern expansions in the nature of two of the most valuable types of intellectual property rights: trade marks and patents. Sam Ricketson's Chapter considers the right to prevent dilution of trade marks, a right that was recently federalised in the United States with the passage of important amendments to section 43 of the Lanham Act. Moving beyond the principle of preventing market place confusion, the broad purpose of the anti-dilution right is to allow the trade mark owner to prevent actions that blur the distinctiveness of the mark and reduce its "advertising value". The scope of patent rights is also expanding. As the Chapters by Jay Thomas and John Smillie describe, in some jurisdictions patent rights are now recognised in business systems and in new uses for known pharmaceutical products.

Expansion of intellectual property rights is seldom without controversy. One of the most sharply contested areas of intellectual property law is the protection of industrial designs. Providing protection for the visual features of commercial products, design rights sit uneasily between copyright and patents; a key challenge in this area is to ensure that the scope of protection for industrial designs undermines the policies of neither. In Chapter 9, Sir Nicholas Pumfrey surveys the latest United Kingdom developments in this area. In addition, Sir Nicholas discusses some of the key European Union initiatives in this area, a topic that is picked up in the Chapter by John Adams, which discusses choice of law and choice of forum in the intellectual property context.

6

Dilution and Confusion: The Bases of Trade Mark Infringement or the new Australian Trade Marks Anti-dilution Law 1999

SAM RICKETSON

SAM RICKETSON

I INTRODUCTION—THE EVER-CHANGING FACE OF INTELLECTUAL PROPERTY LAW

Of all the major intellectual property rights, registered trade marks are probably the most valued and valuable intangible assets possessed by many undertakings: they are the standard bearers and flagships behind which products and services can line up and launch themselves into the world of commerce and consumers. Despite this importance, however, the rationale of trade marks protection is perhaps the most contested of all the intellectual property rights and remains so, notwithstanding the passing of new trade marks statutes in many common law jurisdictions in recent years.

The purpose of this chapter, as initially assigned to me, was to examine this conflict in the light of these recent developments, with particular attention to the topic of infringement. To what extent are trade marks concerned with the actions of competitors which confuse and deceive, and to what extent can they be protected against third party actions that may neither confuse nor deceive but that may nonetheless dilute, "blur", "tarnish" or otherwise damage the mark? Confusion and dilution were the twin themes that I was to explore, and I was in the process of developing an elegant argument to the effect that trade marks law, at least in common law jurisdictions such as Australia, sat unhappily between both poles and was in dire need of reform. But the advantage, or perhaps disadvantage, of long lead times is that fresh events intervene, and cast all well-laid plans into disarray. So it was here: in the last week of June 1999, I had a blissful dream that the Australian Parliament had just amended the whole basis of the Australian trade marks system. The Trade Marks Amendment (Anti-Dilution Protection) Act 1999 had been passed late at night in a matter of minutes, with virtually no debate on its provisions, and this had changed the whole basis of trade mark infringement in Australia.

A possible explanation for the speed of this enactment, at least according to my dream, was that, as usually happens in June each year in Australia, the government of the day was faced with a legislative logjam of bills that had met with concerted opposition in the upper house of the parliament, the Senate. In the absence of progress, as it then appeared, on such matters as tax and corporate law reform, the government was therefore determined to get at least one bill through. But why trade marks, and why so little notice? The truth was that the legislation was easy to pass, given that there had been so little notice of it, and the government was able to say that it was responding to a number of pressures, of which the following were the most important:

(a) Representations from a number of trade mark owners, particularly in the luxury goods area, to the effect that the Australian trade marks law gave insufficient protection to famous and well known marks.
(b) Representations to similar effect from several industry groups and professional organisations.
(c) The possibility that Australia was failing to give proper effect to its international obligations with respect to the protection of trade marks.
(d) The desirability of bringing Australian trade mark law into conformity with that of its principal trading partners, notably the United States.

At one stroke, therefore, or so I dreamed, my task in this chapter was made easier: all I needed to do now was to present an overview of this new legislation, together with a critique of its pertinent points. At the very least, this might be of use to lawyers from other countries, particularly those with common law traditions, that were contemplating similar initiatives. It might also provide a valuable object lesson in the difficulties and pitfalls involved in proceeding too quickly to judgement on the questions of confusion and dilution! Subsequently, of course, I have awoken and discovered that the Australian trade mark law remains unchanged, and that anti-dilution measures have not, in fact, become part of our law. But the dream remains worth telling, and may still provide a useful starting point for a discussion of the proper basis for trade mark infringement.

II   OTHER INTELLECTUAL PROPERTY RIGHTS COMPARED AND CONTRASTED

It is as well to begin our discussion of the dream[1] amendments with some general comments about trade marks as a species of intellectual property. The grouping of trade marks with other kinds of intellectual property rights is, at first sight, an odd one. Patents, designs, copyright and even trade secrets are concerned with acts of origination—with the creative and organisational efforts

---

[1] I have decided to adopt this adjective throughout so that no one is under any misapprehension as to the fact that these amendments are only a figment of my fevered imagination!

that go into bringing into existence a new product or process, a literary or artistic production, or a new design. While the innovation thresholds set for these subject matters may differ, for example, as between a patent and a copyright, they are "fresh starts" or points of departure, where persons have produced something that they will usually then want to exploit, or have others exploit for them, in the relevant market place. Registered trade marks, and their accompanying common law regimes such as passing off, are not concerned with this first stage of origination, but with the subsequent stages of marketing and distribution. Protection for these subsequent stages, in fact, follows logically from the recognition of protection at the first. It is almost a truism that the creation of a new product, process or work does not ensure its commercial success, however worthy it may be. To be successful, it must be marketed and the vehicle for achieving this is to build up some presence in the market place which attracts prospective purchasers. This "presence" will usually be concentrated on some name, symbol, device or get-up, which signifies to the public a particular trade source. Without this, the financial return of the most brilliant inventor, author or artist may be very small. As Lord Diplock remarked in the *Erven Warnink* case:[2]

> Emerson's maker of the better mousetrap if secluded in his house built in the woods would today be unlikely to find a path beaten to his door in the absence of a costly advertising campaign to acquaint the public with the excellence of his wares.

As a consequence, much of the innovative process, whether in industry, commerce or the arts, is concerned with the advertising and merchandising of the various products and services which may have been fostered or assisted by the grant of a patent, copyright, registered design or trade secret protection. More generally, of course, distribution and marketing is critical for any business or commercial activity, regardless of whether these have involved the use of other intellectual property rights. Of special importance in each instance, however, will be the particular designation or indicia by which a product or service is known in the market place and under which it is marketed to consumers. That these insignia should become the subject of rights is hardly surprising, particularly in light of the forms of protection available at the prior stage of origination (through the patent, copyright, designs and trade secrets systems). The difficulty, however, for any legal system is the nature and scope of the protection that should be accorded, and here it is that the difficulty alluded to in the title of this chapter arises. Should the marks and insignia of traders receive analogous protection to that accorded to other intellectual property rights holders? For example, should there be an absolute monopoly accorded in the nature of a patent, which would mean that third parties cannot use the mark in any circumstances, on the basis that this will impair its exclusivity in the hands of the particular trader? Or should some lesser protection against imitation or copying

---

[2] *Erven Warnink BV v. J. Townend & Sons (Hull) Ltd* [1979] AC 731, 740.

be granted, as in the cases of a copyright or design? And if protection should be accorded, what should be the pre-conditions and qualifications for this?

Intellectual property rights in common law jurisdictions have usually represented pragmatic compromises between competing interests, where the grant of protection has been viewed in a instrumentalist fashion, which gives the minimum of protection that is required to achieve the desired goal. This is well exemplified in the famous passage from the judgment of Dixon J in *Victoria Park Racing and Recreation Grounds Co Ltd v. Taylor*:[3]

> [The courts] have not in British jurisdictions thrown the protection of an injunction around all the intangible elements of value, that is, value in exchange, which may flow from the exercise by an individual of his powers or resources whether in the organisation of a business or undertaking or the use of ingenuity, knowledge, skill or labour. This is sufficiently evidenced by the history of the law of copyright and by the fact that the exclusive right to invention, trade marks, designs, trade name and reputation are dealt with in English law as special heads of protected interests and not under a wide generalisation.

Where, then, do the pragmatic compromises arise in the case of trade marks and trade designations?

III SOME HISTORICAL BACKGROUND

There are disparate strands of doctrine and theory that go to explain, first, the development of the common law action of passing off, and then the introduction of the registered trade marks system. Like so many common law actions, the origins of the action of passing off are clouded in some mystery, but it appears that they are to be found in the action of deceit. An old Elizabethan case involving clothiers is often referred to as the basis of the action. This case, however, was not reported and the only references to it are to be found in dicta of Doderidge J in two early seventeenth century cases, *Southern v. How*,[4] a case of deceit, and *Dean v. Steel*,[5] a case of defamation. In addition, the facts of this Elizabethan case are unclear, although it appears that the defendant had used the mark of an eminent clothier on his poor quality cloth, thereby defrauding an innocent purchaser into thinking that he was getting the other's cloth. It is not certain, however, whether it was the purchaser or the injured clothier who brought the action. If it was the former, it is easy to accommodate the purchaser's action under the old action of deceit, and it is only if the clothier himself was the plaintiff that the action parallels the typical fact situation of a modern passing off case. Neither the facts of *Southern v. How* nor those of *Dean*

---

[3] (1937) 58 CLR 479, 509.

[4] (1659) Bridg J 125, 123 ER 1248; (1659) Cro Jac 468, 87 ER 889; (1656) Pop 143, 79 ER 1243; (1676) 2 Rolle 5, 81 ER 621; (1676) 2 Rolle 26, 81 ER 635.

[5] (1626) Latch 188, 82 ER 339.

v. *Steel*, however, involved the passing off by the defendant of the plaintiff's
product as his own and this further diminishes the authority of Doderidge J's
recollections of the earlier Elizabethan case.[6]

It is, perhaps, quaint that the basis for the modern action of passing off (and
the modern system of registered trade marks) should rest on such thin foundations, although this can readily be seen as yet another example of the ingenuity
of the common law in constructing new forms of action on the basis of creative
interpretations of the past. Curiously, after these two seventeenth century cases,
the issue was not reported as arising before the courts until well into the eighteenth century.[7] When it did, the courts, perhaps recalling *Southern* v. *How*,
treated it as a special form of deceit, albeit one where the action was not by the
person deceived but by the person whose mark was used to deceive.[8] The effect
of this was to reduce the operation of the tort to cases where fraud or intention
to deceive was proved.[9] Nevertheless, this requirement was avoided by the
Court of Chancery which, from 1838 on, would grant injunctive relief to
restrain a passing off without proof of fraud.[10] It could be said here that equity
was only acting in its auxiliary jurisdiction and therefore was intervening to
restrain what would be a fraud if it were allowed to continue once the defendant
had notice of the plaintiff's claim.[11] Alternatively, it could be said that fraud was
to be imputed to a person who was found to have imitated another's mark and
therefore that equity was entitled on this basis to intervene to restrain the
further use of that mark.[12] Further differences arose when Courts of Equity
awarded other equitable remedies, such as an account of profits or damages
under Lord Cairns's Act, without proof of fraud.[13] After the Judicature Acts,
however, it became the general practice for courts to award such relief without

---

[6] A very clear and scholarly analysis of the different reports of these cases is to be found in an
unpublished LLM thesis by G. Owen, "The Development, Present Ambit and Future of the Tort of
Passing Off" (Melbourne University Law Library, 1980), 1–24. See also F.I. Schetcher, *The
Historical Foundations of the Law Relating to the Trade Marks* (New York, Columbia UP, 1925)
(reprinted, Union, N.J., Lawbook Exchange, 1999), 8; W.L. Morison, "Unfair Competition and
Passing Off" (1956) 2 *Syd LR* 50, 53.

[7] *Blanchard* v. *Hill* (1742) 2 Atk 484, 26 ER 692. Schetcher suggests that the reason the action for
passing off took so long to develop was because of the influence exercised by the mediaeval guilds
over the trading activities of their members: Schetcher, n. 6 above, 16. Note also that special Acts,
such as the Cutler's Company Act 1623 (21 Jac 1, C 31) were passed during the seventeenth century
to protect craftsmen and their marks after the collapse of the guild system: Owen, n. 6 above, 12–13.

[8] *Blanchard* v. *Hill*, n. 7 above, *Singleton* v. *Boulton* (1783) 3 Doug 293, 99 ER 661; *Knott* v.
Morgan (1836) 2 Keen 219, 48 ER 610; *Crawshay* v. *Thompson* (1842) 4 Man & G 357, 134 ER 146.

[9] E.g., *Hogg* v. *Kirby* (1803) 8 Ves 215, 32 ER 336; *Canham* v. *Jones* (1813) 2 V & B 218, 35 ER
302; *Sykes* v. *Sykes* (1824) 3 B & C 541, 107 ER 834; *Knott* v. *Morgan*, n. 8 above; *Crawshay* v.
Thompson, n. 8 above; *Lord Byron* v. *Johnston* (1816) 2 Mer 29, 35 ER 851.

[10] *Millington* v. *Fox* (1838) 3 My Cr 338, 40 ER 956; *Edelsten* v. *Edelsten* (1863) 1 De G J & S 184,
199, 46 ER 72.

[11] *McAndrew* v. *Bassett* (1864) LT (NS) 442, 443; *Cartier* v. *Carlile* (1862) 31 Beav 292, 54 ER
1151; *Lazenby* v. *White* (1871) 41 LJ Ch 354n.

[12] *Cartier* v. *Carlile*, n. 11 above. See also *Walter* v. *Emmott* (1885) 54 LJ Ch 1059 (CA).

[13] As in *Edelsten* v. *Edelsten* (1863) 1 De G J & S 184, 46 ER 72; *Farina* v. *Silverlock* (1855) 1 K
& J 509, 69 ER 560.

proof of fraud[14] and it seems today that there are no differences between common law and equity in this regard.[15]

For our present purposes, these historical and jurisdictional questions need not detain us: it is enough to note that there was a consumer protection aspect of the protection accorded to common law marks by the action of passing off, with its origins, however uncertain, in the action of deceit and the need for there to be some element of deception or confusion to consumers before liability in passing off arose. The genius of the common law lies in the way in which an action to protect consumers (deceit) was transformed into an action to protect traders, through a showing of confusion to consumers who would be misled into buying the goods or services of another trader. When it became necessary for the courts, particularly those exercising equitable jurisdiction, to identify some proprietary interest that was affected by the passing off, this was soon found in the damage or likely damage that would be caused to the goodwill attached to, or focussed on, the mark or indicia used by a trader. But the damage to that goodwill was to be found in the act of deception or confusion on the part of the defendant that would lead consumers to believe that the defendant's goods or services were those of the plaintiff or were in some way associated with the latter. In this way, a balance was achieved between the interests of traders in maintaining their marketing channels and customer connection (through the protection of his mark), and the interests of consumers (in not being the subject of confusion).

IV STATUTORY PROTECTION OF TRADE MARKS

The deception/confusion basis for common law marks was then enshrined in the first trade mark registration statutes, where a registration system established certain efficiencies in the obtaining and enforcement of protection (through statutory requirements of distinctiveness and the like which obviated the evidentiary requirements of the common law as to proof of reputation and damage).[16] Infringement of statutory marks, however, was limited by the scope of

---

[14] See, e.g., *Johnston & Co v. Orr Ewing* (1882) 7 App Cas 219 (HL); *Daniel & Arter v. Whitehouse* (1898) 15 RPC 134 (Ch D); *Hodgson & Simpson* v. *Kynoch Ltd* (1898) 15 RPC 465 (Ch D); *Pneumatic Rubber Stamp Co Ltd* v. *Lindner* (1895) 15 RPC 525 (Ch D); *Cusenier etc. Co* v. *Gaiety Bars & Restaurant Co Ltd* (1902) 19 RPC 357 (Ch D); *Iron-Ox Remedy Co Ltd* v. *Leeds Industrial Co-op Society Ltd* (1907) 24 RPC 634 (Ch D); *Spalding & Bros* v. *Gammage Ltd* (1915) 32 RPC 273 (HL); *Ronson Products Ltd* v. *James Ronson Ltd (No 2)* [1957] VR 31 (Full Ct). There are, however, a number of post-Judicature Act cases in which judicial reference to the need to show fraud at common law are to be found: *Jamieson & Co* v. *Jamieson* (1898) 15 RPC 169, 191 *per* Vaughan Williams LJ; *Reddaway* v. *Bentham Kemp-Spinning Company* [1892] 2 QB 639, 644 *per* Lindley L, 646 *per* Lopes LJ, 648 *per* A.L. Smith LJ; *Edge* v. *Johnson* (1892) 9 RPC 134, 136 *per* Lord Esher MR, 138 *per* Fry LJ, 140 *per* Lopes LJ.

[15] Except, possibly, where the award of damages is concerned; see further *Draper* v. *Trist* [1939] All ER 513 (CA) and *Marengo* v. *Daily Sketch Ltd* (1948) 65 RPC 242 (HL).

[16] See, e.g., Trade Marks Registration Act 1875 (38 & 39 Vict, c 91), s. 10.

the registration that had been achieved.[17] This was a statutory intellectual property right, but one that was severely qualified and one that was not even described as "property" in the statute.[18] As trade marks became more separated from their common law origins, more elaborate justifications for protecting them began to be articulated, and these began to move away from the deceit/confusion explanations. For example, trade marks were not simply indications of the source or origins of goods or services: they were guarantees of continuity and quality.[19] Again, this was an explanation directed at consumers: the latter purchased or consumed goods or services on the basis of a guarantee held out by the mark that these were the same as had been bought previously and would remain so when bought in the future. In economic terms, the registered mark could be seen as a means of reducing search costs to consumers who need not lay out further resources and time in ascertaining these facts for themselves each time they desired to purchase that good or service.[20] From the trader's point of view, too, there were efficiencies: the mark provided a shorthand means of designating not only the goods or services but of referring, perhaps subliminally or indirectly only, to certain qualities or characteristics associated with those goods or services. Other efficiencies arose in the case of infringement proceedings: confusion could be presumed to have occurred where an identical mark was used on the same goods or services; the same could occur where a deceptively similar or substantially identical mark was used.[21] On the other hand, the rights of other traders were preserved through doctrines of honest concurrent user and defences of descriptive use[22] and the like, while the broader public domain was maintained through requirements of use and prohibitions on marks becoming generic or deceptive or confusing.[23]

So, all was well in trade marks heaven, and little argument was heard to the effect that the protection given should be broader and perhaps should approximate that accorded under other statutory intellectual property rights. Or was this really the case? Dynamic change is a common feature of all intellectual property rights, and trade marks are no exception. Just as the inventions of printing, phonograms, films and computer programs have led to the recognition

---

[17] See, e.g., Trade Marks Registration Act 1875 (38 & 39 Vict, c 91), s. 2.

[18] This continued to be the case in Australia so far as both the Trade Marks Act 1955 and 1995 were concerned, as well as in the UK Trade Marks Act 1938. However, see now Trade Marks Act 1994 (UK), s. 22.

[19] See further J.R. Lunsford, "Consumer and Trademarks: The Function of Trademarks in the Market Place" (1974) 64 *The Trademark Rep* 75; E.W. Hanak, "The Quality Assurance Function of Trademarks" (1975) 65 *The Trademark Rep* 318; M. Gabay, "The Role of Trademarks in Consumer Protection and Development in Developing Countries" [1981] *Industrial Prop* 102; L.B. Burgunder, "An Economic Approach to Trademark Genericism" (1985) 23 *Am Bus L J* 391.

[20] See generally W.M. Landes and R.A. Posner, "The Economics of Trademark Law" (1988) 78 *The Trademark Rep* 267; S.L. Carter, "The Trouble with Trademark" (1990) 99 *Yale L J* 759. See also P.J. Kaufmann, *Passing Off and Misappropriation,* (IIC Studies in Industrial Property and Copyright Law (VCH, Weinheim, 1986), chap. 1.

[21] In the case of Australia, see the Trade Marks Act 1955 (Cth), ss. 58 and 62.

[22] Trade Marks Act 1955 (Cth), ss. 34 and 63.

[23] Trade Marks Act 1955 (Cth), ss. 23, 28 and 56.

of successive new copyrights, and just as developments in biotechnology and information technology have led to reformulations and extensions of traditional patent doctrines, so too have changes in marketing and distribution led to a reconceptualisation of the basis of trade mark protection. There is nothing particularly new in this statement. As early as the 1920s, the American commentator Schechter pointed to the changing nature of trade marks where the latter could now be regarded as valuable assets in themselves, independent of their attachment to a particular product, service or business.[24] The value of these assets could be "whittled away" or diluted by the actions of third parties using the mark, even where this did not occur in relation to the same goods or services for which the mark was registered and even in the absence of confusion to consumers or of competition between "senior" and "junior users". Thus, the use of a mark that was well known in relation to quite different products would, over time, dilute the distinctiveness or exclusiveness of the mark, to the ultimate detriment of the trade mark owner.[25]

In one sense, this was a revolutionary notion that began to equate the basis for trade marks protection to trespass (a true proprietary remedy) rather than deceit and deception (the traditional basis for passing off and trade mark infringement). But even before this, it had been acknowledged by Anglo-Australian courts that trade marks and trade names, or at least well-known ones, could have a much greater umbrella of protection. Consider, for example, the following:

(a) The protection granted to *The Times* newspaper against the use of the word "Times" in relation to bicycles.[26]

(b) The protection gained by the Kodak and Eastman Camera Company against the use of the mark "Kodak", also in relation to bicycles.[27]

And, more recently:

(c) The refusal by the High Court of Australia of the registration of a Mickey Mouse and Minnie Mouse trade mark in respect of radio receiving sets and kits, following objections by the Walt Disney Corporation that this would deceive and confuse consumers who were familiar with the cartoon character of that name.[28] Latham CJ succinctly expressed the reason for the opponents' success as follows:[29]

---

[24] F. Schechter, "The Rational Basis of Trademark Protection" (1927) 40 *Harv L Rev* 813.

[25] For further reflections on the development of "dilution theory", see the interesting collection of articles in (1996) 59 *Law and Contemp. Prob.*, celebrating the first 50 years of the US Lanham Act, in particular the articles by M. Handler at 5 ("A Personal Note on Trademark and Unfair Competition Law Before the Lanham Act"); R.C. Denicola at 76 ("Some Thoughts on the Dynamics of Federal Trademark Legislation and the Trademark Dilution Act of 1995"); and M.J. Alexander and M.K. Heilbronner at 93 ("Dilution under Section 43(C) of the Lanham Act").

[26] *Walter v. Ashton* [1902] 2 Ch 282.

[27] *Eastman Photographic Materials Co Ltd v. John Griffiths Cycle Corp. Ltd* (1898) 15 RPC 105.

[28] *Radio Corporation Pty Ltd v. Disney* (1937) 57 CLR 448.

[29] *Ibid.*, 453. Affirmed on appeal: [1999] FCA 1655 (26 November 1999).

The opponents have, in my opinion, shown that the names and the figures are so closely associated in the public mind, in Australia and elsewhere, with Walter E. Disney and his activities, that the use of either the names or the figures in connection with any goods at once suggests that the goods are "in some way or other connected" with Walter E. Disney. . . . This, the evidence shows, would be the case whatever the nature of the goods to which the names were attached. It is very seldom indeed that there can be a world-wide association of ideas in connection with a particular name or figure, but the evidence shows that this association does exist in the present case. A proposed trademark should not be registered if it involves "a misleading allusion or a suggestion of that which is not strictly true". . . . Thus, in my opinion, these marks should not be registered.

(d) The professional ballroom dancers who were able to prevent the use of their photographic likeness on the cover of a sound recording of dance music,[30] and the succession of subsequent cases in Australia, the United Kingdom and other common law jurisdictions that have recognised and sanctioned the practice of character and personality merchandising.[31]

These are but straws in the wind, it can be said, and each can be explained by reference to the likelihood of confusion and hence damage that could be inferred to follow from the conduct in question. On the other hand, they signalled an increasing judicial readiness to interpret the scope of passing off and trade mark protection more widely, and a growing awareness of the likely damage that may occur even where fields of activity are widely diverging. Indeed, the subsequent development of character merchandising represents a striking instance of judicial acceptance of the new means of marketing and promotion that were developing. Confusion remained the basis for these developments, but, like a rubber band, it stretched and began to fall out of shape as judges pushed the envelope ever further. Thus, to take three other well known and more recent cases, consider the following:

(e) The *Spanish Champagne* case,[32] where the French producers of the "real" champagne sparkling wine were able to restrain the use of their name in the combination "Spanish champagne". While the latter was geographically correct (the wine in question was made in Spain), the usage nonetheless diminished the exclusiveness of the champagne image by deceiving potential consumers into thinking that this was the "real thing". In a later case, the English Court of Appeal restrained the use of the name "Elderflower Champagne" in respect of a non-alcoholic sparkling drink at the behest of the champagne producers.[33]

---

[30] *Radio Corporation Pty. Ltd* v. *Henderson* [1960] NSWR 279.

[31] See generally S. Ricketson, "The Theory and Practice of Character Merchandising . . ." (1991) 1 *IPJ* 191 (renamed as *Australian IPJ*).

[32] *J. Bollinger* v. *Costa Brava Wine Co Ltd* [1966] RPC 116.

[33] *Taittinger SA* v. *Allbev Ltd* [1993] FSR 641. See further the discussion of this case by H. Carty, "Dilution and Passing Off: Cause for Concern" (1996) 112 *LQR* 632, 635ff.

(f) The use of the Crocodile Dundee persona by a small Queensland tourist store in a parodic but referential sense that implied an association with the creator of Crocodile Dundee.[34] If there was confusion here, it was of the most refined and artificial kind, and was a mere window dressing for the fact that liability was imposed for an outright appropriation of another's image. As Burchett J of the Federal Court of Australia remarked in another case involving Crocodile Dundee:[35]

> No logic tells the consumer that boots are better because Crocodile Dundee wears them for a few seconds on the screen . . . but the boots are better in his eyes, worn by his idol. The enhancement of the boots is not different in kind from the effect produced when an alpine pass makes a greater impact on the tourist whose mind's eye captures a vision of Hannibal urging elephants and men to scale it.

(g) At the most extreme, the use of the name of a fictional beer ("Duff"), derived from the famous *Simpsons* series, by the South Australian Brewing Company in relation to an actual beer product of their own.[36]

It is clear that the courts in both Australia and the United Kingdom in passing off cases have been moving back the boundaries of confusion so as to embrace confusion not only as to source but also as to product.[37] In addition, the kinds of damage, or likelihood of damage, that such confusion may lead to have been interpreted generously, so as to give protection to traders in relation to "brand extension" (the possibility that they may extend their activities into areas in which they do not presently trade) or, more generally, the granting of licences or sponsorships (as in the case of character merchandising).

On the other hand, courts in both countries have generally shied clear of enunciating any broader basis for protection, for example, through the development of a general tort against unfair competition or misappropriation pursuant to which any unauthorised taking or use of another's mark, name or other indicia will be actionable, irrespective of the presence of some element of deception or confusion.[38] There is a judicial commitment to free competition in the market place, and a strong presumption that this will be undermined by the grant of protection that is too wide. This view was well expressed by Goldberg J of the Federal Court of Australia in a recent case involving the alleged copying of the "trade dress" of the plaintiff's boots:[39]

> There is a substantial body of evidence to the effect that interpreting and copying fashion styles and fashion looks is endemic in the fashion and footwear industries and is

---

[34] *Hogan* v. *Koala Dundee Pty. Ltd* (1988) 83 ALR 87.

[35] *Pacific Dunlop Ltd* v. *Hogan* (1989) 14 IPR 398, 429.

[36] *Twentieth Century Fox Film Corporation and Matt Groening Productions, Inc* v. *The South Australian Brewing Co Ltd and Lion Nathan Australia Pty. Ltd* (1996) 34 IPR 225.

[37] See further Carty, n. 33 above.

[38] See, e.g., *Cadbury-Schweppes Pty. Ltd* v. *Pub Squash Co Pty. Ltd* [1981] RPC 429; and *Moorgate Tobacco Co Ltd* v. *Philip Morris Ltd* (1984) 3 IPR 545.

[39] *Dr Martens Australia Pty. Ltd* v. *Figgins Holdings Pty. Ltd* (includes corrigenda dated 16, 22 and 28 April 1999) [1999] FCA 461 (16 April 1999), (1999) 44 IPR 281.

therefore justifiable. Such a proposition depends upon whether a right is infringed or a statutory provision is contravened by such copying. In the absence of copyright, design or trade mark protection there is no infringement of any right by such inter-pretation and copying unless the copy product can be said to be passed off as and for the genuine product or that consumers are misled and deceived into believing that the copy product is a genuine product or as emanating from the trade source of the gen-uine product, or has the sponsorship of, or an association with, the manufacturer of the genuine product. The tenor of some of the cross-examination of the respondents' witnesses was that in principle there was something wrong or illegitimate about copy-ing somebody else's product. Whatever view one may have about the moral or social propriety of such copying that is not a matter for the Court. The matter was put suc-cinctly by Lord Scarman speaking for the Privy Council in *Cadbury-Schweppes Pty Ltd v The Pub Squash Co Pty Ltd* (1980) 32 ALR 387 at 393:

> "But competition must remain free: and competition is safeguarded by the necessity for the plaintiff to prove that he has built up an 'intangible property right' in the advertised descriptions of his product: or, in other words, that he has succeeded by such methods in giving his product a distinctive character accepted by the market. A defendant, however, does no wrong by entering a market created by another and there competing with its creator. The line may be difficult to draw: but, unless it is drawn, competition will be stilled. The test applied by Powell J in the instant case was to inquire whether the consuming public was confused or misled by the get-up, the formula or the advertising of the respondent's product into thinking that it was the appellants' product. And he held on the facts that the public was not deceived. Their Lordships do not think that his approach in law (save in one respect, as will later appear), to the central problem of the case can be faulted."

The issue for the Court is whether there has been an infringement of a right given by law or the contravention of any statutory provision. Accordingly, it forms no part of my task to be critical of persons for copying products unless they have infringed such a right or brought about such a contravention.

Yet, if the common law still adheres to a notional commitment to the need for confusion and deception, the same is not necessarily true in the case of registered trade marks. As noted above, statutory registration systems are, at the same time, both efficient and limiting: "efficient" in the sense that they reduce trans-action and enforcement costs once registration is achieved, and "limiting" in the sense that preconditions and boundaries to protection have to be set in a way that is not required with a more flexible common law right of action. Accordingly, while confusion has remained at the core of registered trade mark protection, the pressure for a wider umbrella of protection has steadily increased. In the case of the previous Australian Trade Marks Act 1955, this manifested itself in a number of ways:

(a) A general prohibition on the registration of marks that were confusing or deceptive[40]; as the case of Mickey Mouse referred to above shows,[41] this

---

[40] Trade Marks Act 1955 (Cth), s. 28(a).
[41] *Radio Corporation Pty. Ltd v. Disney* (1937) 57 CLR 448.

could provide a negative protection for a well known mark, even for one that was not already registered and had not been used in relation to the same goods or services that were the subject of an application for registration, if the grant of this application would lead to confusion and deception.

(b) A limited prohibition on invalidity arising through genericism, under which such an objection could only be made on the basis of trade usage rather than on the basis of generic usage by consumers.[42]

(c) A limitation on subsequent invalidity arising where a registered mark became deceptive or confusing and this was not due to blameworthy conduct on the part of the registered proprietor.[43]

(d) Provision for the defensive registration of trade marks in relation to goods or services for which the marks were not actually used.[44]

While it was possible to explain such provisions as being necessary to avoid confusion (which remained the clear basis for infringement), they nonetheless pushed this notion further, and it was possible to see them as also being concerned, albeit in a piecemeal and limited fashion, with the maintenance of the exclusiveness and distinctiveness of trade marks as subjects of protection in themselves. This suggested that the basis or rationale for trade mark protection was extending in an analogous way to that which had occurred with passing off, although it would be difficult to describe this as embodying a dilution rationale as such. On the other hand, in other jurisdictions, as well as internationally, such a basis for protection was being articulated. This approach was focussed on the specific case of "famous" or well-known marks, where the clear concern was to prevent dilution of the marks rather than just confusion. It is therefore necessary to consider this international and comparative background more fully, before examining the ways in which these issues are dealt with under the current Australian law and under the dream amendments. But first, a little more needs to be said about the concepts of dilution and fame.

V THE CONCEPTS OF DILUTION AND FAME

As noted above, the notion of dilution was given an initial impetus in Anglo-American thinking through the writings of Schechter, who described it in the following terms:[45]

[the] gradual whittling away or dispersion of the identity and hold upon the public mind of the mark or name by its use on noncompeting goods. The more distinctive or unique the mark, the deeper is its impress upon the public consciousness and the

---

[42] Trade Marks Act 1955 (Cth), s. 55; see further *F.H. Faulding & Co Ltd* v. *Imperial Chemical Industries Ltd* (1964) 112 CLR 537.

[43] Based on s. 28(a) and (d) of the Trade Marks Act 1955 (Cth); see further *New South Wales Dairy Corporation* v. *Murray Goulburn Co-operative Company Ltd* (1990) 97 ALR 73.

[44] Trade Marks Act 1955 (Cth), Part XII (ss 93–97).

[45] Schechter, n. 24 above, 825.

greater its need for protection against vitiation or disassociation from the particular product in connection with which it has been used.

Slowly, the notion took root in a number of American States where, from 1947 onwards,[46] anti-dilution statutes were passed which granted protection to State trade marks, generally in the absence of some showing of confusion about the source of the goods or services in question. As will be seen below, an anti-dilution remedy has now been incorporated into US Federal law. The notion of dilution, however, remains somewhat open-ended. US courts have used vivid language to describe the effect of the conduct that is embraced by the concept.[47] Thus, one court has described it as "an infection which, if allowed to spread, will inevitably destroy the advertising value of the mark",[48] another has referred to the "cancer" which feeds on the business reputation of established marks,[49] and a third has likened it to the stone by stone demolition of a building.[50] More precise formulations, however, refer to uses which diminish the "distinctiveness, effectiveness and, hence, value" of a mark through a blurring of the mark's product identification or by damaging the positive associations that have attached to it (sometimes called "tarnishment").[51] It is also possible that dilution can occur through parodic uses of the mark,[52] although this might simply be another aspect of tarnishment, rather than a distinct form of dilution. A further kind of dilution might occur where a mark is made generic, through the increasing use of it as the name of goods or services rather than as a mark.[53] It seems that Schechter saw trade mark dilution as being limited to cases where the mark was used in relation to non-competing goods, although this is not required under the most recent statutory formulation of the doctrine in section 43(c) of the Lanham Act (see further below).[54] Nonetheless, it is clear that dilution, in the sense of diminishing the distinctiveness and exclusiveness of a mark, can occur even where there is a non-confusing use in relation to the same goods or services, for example, where a defendant uses the mark as a point of reference in relation to their own goods or services through comparative advertising or some

---

[46] See generally the excellent review of the history and operation of these statutes in P. Fields, "Trade Mark Anti-Dilution Remedies—Now on a US Federal Level" [1998] *Intell Prop Forum* 30, 31–3. See further the interesting collection of articles in (1996) 59 *Law and Contemp. Prob.*, celebrating the first 50 years of the US Lanham Act, in particular the articles by Handler, n. 25 above; Denicola, n. 25 above; and Alexander and Heilbronner, n. 25 above. See also J.T. McCarthy, "The 1996 United States Federal Anti-dilution Statute" (1998) 9 *AIPJ* 38.

[47] The following references are taken from Fields, n. 46 above, 33.

[48] *Mortellito* v. *Nina of Cal., Inc.*, 335 F Supp. 1288, 1296 (SDNY 1972).

[49] *Allied Maintenance Corp.* v. *Allied Mechanical Trades, Inc.*, 369 NE 2d 1162, 1165 (NY 1977).

[50] *Eastman Kodak Co* v. *Rakow*, 739 F Supp. 116, 119 (WDNY 1989).

[51] *Ameritech, Inc.* v. *American Info Technologies Corp.*, 811 F 2d 960 (6th Cir. 1987); *Mead Data Central, Inc.* v. *Toyota Motor Sales, USA, Inc.*, 875 F 2d 1026, 1036 (2nd Cir. 1989).

[52] See further Fields, n. 46 above, 37–8.

[53] See further Carty, n. 33 above, 645.

[54] See further McCarthy, n. 46 above, 40.

other kind of referential use. However, it is clear that the diluting consequences of each of these kinds of use are obviously more likely to occur where the trade mark is a well known or "famous" one, and hence it has been the owners of these kinds of marks who have sought this wider form of protection. Logically, such marks must be the most vulnerable to dilution, although it is not always easy to define the point at which a broadened concept of confusion ceases to provide protection and dilution proper takes over. There are two extremes to consider here:

(a) X has a trade mark registered in respect of a wide range of goods or services, and has a habit of extending these registrations and using or licensing the use of the mark accordingly. The mark is highly distinctive and is well known throughout the community. Here confusion might be a sufficient reason for liability on the basis that a connection with the registered owner will be easy to make where it is used by Y on goods or services without the registered owner's authority, regardless of whether these are different goods or services or whether such conduct can be regarded as blurring or tarnishing X's mark.

(b) X has a trade mark registered in respect of a particular product (for example, sauces) or service (for example, legal information) and has no intention of widening the use of that trade mark in relation to other goods or services. The mark is highly distinctive (either because of its high degree of inherent distinctiveness or distinctiveness acquired through user or both). It is also widely known in other channels of trade and in the wider community, although this knowledge relates to its use in respect of that particular good or service. Confusion, or the likelihood of confusion, may therefore not arise where Y uses the same mark in relation to quite different goods or services, as no one will assume that there is a connection. On the other hand, it might be possible to argue that the capacity of the mark to distinguish in relation to the goods or services for which it is registered is lessened, once it is used by another party on different goods or services that have no apparent connection to the first. Without confusion, this can be regarded as a blurring of the product identification of the trade mark and hence a dilution.

It is only in the second of these cases that the concept of dilution comes into its own, but it is possible to postulate a series of intermediate cases between these two extremes where both the elements of confusion and dilution could be present and overlap with each other. Several further points need to be noted:

(a) Confusion and/or dilution arise only where a mark is used for unrelated goods or services because the mark has some kind of broader notoriety or fame among the public or relevant section of the public. This awareness or recognition of the mark may not have developed because these people have ever used goods or services to which the mark has been applied (the usual recognition function ascribed to trade marks), but may simply be the result of general advertising or promotion. Fame of this kind is not always easy to quantify or prove, but instances immediately come to mind, for example, the fact that words like "Rolls Royce" or "Rolex" can become regular reference points in daily speech for high quality products that few of us may ever possess. While the use of such marks in relation to unrelated goods or services may not cause confusion and resultant loss of sales of the products for which they are registered, clearly it can be argued that such uses will ultimately dilute the distinctiveness of those marks in the sense of diminishing the capacity of the owner to use them to identify their own goods or services or to extend them to other goods or services as part of a planned programme of brand extension.

(b) If dilution of a mark that is well known can occur through use in respect of unrelated goods or services, it can also be argued that it is just as likely to occur through any other kind of unauthorised use, for example:

  (i) descriptive uses, where the mark is used to describe or refer to the characteristics of a particular good or service (whether related or not), such as the "Rolls Royce of household cleaning services".

  (ii) uses that tend to make the mark generic for particular goods or services, such as "champagne" for all sparkling wines.

  (iii) comparative or referential uses, such as in the practice of comparative advertising.

  (iv) parasitic uses with respect to the same or related goods or services that clearly distinguish the two, e.g. cheap perfume sold as a "copy of Chanel No 5".[55]

  (v) uses in quite unrelated contexts, such as "for a Rolls Royce treatment of this topic, see *Ricketson on Intellectual Property* at p . . .".

Each of these uses may tend to dilute the mark in some way, but clearly a policy decision will have to be made about which, if any, will be prohibited under a dilution rationale. If all are to be prohibited, this will give the trade mark owner a near absolute right of property in the particular trade mark. In such cases, the protection of the distinctiveness and reputation of the mark becomes intertwined with the more absolute protection of the mark as the exclusive asset of the trade mark owner. Any intellectual property right, however, in our tradition represents a balancing of public and private interests, and this will need to be embodied in specific defences or exceptions to infringement. Possible examples of appropriate defences might be exceptions for non-commercial uses, good faith descriptive uses, uses for the purposes of news reporting, and so on.

(c) If protection against dilution is to be accorded to famous or well known marks, do the same justifications for this protection apply, as in the case of

---

[55] This example is given by Landes and Posner, n. 20 above, 304.

ordinary trade marks? Are, for example, search costs to consumers reduced where the owner of a famous mark can prevent the use of the mark by third parties for unrelated goods or services in the absence of confusion? It seems more difficult to make this argument, as consumers will, by definition, be able to distinguish between the marks in the different areas of use. Nonetheless, it is still possible to argue that such uses will affect search costs, albeit in a more subtle way. Thus, it can be said that they inevitably diminish the distinctive quality of a famous mark and lessen its capacity to convey a single, unqualified message to consumers. Even if not confused about whether there is a connection between senior and junior users, consumer search costs will increase as they try to sort out what each message conveys. In particular, the guarantee of quality which is embodied in the famous mark will inevitably be reduced or "blurred" by the unauthorised second use. This will occur whether or not the second use is in respect of the same goods or services (the Chanel No 5 example) or completely unrelated goods or services.

(d) A further justification for protection can be found in arguments based on "external benefits".[56] Diluting uses represent free riding on the efforts of the owner of the famous mark who has invested considerable resources and effort in building up the mark as the sign of a prestigious product or product range. In economic terms, the second user of the mark is able to appropriate some of the benefits of this investment without compensating the famous mark's owner and without having to undertake investments of their own in the creation of a distinctive trade mark. Clearly, without protection against diluting uses, the owner of a famous trade mark will have little incentive to undertake the necessary initial investment in building up the reputation and renown of the famous mark.

Against this background, how are the topics of famous marks and dilution treated under international instruments and in the laws of other relevant common law jurisdictions?

VI INTERNATIONAL OBLIGATIONS

Australia, like most other common law jurisdictions, has substantive obligations with respect to trade marks that arise under two principal agreements: the Paris Convention for the Protection of Industrial Property, and the 1994 Agreement on Trade Related Aspects of Intellectual Property (herein TRIPS). The Paris Convention is concerned primarily with matters of national treatment[57] and priority periods for the making of applications in member countries

---

[56] Landes and Posner, n. 20 above, 304.
[57] Arts. 2 and 6.

pursuant to the Convention,[58] but contains the following provision in Article 6[bis] with respect to the protection of well-known marks:

(1) The countries of the Union undertake, *ex officio* if their legislation so permits, or at the request of an interested party, to refuse or to cancel the registration, and to prohibit the use, of a trademark which constitutes a reproduction, an imitation, or translation, liable to create confusion, of a mark considered by the competent authority of the country of registration or use to be well known in that country as being already the mark of a person entitled to the benefits of this Convention and used for identical or similar goods. These provisions shall also apply when the essential part of the mark constitutes a reproduction of any such well-known mark or an imitation liable to create confusion therewith.

(2) A period of at least five years from the date of registration shall be allowed for requesting the cancellation of such a mark. The countries of the Union may provide for a period within which the prohibition of use must be requested.

(3) No time limit shall be fixed for requesting the cancellation or the prohibition of the use of marks registered or used in bad faith.

These provisions are hardly onerous, and moreover are tied to a confusion rationale and to uses in relation to goods that are "identical or similar". In the case of the Australian Trade Marks Acts of 1955 and 1995, they were readily satisfied by provisions which prohibited the registration and continued registration of marks that were deceptive or confusing, as well as the provision of defensive registration. From the perspective of trade mark proprietors, particularly those concerned to maintain the uniqueness of their famous or well-known marks, such protection was hardly sufficient to address their concerns over the prospects of dilution, particularly where use on unrelated goods or services was concerned. While these concerns were clearly ventilated during the negotiations that led to the adoption of the TRIPS Agreement,[59] the final provisions of that instrument do not take matters much further, although they do provide some useful amplification of the Paris Convention obligations. Thus, all member countries bound by TRIPS must apply the provisions of Articles 1–12 and 19 (including, obviously, Article 6[bis]) of the Paris Convention[60] and, in addition, must comply with the following obligation under Article 16 of TRIPS:

(1) The owner of a registered trademark shall have the exclusive right to prevent all third parties not having his consent from using in the course of trade identical or similar signs for goods or services which are identical or similar to those in respect of which the trademark is registered where such use would result in a likelihood of confusion. In case of the use of an identical sign for identical goods or services, a likelihood of confusion shall be presumed. The rights described above shall not prejudice any existing prior rights, nor shall they affect the possibility of Members making rights available on the basis of use.

[58] Art. 4.
[59] See M. Blakeney, *Trade Related Aspects of Intellectual Property Rights: A Concise Guide to the TRIPS Agreement* (London, Sweet & Maxwell, 1996).
[60] TRIPS Agreement, Art. 2(1).

(2) Article 6bis of the Paris Convention (1967) shall apply, mutatis mutandis, to services. In determining whether a trademark is well-known, account shall be taken of the knowledge in the relevant sector of the public, including knowledge in that Member obtained as a result of the promotion of the trademark.

(3) Article 6bis of the Paris Convention (1967) shall apply, mutatis mutandis, to goods or services which are not similar to those in respect of which a trademark is registered, provided that use of that trademark in relation to those goods or services would indicate a connection between those goods or services and the owner of the registered trademark and provided that the interests of the owner of the registered trademark are likely to be damaged by such use.

So far as international obligations with respect to registered trade marks are concerned, Article 16 of TRIPS provides the first "codification" of the scope of this protection, namely:

(a) Protection generally is based on likelihood of confusion, with an application beyond the goods or services for which the mark is registered to goods or services which are "similar".

(b) Likelihood of confusion is to be presumed where there is an unauthorised use of an identical mark on identical goods or services for which the mark is registered.

(c) Article 6bis of the Paris Convention is extended to apply to well-known marks with respect to services. In addition, it is extended to apply to unauthorised uses in relation to goods or services which are "not similar" to those in respect of which the trade mark is registered. A criterion for determining whether a mark is well-known is also provided, namely "the knowledge of the trademark in the relevant sector of the public, including knowledge in that Member obtained as a result of the promotion of the trademark". This is not an exhaustive statement of how to determine how well-known a mark is, but it indicates that knowledge in the member country need not be based only on knowledge arising from the use of that mark but may arise from advertising and other promotional activities in that country. Whether or not this is enough, in the absence of some actual user, is not made clear.

(d) Protection of well-known marks is not qualified by reference to the notion of confusion, but by a differently worded criterion, namely that the unauthorised usage must be such that it indicates a "connection between those goods or services and the owner of the registered trade mark". The nature of this "connection" is undefined, but would presumably extend to a "likelihood of association", such as appears in section 10(2) of the UK Trade Marks Act 1994. "Connection" need not necessarily entail confusion, although this is the way that some national laws, such as those in the UK and Australia, have traditionally interpreted this phrase.[61] On the other hand, it is conceivable that the unauthorised use of a trade mark on quite

---

[61] *Wagamama Ltd* v. *City Centre Restaurants plc* [1995] FSR 713, 720–1 (*per* Laddie J).

different goods or services could well hold out an alleged connection or association with the registered trade mark owner without there being any necessary confusion on the part of consumers that the goods emanate from the trade mark owner or are, in some sense, authorised or licensed by him. This, in fact, can be regarded as the classic dilution situation where the exclusivity or distinctiveness of a famous mark is diluted or "whittled away" by the activities of a another user in quite a different domain. It is unclear whether Article 16(3) of TRIPS was intended to have such a wide application, and a strong argument can be mounted in favour of restricting "connection" to confusing uses in view of the fact that the provision operates as an application of Article 6*bis* of the Paris Convention which is clearly so limited. On the other hand, it is worth noting that Article 16(3) contains a further qualification that could be treated as being consistent with a "dilution" interpretation of that provision, namely that the "interests of the owner of the registered trade mark are likely to be damaged by such use". As a matter of logic, there is no reason why damage to the interests of trade mark owners should flow only from those acts which of third parties which give rise to confusion.

VII OTHER NATIONAL COMPARISONS

In this regard, it is useful to consider briefly the approaches taken in two other relevant common law jurisdictions, the United Kingdom and the United States of America.

A The United Kingdom

Unlike Australia and New Zealand, the United Kingdom marches not only to the beats of TRIPS and the Paris Convention but also to those of the European Communities. In this regard, the UK Trade Marks Act 1994 gives effect to the provisions of an EC Directive[62] which has sought to "approximate" the trade marks law of all Community members and has "swept away the old law".[63] The relevant provisions concerning infringement are to be found in sections 9 and 10, with section 9 being "no more than a chatty introduction"[64] to the details of infringing acts that are set out in section 10. The latter follows a structure which also reflects that contained in Article 16 of TRIPS, and treat as infringing the following uses of "signs" that are:

(a) "identical" with a registered trade mark in respect of the same goods or services—infringement here is presumptive: section 10(1).

---

[62] 189/104/EEC, 21 December 1988.

[63] *British Sugar plc* v. *James Robertson & Sons Ltd* [1996] RPC 281, 290 (*per* Jacob J). The "old law" here, of course, was the Trade Marks Act 1938.

[64] *Ibid.*, 291.

(b) "identical" or "similar" to a registered trade mark in respect of the same or similar goods or services—infringement occurs where a "likelihood of confusion on the part of the public" exists (this includes a "likelihood of association" which Laddie J has interpreted to be a subset of confusion):[65] section 10(2).

(c) "identical" or "similar to" a trade mark in respect of dissimilar goods or services: infringement occurs here where the "trade mark has a reputation in the United Kingdom and the use of the sign, being without due cause, takes unfair advantage of, or is detrimental to the distinctive character or the repute of the trade mark": section 10(3).

The last-mentioned provision appears to provide protection against dilution in relation to different goods or services, without the need for a showing of confusion on the part of consumers. The term "dilution", of course, does not appear, but other similar concepts are used, for example, the taking of "unfair advantage" and uses that "are detrimental to the distinctive character or the repute of the trade mark". The words "repute of the trade mark" are potentially very broad, and appear to be used in contrast to the words "distinctive character". It seems likely that the former refers only to the distinctiveness, inherent and acquired, of the mark, i.e. the factors which entitle the mark to registration in the first place, whereas the reference to "repute" goes wider to encompass the more amorphous notion of the general image or notoriety enjoyed by the mark. Uses which are detrimental to these aspects of the trade mark are obviously very much at large, as are uses that take "unfair advantage" of them. It is, perhaps, for this reason that several UK decisions have limited such a wide ranging interpretation of section 10(3) by holding that a likelihood of confusion must exist in order for there to be a taking of unfair advantage of the plaintiff's mark or for this to be detrimental to its distinctive character or repute.[66] On the other hand, in the *British Sugar* case, Jacob J appeared to accept (though this was by way of obiter) that section 10(3) might be infringed in circumstances where there was no confusion, citing Benelux authority to this effect.[67] More recently, the Court of Appeal has indicated support for this view, although only by way of obiter.[68] One commentator has noted, however, that such cases are likely to be "unusual", suggesting that these will more likely involve instances of tarnishment, where the mark is used with unpleasant connotations.[69]

---

[65] *Wagamama Ltd* v. *City Centre Restaurants plc* [1995] FSR 713, 721 ff. See further D. Llewelyn, "The New Law on Infringement of Registered Trade Marks in the United Kingdom: Early Developments" (1996) 7 *AIPLJ* 149.

[66] *BASF plc* v. *CEP (UK) plc*, 26 October 1995 (Knox J); *Baywatch Production Co Inc.* v. *The Home Video Channel* [1997] FSR 22, 30–1 *per* Michael Crystal QC.

[67] *British Sugar plc* v. *James Robertson & Sons Ltd* [1996] RPC 281, 295.

[68] *British Telecommunications plc* v. *One in a Million Ltd* [1999] FSR 1, 25 *per* Aldous LJ, Swinton Thomas and Stuart-Smith LJJ agreeing.

[69] Llewelyn, n. 65 above, 158.

Two further points about the UK Trade Marks Act 1994 should be noted:

(a) Registered trade marks are specifically stated to be "personal property",[70] which tends to underline the proprietary aspect of a trade mark as a free-standing intangible asset (the Trade Marks Act 1938 was silent on this point).

(b) Defensive registration of well known marks has been deleted, and has been replaced by a section which provides that owners of well known marks entitled to protection under Article 6*bis* of the Paris Convention are entitled to seek protection in the United Kingdom (by way of an injunction) against the use of an identical or similar trade mark in relation to identical or similar goods where the use is likely to cause confusion.[71] This can be done regardless of whether or not the trade mark owner carries on business or has any business in the United Kingdom. This gives more precise effect to the requirements of Article 6*bis* than did the previous defensive registration provisions which proved to be highly restrictive in practice.[72] Liability under section 56 is, however, qualified by the requirement of a likelihood of confusion.

B   The United States of America

The position here, with respect to dilution, is clearer in that the term expressly appears in US legislation, and it is also made explicit that protection is not dependent upon the presence of confusion or deception. Following the enactment of a number of State anti-dilution statutes over a period of some 40 years or more, the Lanham Act was amended in 1996[73] to include protection for famous marks against acts of dilution on the part of third parties. Thus, section 43(C) provides:

(1) The owner of a famous mark shall be entitled, subject to the principles of equity and upon such terms as the court deems reasonable, to an injunction against another person's commercial use in commerce of a mark or trade name, if such use begins after the mark has become famous and causes dilution of the distinctive quality of the mark, and to obtain such other relief as is provided in this subsection. In determining whether a mark is distinctive and famous, a court may consider factors such as, but not limited to—

A. the degree of inherent or acquired distinctiveness of the mark;

B. the duration and extent of use of the mark in connection with the goods or services with which the mark is used;

---

[70] Trade Marks Act 1994 (UK), s. 22.

[71] S. 56.

[72] Llewelyn, n. 65 above, 158. See also M. Blakeney, "'Well Known' Marks" [1994] *EIPR* 481.

[73] 15 USC § 1125c(1). See further Fields, n. 46 above, 31–3; and the relevant articles in (1996) 59 *Law and Contemporary Problems* (No 2), especially those by Denicola, n. 25 above, and Alexander and Heilbronner, n. 25 above. See also McCarthy, n. 46 above.

C. the duration and extent of advertising and publicity of the mark;

D. the geographical extent of the trading area in which the mark is used;

E. the channels of trade for the goods or services with which the mark is used;

F. the degree of recognition of the mark in the trading areas and channels of trade used by the mark's owner and the person against whom the injunction is sought

G. the nature and extent of use of the same or similar marks by third parties; and

H. whether the mark was registered under the Act of March 3, 1881, or the Act of February 20, 1905, or on the principal register.

In an action brought under this subsection, the owner of the famous mark shall be entitled only to injunctive relief unless the person against whom the injunction is sought wilfully intended to trade on the owner's reputation or to cause dilution of the famous mark. If such wilful intent is proven, the owner of the famous mark shall also be entitled to the remedies set forth in sections 35(1a) and 36, subject to the discretion of the court and the principles of equity.

(2) ...

(3) The following shall not be actionable under this section:

A. Fair use of a famous mark by another person in comparative commercial advertising or promotion to identify the competing goods or services of the owner of the famous mark.

B. Noncommercial use of a mark.

C. All forms of news reporting and news commentary.

Finally, "dilution" is defined in section 45 as meaning:

the lessening of the capacity of a famous mark to identify and distinguish goods or services, regardless of the presence or absence of—

1. competition between the owner of the famous mark and other parties, or
2. likelihood of confusion, mistake or deception.

This is, perhaps, the most comprehensive national statement of an anti-dilution remedy, but the following limitations need to be borne in mind:

(a) Like the Paris Convention, the TRIPS Agreement and the UK provisions, it is confined to famous marks: this raises difficult issues of definition (although quite detailed guidelines to assist in this determination are provided in section 43(C)(1)), as well as the question whether similar protection for lesser known marks is not also justifiable.

(b) Dilution through "tarnishment" is not specifically referred to in section 43(C), but, despite some suggestions to the contrary by commentators,[74] it appears that the US courts have regarded these kinds of activities as coming within the provision.[75]

---

[74] See, e.g., Denicola, n. 25 above, 88–90; and Alexander and Heilbronner, n. 25 above, 124.

[75] McCarthy, n. 46 above, 42. Note, however, one instance referred to by McCarthy where it has been held that the use of a famous mark in relation to an allegedly "cheap knock-off" product did not amount to tarnishment: *Clinique Laboratories, Inc.* v. *Dep Corp.*, 945 F Supp. 547, 562 (SDNY 1996).

(c) It covers diluting activities in relation to any goods or services; regardless of the likelihood of confusion or the presence of competition between senior and junior users.

(d) The defences listed in section 43(C)(3) possibly go beyond what is contemplated by Article 17 of TRIPS which allows members to make "limited exceptions to the rights conferred to a trade mark, such as fair use of descriptive terms, provided that such exceptions take account of the legitimate interests of the owner of the trade mark and of third parties".

VIII THE 1995 AUSTRALIAN ACT

In some ways, the Australian Trade Marks Act 1995 follows the pattern of the 1994 UK Act; in other significant respects it does not. Thus, the definition of "trade mark" is in similar, though not identical, terms, namely "a sign used, or intended to be used, to distinguish goods or services dealt with or provided in the course of trade by a person from goods or services so dealt with or provided by any other person".[76] Likewise, the requirements for registration are similar, requiring that a mark should be "capable of distinguishing" the applicant's goods or services from those of other persons and providing further that this may be established through a showing of inherent distinctiveness or through acquired or factual distinctiveness or a combination of both.[77] Significant differences, however, arise in relation to the provisions concerned with infringement. Section 20(1) defines the exclusive rights given by registration of a trade mark to be the rights to use the trade mark and to authorise other persons to use the trade mark in relation to the goods and/or services in respect of which the mark is registered. However, the acts that will infringe a registered trade mark are specified separately in section 120 as follows:

(a) Use "as a trade mark" of a sign that is "substantially identical with, or deceptively similar to" the registered trade mark in relation to goods or services for which the mark is registered: section 120(1). Infringement is presumed, once these matters are established.

(b) Use "as a trade mark" of a sign that is "substantially identical with, or deceptively similar to", the registered trade mark where this use is in respect of goods or services of "the same description" as those in respect of which the trade mark is registered or goods or services that are closely related to the registered services or goods: section 120(2). However, infringement will not be taken to have occurred if the person using the sign establishes that such use was not likely to deceive or cause confusion. It will be noted here

---

[76] Trade Marks Act 1995 (Cth), s. 17. The equivalent definition in the UK Act (s 1(1)) provides that a trade mark means "any sign capable of being represented graphically which is capable of distinguishing goods or services of one undertaking from those of another undertaking".

[77] Trade Marks Act 1995 (Cth), s. 40, cf Trade Marks Act 1994 (UK), s. 3.

that, unlike section 10(2) of the UK Act, the onus of showing lack of likelihood of confusion is imposed on the defendant (in the UK provision, likelihood of confusion is one of the elements of infringement to be established by the trade mark owner). Section 120(2) of the Australian Act also does not indicate who it is who should be confused or deceived, whereas section 10(2) of the UK Act makes it clear that the likelihood of confusion must exist "on the part of the public".

(c) Use "as a trade mark" of a sign that is "substantially identical with, or deceptively similar to", the registered trade mark where the trade mark is "well known" in Australia and is in relation to "unrelated goods" or "unrelated services", i.e. goods or services that are not of the same description or closely related to goods or services in respect of which the trade mark is registered: section 120(3). Infringement will arise where, because such a mark is well known, the use of the sign by the defendant would be "likely to be taken as indicating a connection between the unrelated goods or services and the registered owner of the trade mark", and, for that reason, the "interests of the registered owner are likely to be adversely affected". So far as the phrase "well known in Australia" is concerned, account is to be taken of the "extent to which the trade mark is known within the relevant sector of the public, whether as a result of the promotion of the trade mark or for any other reason".

In general, it will be seen that this provision follows the structure of infringing acts contained in Article 16 of TRIPS. However, the following differences should be noted.

A "Use as a Trade Mark"

Each act of infringement defined in section 120 requires the use of a sign "as a trade mark", whereas this is not specifically required in Article 16 which refers to use in the "course of trade" (Article 16(1)) and, in the case of well known marks, to "use of that trade mark" (Article 16(3)). The phrase "use as a trade mark" does not appear in section 10 of the UK Act, and Jacob J in the *British Sugar* case made it clear that such a gloss was not to be added to that provision.[78] Likewise, in the 1955 Australian Act, there was no explicit reference to the need for an infringing use of a trade mark to be "use as a trade mark", but the phrase "use in the course of trade" was interpreted by the courts to have this meaning.[79] Accordingly, it would seem that the reference to "use as a trade mark" in section 120 of the 1995 Act was intended to give legislative effect to this prior judicial interpretation. Nonetheless, a requirement that an infringing use of a trade mark should be a "use as a trade mark" may impose a considerable

---

[78] *British Sugar plc* v. *James Robertson & Sons Ltd* [1996] RPC 281, 291.
[79] *Johnson & Johnson Australia Pty. Ltd* v. *Sterling Pharmaceuticals Pty. Ltd* (1991) 101 ALR 700.

limitation on the scope of infringement. It is possible that a trade mark may be used in the "course of trade", for example, in a descriptive or comparative sense, and not therefore be used as a trade mark in the sense of distinguishing the goods or services dealt in or provided in the course of trade from the goods or services of others (definition of "trade mark" in section 17 of the 1995 Act).

Several decisions of Australian courts on the 1955 Act have given effect to such an interpretation, without any need to rely upon the exceptions to infringement that were contained in that Act.[80] Thus, in *Johnson & Johnson Australia Pty. Ltd v. Sterling Pharmaceuticals Pty. Ltd*,[81] the Full Court of the Federal Court of Australia held that the use of the mark CAPLETS on its pharmaceutical products by Johnson & Johnson was not an infringing use of the trade mark but was merely descriptive, even though the decision by Johnson & Johnson to use the mark was "prompted by an international strategy to make the word into a generic word to the detriment of the applicant [respondent]".[82] In *Pepsico Australia Pty. Ltd v. Kettle Chips Co Pty. Ltd*,[83] the Full Court reached a similar conclusion in relation to an alleged infringement of the registered trade mark "Kettle" where the appellants used the words "Kettle Cooked" on the wrapping of their potato chips. This was on the basis that there was no use of "Kettle" as a trade mark, but this was simply done as a way of describing the process by which the chips were made, i.e. cooked in a kettle. Most recently, in relation to the 1995 Act, Merkel J of the Federal Court has held there was no infringement of a "contour" mark consisting of a representation of the famous shape of the Coca Cola bottle where the respondents produced and sold confectionery in the same shape.[84] The relevant provision here was section 120(3) (unrelated goods), but Merkel J found there was no use of the contour mark as a trade mark:[85]

> *the cola bottle confectionery, as such, does not indicate or connote origin of the goods and hence application or use of the contour bottle (represented by the confection) as a trade mark or, to put the matter in terms of s 17 of the Act, the confectionery does not distinguish the goods so as to indicate they were goods dealt with or provided by any particular person;
>
> *whilst the cola bottle confection is recognisable as having the shape of the contour bottle, consumers would not be likely to believe or expect it to have a commercial or trade connection of some kind with the applicant by reason of having that shape;
>
> *consumers would not be led to wonder whether it might be the case that the confectionary comes from the same source as Coca-Cola.

---

[80] Trade Marks Act 1955 (Cth), s. 64(1). See now Trade Marks Act 1995 (Cth), s. 122. For decisions on the 1955 Act and its predecessors, see *Mark Foy's Ltd* v. *Davies Coop & Company Ltd* (1956) 95 CLR 190; *Shell Company of Australia Ltd* v. *Esso Standard Oil (Australia) Ltd* (1963) 109 CLR 407.

[81] (1991) 101 ALR 700.

[82] *Ibid.*, 731 *per* Gummow J. See further the discussion of this case by M. Richardson, "An Economic Perspective on Distinctiveness in the Trade Marks Act 1994" (1995) 6 *AIPJ* 65, 71–2.

[83] (1996) 33 IPR 161.

[84] *Coca Cola Co* v. *All-Fect Distributors Ltd, trading as Millers Distributing Co* (1999) 43 IPR 47.

[85] *Ibid.*, 65. This decision was reversed on appeal [1999] FCA 1721 (10 December 1999).

I can shortly state my reasons for arriving at these conclusions. Use as a mark requires that the mark be used in such a way as to indicate or connote origin of the goods. In my view a number of factors support the conclusion that the cola bottle confectionary does not indicate or connote origin of the goods and hence *use* of the contour bottle represented by the confection as a trade mark. The inscription "Cola" and the colour of the confectionery is descriptive of the flavour rather than the origin of the goods. Further, the elongated and distorted form and appearance of the cola bottle confectionery, although generally recognisable as having the shape and basic markings of the contour bottle, is dissimilar to it in significant respects and is far from an exact copy of it. Thus, the product itself does not present as indicating or connoting its origin. Insofar as the packaging, labelling and get-up of the tub containing the confectionery uses a shape similar to that of the contour bottle, they do not do so in a manner that indicates or connotes origin. To the extent origin is indicated, the predominantly blue and green label depicts the origin of the product to be "Efruti". Of particular importance is my impression and estimation that the cola bottle confectionery is presented as a fun product "perhaps cheekily" imitating the contour bottle but not as representing any other connection with it. Thus, the cola bottle confectionery is merely recognisable as having the well known shape of the contour bottle but would not be likely to be believed or expected to have a trade or commercial connection of some kind with the applicant by reason of having that shape. Likewise consumers would be unlikely to be led to wonder whether it might be the case that the confectionery comes from the same source as Coca-Cola.

Each of these decisions limits the efficacy of the separate defences to infringement that were provided in both the 1955 and 1995 Acts, for example, in relation to good faith descriptive uses, although, in *Coca Cola*, the decision of Merkel J was specifically dictated by the fact that the words "use as a trade mark" now appear in section 120. Nonetheless, the pre-1995 judicial gloss and the 1995 statutory wording seem inconsistent with the thrust of Article 16 of TRIPS. This point was made eloquently by Jacob J in the *British Sugar* case where he rejected the insertion of such a gloss into the UK provision, noting that the words "use as a trade mark" did not appear in the EC Directive, and that there was no reason so to limit the provisions of section 10:[86]

> That is not to say a purely descriptive use is an infringement. It is not, but not because it does not fall within section 10 but because it falls within section 11(2) [the equivalent to section 122 of the 1995 Australian Act]. I see no need to put any gloss upon the language of section 10. It merely requires the court to see whether the sign registered as a trade mark is used in the course of trade and then to consider whether that use falls within one of the three defining subsections . . .

It is possible to argue that the CAPLETS and "Kettle" decisions are justifiable as a matter of policy, because of the low inherent distinctiveness of those marks,[87] but the same result could have been achieved by reference to statutory defences concerning descriptive uses but with the added qualification that the

---

[86] *British Sugar plc* v. *James Robertson & Sons Ltd* [1996] RPC 281, 291.
[87] See further the discussion of this point by Richardson, n. 82 above, 71–2.

court could have considered the good faith aspect of such use. In the case of "Coca Cola", however, there can be little doubt about the fame and high inherent distinctiveness of this mark, but it was still rendered a non-infringing use by reason of the fact that it was not used as a trade mark.

B "Substantially Identical" and "Deceptively Similar"

Each of the signs used for the purposes of section 120 must be "substantially identical with" or "deceptively similar to" the registered trade mark, rather than "identical or similar", the language used in Article 16 of TRIPS and section 10 of the UK 1994 Act. The wording used in section 120 is the same as that used in the 1955 Act, and it may be that the draftsman wished to maintain this wording for the convenience of users of the new Act. "Substantial identity" is not defined, but there is a definition of "deceptive similarity" to the effect that a mark will be taken to be deceptively similar to another mark if "it so nearly resembles that other trade mark that it is likely to deceive or cause confusion".[88] No specific reference is made to the persons who must be deceived or confused, but it seems reasonable to interpret this as meaning the relevant public for the goods or services in respect of which the mark is registered. In addition, the words have received interpretation by the courts, to the effect that substantial identity requires a side by side inspection of the marks whereas deceptive similarity arises where the marks are seen at different times, but the second brings the first to mind as the result of "imperfect recollection".[89]

The differences between the terminology in section 120 and Article 16 may not be of any practical significance, but the following points may still give rise to difficulty:

(a) "Identical" signs are not strictly embraced by the phrases "substantially identical" or "deceptively similar", but it cannot be supposed that the use of an identical sign should escape liability for the purposes of infringement. Under the 1955 Act, it was possible to argue that the use of the identical mark was covered by a separate section (section 58(1)) that gave the registered proprietor of a trade mark the right to the exclusive use of the mark in respect of the goods or services for which it was registered and to obtain relief in respect of infringement of that mark.[90] The use of substantially identical and deceptively similar marks was then treated as further acts of

---

[88] Trade Marks Act 1995 (Cth), s. 10.

[89] See further *Sym Choon & Co Ltd* v. *Gordon Choon Nuts Ltd* (1949) 80 CLR 65, 78 *per* Williams J; *Shell Co of Australia Ltd* v. *Esso Standard Oil (Australia) Ltd* (1963) 109 CLR 407, 415 *per* Windeyer J; *Polaroid Corporation* v. *Sole N Pty Ltd* [1981] 1 NSWLR 491, 498 *per* Kearney J; *Mid Sydney Pty Ltd* v. *Australian Tourism Company Ltd* (1999) 42 IPR 561, 569 (Full Court, Federal Court of Australia).

[90] *Mark Foy's Ltd* v. *Davies Coop & Company Ltd* (1956) 95 CLR 190; *Angoves Pty Ltd* v. *Johnson* (1982) 43 ALR 349.

infringement under another section (section 62(1)). The wording of the corresponding provisions of the 1995 Act (sections 20 and 120) is somewhat different, and it may not be so easy to make the argument that the exclusive right to "use the trade mark" in section 20(1)(a) enables the trade mark owner to bring infringement proceedings in respect of the unauthorised use of an identical mark by a third party. This is because section 120 appears to be an exclusive statement of what acts constitute infringements of the registered mark. If this is so, then the use of identical signs will need to be embraced within the concept of substantially identical or deceptively similar signs under section 120. Given the absurdity of holding otherwise, it is to be assumed that this will be the decision of any Australian court which is confronted with this particular situation. On the other hand, the need for uncertainty would have been avoided had the wording from Article 16 of TRIPS been adopted.

(b) While it is possible that the concepts of "similarity" and "substantial identity" will cover the same ground, it does not follow that this will occur as between the concepts of "similarity" and "deceptive similarity". It is clear from a number of Australian decisions, on both the 1955 and 1995 Acts, that a mark may not be substantially identical to the registered mark when compared side by side, but it may nonetheless be deceptively similar where it brings to mind the "idea" of the registered mark when it is seen or observed in the course of ordinary use. There is nothing in Article 16 to indicate that the term "similarity" should have this extended meaning, and it is possible therefore that the Australian reference to "deceptively similar" has a wider operation than the unqualified word "similar" which appears in Article 16. On the other hand, it is worth noting the decision of Laddie J in *Wagamama Ltd* v. *City Centre Restaurants plc*,[91] in which his Lordship held that the reference to "similar" marks in section 10 of the UK 1994 Act covered the use of marks in circumstances which would be regarded "deceptively similar" in the Australian context.

(c) Quite apart from the difference of language as between section 120 of the 1995 Australian Act and Article 16 of TRIPS, there is a possible redundancy in the retention of the phrase "deceptively similar to" in section 120(2), which deals with uses of signs in relation to goods or services of the same description or which are closely related to those in respect of which the mark is registered. Thus, "deceptively similar" means "so nearly resembles that other trade mark that it is likely to deceive or cause confusion" (see section 10). This, then, will be a matter for the registered owner of the trade mark to prove when he or she brings infringement proceedings against an alleged infringer under section 120(2). On the other hand, the latter will be taken not to have infringed the trade mark if they can establish that using

---

[91] [1995] FSR 713, 720–1, 731–3. See also *Origins Natural Resources, Inc* v. *Origin Clothing Ltd* [1995] FSR 280, 284 *per* Jacob J and *The European Ltd* v. *The Economist Newspapers Ltd* [1996] FSR 431.

the sign as the person did is not likely to deceive or cause confusion. As a matter of drafting, it is undesirable to use the same language in relation to what must be proved by the plaintiff (the use of a sign that is likely to deceive or cause confusion) and what must be shown to avoid liability (the use of a sign in a way that is not likely to deceive or cause confusion). Given that this must be use as a trade mark in the first instance (see above), it is not clear what the proviso to section 120(2) requires. Does it mean that the defendant needs to show that the sign he used was not deceptively similar (in the sense of being liable to deceive or cause confusion)—something which the trade mark owner is required to establish—or is this a reference only to the particular use of the sign that was made by the defendant? On the first of these interpretations, it would be difficult for a defendant ever to succeed in relying on the proviso once the plaintiff had established that the defendant's sign was likely to deceive or cause confusion: by definition, it would be impossible for the defendant to displace the likelihood of deception or confusion once the plaintiff had shown this on the balance of probabilities. On the second interpretation, the sign used by the defendant would be deceptively similar, but the latter will be able to escape liability by establishing that his use of it was not likely to deceive or confuse. Given that this will have to be a "trade mark use", it is unclear how a defendant will ever be able to show that he has used the sign, which is admittedly deceptive or confusing, in a way that is not. Either the sign itself is deceptive or confusing or it is not. It is possible that the reference to "using the sign as the person did" in the proviso to section 120(2) includes reference to the surrounding circumstances of the use. This was certainly the case in relation to infringement of Part B marks under the 1955 Act,[92] but the situation dealt with in section 120(2) is quite different from the case of the old Part B marks where the alleged infringing use was still required to be in relation to the goods or services for which the mark was registered. Such an interpretation, however, would make the proviso to section 120(2) more meaningful, and would make the kind of usage envisaged by that subsection akin to the type of considerations that are relevant to a passing off action. Whether this is consistent with the requirements of Article 16(1) of TRIPS is another matter.

C Well-known Marks

Section 120(3), which deals with these, tracks the TRIPS obligations more closely, but again there are problems of the same kind already noted above in relation to the TRIPS provisions and those in the UK 1994 Act. The following points can be made:

---

[92] Trade Marks Act 1955 (Cth), s. 62(2). See further *Marc A Hammond Pty. Ltd* v. *Papa Carmine Pty Ltd* (1977) 15 ALR 179, 182 (SCNSW).

(a) The mark must be "well known" in Australia, a phrase that is defined by precise reference to Article 16(2) of TRIPS, namely that account must be taken of the "extent to which the trade mark is known within the relevant sector of the public, whether as a result of the promotion of the trade mark or for any other reason". It is clear that "well-knownness" (a terrible word!) is a matter of evidence for the court to decide, but that use of the mark may not be necessary for this purpose. Thus, it may be possible to take account of promotional and advertising campaigns, or other means of raising awareness, for example, through television shows, films or recordings. On this basis, such marks as DUFF or STAR WARS would be able to satisfy the requirement of being well-known, even if they had not actually been used with respect to any goods or services in Australia at the relevant time.

(b) The sign that is used must be "substantially identical with, or deceptively similar to", the registered mark: on the meaning of these phrases, see the discussion above.

(c) Because the trade mark is well-known, the sign (used by the defendant) is likely to be taken as indicating a "connection between the unrelated goods or services and the registered owner of the trade mark". This language, again, comes directly from Article 16(3) of TRIPS and it was suggested above that this might well encompass the indicating of a connection that was not deceptive or confusing. It is noteworthy that a similar usage of "connection" occurs in Part 17 of the 1995 Act which deals with defensive registration of trade marks. This is another method for protection of well-known marks in Australia, although little effective use of it or its predecessor under the 1955 Act seems to have occurred.[93] On the other hand, the initial requirement in section 120(3) that the defendant's sign should be substantially identical with, or deceptively similar to, the well-known mark seems to require a likelihood of confusion, although this is not part of Article 16(3) of TRIPS which makes no reference to whether the defendant's sign is identical or similar. While specifically directed at the case of well-known marks, section 120(3) can hardly be seen, therefore, as providing a remedy against dilution of such marks.

(d) Given that it is likely that the "connection" for the purposes of section 120(3) will need to be deceptive or confusing, it is difficult to know what the final requirement in paragraph (d) of that provision adds, namely that "for that reason [the indication of a connection between the unrelated goods or services and the registered owner of the trade mark] the interests of the registered owner are likely to be adversely affected". On its own, this formulation could encompass diluting activities, i.e. damage that flowed from a diminution in the distinctiveness of the registered mark (blurring) or from the holding out of some inappropriate association (tarnishment). However,

---

[93] See further D. Shavin, "Famous Marks—Have They Ever Had Effective Protection? Post TRIPS—Has Anything Changed?" [1998] *Intell Prop Forum* 30.

the requirement of some element of deception or confusion should make such damage to the trade mark owner's interests inevitable, in any event.

IX THE 1999 DREAM AMENDMENTS

Had my dream been true, it would have been strange, indeed, that the Australian Parliament, having passed as many as two separate trade marks statutes within the space of a year,[94] should now have made major amendments to the 1995 Act so as to cover the dilution of registered trade marks. It will be apparent from the above account that, to date, dilution has not been a basis for trade mark infringement in Australia, either under the 1995 Act or its predecessors, or at common law under the action of passing off in all its extended forms. The origins of my dream amendments may have been somewhat uncertain, but they sprang full-grown into the world and purported to cover all significant forms of trade mark dilution in relation to well-known marks. At the same time, they embodied a complete reworking of the provisions of the 1995 Act relating to infringement generally. In particular, section 120 would have been replaced with the following:

"When is a registered trade mark infringed?
120 (1) A person infringes a registered trade mark if the person uses a sign that is identical or similar to the trade mark in relation to goods or services in respect of which the trade mark is registered.

(2) A person infringes a registered trade mark if the person uses a sign that is identical or similar to the trade mark in relation to goods or services that are identical, similar or closely related to those in respect of which the trade mark is registered where the result of such use is the likelihood of confusion on the part of the public, including the likelihood of confusion as to the association of the registered owner with the goods or services in respect of which the sign is used.

(3) A person infringes a registered trade mark if the person uses a sign that is identical or similar to the trade mark in relation to any goods or services where the trade mark is well known within Australia and the result of such use is to dilute the distinctive character or reputation of the mark.

(4) In determining whether a registered trade mark is well known within Australia for the purposes of subsection (3), one must take account of, but not be confined to, the following factors:

(a) the degree of inherent or acquired distinctiveness of the mark;
(b) the duration and extent of use of the mark in connection with the goods or services with which the mark is registered;
(c) the duration and extent of use of the mark in connection with any other goods or services;

---

[94] The present 1995 statute was preceded by the Trade Marks Act 1994 (never proclaimed) which was passed in order to comply with immediate TRIPS deadlines but which was then re-enacted with some further changes in 1995.

(d) the channels of trade for the goods or services for which the owner's mark is used;

(e) the duration and extent of advertising and publicity of the mark and the extent to which the mark is known within the relevant sector of the public;

(f) the degree of recognition of the mark in the trading areas and channels of trade used by the mark's owner and the person against whom the injunction is sought;

(g) the nature and extent of use of the identical or similar marks by third parties; and

(h) the extent to which the trade mark is known within the Australian community or a within a part of that community, as a result of the promotion of the mark that has occurred whether within or outside Australia or for any other reason.

(5) For the purposes of subsection (3), to "dilute the distinctive character or reputation" of a registered trade mark that is well-known in Australia means actions of a person that:

(a) lessen the capacity of the trade mark to distinguish goods or services; or

(b) diminish the general reputation of the trade mark within the Australian community or a section of that community;

regardless of whether the registered owner of the mark and that person are in competition with each other or whether these actions give rise to a likelihood of confusion or deception on the part of the relevant public.

(6) Without limiting the generality of actions which have the consequences referred to in paragraphs (a) and (b) of subsection (3), these include the following:

(a) acts which place the mark in an inappropriate or damaging context or hold out the mark as having inappropriate or damaging associations;

(b) acts which hold the mark out to inappropriate ridicule or contempt; and

(c) acts which tend to make the mark a descriptive or generic indication of a particular good or service."

New defences to infringement were also contained in an amended section 122(1) as follows:

When is a trade mark not infringed?

122 (1) In spite of s 120, a person does not infringe a registered trade mark where:

(a) the person uses a sign otherwise than in the course of trade;

(b) the person uses in good faith

   (i) the person's name or the name of the person's place of business; or

   (ii) the name of a predecessor in business of the person or the name of the predecessor's place of business;

(c) the person uses a sign in good faith to indicate the kind, quality, quantity, intended purpose (including as accessories or spare parts), value, geographical origin, or some other characteristic of goods or services, or the time of production of the goods or the rendering of the services;

(d) the person makes fair use of the trade mark for the purposes of comparative commercial advertising or promotion to identify the competing goods or services of the registered owner;

(e) the person uses the trade mark in course of reporting news;

(f) the person uses the trade mark by way of a fair parody or satire;

(g) the person exercises a right to use a trade mark given to the person under this Act;

(h) the court is of the opinion that the person would obtain registration of the trade mark in his or her name if the person were to apply for it; or

(i) the person, in using a sign referred to in subsection 120(1) or (2) in a manner referred to in that subsection, does not (because of a condition or limitation subject to which the trade mark is registered) infringe the exclusive right of the registered owner to use the trade mark.

Another significant amendment was to delete the provisions of the 1995 Act dealing with the defensive registration of trade marks (Part 17) and to replace them with an equivalent provision to section 56 of the UK Trade Marks Act 1994 (see above).

A Explanation of the Dream

What advance, if any, did the above provisions represent over the existing Australian law? The following points may be noted:

(a) Confusion, or rather presumed confusion, remained the basis of infringement where the same mark was used in relation to the same goods or services for which the mark was registered.

(b) Confusion or likelihood of confusion also remained the principal basis for infringement where a sign was used in relation to the same or similar goods or services in respect of which the mark was registered (there was, of course, no requirement in section 120(2) that the similar or closely related goods or services in respect of which the sign is used by the defendant should be within the registration of the mark).

(c) In all three infringement provisions (section 120(1), (2) and (3)), the words "substantially identical with" and "deceptively similar to" were replaced with the words "identical" and "similar". As explained above, this was in keeping with the terminology employed in Article 16 of TRIPS and also finds a parallel in the 1994 UK Act.

(d) "Use as a trade mark" was no longer required for the purposes of infringement under any of the subsections. Any use of a sign that was identical or similar would suffice, unless it fell within one of the specific exceptions outlined in section 122.

(e) Most controversial was the addition of a widely drafted remedy against dilution of well-known marks in section 120(3). This was quite clearly divorced from any need to show likelihood of confusion or competition between the parties, and appeared to be an amalgam of the US and UK approaches, together with some specifically Australian glosses. In the absence of further legislative direction, it could have been assumed that both blurring and tarnishment were covered by subsection (3)(a) and (b), but subsection (6) put it beyond question that all derogatory actions in relation to a well known mark were covered (shades of moral rights). This also includes actions of a third party that tend to make a mark descriptive or generic.

(f) Unlike the UK provisions, the dilution remedy was not confined to actions with respect to unrelated goods or services. Thus, it would cover equally the case of "Chanel No 5 trucks" (goods unrelated to perfumes) and the use of Chanel No 5 in relation to cheap "copies of Chanel No 5" perfume (a non-confusing use in relation to the same goods). The adverse consequences that must be shown for the purposes of dilution were those referred to in subsection (5), namely the lessening of the capacity of the well known mark to distinguish goods or services; or the diminishing of the general reputation of the mark within the Australian community or a section of that community. Unlike section 10(3) of the UK Act, these were objective criteria to be determined by the court, rather than more open-ended tests, such as whether the use had taken an "unfair advantage of, or is detrimental to", the distinctive character or repute of the mark. A distinction here appeared to be made between the distinctiveness of a mark and its general reputation. In practice, however, these concepts must surely have overlapped.

(g) Was the limitation of the dilution remedy in section 120(3) to marks that were well-known justifiable? It is true that the requirement of being "well-known" imposed a less rigorous condition than being "famous" or "notorious", and that the guidelines in section 120(4) suggested that this would be a question of fact and degree to be assessed by the court in each case. On the other hand, should activities of the kind that occurred in the CAPLETS and "Kettle" cases described above escape liability?[95] These would probably not be capable of being regarded as well-known marks within the new section 120(3), because of their low levels of inherent distinctiveness. On the other hand, the activities of the defendants in each case had a clear diluting tendency, and entailed the same kind of free riding that would have occurred had these been famous marks. Under the dream amendments, however, such activities would now fall within section 120(1) or (2), on the basis that they do not have to be uses "as a trade mark" and would undoubtedly be confusing. Liability would only be avoided if they could then fall within one of the exceptions in section 122, such as good faith descriptive use, and the "good faith" of these uses would be very doubtful, particularly in the CAPLETS case.

(h) The exceptions to infringement in the new section 122 covered most, if not all, of the exceptions that were previously allowed, but also included specific exceptions that would become important once there was a dilution

---

[95] *Johnson & Johnson Australia Pty. Ltd* v. *Sterling Pharmaceuticals Pty. Ltd* (1991) 101 ALR 700 and *Pepsico Australia Pty. Ltd* v. *Kettle Chips Co Pty. Ltd* 1996) 33 IPR 161.

remedy for well-known marks. These included a general exception in respect of non-commercial use, an exception in favour of news reporting, one for comparative advertising (which was already allowed under section 122 of the 1995 Act) and one for "fair parody and satire". The last was the most uncertain in its scope—how can a parody or satire ever be fair?—but was inserted at the end of my dream as a last minute amendment by an independent senator who was concerned that Australian judges have, in the past, taken a somewhat restrictive attitude to the use of parody as a justification for passing off and copyright infringement[96] (the same senator, however, was at pains to point that he did not think that these judges were bereft of a sense of humour, simply that they were generally inclined to disregard the effect of humour when assessing the commercial impact of parodic usages!).

(i) It is instructive to consider how the new dilution provision in section 120(3) might have operated in several recent Australian cases involving well-known trade marks.

- In *McIlhenny Co v. Blue Yonder Holdings Pty. Ltd*,[97] the trade mark "Tabasco" was registered in respect of a certain kind of sauce, and the use complained of was in relation to design services. Lehane J of the Federal Court of Australia found that, although the mark "Tabasco" was highly distinctive and well-known in relation to sauce, there was no likelihood of deception or confusion where this was used in relation to design services, even though the use was perhaps a "cheeky" one intended to indicate that these services were "hot" (this case was brought in passing off as well as under section 52 of the Trade Practices Act 1974, rather than as a trade marks infringement claim). Under the new section 120(3), it is arguable that, despite the absence of confusion or deception, this conduct would have fallen within subsection 3(a) or (b) as tending to lessen the distinctive character or reputation of the mark; in addition, such a use might be argued to prejudice the legitimate interests of the trade mark owner by reducing the possibilities for "brand extension", i.e. the exploitation of the "Tabasco" trade mark in related products or services.
- In *Coca Cola Co v. All-Fect Distributors Ltd*,[98] there was no liability for trade mark infringement under the present section 120(3) because the contour bottle shaped confectionery was held not to constitute a use of the contour bottle trade mark as a trade mark. It was not strictly necessary for Merkel J to consider the issue of likelihood of confusion, although he noted a number of US cases where relief had been given for infringement

---

[96] See, e.g., *Pacific Dunlop Ltd* v. *Hogan* (1989) 14 IPR 398, 429 and *AGL Sydney Ltd* v. *Shortland County Council* (1989) 17 IPR 99.

[97] (1997) 39 IPR 187.

[98] (1999) 43 IPR 47. This decision was reversed on appeal: [1999] FCA 1721 (10 December 1999).

with respect to use on non-competing goods and services.[99] Assume, however, that no likelihood of confusion or deception had been found: would this use nonetheless have amounted to a dilution of the contour bottle trade mark? It is arguable that it would have done so, on the basis that this kind of use would diminish both the distinctive character and reputation of the mark.

- An instance of a possibly tarnishing use might be found in the facts of the English case of *Baywatch Production Co, Inc* v. *The Home Video Channel*,[100] where the complaint was that the trade mark BAYWATCH (derived from the television series of that name) and registered in respect of various items of merchandise had been infringed under section 10(3) of the UK 1994 Act by the use of the sign BABEWATCH in relation to an adult television programme. In the absence of likelihood of confusion, Michael Crystal QC held that there could be no action that took advantage of, or was detrimental to, the distinctive character or repute of the mark. Under section 120(3) and (6) of the dream amendments, this would clearly be an act that placed the mark in an inappropriate or damaging context or which held it out as having inappropriate or damaging associations, or more generally to inappropriate ridicule or contempt.

X CONCLUSION REMARKS—WAS IT ONLY A DREAM?

The above account is an attempt to describe one possible way in which the basis for trade mark infringement might be reformed in a common law jurisdiction such as Australia. While changes of this magnitude are not specifically dictated by international instruments, such as TRIPS, they are certainly consistent with those instruments as well as with developments in such important jurisdictions as the USA. On the other hand, are such reforms necessary or, indeed, justifiable? On a number of matters, such as the requirement of "use as a trade mark" and the replacement of terms such as "substantially identical" and "deceptively similar", I believe that there can be little criticism of the changes made in the dream amendments. These are areas in which the existing Australian provisions are out of kilter with the equivalent provisions in other national laws, and

---

[99] Thus, Merkel J said (at 64): "[g]enerally, in the United States famous trade marks have been given broad protection against use on non-competing products. For example, the 'Rolls Royce' mark for autos and planes was enforced against 'Rolls Royce' for radio tubes: see *Wall* v *Rolls-Royce of America Inc* 4 F.2d 333 (3d Cir. 1925). The 'Tiffany' mark for jewellery, silver, and other expensive items has been enforced against 'Tiffany' for a theatre (see *Tiffany & Co* v *Tiffany Productions* 264 N.Y. Supp. 459 (1932)), a restaurant (see *Tiffany & Co* v *Boston Club Inc* 231 F.Supp. 836 (D. Mass. 1964)) and ceramic tiles: see *Tiffany & Co* v *Tiffany Tile Co* 345 F.2d 214 (C.C.P.A. 1965). The 'Dunhill' trade mark for tobacco, cigars, pipes, toiletries, and gift items has been enforced against 'Dunhill' on scotch whisky: see *Alfred Dunhill of London Inc* v *Kasser Distillers Prods Corp* 350 F.Supp. 1341 (E.D. Pa. 1972), aff'd per curiam, 480 F.2d 714 (3d Cir. 1973)."

[100] [1997] FSR 22.

changes in Australian law are clearly required. On the more fundamental question of dilution of well-known marks, however, there are strong criticisms which can be made. These include the following:

(a) Allowing relief against dilution of a trade mark, whether famous, well-known or otherwise, represents a radical departure from the traditional conception of a trade mark as a badge of origin, severing it from its historic origins in deceit and consumer protection. Under such a development, trade marks will become property rights in themselves, capable of protection from any intrusion or trespass from third parties. The public domain aspect of trade marks, under which courts sought assiduously to preserve the "common heritage" of words and signs,[101] will disappear and the rights of rival traders, and the public generally, will be diminished.

(b) Any property right so recognised must meet the inevitable objection that arises when the need for a remedy is deduced from the application of labour and effort that then provides its own justification for protection from appropriation by third parties. There is a bootstraps element here that has usually been rejected by common law courts, as exemplified by the famous statement of Dixon J in *Victoria Park Racing and Recreational Grounds Co Ltd* v. *Taylor*, quoted at the start of this chapter. Extensions of protection, particularly under statute, require further justification, and a proper assessment of the ramifications of according such protection.

(c) Dilution remedies will inevitably favour one class of trade mark owners, namely those who possess famous or well-known marks. Leaving aside any deep-seated visceral feelings one may have about the activities and influence of dreaded multinationals, according such marks a wider sphere of protection inevitably cuts into the freedoms and usages of other traders, particularly at the local level, as well as affecting the interests of consumers generally. In jurisdictions such the USA, constitutional guarantees of freedom of expression can moderate the scope of such claims and bring them within reasonable compass. This is not the case in a country such as Australia, although clearly specific legislative provision for this can be made (as in the dream amendments to section 123 outlined above).

Against these objections, the following arguments may be advanced:

(a) Allowing for recognition of a dilution remedy, at least in the case of famous marks, reflects the changing conditions of modern marketing and

---

[101] The phrase is that of Kitto J in *Clark Equipment Co* v. *Registrar of Trade Marks* (1964) 111 CLR 511, 514. See also the words of Lord Macnaghten in *Eastman Photographic Materials Company Ltd's Application* (1898) 15 RPC 476, 486: "[t]he object of putting a restriction on words capable of being registered as Trade Marks was, of course, to prevent persons appropriating to themselves that which ought to be open to all. There is a 'perpetual struggle' going on as Lord Justice Fry has observed, 'to enclose and appropriate as private property certain little strips of the great open common of the English language. That', he added, 'is a kind of trespass against which I think the Courts ought to set their faces'."

distribution of goods and services. This is particularly so in a global trading community where digital networks allow for the instantaneous transmission of symbols and information across national borders. As Schechter noted over 70 years ago, these changes mean that the function of trade marks has changed fundamentally and that this should be reflected in the scope of legal protection they receive.[102] If this means a shift from a deceit to a trespass basis, this is simply an inevitable reflection and consequence of the underlying changes that are occurring in the market place. The effort and investment that go into the creation and deployment of such marks are therefore as deserving of protection as any other form of endeavour protected by rights such as copyrights, designs or patents. The famous statement of Peterson J in *University of London Press Ltd* v. *University Tutorial Press Ltd*[103] has the same intuitive appeal here as it does in the context of copyright, namely that "as a rough practical test . . . what is worth copying is prima facie worth protecting".

(b) While the bootstraps argument may be acknowledged, it is nonetheless possible to mount a credible argument that protection against dilution is required in order to provide the necessary incentive for trade mark owners to invest in the development of high quality products and services. This, again, is a familiar argument for the recognition of new or extended intellectual property rights, and is always difficult to assess in empirical terms.

(c) While recognition of "new rights" inevitably carry with them consequential restrictions on others (competitors, other traders and consumers), these restrictions are by no means absolute and can be modified by appropriate limitations and exceptions (as in the dream amendments to section 123 above).

It will be clear that there are tough policy debates that need to be conducted before any kind of dilution remedy is introduced into domestic law. In my dream, the new amendments came out of the blue and were passed with no notice or discussion. But would the reality have been any different? Would the proposals have been outlined, first, in some kind of Green Paper, followed by White, lengthy government consultations and public submissions, and scrutiny by a Senate Committee? This has certainly been the pattern in Australia with respect to reforms in such areas as copyright, corporations law and taxation. But it is less certain that such a process would occur in the case of trade marks, because the latter do not often attract the same kind of attention that attaches to the formulation of exclusive rights and defences (as in the case of copyright), the reformulation of directors' duties (as in the case of corporations) or the introduction of a new tax. Thus, the Trade Marks Act 1995 grew out of a relatively informal process of governmental consultation and policy development in which questions of substance were mostly subordinated to matters of adminis-

---

[102] Schechter, n. 24 above.
[103] [1916] 2 Ch 601, 610.

trative detail. And, at the international level, the discussions of famous marks by the expert committees of WIPO seem to have foundered upon definitional issues rather than questions of policy. So, it could well be, in another year or so, when the Australian Parliament runs into its annual silly season and an anxious government wishes to be seen as doing something—or anything at all—that an anti-dilution measure could be slipped through, without too much fuss and bother. Yet, in our everyday transactions and usage, trade marks affect us all. It would be a great pity, therefore, if such changes were to be introduced, as in a dream and without a far-reaching public discussion of the merits and necessity for such extended forms of protection.

ADDENDUM

In a recent decision, too late for inclusion in the principal text, the High Court of Australia has expressly acknowledged the damage that may arise to a long established mark from the diluting effects of another mark which is the same or similar. In *Campomar Sociedad, Limitada* v. *Nike International Ltd.*,[104] the parties were the owners of the mark NIKE which was registered in respect of different classes of goods: perfume products, laundry products and soaps, on the one hand, and athletic footwear and sports clothing, on the other. The competition between the marks became obvious as the activities of the parties began to move more closely together in the marketplace, and there were claims by the respondent for the removal of the appellant's marks as entries wrongly made or remaining in the register, for misleading or deceptive conduct under s 52 of the Trade Practices Act 1974, and for passing off. The judgment of the High Court (which was a unanimous one) ranges widely and learnedly over each of these areas, and will do much to clarify a number of uncertainties, in particular with respect to the operation of s 28(a) of the Trade Marks Act 1955 (as it then was). Nonetheless, although keenly aware of the dilution effects that may arise in a case like this, the Court has refrained from moving beyond the existing limits to protection, although these heads of protection may very well provide adequate protection in many cases on the basis of an extended deception/confusion theory. The brave new step into the world of dilution therefore awaits the legislative intervention foreshadowed in the principal text.

A further addendum needs to be given concerning the decision of Merkel J in *Coco Cola Co* v. *All-Fect Distributing Corp* (1999) 43 IPR 47. This was reversed on appeal by the Full Federal Court on 10 December 1999: [1999] FCA 1721 which held that the mark had, in fact, been used as a trade mark. Furthermore, in a significant finding, the court held that it was unnecessary that this usage should indicate a connection with the registered owner of the mark: it was enough that the use indicated a connection with the person using the mark, i.e. the alleged infringer.

---

[104] (2000) 46 IPR 481.

7

New Challenges for the Law of Patents

JOHN ROBINSON THOMAS

I INTRODUCTION

The topic of "New Challenges for the Law of Patents" at a conference devoted to "International Intellectual Property and the Common Law World" presents a double predicament. Despite the heightened station assumed by the patent system in the past decade, it seems unlikely that any of the current issues facing the patent system fulfill the standards of novelty and inventive step so familiar to patent practitioners. The patent community has staged heated debates over such points as patentable subject matter, claim interpretation and the costs of patent enforcement before. Whether we should derive comfort from this familiarity, or despair over our continued inability to achieve a satisfactory resolution of these points, seems more difficult to say.

Focus upon the common law world also seems to present a rather cabined view of the international patent order, at least at first blush. Actors in common law countries also seek protection for their proprietary technologies in jurisdictions with differing legal traditions. Depending upon those markets a client judges significant, rulings from Kasumigaseki or the banks of the Isar may be more important to the common law patent practitioner than those from Crystal City or Cardiff.

But there are merits too to this posture. Our shared traditions lend focus to discussion of the patent issues of the day. Yet the enormous diversity that exists in the common law world, in terms of extra-legal culture, economic conditions and the technological interests of its members, results in the robust presentation of competing views. And surely our long collective experience will contribute to the resolution of the patent issues that sometimes strain our trading relations and traditional bonds of friendship. After all, the Statute of Monopolies, the Jacobean legislation that continues to inform the workings of the contemporary patent order, arose from the common law tradition.[1]

The Statute of Monopolies is a good starting point for thinking about one of the central concerns of the modern patent law, the extent of patentable subject matter. The Statute extended the possibility of patenting only to

---

[1] 21 Jac 1, c 3 (1623). See generally C.R. Kyle, "But a New Button to an Old Coat: the Enactment of the Statute of Monopolies" (1998) 19 *J of Legal History* 203.

"manufactures". Although the usual sense of that term suggests human-made artifacts, the rationalisation of production techniques brought about by the Industrial Revolution led courts to entertain a widening conception of what was patentable. By the mid-nineteenth century, the English patent system had extended fully to both products and processes.[2] Yet discomfort with the potential scope of process protection remains today. Common law courts that continued to interpret the term "manufactures" sought to limit the patent system to so-called "manual arts",[3] an "artificially created state of affairs"[4] or the production or preservation of vendible products.[5] Yet the seemingly inevitable tendency is to broaden the ambit of patentable subject matter, a trend achieved in part through artful claims drafting. Two recent opinions deserving of further discussion best illustrate the trend towards a more ambitious sense of what is patentable.[6]

The first is the decision of the Court of Appeal of New Zealand in *Pharmaceutical Management Agency Ltd* v. *Commissioner of Patents* (hereafter "*Pharmac*").[7] The Court held that so-called Swiss-type claims, that recite an additional use of a known pharmaceutical, are valid in New Zealand. The opinion is controversial because it essentially allows proprietary rights in inventions formerly believed to be unpatentable, so long as the inventor maintains the appropriate claim drafting protocol. This chapter offers perspectives from US patent practice regarding the significance of the claim format in the substantive patent law, as well as commentary on the appropriate disposition of the case on appeal.

Second is the opinion in *State Street Bank & Trust Co* v. *Signature Financial Group, Inc.*,[8] authored by the United States Court of Appeals for the Federal Circuit. There the plaintiff held a patent for a data processing system consisting of software for managing a stock mutual fund. The Federal Circuit not only held that data transformation through a series of mathematical calculations presented a patentable technique, but it also took the opportunity to obliterate the venerable proscription on patenting so-called "methods of doing business". Keenly aware of the *State Street* judgment, applicants have besieged the United States Patent and Trademark Office (herein PTO) with applications ranging

---

[2] See *Crane* v. *Price* (1842) 4 Man & G 580, 134 ER 239.

[3] See *Maeder* v. *Busch* (1938) 59 CLR 684.

[4] See *National Reseach Dev. Corp's. Application* [1961] RPC 134 (HCA 1964). See also (1959) 102 CLR 252.

[5] *Boulton* v. *Bull* Z Hy Bl 463, 482–3, (1795) 126 ER 651, 661.

[6] The new ambitions of the patent system have been realised in fits and starts, and not without exception. Two recent opinions have suggested a more confined view of patent eligibility, in particular dicta regarding methods of medical treatment in Australia (see *Bristol-Meyers Squibb Co* v. *F.H. Faulding & Co*, (1998) 41 IPR 467; appeal dismissed (2000) 46 IPR 553 as well as the invalidation of the oncomouse patent by a court in first instance in Canada (see *President and Fellows of Harvard College* v. *Commissioner of Patents* (1998) 79 CPR (3d) 98). But these opinions appear anomalous and hardly indicative of a narrowing trend in global patent law.

[7] (2000) 46 IPR 655.

[8] 149 F 3d 1368 (Fed. Cir. 1998).

from financial software to Internet-based business models.[9] This chapter thoroughly reviews the *State Street* opinion and more briefly explores the wisdom of its ambitious sense of patentable subject matter.

Before discussing these cases and their ramifications, it should be noted at the outset that statutory subject matter presents a crucial topic in the patent law. Determining the appropriate subject matter for patenting is important because a paucity of constraining doctrines allays the proprietary rights associated with granted patents.[10] The adjudicated infringer need not have derived the patented invention from the patentee, as liability rests solely upon a comparison of the text of the patent instrument with an alleged infringement.[11] The patent law as well lacks a robust experimental use exemption in the nature of copyright law's fair use privilege.[12] The decision to subject particular areas of endeavour to the patent system is therefore of great moment, in effect subjecting entire industries to a private regulatory environment with constantly shifting contours. Given the contemporary movement towards an increasingly ambitious sense of patentable subject matter, further reflection upon the appropriate grasp of the patent system appears worthwhile.

II   ON *PHARMAC* AND THE FORMATTING OF PATENT CLAIMS

The *Pharmac* opinion concerns the propriety of so-called "Swiss-type claims" under the patent law of New Zealand. Such claims relate to an additional use of a known pharmaceutical, typically reciting "the use of a particular pharmaceutically active compound in the manufacture of a medication to treat a particular disorder". One might imagine that an inventor who discovered an additional use for a known composition would claim her discovery more straightforwardly, in terms of a method of treating the disorder. However, the leading New Zealand case of *Wellcome Foundation Ltd* v. *Commissioner of Patents*[13] held that methods of treating disease in humans were not patentable under the Patents Act 1953 (NZ). The *Wellcome Foundation* judgment comports with Article 27(3) of the TRIPS Agreement and with the express terms of various

---

[9] See J. Bick, "Adapting Process Patents to Cyberspace" 220 *NYLJ*, No 98 at 1, col 1 (19 November 1998); M. Walsh, "Internet Companies Seek Protection: Apply For Patents to Guard Technology, But Litigation May Slow Commerce", *Crain's N Y Bus* (21 December 1998); "'Boom' in Business Method Patent Filings Has Followed 'State Street' Ruling, PTO Says", (1998) 57 *Patent, Trademark & Copyright J* 115 (PTO Deputy Commissioner Dickinson expects approximately 300 business method patents to issue in 1999).

[10] See 35 USC § 271(a) (1994) (the patentee has the exclusive right to make, use, sell, offer to sell or import into the United States the patented invention).

[11] See M.J. Adelman *et al.*, *Patent Law* (St Paul, Minn., West Publishing Co, 1998), 860–1.

[12] See R.S. Eisenberg, "Patents and the Progress of Science: Exclusive Rights and Experimental Use" (1989) 56 *U of Chic L Rev* 1017, 1023; R S Eisenberg, "Proprietary Rights and the Norms of Science in Biotechnology Research" (1987) 97 *Yale L J* 177, 222.

[13] [1983] NZLR 385.

patent statutes elsewhere, most notably Article 52(4) of the European Patent Convention.

Claims drafters quickly attempted to obtain nearly identical protection to that disallowed in *Wellcome Foundation* by articulating inventions in a slightly different fashion. Swiss-type claims instead recite a method of making a medication, a traditional industrial process understood to lie within the patent system. Well-drafted Swiss-type claims additionally employ the magic word "manufacture", the original definition of patent-eligible subject matter in the Statute of Monopolies.

A 1990 decision of the New Zealand Commissioner of Patents, which stressed substance over form, nonetheless held that such claims would not be issued in New Zealand. Undoubtedly influenced by developments overseas, which were increasingly accepting of Swiss-type claims, the Commissioner overturned this judgment in January 1997. Pharmac, a government agency concerned with the subsidisation of pharmaceuticals, subsequently brought an action in the High Court challenging the latter decision.

The judgment of Gallen J in the High Court of New Zealand was that so-called Swiss-type claims were appropriate under the New Zealand patent law.[14] The Court found persuasive the European Patent Office Board opinion in *Eisai*, which upheld such claims within European Patent Office practice. Pharmac sought review of the matter from the Court of Appeal.

The Court of Appeal responded on 17 December 1999 with an opinion affirming the lower court. The Court of Appeal acknowledged the view of Jacob J that claims in Swiss form amounted to "devices and sophistry".[15] The Court nonetheless observed that Article 27 of the TRIPS Agreement required New Zealand to allow patents to issue "for any inventions, whether products or processes, in all fields of technology, provided that they are new, involve an inventive step and are capable of industrial application". Believing that the discovery of a new property of a chemical compound constituted an "invention" within the meaning of this broad language, the Court reasoned that the TRIPS Agreement compelled the conclusion that claims in Swiss form were allowable.[16]

Existing commentary on *Pharmac* has largely centred on the traditional debate whether medical methods as such are patentable. As such, US patent practice may not initially seem a useful source of consultation, for the simple reason that medical practitioners have for decades obtained US patents directly upon methods of medical treatment.[17] However, this environment may be shift-

[14] [1999] RPC 752.

[15] (2000) 46 IPR 655, 669, citing *Bristol-Myers Squibb Co v. Baker Norton Pharmaceuticals, Inc.* [1999] RPC 253, 280.

[16] *Ibid.*, 671–2.

[17] See W.D. Noonan, "Patenting Medical and Surgical Procedures" (1995) 77 *J Pat & Trademark Off Soc'y* 651; United States Patent No 5,364,838 (15 November 1994) (method of intrapulmonary administration of insulin); United States Patent No 5,456,663 (10 October 1995) (method of treating cancer).

ing in the USA. Although, traditionally, few patentees had attempted to enforce such patents,[18] in the early 1990s a Dr Samuel Pallin alleged that another physician had infringed his patented cataract surgery procedure.[19] The lawsuit led to a raging debate that questioned the impact of patents upon medical ethics, patient care and professional autonomy. Although some urged that such patents offered individuals incentives to invent and disclose new medical methods, others pointed to the possibility that patents might restrict access to life-saving techniques, lead to invasions of patient privacy and override the culture of disclosure and peer review that pervades the medical community.[20]

Following the condemnation of patents on methods of medical treatment by the American Medical Association House of Delegates, the United States Congress reacted by amending the Patent Act. As codified in § 287(c), the new statute deprives patentees of remedies against medical practitioners engaged in infringing "medical activity".[21] Although the PTO may still issue patents on medical methods, the inability of such instruments to provide their owner with any relief essentially renders them a legal nullity. The result of these amendments, in addition to a likely TRIPS Agreement violation, is that we may see more Swiss-type claims in the United States as well.

Pharmac does exemplify a broader movement, however, one worthy of discussion here. Courts have long recognised and policed attempts to contract around the patent code.[22] For example, settled US law establishes that the proprietor of a patent which enjoys market power cannot extend that patent beyond its statutory term or restrain competition in an unpatented product via contract.[23] Yet today a far more subtle and fundamental mechanism for drafting around the statute has materialised: the humble patent instrument itself. Patent drafters have only partially realised the remarkable set of tools they now possess for expanding the scope of patent-eligible subject matter, augmenting the market power of issued patents, and avoiding core precepts of the patent canon.

The source of these new-found resources is case law concerning the claims, the tightly drafted technical aphorisms that close the contemporary patent instrument. It is these few, carefully chosen words of limitation that have traditionally served to define the inventor's patentable advance.[24] *Pharmac* typifies a

---

[18] C.J. Katopis, "Patients v. Patents?: Policy Implications of Recent Patent Legislation" (1997) 71 *St John's L Rev* 329, 354–5.

[19] See *Pallin* v. *Singer*, 36 USPQ 2d 1050 (D Vt. 1995).

[20] See B. Gocyk-Farber, "Patenting Medical Procedures: A Search for a Compromise Between Ethics and Economics" (1997) 18 *Cardozo L Rev* 1527.

[21] 35 USC § 287(c). See G.J. Mossinghoff, "Remedies Under Patents on Medical and Surgical Procedures" (1996) 78 *J Pat & Trademark Off Soc'y* 789.

[22] See R.P. Merges, *Patent Law and Policy* (2nd edn, Charlottesville, Va., Mitchie Law Publishers, 1997), 1172.

[23] See, e.g., *B. Braun Medical, Inc.* v. *Abbott Labs., Inc.*, 124 F 3d 1419, 1426 (Fed. Cir. 1997).

[24] E.g., *Markman, Inc.* v. *Westview Instruments*, 52 F 3d 967, (Fed. Cir. 1995), aff'd, 517 US 370 (1996).

trend wherein the claims have assumed a new, more malleable role. Patent claims have become as well a sort of well-pleaded complaint, easily manipulated to comply with or diverge from the patent statute or judicial precedent.

The format of a patent claim is pivotal because substantive rights hinge upon whether the claimed invention comprises artifact or technique. For example, infringement of an artifact claim occurs due to the unauthorised making of, using, selling, offering for sale or importing into the claimed physical techno-logy.[25] In contrast, courts have traditionally held that one infringes a claim directed towards technique only by performing the steps of the claimed process.[26] Patentees have been held to exhaust the rights provided by artefact claims upon the first sale of their commercial embodiment; yet technique claims have traditionally been exempted from the exhaustion principle, allowing patentees downstream control of technologies within the market place.[27] As a final example, the patent statute limits the remedies owing to patentees that do not mark their patented products with the appropriate legend, but the courts have held that the incorporeal steps of a technique claim lie without the mark-ing requirement.[28] For these and other reasons, technologists have recognised that claims directed towards technique offer a different bundle of rights from that provided by artefact claims.

Given the significance of patent claim format and the ease with which claims may be converted from one format to another,[29] inventors have long attempted to manipulate substantive patent doctrine through claim drafting protocols. This chapter next discusses three episodes in the United States exemplifying this trend: the demise of the so-called "function of a machine" doctrine, the rela-tionship between product and process in biotechnology, and the rise of claims to encoded recording media in the computer arts.

A The "Function of a Machine" Doctrine

As claims of the patent instrument were increasingly relied upon as the measure of its owner's proprietary rights throughout the nineteenth century,[30] US claims drafters attempted to paint more than a merely accurate verbal portrait of a spe-cific artefact. In an effort to obtain broader coverage, they quickly attempted to

---

[25] 35 USC § 271(a) (1994).

[26] See *Joy Technologies* v. *Flakt, Inc.*, 6 F 3d 770, 773 (Fed. Cir. 1993).

[27] See *Bandag, Inc.* v. *Al Bolser's Tire Stores*, 750 F 2d 903, 924 (Fed. Cir. 1984) ("The doctrine that the first sale by a patentee of an article embodying his invention exhausts his patent rights in that article . . . is inapplicable here, because the claims of the [asserted] patent are directed to a 'method'"); see also *United States* v. *Univis Lens Co*, 316 US 241, 251–2 (1942).

[28] See *Bandag, Inc.* v. *Gerrard Tire Co*, 704 F 2d 1578, 1581 (Fed. Cir. 1983) (It is "settled in the case law that the notice requirement of the statute does not apply where the patent is directed to a process or method").

[29] See R.H. Stern, "Tales from the Algorithm War: *Benson* to *Iwahashi*, It's Déjà Vu All Over Again" (1991) 18 *Am Intell Prop L Ass'n Q J* 371, 378.

[30] See *Markman, Inc.* v. *Westview Instruments*, 517 US 370, 378–9 (1996).

augment their patent instruments with additional claims drawn to broader technical effects. Among the first efforts to result in litigation was made by Nathaniel J. Wyeth, inventor of a machine for cutting ice into uniformly sized blocks. Wyeth's patent claimed the machine as well as the method of cutting ice into blocks of a uniform size. Justice Story held the technique claim void, declaring that "[a] claim broader than the actual invention of the patentee is, for that very reason, upon the principles of the common law, utterly void, and the patent is a nullity".[31]

The function of a machine doctrine emerged from this early sense of claim breadth. As the system of claiming became increasingly refined in the US patent system, the courts were generally hostile to attempts at claiming a technology both as artefact and technique. The US Supreme Court concluded in *Corning* v. *Burden* that "it is well settled that a man cannot have a patent for the function or abstract effect of a machine, but only for the machine that produces it".[32] The Court offered the following illustration to point to the difference between artefact and technique:[33]

> As, for instance, A has discovered that by exposing India rubber to a certain degree of heat, in mixture or connection with certain metallic salts, he can produce a valuable product or manufacture; he is entitled to a patent for his discovery, as a process or improvement in the art, irrespective of any machine or mechanical device. B, on the contrary, may invent a new furnace or stove, or steam apparatus, by which this process may be carried on with much saving of labor, and expense of fuel; and he will be entitled to a patent for his machine, as an improvement in the art. Yet A could not have a patent for a machine, or B for a process . . .

Here the Court seemed to rely upon nothing more than its intuition whether a technologist had invented artefact or technique. Yet even a moment's reflection indicates the profound limitations of this positivist statement, so typical of nineteenth century patent decisions. "A" could just as well have drafted a narrower claim directed towards a specific artefact that cures rubber, or "B" presented claims stating the technique by which he built his stove or through which his steam apparatus operated. The Court's bold pronouncement does not explain why these alternative descriptive formats are improper, or capture the realisation that invention itself is activity that can be expressed as technique. Varying results in subsequent cases betrayed this lack of analytical rigour: although the Court on occasion upheld patents directed towards mechanical processes,[34] its 1894 decision in *Risdon Locomotive Works* v. *Medart*[35] vigorously reaffirmed the function of a machine doctrine *en route* to striking down a patented method of making belt pulleys.

---

[31] *Wyeth* v. *Stone*, Fed Cases No. 18, 107 (CC Mass. 1840).
[32] 56 US (15 How) 252 (1853).
[33] *Ibid.*, 268.
[34] See *Tilghman* v. *Proctor*, 102 US 707 (1880); *Cochrane* v. *Deener*, 94 US 780 (1877).
[35] 158 US 68 (1894).

US courts began to demonstrate a more wholesale weariness with the function of a machine doctrine by the mid-twentieth century. The final Supreme Court decision considering this doctrine, *Waxham v. Smith*,[36] confirmed a distinction that arose in lower tribunals between claims drawn to the mere effects and results of a machine and those that described mechanical operations without specified instruments of performance. The former were not patent eligible, but for the latter a technique claim could be obtained. Thus the Court concluded:[37]

> A method, which may be patented irrespective of the particular form of the mechanism which may be availed of for carrying it into operation, is not to be rejected as "functional", merely because the specifications show a machine capable of using it.

In years to come, the battleground for the "function of a machine" doctrine would become a lower court, the Court of Customs and Patent Appeals. In *In re Conover*,[38] the applicant claimed a method of making a roller bearing as well as the roller bearing itself. The Patent Office Board had rejected the claims on the ground of obviousness. Following an appeal to the Court of Customs and Patent Appeals (herein CCPA), predecessor to the Federal Circuit, the applicant obtained a reversal. Regarding the applicant's use of both artefact and technique claims, Judge Smith briefly stated:[39]

> [I]t is our conclusion that the invention for which a patent is sought here is one of those inventions where it is doubtful whether the invention resides in the process or the structure and which may be claimed with equal facility in terms either of method or structure. Since both types of claims are recognised by the statute, . . . it is our opinion that both types of claims may properly be allowed to issue in a single patent where, as here, they are but alternative expressions for defining a single invention.

Judge Smith seemed to have underestimated the number of circumstances in which a technology may be claimed in either format. As demonstrated previously, conversion from one sort of claim to another is a straightforward matter indeed. Judge Smith also provided little guidance on how to determine whether a particular invention "resides" in the category of artefact or technique.

A need for guidance would soon be unnecessary in light of the CCPA's subsequent decision in *In re Tarczy-Hornoch*.[40] There, the applicant appealed an adverse opinion from the Patent Office Board of Appeals. The Board had affirmed the examiner's rejection of certain claims of an application directed towards a "Pulse Sorting Apparatus and Method". While the examiner had allowed the applicant's apparatus claims, those claims directed towards a method of using were rejected for merely defining the function of the apparatus.

---

[36] 294 US 20 (1934).
[37] *Ibid.*, 22.
[38] 304 F 2d 680 (CCPA 1962).
[39] *Ibid.*, 684–5.
[40] 397 F 2d 856 (CCPA 1968).

On appeal, the CCPA reversed in a three to two opinion. Judge Rich authored a magisterial majority opinion that flatly overruled earlier CCPA decisions relying upon the function of a machine doctrine. Judge Rich seemed unconcerned that several Supreme Court opinions, including *Corning* and *Risdon*, had uniformly been read to establish this doctrine. According to his Honour's opinion, which traced the function of a machine doctrine from its earliest underpinnings, these decisions were not directed to process claims *per se* but instead to claim breadth.[41] Judge Rich also found the doctrine unsupportable on policy grounds, concluding that:[42]

> The essential difficulty is in the fact that, although at the time of the application only one apparatus may be known which is capable of carrying out the process, others may become available later. In which case, of course, the inventor is cheated out of his invention. It is peculiarly our responsibility to see that the decisional law does not require this kind of inequity.

Two of the five members of the CCPA dissented. According to Judges Kirkpatrick and Worley, whether the "function of an apparatus" curtailed the rights of inventors to a substantial extent was an open question. In light of this perceived uncertainty, the dissenters reasoned that the rule of *stare decisis* counselled against overturning "a well established and accepted rule of nearly seventy years' standing".[43]

Despite the closeness of the vote in the case and the significant body of precedent reciting the "function of a machine" mantra, scant controversy surrounded *Tarczy-Hornoch*. The Patent Office and other courts readily accepted its holding.[44] Judge Rich's approval of the conversion of machine claims into processes nonetheless marks a point of departure in the patent law. Fuelled by *Tarczy-Hornoch*, the patent system has increasingly embraced inventions of greater abstraction.[45] Psychological techniques,[46] sports methods,[47] commercial strategies[48] and other inventions that many would judge not to be fundamentally technological in character are now within the ambit of the United States patent regime. The controversy between technique and artefact would soon begin to run in other venues, however, especially those of chemistry and biotechnology.

[41] *Ibid.*, 867.

[42] *Ibid.*, 868.

[43] *Ibid.*, 868–70.

[44] See *Federal Sign and Signal Corp* v. *Bangor Punta Operations, Inc.*, 357 F Supp. 1222, 1234 (SDNY 1973); United States Patent and Trademark Office, *Manual of Patent Examining Procedure*, § 2173.05(v) (1996) (reciting rule of *Tarczy-Hornoch*).

[45] A point recognised by Justice Stevens and discussed in his dissenting opinion in *Diamond* v. *Diehr*, 450 US 175, 198 (1981). See also M.J. Adelman, *Cases and Materials on Patent Law* (St Paul, Minn., West Publishing Co, 1998), 104–5.

[46] See United States Patent No 5,190,458, granted on 2 March 1993 to Valma R. Driesner (directed towards a "Character Assessment Method").

[47] See United States Patent No 5,616,089, granted on 1 April 1997 to Dale D. Miller (directed towards a "Method of Putting").

[48] See United States Patent No 5,668,736, granted on 16 September 1997 to Edwin S. Douglas and Daryl V. Turner (directed towards a "Method for Designing and Illustrating Architectural Enhancements to Existing Buildings").

B Product and Process in Chemistry and Biotechnology

Method claims have also raised perplexing issues with regard to chemistry and biotechnology. It is often the case that skilled artisans would have been readily able to generate a new chemical compound or biotechnological product, using well-known, conventional processes, once they learn the precise composition of the end product. However, they would have lacked motivation to perform this process without knowledge of the special properties of the new product. In terms of the patent law, the question then becomes whether claims directed towards such a method of making would have been obvious. In one sense, since the method is being used to produce a novel and non-obvious product, the method too must be novel and non-obvious. But, on the other hand, if the process is used in a conventional way to generate a product, perhaps we should view the process as novel but not necessarily non-obvious. In appropriate cases, the same reasoning applies not just to end products, but also to starting materials.

A simple analogy may focus attention on the nub of this problem.[49] Consider a team of botanists which jointly invents a new sort of fruit hybrid, such as a fanciful "kiwiberry". They file an application at the PTO claiming the kiwiberry and a method of making a kiwiberry pie. Plainly the applicants' kiwiberry pie recipe is novel. Indeed, it could not have possibly existed prior to the invention of the kiwiberry. But should the mere substitution of a new filling entitle the botanists to a patent on a method of making a fruit pie? The rejection of the botanists' method claims on the ground of non-obviousness amounts to the policy judgement that they should not.

The Federal Circuit addressed these issues in *In re Durden*.[50] There, the applicants had filed applications claiming oxime compounds, insecticidal carbamate compounds, and a process for producing the carbamate compounds using the oxime compounds as starting materials. Patents had issued on the oxime and carbamate compounds, but the PTO had rejected the process claims over a prior art patent.

On appeal, the applicants conceded that "the claimed process, apart from the fact of employing a novel and unobvious starting material and apart from the fact of producing a new and unobvious product, is obvious". The Federal Circuit stated the issue to be resolved as "whether a chemical process, otherwise obvious, is patentable *because* either or both the specific starting material employed and the product obtained, are novel and unobvious". The Court affirmed the rejection, concluding that:

> Of course, an otherwise old process becomes a *new* process when a previously
> unknown starting material, for example, is used in it which is then subjected to a con-

---

[49] This example follows from Merges, n.22 above, 606.
[50] 763 F 2d 1406 (Fed. Cir. 1985).

ventional manipulation or reaction to produce a product which may also be *new*, albeit the *expected* result of what is done. But it does not necessarily mean that the whole process has become *unobvious* in the sense of § 103. In short, a *new* process may still be obvious, even when considered "as a whole," notwithstanding the specific starting material or resulting product, or both, is not to be found in the prior art.

Durden proved a burdensome precedent for actors in the recombinant biotechnology industry. Broadly speaking, recombinant technologies involve the alteration of a host cell so that it produces a desirable protein. The resulting products, including erythropoietin, interferon, and tissue plasminogen activator (tPA), are identical or similar to naturally occurring products. As such, the valuable protein product is often not patent eligible in and of itself. Biotechnologists do claim the transformed host cells as a sort of "machine" capable of producing a desirable protein. They also seek to claim the method of making the end product. Biotechnologists discovered significant opposition to such method claims within the PTO, however. Based upon *Durden*, many examiners rejected such claims because the process of obtaining desirable protein products from transformed host cells is ordinarily well understood by skilled artisans. This set of skills applies even to host cells that are themselves patentable starting materials.

Congress responded by enacting the Biotechnological Process Patents Act 1995.[51] This legislation created section 103(b), a complex statute that applicants may elect to employ. Section 103(b) provides that a "biotechnological process" that uses or results in a novel, non-obvious composition of matter will be considered non-obvious if (i) the inventor files an application or applications claiming the process and the composition of matter at the same time; and (ii) the process and composition of matter were owned by the same person at the time they were invented. The term "biotechnological process" is elaborately defined to tie the statute to contemporary biotechnology research, including such processes as "cell fusion procedures yielding a cell line that expresses a specific protein, such as a monoclonal antibody".

The Federal Circuit opinion in *In re Ochiai*,[52] issued just a few weeks after Congress enacted section 103(b), suggests that this legislative effort may have been unnecessary. Claim 6 of Ochiai's application recited a process for preparing a cephem compound. Although the cephem compound generated by this process was novel and non-obvious, the PTO reasoned that the process recited in claim 6 would have been obvious. Several prior art references taught the use of an extremely similar process to create a slightly different final product from that claimed by Ochiai. The PTO concluded that the holding of *Durden* mandated the rejection of claim 6.

On appeal, the Federal Circuit reversed the PTO rejection. The Court reasoned that the claimed starting material was unknown to skilled artisans prior to the filing of Ochiai's application. The Court then concluded that although the

---

[51] Pub L 104–41, 109 Stat 351.
[52] 71 F 3d 1565 (Fed. Cir. 1995).

claimed method was extremely similar to teachings of the prior art, the prior art nonetheless offered no suggestion or motivation to perform the claimed process. According to the *Ochiai* panel, "[s]imilarity is . . . not necessarily obviousness". The Court distinguished *Durden*, stating that that case presented no more than an application of the general rule "that section 103 requires a fact-intensive comparison of the claimed process with the prior art rather than the mechanical application of another *per se* rule". Because non-obviousness cases involve complex factual issues and "applications of a unitary legal regime to different claims and fields of art to yield particularised results", reasonable persons could well disagree about the outcome of a particular non-obviousness determination.

The PTO Commissioner responded to *Ochiai* with a Notice that resembled a sigh of relief. Recognising the holding of *Ochiai*, the Commissioner discouraged use of section 103(b) and additionally announced that the Patent Office would not issue regulations to implement that statute. Instead, applicants wishing to employ the statute were invited to petition the Commissioner. The Notice further instructed examiners that "language in a process claim which recites making or using a unobvious product must be treated as a material limitation".

Although difficult to reconcile with *Durden*, *Ochiai* has been favourably received by most commentators. Nonetheless, its consistency with the Congressional intent underlying section 103(b) may be questioned. Congress enacted section 103(b) as a narrow provision that solved a specific problem for a single industry. More broadly worded proposals that would have applied to all technologies had been considered and rejected. For example, because *Ochiai*'s application involved a chemical technology, it would not be considered a "biotechnological process" under the statute ultimately enacted. Plainly, *Ochiai*'s holding considerably opens up what Congress had crafted as a narrow exception to the prevailing case law.

C *Beauregard* Claims

An even more recent manifestation of these trends has led to the drafting of encoded software instruction as artefact. No longer content with claims directed towards software methods for completing a certain task, drafters are additionally fashioning claims directed towards a computer-usable storage medium, such as a floppy disk, hard disk or CD-ROM, on which software instructions have been recorded. Such a claim might recite:[53]

16. A noise-tolerant address transmission system for a digital telecommunications network, stored on a floppy diskette having a programmed surface, the diskette comprising:

---

[53] See United States Patent No 5,437,023, issued on 25 July 1995 to Laurence Sheets and Guy Cerulli (directed towards a "Noise-tolerant Address Transmission System for Digital Telecommunication Network").

a first plurality of magnetic media formed within a first portion of said programmed surface which are spatially configured to provide a first set of binary values for detecting a maintenance code; and

a second plurality of magnetic media formed within a second portion of said programmed surface which are spatially configured to provide a second set of binary values for introducing a responsive communication signal into a stream of encoded data.

The only formal treatment of claims of this sort in the United States, *In re Beauregard*,[54] comprises an unpublished decision from the Patent Office Board of Appeals. There, the Patent Office initially rejected this sort of claim on the basis of venerable "printed matter" cases. Those decisions had found unpatentable "claims defining as the invention certain novel arrangements of printed lines or characters, useful and intelligible only to the human mind".[55] The Patent Office Board had previously reasoned that the printed matter rule acted to preserve statutory limits on patentable subject matter. According to the Board, "when the real substance of the contribution by its originator clearly is unpatentable in its own right", the printed matter rule cut off attempts to obtain a patent "by indirection".[56]

Beauregard quickly filed an appeal, cognizant that the printed matter rule had not fared well at the Federal Circuit. Commencing with one of its earliest decisions, the Federal Circuit had referred to the printed matter rule as one of "questionable legal and logical footing".[57] A later opinion, *In re Lowry*,[58] had denied the rule's applicability to a computer memory storage system. The Court there held that the claimed computer "memory for storing data" did not recite merely the information content of the memory, but instead "specific electronic structural elements which impart a physical organisation on the information stored in memory".[59]

The Federal Circuit never heard oral argument in *In re Beauregard*. The position of the Solicitor of the Patent Office changed hands during the pendency of Beauregard's appeal, with the new incumbent quickly filing a motion to dismiss. According to the Solicitor, the Patent Office now accepted "that computer programs embodied in a tangible medium, such as floppy diskettes, are patentable subject matter . . .".[60] The Federal Circuit granted the motion, vacating the Board's opinion and remanding the case to the Patent Office for further consideration on other requisites of patentability.

---

[54] 53 F 3d 1583, 1383 (Fed. Cir. 1995).
[55] *In re Bernhart*, 417 F 2d 1395, 1399 (CCPA 1969). See also *In re Jones*, 373 F 2d 1007 (CCPA 1967); Note, "The Patentability of Printed Matter: Critique and Proposal" (1950) 18 *Geo Wash Univ L Rev* 475.
[56] *In re Bernhart*, n. 55 above, 1398 (CCPA 1969) (quoting unpublished opinion of the Board).
[57] *In re Gulack*, 703 F 2d 1381, 1385 n. 8 (Fed. Cir. 1983).
[58] 32 F 3d 1579 (Fed. Cir. 1994).
[59] *Ibid.*, 1583.
[60] *Ibid.*, 1584.

Although the Federal Circuit's dismissal of Beauregard's appeal hardly amounts to judicial imprimatur, an increasing number of US patents are employing this format. Both the European and Japanese Patent Offices have also approved of this claim format. Regrettably, subsequent discussion of the propriety of *Beauregard*-style claims has largely been confined to whether such claims comprise printed matter or not. Seen in combination with *Ochiai* and *Tarczy-Hornoch*, however, *Beauregard* holds far more dramatic consequences for the patent system than can be expressed by the bankrupt printed matter rule. It instead suggests potent possibilities for claims drafters under prevailing notions of claim format, and as well a significant reinterpretation of core notions of the United States patent regime. This chapter turns to this effort next, articulating potential uses and abuses of claim formatting within the patent law.

D   Drafting Around the Infringement Statute

The insight that *Tarczy-Harnoch*, *Ochiai* and *Beauregard* each concerns the boundary between object and action allows the exploration of a tension within the patent law. The system of patents is one that is fundamentally concerned with the abstraction of technology into text.[61] Yet this process of mapping is hardly an orderly one. Instead, it presents numerous ambiguities that obscure the determination of whether a drafter's chosen claim format is appropriate or not. The next portions of this chapter explore more fully the consequences of the favourable reception of their efforts by the courts and the PTO. In so doing, it presents something of a primer on how to avoid substantive patent law rules through skilful claim drafting.

(i)   Drafting into Direct Infringement

One of the significant limitations surrounding technique claims is that they are infringed only through performance. A key US decision tracking this distinction is *Joy Technologies, Inc.* v. *Flakt, Inc.*[62] The litigants both designed and built flue gas desulphurisation technology. The patentee, Joy Technologies, Inc., successfully enforced United States Patent No 4,279,873 against Flakt, Inc. Each of the '873 patent claims was directed towards a recursive technique for desulphurising fly ash-containing flue gas that resulted from coal combustion. For example, claim 1 of the '873 patent included the steps of "collecting a fly ash-containing dry powder" and "atomising an aqueous feed suspension comprising $Ca(OH)2$ and fly ash".

The District Court faced a difficult task when framing the remedies owed to Joy. The Court recognised that power plant construction often consumed five

---

[61] See P. Drahos, *A Philosophy of Intellectual Property* (Brookfield, Vt., Dartmouth, 1996), 145–64.

[62] 6 F 3d 770 (Fed. Cir. 1993).

or more years. If Joy were unable to obtain an injunction preventing Flakt from constructing devices that performed the patented process, then it could essentially deduct the lengthy construction time from the term of the '873 patent. In contrast, Flakt, recognising the narrower scope accorded to technique claims, argued that its equipment sales did not comprise an infringement so long as the equipment was not operated. The Court ultimately sided with Joy, enjoining Flakt from entering into any contracts during the term of the '873 patent for sales of devices designed to carry out the patented process.

On appeal, the Federal Circuit vacated the injunction and remanded the matter of the injunction to the District Court for reconsideration. The Court expressly recognised that the "law is unequivocal that the sale of equipment to perform a process is not a sale of the process within the meaning of section 271(a)".[63] Not only did Flakt not directly infringe Joy's technique claims, the Court reasoned, but Flakt's equipment sales neither induced infringement nor constituted contributory infringement. According to the Court, if the equipment sold by Flakt was not employed by the purchaser, then no direct infringement occurred at all, and therefore no form of indirect infringement was possible.

Joy Technologies reads as a solemn and well-reasoned opinion. Nonetheless, it appears to be entirely irrelevant, at least to informed claims drafters. *Joy Technologies* is merely a case about the recitation of a few formalisms within the language of patent claims.

To see why this is so, consider the absence of artefact claims in the '873 patent. The Federal Circuit offered no explanation for the lapse, but two possibilities present themselves. The first, and most likely, possibility is that Joy would have been able to obtain apparatus claims in view of the prior art and the holding of *Tarczy-Hornoch*, but did not. Given the patentability of the Joy process, the possibility that a device capable of carrying out the process was already used in some other context, such as to remove pollutants from automobile emissions, is quite unlikely. In that case, Joy was essentially punished for failing to recite the word "machine" rather than "process" in its claim preamble, and to place the words "means for" in front of each of its claimed steps.

The second possibility is that the prior art actually would have prevented Joy from obtaining apparatus claims. Even in that case, the reasoning of *Ochiai* allows even minimally competent drafters to place a sort of "method of making" claim within Joy's '873 patent. Such claim would recite "*a process for building machinery to be used* in a process for desulphurising fly ash-containing flue gas" and include such steps as "*building machinery capable of* collecting a fly ash-containing dry powder" and "*building machinery capable of* atomising an aqueous feed suspension comprising Ca(OH)2 and fly ash". The mere addition of the italicised language to the actual '873 patent claim language precisely describes the competitive behaviour with which Joy was concerned. Flakt could have been

---

[63] *Ibid.*, 773.

prevented from manufacturing machines that would carry out the patented process even though no artefact claim appeared in the '873 patent.

Although this style of claim is not a common one, *Ochiai* may be read to confirm its propriety. The proposed method of making a claim that would have proved useful to Joy is analogous to the acylation reaction that, despite its conventionality, was upheld in *Ochiai*. Undoubtedly skilled chemical engineers and machinists would be readily able to manufacture devices capable of performing Joy's patentable process once they knew of it. But, via *Ochiai*, such knowledge may not be on the table when the non-obviousness determination is made. Competent artisans would possess no motivation to build a device to perform an unknown process, and even the presence of similar devices within the prior art does not change this result.

(ii) *Drafting Around* Deepsouth

The US Supreme Court's controversial opinion in *Deepsouth Packing Co* v. *Laitram Corp*[64] formed the impetus for another paragraph of the infringement statute. Deepsouth was the proprietor of a patent claiming a "shrimp de-veining machine" that consisted of knives spaced above an inclined trough along with a water supply. Its competitor, Laitram, assembled the parts necessary to construct the patented machine, but did not finally assemble them in the United States. Laitram instead shipped the parts to a Brazilian customer which could quickly assemble them to form a functioning device. The Louisiana District Court had refused to enjoin this activity, reasoning that Deepsouth's patent protected only the combination of the claimed parts.[65] The Court of Appeals for the Fifth Circuit reversed after finding the lower court's reasoning "an artificial, technical construction" that did not further the constitutional mandate of promoting the useful arts.[66]

Following its grant of certiorari,[67] the Supreme Court again reversed. According to the Court, the precedent was clear that a combination patent protected only against the operable assembly of the whole, not the sum of its parts. The Court reasoned that to hold otherwise would mark a significant expansion of the scope of a patent. The Court closed by suggesting that Congress send a "clear and certain" signal to supplement those acts that would infringe artefact claims.

Congress responded by enacting section 271(f). That statute in essence declares that the supply of uncombined components comprising a substantial portion of a patented invention constitutes a patent infringement. The components of the patented invention need not be combined within the United States under section 271(f), but the statute does require that defendants possessed the

---

[64] 406 US 518 (1972).
[65] 310 F Supp. 926, 929 (ED La. 1970).
[66] 443 F 2d 936, 938 (5th Cir. 1971).
[67] 404 US 1037 (1972).

intent to infringe. The Senate Committee Report remarked that section 271(f) would "prevent copiers from avoiding U.S. patents by shipping overseas the components of a *product* patented in this country so that the assembly of the components will be completed abroad",[68] suggesting that section 271(f) applies only to artefact claims.

Throughout this episode, both Court and Congress spoke reverently of constitutional mandates, basic tenets of the patent system and "this Nation's historical antipathy to monopoly".[69] Properly seen, however, *Deepsouth* presented simply another case of poor claim drafting. Deepsouth could have drafted a so-called "kit" claim of the type approved by the Court of Customs and Patent Appeals in *In re Venezia*.[70] There, the applicant offered the following claim:[71]

> A splice connector kit having component parts *capable of being assembled* in the field . . ., the kit comprising the combination of:
>   a pair of sleeves of elastomeric material, each sleeve of said pair *adapted to be fitted* over the insulating jacket of one of said cables . . .;
>   electrical contact means *adapted to be affixed* to the terminus of each exposed contact . . .;
>   a pair of retaining members *adapted to be positioned* respectively between each of said sleeves . . .; and
>   a housing, . . . *whereby said housing may be slidably positioned* over one of said cables . . .

The PTO had rejected the claim based upon two grounds. First, the PTO held that the claim language was indefinite[72] because "the elements are recited without present co-operation. The language is futuristic and conditional in character . . .".[73] The PTO additionally held that the claimed kit did not qualify as an "article of manufacture" within the terms of the Patent Act because a "kit" comprised a plurality of separate manufactures, rather than a single manufacture.

On appeal to the Court of Customs and Patent Appeals, the Court overturned the PTO on both grounds. According to Judge Lane, the claim language was not "a mere direction of actions to take in the future" but a structural limitation upon the claim elements. Further, a skilled artisan would possess no difficulty in determining whether a collection of interrelated parts would infringe. Regarding patent eligibility, the Court concluded:

> To hold that the words "any manufacture" exclude from their meaning groups or "kits" of interrelated parts would have the practical effect of not only excluding from patent protection those "kit" inventions which are capable of being claimed as a final assembly (e.g., a splice connector), but also many inventions such as building blocks, construction sets, games, etc. which are incapable of being claimed as a final assembly.

[68] S Rep No 98–663 (1984), 6 (emphasis added).
[69] 406 US 518, 530 (1972).
[70] 530 F 2d 956 (CCPA 1976).
[71] *Ibid.*, 957.
[72] Under 35 USC § 112 (1994) ¶ 2.
[73] 530 F 2d 956, 958 (CCPA 1976).

Although the Court of Customs and Patent Appeals plainly could have allowed kit claims only in the latter instance, its sweeping ruling provides a useful tool for claim drafters. Following *Venezia*, for example, Deepsouth simply could have drafted a claim towards "a shrimp-deveining kit having component parts capable of being assembled". Curiously, although *Deepsouth* was decided less than four years prior to *Venezia*, and within in an era where the Supreme Court only infrequently turned to patent cases, the Court of Customs and Patent Appeals made no mention of *Deepsouth* in its opinion.

A *Venezia*-style claim is not the only mechanism for avoiding *Deepsouth*. Perhaps, after *Ochiai*, one could also draft an additional claim directed towards "*a method of gathering components in order to construct* the shrimp de-veining machine of claim 1". The advantage of such a claim is that it does not require connection of the claimed parts.

(iii) Drafting Around the Indirect Infringement Statutes

The current environment of claim drafting provides even more possibilities for skirting the indirect infringement statutes, section 271(b) and (c).[74] Contemporary case law has empowered claims drafters with the ability to recite those technologies directly practised or sold by their competitors. The need for patentees to resort to section 271(b) and (c) thus becomes more limited. Given the stricter requirements associated with indirect infringement as compared to direct infringement, this trend marks a significant augmentation of the rights of patentees.

This realisation appears to be among the chief motivations of Beauregard in drafting patent claims directed towards a storage device encoded with software instructions.[75] Earlier inventors of software technologies usually wrote patent claims solely in the form of technique. Among the consequences of this drafting choice was that retailers or other actors that sold encoded disks were essentially immune to charges of infringement. Such individuals did not perform the patented methods themselves, at least in commercially significant ways, so they did not commit direct infringement. The majority of downstream actors were also oblivious to patent rights associated with various software products and therefore lacked the requisite intent associated with indirect infringement. Only at such time as they were informed of the patentee's rights could a charge of indirect infringement hold.

Even if intent could be proven, proprietors of software patents claiming techniques would be required to tie the contributory or induced infringement to the directly infringing acts—in this case, the practice of the method claims by

---

[74] S. 271(b) mandates that "[w]hoever actively induces infringement of a patent shall be liable as an infringer". S. 271(c) makes an infringer of one who sells a component of a patented invention "knowing the same to be especially made . . . for use in an infringement . . . and not a staple article . . . of commerce".

[75] See E.P. Heller, III, "Letter to the Editor" (1996) 78 *J Pat & Trademark Off Soc'y* 188.

individual customers. Not only might the extent of customer use prove burdensome to demonstrate in court, patentees are typically reluctant to sue or seek discovery from their own potential customers.

The augmentation of software patent with artefact claims allows patentees to avoid such difficulties. Inventors such as Beauregard have instead claimed precisely the things that all actors in the stream of commerce ultimately make, use or sell: encoded diskettes, compacts disks and other media. Such claims therefore present far more than a procedural quibble. They significantly enhance the scope of the patentee's rights, streamlining the cause of action for infringement while simultaneously expanding the set of potential defendants.

(iv) Other Infringement Doctrines

The ability of patentees to obtain freely both artefact and technique claims carries with it still further consequences in terms of patent infringement law. A review of additional infringement principles reveals at least one patent-limiting rule that claims drafters can readily circumvent and one patent-strengthening rule that nearly any patentee can invoke through skilful drafting.

The exhaustion, or "first sale", doctrine is one that now can be readily avoided through well-drafted claims. Patent applicants need merely to include technique claims involving the manufacture or use of an artefact that has been directly claimed elsewhere. Then the patentee could avoid altogether the usual principle that artefact claims are exhausted through the sale of artefacts. Its process claims will survive numerous transactions regarding the patented good, allowing the force of the patent to intrude deeply into the stream of commerce. Given that the exhaustion doctrine ordinarily places significant limitations upon the market power of a particular patent, this trivial drafting exercise appears exceptionally worthwhile for patent applicants.

In contrast, the presumption afforded to patentees by section 295 of the US patent statute appears readily appropriated into every patentee's bundle of rights. Like section 68A of the New Zealand patent statute, section 295 allows holders of process patents to shift the burden of proof of infringement upon the accused infringer. Again, one need only draft claims directed towards the technique of making an artefact that is itself claimed elsewhere. This strategy allows the patentee to invoke the altered presumption of section 295, essentially placing the burden upon defendants not to practise the claimed technique.

E Drafting Around the Marking Statute

Patent marking doctrine, too, places considerable weight upon whether the infringed claim is artefact or technique.[76] The marking requirement arises out

---

[76] See J.M. Markarian, "Can the Marking Requirements for a Patented Article Be Circumvented By Obtaining A Process Patent?" (1997) 79 *J Pat & Trademark Off Soc'y* 365; J. Voelzke, "Patent

of section 287(a) of the US Patent Act, which limits the recoverable damages of patentees that make or sell "any patented article" without labeling the article or its package with the appropriate patent number. Patentees that fail to do so cannot recover damages until they actually notify the accused infringer.[77] The marking statute serves "to give patentees the proper incentive to mark the products and thus place the world on notice of existence of the patent".[78]

The apparent difficulty of marking the incorporeal has not failed to impress US courts. The Supreme Court held in *Wine Railway Appliance Co* v. *Enterprise Railway Equipment Co* that:[79]

> The idea of a tangible article proclaiming its own character runs through this and related provisions. Two kinds of notice are specified—one to the public by a visible mark, another by actual advice to the infringer. The second becomes necessary only when the first has not been given; and the first can only be given in connection with some fabricated article.

This language implies only that the patentee sell a "tangible article", not necessarily that the patentee has claimed one. Nonetheless, the Federal Circuit declared early in its history that it is "settled in the case law that the notice requirement of this statute does not apply where the patent is directed to a process or method".[80] This law seems quite similar to that of section 68(1) of the New Zealand patent statute, which on its faces applies only to "articles".

Perhaps cognisant of the restrictiveness of its early reading, the Federal Circuit refined this principle in its subsequent case law. *American Medical Sys., Inc.* v. *Medical Eng'g Corp.*[81] involved a patent with claims directed towards both a medical prosthesis and a method of packaging it in a sterile state. The Court provided that where a particular patent instrument contains both apparatus and method claims, "to the extent that there is a tangible item to mark by which notice of the asserted method claims can be given", that a party must mark in order to take advantage of the constructive notice provision of section 287.

In yet another decision, however, the Federal Circuit seemingly provided clever claim drafters with the tools to write their way around even this refinement. In *Hanson* v. *Alpine Valley Ski Area, Inc.*,[82] the asserted patent covered a method and apparatus for making artificial snow. The infringer, Alpine, sought to avoid an assessment of damages because Hanson's licensee had not marked its patented snow-making machines. The Federal Circuit opted not to apply

---

Marking Under 35 U.S.C. § 287(a): Products, Processes, and the Deception of the Public" (1995) 5 *Fed Circuit B J* 317.

[77] 35 USC § 287 (1994).

[78] *American Med. Sys., Inc.* v. *Medical Eng'g Corp.*, 6 F 3d 1523, 1538 (Fed. Cir. 1993) (quoting *Laitram Corp.* v. *Hewlett-Packard Co*, 806 F Supp. 1294, 1296 (ED La. 1992)).

[79] 297 US 387, 395 (1936).

[80] *Bandag, Inc.* v. *Gerrard Tire Co*, 704 F 2d 1578, 1581 (Fed. Cir. 1983) (quoted in *Hanson* v. *Alpine Valley Ski Area, Inc*, 718 F 2d 1075, 1083 (Fed. Cir. 1983)).

[81] 6 F 3d 1523 (Fed. Cir. 1993), cert. denied, 511 US 1070 (1994).

[82] 718 F 2d 1075 (Fed. Cir. 1983).

section 287, reasoning only that "[t]he only claims that were found infringed in this case [were] drawn to '[t]he method of forming, distributing and depositing snow upon a surface . . .'".[83] Because only technique claims had been found to have been infringed, the Court reasoned that the marking requirement did not apply even though Hanson's patent included parallel artefact claims.

Reconciliation of *Hanson*, which presents a sort of well-pleaded complaint rule, with *American Medical*, which concentrates on the need to supply notice whenever a tangible item presents the opportunity, appears difficult.[84] *Hanson* and *Wine Railway* remain in the reporters, however, and, as they predate *American Medical*, are presumptively the controlling precedent on this matter.[85] In combination with *Tarczy-Hornoch* and *Ochiai*, these decisions present claim drafters with potent mechanisms for drafting around the marking statute. Simply put, few wise technologists need mark their products in order to maximise an award of damages under section 287. Instead, they are well-advised to draft additional method claims and to segregate them into distinct patent instruments, or, at the least, to assert only method claims during enforcement litigation.

F Drafting into Patent Eligibility

Statutory restrictions upon the subject matter suitable for patenting have also been manipulated by the claims drafter. As in *Pharmac*, technologists the world over have proven adroit in partially surmounting bans against patents directed towards methods of medical treatment.[86] In contrast, American claims drafters have principally directed their efforts towards computer-related inventions. Over the past two decades, they have successfully overcome PTO resistance to such claims in what is best described as a war of attrition. Full appreciation of the latest skirmish, in which the PTO acquiesced to Beauregard's encoded instruction claims, suggests that the greatest spoils of victory for potential patentees may yet lie ahead.

Beauregard's encoded software claims again call upon the caretakers of the patent system to determine the limits of patentable subject matter. The patent law traditionally concerned itself with industrial technologies; innovations in the ordering and representation of information were left to the realm of

---

[83] *Ibid.*, 1083.

[84] The Federal Circuit's loose handling of the marking statute also seems puzzling in light of its much stricter interpretation of notice, a damages requisite that occurs when the patentee is found not to have marked in accordance with the statute: see *Amsted Industries Inc* v. *Buckeye Steel Castings Co*, 24 F 3d 178 (Fed. Cir. 1994).

[85] See *Atlantic Thermoplastics Co* v. *Faytex Corp.*, 974 F 2d 1279, 1281 (Fed. Cir. 1992) ("no [Federal Circuit] precedent can be disregarded or overruled save by an *in banc* court") (Rich J dissenting from the denial of rehearing *in banc*).

[86] See *John Wyeth & Brother Ltd's Application* [1985] RPC 545 (English Patent Court).

copyright.[87] Manifestations of this principle included the printed matter doctrine as well as a rule disallowing patents on "mental steps",[88] the latter leading to decisions banning patents concerning mathematical algorithms. The Supreme Court judged such inventions to represent "abstract intellectual concepts" that comprised the "basic tools of scientific and technological work".[89]

Computer technology tremendously strained these historical distinctions. Software programs appear as text, yet when appropriately processed by a computer come to represent functional steps.[90] Further, artisans commonly describe even the electronic signals and components that comprise computer hardware through mathematical terminology. One can appreciate that the processing of electrocardiographic signals requires operations that may be expressed in terms of mathematical functions, but represent the tangible manipulation of electrical signals that regulate the function of the human heart.[91]

Not only do perplexing conceptual issues attend computer-related inventions, but they bring with them complex issues for claims drafters. Within this discipline, engineers may accomplish identical technical behaviours through differently phrased software texts[92] and a wide variety of hardware arrangements.[93] Specific structural claiming is of extremely limited utility within the computer-related arts. Yet broad functional claiming only makes the technology appear more abstract and contributes to the sense that such inventions lie without the patent system.

Claims drafters responded to these competing pressures by reciting apparatus, but at its broadest conceptual level. The ordinary mechanism for achieving this goal was the phrase "means for", followed by the specific function to be performed. Thus, instead of drafting the abstract step of multiplying two numbers, or the overly specific combination of capacitors, transistors and other elements that comprise a multiplier circuit, the drafter would simply recite "means for multiplying". Professor Richard Stern has aptly termed such a claim element as "nominal hardware" out of the recognition that the presence of the hardware limitation in the claim does not, as a practical matter, limit the scope of the claim any more than if it were omitted.[94]

The PTO identified this claim drafting technique and initially rejected such claims as identifying non-statutory subject matter. Often examiners would reason that these claims actually described an abstract technique, yet recited

---

[87] See P. Samuelson *et al.*, "A Manifesto Concerning the Legal Protection of Computer Programs" (1994) 94 *Colum L Rev* 2308, 2344.

[88] See *Hallibuton Oil Well Cementing Co* v. *Walker*, 146 F 2d 817 (9th Cir. 1944), rev'd on other grounds, 326 US 705 (1945).

[89] *Gottschalk* v. *Benson*, 409 US 63 (1972).

[90] See Samuelson *et al.*, n. 87 above, 2315–6.

[91] See *Arrhythmia Research Technology, Inc.* v. *Corazonix Corp.*, 958 F 2d 1053 (Fed. Cir. 1992).

[92] Samuelson *et al.*, n. 87 above, 2317.

[93] Stern, n. 29 above, 382–4.

[94] *Ibid.*, 382.

hardware only through the guile of the drafter.[95] The Federal Circuit ultimately adopted a far more formalistic approach, however, as indicated by its opinion in *In re Iwahashi*.[96] In that case Iwahashi, who had submitted a patent application entitled "Auto-Correlation Circuit for Use in Pattern Recognition", appealed from the rejection of a single claim on the grounds of ineligible subject matter. Iwahashi's application disclosed a schematic, flow-chart-like diagram of his invention as well as more detailed diagram with specific electronic elements. Iwahashi had drafted his claim almost exclusively in functional terms, however, including such elements as the "means for calculating the sum" of two sample values. One of Iwahashi's claim limitations did facially define structure, however: "a read only memory associated with said means for calculating". In lay terms, a "read only memory", or ROM, amounts to an information storage device, programmed to respond to given inputs with a predetermined output. Iwahashi's application specified that the ROM would output the square of the number provided to it.

In issuing its rejection, the PTO reasoned that each of the claimed "means" was in fact merely a mathematical step. The recited "means for calculating the sum", for instance, amounted merely to the step of adding two numbers. Further, the sole structural limitation, the ROM, comprised nothing more than a multiplication table on a chip. The PTO concluded that the invention as a whole consisted of a mathematical technique that was not patent eligible.

On appeal, the Federal Circuit reversed the PTO rejection. The Court sharply disagreed that Iwahashi's claims solely recited mathematics. According to Judge Rich, the recited ROM was a "specific piece of apparatus", and the claim as a whole "a combination of interrelated means". The Court dismissed the PTO's conclusion that the claim was in reality a cleverly disguised technique, concluding that the Court's precedent "held some claims statutory and other claims non-statutory, depending entirely on what they said. We have to do the same here."[97]

The *Iwahashi* reasoning was criticised as emphasising claim drafting manipulations over the substance of what had been invented.[98] Nonetheless, *Iwahashi* came to represent the contemporary stance of the PTO and Federal Circuit. Subsequent holdings, in particular the *in banc* decision in *In re Alappat*,[99] have confirmed that so long as the claims drafter formalistically recites some sort of structure, inventors may obtain patents for what many technologists would describe as a mathematical discovery.[100]

The claiming concept presented by the applicant in *In re Beauregard* appears to take the reasoning of *Iwahashi* and *Alappat* one step further. Even the abstract artefacts that were claimed by Iwahashi appear to be of a different

[95] See *In re Alappat*, 33 F 3d 1526, 1540 (Fed. Cir. 1994) (*in banc*).
[96] 888 F 2d 1370 (Fed. Cir. 1989).
[97] *Ibid.*, 1374.
[98] See Stern, n. 29 above.
[99] 33 F 3d 1526 (Fed. Cir. 1994).
[100] *Ibid.*, 1561–2 (Archer CJ dissenting).

flavour from the computer storage device recited by Beauregard. In *Iwahashi*, the claimed means actually performed the recited functions. But Beauregard's storage medium appears merely as a vessel for housing the encoded software.

Acceptance of *Beauregard*-style claims appears to hold significant consequences for the patent system. Chief among them is that the statutory boundaries of the patent law seem greatly expanded. If any encoded disk comprises a patent-eligible article of manufacture, then few principles appear to restrain the eligibility of any recorded information whatsoever. In particular, æsthetic creations traditionally considered to be within the purview of the copyright statute also suddenly appear to lie within the ambit of the patent system as well. If we allow claims directed toward a CD encoded with Word Perfect™ 6.0, for example, there seems scant reason to deny a patent on a CD recording of Peter Ilyich Tchaikovsky's Sixth Symphony.[101]

Recognising this concern, the PTO issued Guidelines for Computer-related Inventions that attempt to distinguish between "functional descriptive material" such as a data structure and "non-functional descriptive media" including music and literary works.[102] The Software Guidelines provide:[103]

> When functional descriptive material is recorded on some computer-readable medium it becomes structurally and functionally interrelated to the medium and will be statutory in most cases. When non-functional descriptive material is recorded on some computer-readable medium, it is not structurally and functionally interrelated to the medium but is merely carried by the medium. Merely claiming non-functional descriptive material stored in a computer-readable medium does not make it statutory. Such a result would exalt form over substance.

This sort of conclusory reasoning hardly inspires confidence that the PTO will be able successfully to distinguish between industrial and æsthetic works. Whether users value the encoded data for use as a word processor or musical composition, no difference exists between the manner in which the media record the information. Indeed, the computer software that audibilises encoded musical compositions could likely play data that were intended to be a spreadsheet program, although the generated sounds may not suit the tastes of many individuals.[104] Stating that one set of data is merely recorded on a medium, while the other bears a functional relationship towards that medium is simply a misstatement of fact.

Further, deciding whether an encoded work is principally æsthetic or functional presents a complex judgement. Many individuals have experienced the

---

[101] The title of the latter work, "The Pathétique," appears as well an appropriate commentary on this possibility.

[102] 61 Fed Reg 7478 (28 February 1996).

[103] *Ibid.*, 7481.

[104] Perhaps some future hacker will succeed in crafting a sort of Nabokov-like pun by generating a software fragment that calculates pi to one thousand places past the decimal point, yet could simultaneously be audibilised as Gustav Mahler's "Symphony of a Thousand". See, e.g., V. Nabokov, *Ada, or Ardor: A Family Chronicle* (London, Weidenfeld & Nicolson, 1969) (referring to a yellow-blue vase; in Russian, "*ya lyublyu vas*" means "I love you").

pleasures that attend the appreciation of an artefact's elegant design, be it a software program, medieval clock or late model automobile. Conversely, issued patents describe how playing music encourages plant growth,[105] induces the interest of customers[106] and discourages shoplifting.[107] The PTO approach takes examiners perilously close to judging the æsthetic merits of the submitted work, an inquiry that the copyright law has declined to enter into.[108] With such a scant basis for distinguishing one sort of encoded data from another, the acceptance of claims towards encoded software suggests a greater place for information products within the patent law, provided the appropriate drafting formalities are observed.

G Consequences of Contemporary Claim Drafting Norms

This review demonstrated that claims drafters have only partially realised the powerful tools they possess to circumvent the legal distinctions between artefact and technique. If unchecked, the newly acquired skills of claims drafters will have a potent impact upon the patent law. Although claims have traditionally been seen as setting forth an inventor's patentable advance, they have now assumed the role of a sort of well-pleaded complaint. The deleterious consequences that flow from this new status of patent claims are worthy of further exploration.

Foremost among the ramifications of these new claim drafting rules is the capability for a dramatic expansion of the market power of a particular patent, a possibility best demonstrated by example. Consider the invention of a patentable shovel. Claims drafters of an earlier era would likely have been content to recite merely the shovel itself. Such a claim would allow the patentee to prohibit others from making, using, offering for sale, selling, or importing into the United States the patented shovel.[109]

Inspired by such decisions as *Tarczy-Harnoch* and *Ochiai*, however, contemporary claims drafters will likely wish to obtain a separate patent claiming a method of using the shovel to extract items from the earth. Not only would the patentee be able to found suits based upon uses of the patented shovel itself, but also using, offering for sale, selling or importing into the United States products of the patented method, such as unearthed minerals, fossil fuels or even

---

[105] See United States Patent No 3,703,051, granted on 21 November 1972 to Pearl Weinberger (directed towards a "Method for Improving the Growth Characteristics of Plant Material Such as Seeds and Growing Plants").

[106] See United States Patent No 5,051,728, granted on 24 September 1991 to Frank Y. Wang (directed towards a "Music Poster").

[107] See United States Patent No 4,395,600, granted on 26 July 1983 to Rene R. Lundy and David L. Tyler (directed towards an "Auditory Subliminal Message System and Method").

[108] See *Bleistein* v. *Donaldson Lithographing Co*, 188 US 239 (1903) (Holmes J) ("It would be a dangerous undertaking for persons trained only to the law to constitute themselves final judges of the worth of pictorial illustrations, outside of the narrowest and most obvious limits").

[109] 35 USC § 271(a) (1994).

excavated cultural artefacts.[110] Although this example may appear fantastic, consider the implications of method of use claims for such devices as oil well drill bits or catheters for extracting human blood.

The claims drafter might also see the advantages of obtaining a third patent directed towards a method of making the shovel. Once asserted against accused infringers, the patentee would be able to employ section 295 of the United States patent statute, or section 68A of the New Zealand statute, to its advantage. If the court found a substantial likelihood that the accused shovels were made by the claimed method and that the patentee made reasonable efforts to determine which process was actually used, it will invert the usual burden of proof and require that the defendant prove the shovel does not infringe.

Individually, any one of these claim formats possesses disadvantages. The exhaustion and marking doctrines would encumber the artefact claim. Sole ownership of a method of using claim would require the patentee to plead indirect infringement against sellers of the shovel that did not use the shovels themselves, requiring some proof of intent. And the method of making a claim would by its own terms not reach actors that did not manufacture shovels. But the combination of the three patents provides the patentee with an impressive array of proprietary rights that earlier notions of claim formatting would have denied.

A new sense of the role of patent claims places a premium upon artful claim drafting, not in the usual sense of capturing the inventor's technological contribution and surmounting the prior art, but in perceiving the legal ramifications of different descriptive formats. Sophisticated applicants have been encouraged to file lengthier patent applications, or even different patent applications, containing repetitively drafted claims. Those lacking the legal knowledge or funds to engage in duplicative drafting exercises will find themselves unable to take advantage of the nuances of these special rules.

The guile of the claims drafter appears to have rendered certain provisions of the Patent Code as doing little more than to influence the PTO fee schedule. A competent claims drafter appears quite capable of bypassing the marking statute and thereby subverting the statutory goal of notifying the public of patent rights. The marking statute has instead been transformed into a PTO revenue raising measure, for rather than encouraging patentees to label their products it will simply spur them into obtaining additional patent instruments with technique claims. Conversely, statutes such as section 271(f) must be seen merely as saving patentees the burden of drafting additional *Venezia*-style "kit" claims and absorbing the additional fees those claims would entail.

H   Closing Thoughts on *Pharmac*

Current claim drafting presents a language game of proportions that would delight any deconstructionist. Yet so long as claim format impacts on the sub-

---

[110] See 35 USC § 154(a)(1) (1994).

stantive patent law, applicants will possess strong incentives to contort claim formats in order to recite patentable subject matter, or to expand the market power of claims relating to subject matter well understood to be patentable. The review completed here suggests that the US patent regime has been far from vigilant in ensuring the integrity not only of individual patent claims, but of its own corpus of statutory and judicially expressed principles. *Pharmac* presents the patent system of New Zealand with a similar policy concern.

In my view, Swiss-type claims present an abuse of language. This distortion of the precedent on the patenting of methods of medical treatment seems little more than a schoolboy's trick. Further, once one legal fiction is created, others must follow quickly along to prop up the first. In particular, one wonders why patentability should rest on the novelty or non-obviousness of the patient delivery mechanism, when this feature really has little to do with the practical knowledge that the inventor bestows upon the public.

The US experience teaches that the New Zealand Court of Appeal would have done far better to stress the substantive effect of Swiss-type claims than somehow to distinguish them from the pure medical method claims considered in *Wellcome Foundation*. The New Zealand courts should be admired for their efforts to find harmony among the prevailing case law, but, with respect, seem to have underestimated the guile of the claims drafter. If the judgment that medical technique patents are "generally inconvenient" remains sound, then surely other sorts of claims with the identical market effect also lie outwith the patent system.

On the other hand, perhaps it is time to revisit *Wellcome Foundation*. The opinion consists less of legal reasoning than of a policy discussion, and is notable for the marked absence of any empirical underpinning. Although that court identified many evils associated with the proprietisation of medical techniques, it seemed to discount the equitable powers of common law courts in fashioning injunctive relief in such cases. Nor did the Court of Appeal seem put off by the lack of a legislative expression of a policy against patented medical techniques in New Zealand.

Further, it is not readily apparent that the patent system provides the most apt mechanism for restraining the parade of public health horrors intoned by the *Wellcome Foundation* court. As also suggested by recent New Zealand legislation supporting the grey market,[111] the intellectual property laws seem to bear a heavy load in that part of the world. That the gutting of the intellectual property laws could somehow compensate for either the lapses of competition law or ethical shortcomings of medical professionals also seems doubtful. At all events, the New Zealand patent system faces a legal issue of considerable subtlety following *Pharmac*. Given the strong tradition of comparative law in New Zealand following *Pharmac*, perhaps the US experience will be of assistance in assessing the impact of Swiss-type claims.

---

[111] See A. Van Melle, "Parallel Importing in New Zealand" (1999) 21 *EIPR* 63.

The *State Street Bank* opinion has attracted enormous attention even outside the United States. Sadly, it was last patentability opinion of Judge Giles S. Rich, who passed away in June 1999 at the age of 95 after serving on the US bench for over forty years. The opinion lifted the venerable ban on patenting business methods so long a part of US patent law, and a more recent opinion, *AT&T Corp.* v. *Excel Communications, Inc.*,[112] suggests that the Federal Circuit continues to hold an exceptionally ambitious view of patentable subject matter. The right of foreign priority suggests that this sort of patent claim may soon be landing on other shores, so a thorough review of the *State Street* opinion and its aftermath in the United States may be of interest. This chapter also briefly considers the status of business methods as a "manner of manufacture" within the Statute of Monopolies.

A The Foundational Law of Business Methods

The first US Congress expressly declared a "useful art" to be within the scope of the 1790 Patent Act, tracking the language of the US Constitution.[113] Section 101 of the current legislation, the Patent Act 1952, extends patentability to "any new and useful process, machine, manufacture, or composition of matter". The statute circularly defines the term "process" to mean any "process, art or method", including "a new use of a known process, machine, manufacture, composition of matter or material".[114] Supreme Court elaborations of this definition have included "a method of doing a thing",[115] "a mode of treatment of certain materials to produce a given result"[116] and "some practicable method or means of producing a beneficial result or effect".[117]

While the United States courts possessed a firmer statutory grounding for processes than their common law peers, they too experienced difficulties in adjudicating disputes involving process patents.[118] Patented processes are often practised in secret, with only the product of the process available to the public. The inchoate nature of processes makes it difficult to evaluate their impact upon

---

[112] 172 F 3d 1352 (Fed. Cir. 1999), cert. denied 120 S Ct 368 (1999).

[113] US Constitution, Art. I, § 8, cl. 8 authorises Congress "[t]o promote the Progress of Science and the useful Arts, by securing for limited Times to Authors and Inventors the exclusive Right to their respective Writings and Discoveries."

[114] 35 USC § 100(b) (1994).

[115] *Expandable Metal Co* v. *Bradford*, 214 US 366, 383 (1909).

[116] *Cochrane* v. *Deener*, 94 US 780, 787–8 (1877).

[117] *Corning* v. *Burden*, 56 US (15 How) 252, 268 (1853).

[118] See D.S. Chisum, "The Patentability of Algorithms" (1986) 47 *U Pitt L Rev* 959, 963 (noting the problems encountered in interpreting the meaning of "process"). Earlier treatments include H. Berman, "Method Claims" (1935) 17 *J Pat Off Soc'y* 713, 789; W.B. Whitney, "Patentable Processes" (1905) 19 *Harv L Rev* 30.

the public domain,[119] assess whether or not they have been infringed[120] and determine how they can be physically marked.[121]

But particularly troubling within the sphere of processes is the demarcation of the limits of patentable subject matter. Seemingly any sort of communicable technique can be articulated as a series of steps and expressed in the style of a patent claim. This sense is reinforced by the legislative history of the current patent statute, which the Supreme Court read as holding "that Congress intended statutory subject matter to 'include anything under the sun that is made by man' ".[122]

Perhaps realising the expansive grasp of proprietarisation made possible by the patent system, the courts developed sundry doctrines to cabin its reach. Variously expressed as bars to patents on business methods,[123] as well as such things as "mental steps", "algorithms" and "printed matter", these doctrines purported to hold certain subject matter unpatentable *per se*. Chief among these limitations was the longstanding sentiment that "[a]n idea of itself is not patentable".[124] "While a scientific truth, or the mathematical expression of it, is not patentable invention, a novel and useful structure created with the aid of knowledge of scientific truth may be."[125] Although the policy underpinnings of this restriction were never articulated well, the Supreme Court once suggested that such abstractions comprised "the basic tools of scientific and technological work",[126] too central to the process of technological development to be appropriable. Just as the copyright law limits itself to protection of expression and permits an author's ideas to enrich the public domain,[127] so too did the patent

---

[119] See, e.g., *Metallizing Eng'g Co Inc.* v. *Kenyon Bearing & Auto Parts Co, Inc.*, 153 F 2d 516 (2nd Cir. 1946), cert. denied, 328 US 840 (1946).

[120] Process Patents Amendment Act 1988, Pub L No 100–418, 9001–07. See generally *Eli Lilly & Co* v. *American Cyanamid Co*, 82 F 3d 1568 (Fed. Cir. 1996); W.B. Haymond, "The Process Patent Amendments Act of 1988: Solving An Old Problem, But Creating New Ones" [1989] *BYU L Rev* 567; G.E.J. Murphy, "Note, The Process Patent Amendments Act of 1988" (1989) 9 *J of L & Com* 267.

[121] See, e.g., *American Medical Sys., Inc.* v. *Medical Eng'g Corp.*, 6 F 3d 1523 (Fed. Cir. 1993), cert. denied, 511 US 1070 (1994).

[122] *Diamond* v. *Diehr*, 450 US 175, 182 (1981) (quoting S Rep No 1979, 82nd Cong, 2nd Sess 5 (1952); HR Rep No 1923, 82nd Cong, 2nd Sess 6 (1952)). But see D.S. Chisum, *Patents: A Treatise on the Law of Patentability, Validity and Infringement* (New York, Matthew Bender, 1999), § 1.01 at 1–6 ("Theoretical or abstract discoveries are excluded as are discoveries, however practical and useful, in nontechnological arts, such as the liberal arts, the social sciences, theoretical mathematics, and business and management methodology"); G.S. Rich, "Principles of Patentability" (1960) 28 *Geo Wash L Rev* 393, 393–4 ("Of course, not every kind of an invention can be patented. Invaluable though it may be to individuals, the public, and national defense, the invention of a more effective organisation of the materials in, and the techniques of teaching a course in physics, chemistry or Russian is not a patentable invention. . . . Also outside that group is one of the greatest inventions of our times, the diaper service").

[123] See generally E.R. Yoches and H.G. Pollock, "Is the 'Method of Doing Business' Rejection Bankrupt?" 3 *Fed Cir B J* (Spring 1993); G.E. Tew, "Method of Doing Business", 16 *J Pat Off Soc'y* 607 (August 1934).

[124] *Rubber-Tip Pencil Co* v. *Howard*, 87 US (20 Wal) 498, 507 (1874).

[125] *Mackay Co* v. *Radio Corp*, 306 US 86, 94.

[126] *Gottschalk* v. *Benson*, 409 US 63 (1972).

[127] 17 USC § 102(b) (1994).

law concern the physical instantiation of technological knowledge rather than that knowledge itself.

The bar on patents directed towards business methods represented an extension of the prescription on patenting abstract principles. As early as 1868, the Patent Commissioner sensed that "[i]t is contrary to the spirit of the law . . . to grant patents for methods of book-keeping".[128] Nineteenth century courts also opined that "a method of transacting common business"[129] or "a mere contract"[130] was unpatentable. Yet it was not until the Second Circuit's 1908 opinion in *Hotel Security Checking Co* v. *Lorraine Co*[131] that the proscription on business method patents was secured in the treatises.[132]

The patent at issue in *Hotel Security Checking* concerned a "method and means for cash-registering and account-checking" designed to prevent fraud by waiters and cashiers.[133] The system employed certain forms that tracked sales and ensured that waiters submitted appropriate funds at the close of business. The Second Circuit invalidated the patent on the basis of prior knowledge, finding that the patented technology "would occur to anyone conversant with the business".[134] However, the Court further observed that:[135]

> It is manifest that the subject-matter of the claims is not a machine, manufacture or composition of matter. If within the language of the statute at all, it must be as a "new and useful art". One of the definitions given by Webster of the word "art" is as follows: "The employment of means to accomplish some desired end; the adaptation of things in the natural world to the uses of life; the application of knowledge or power to practical purposes." In the sense of the patent law, an art is not a mere abstraction. A system of transacting business disconnected from the means of carrying out the system is not, within the most liberal interpretation of the term, an art.

To similar effect had been the earlier statement of the Commissioner in *Ex parte Turner*, which held that "a plan or theory of action which, if carried into practice, could produce no physical results proceeding directly from the operation of the theory or plan itself is not an art within the meaning of the patent laws".[136] Thus both court and Patent Office hinged the patentability of processes upon the presence of a "physical tangible facility" for practising the patented technique.[137] Importantly, both tribunals also held that mere "printed matter"—information inscribed upon a substrate for purposes of presenta-

---

[128] *Ex parte Abraham*, 1868 Comm'r Dec 59, 59 (Comm'r Pat. 1868).

[129] *United States Credit Sys. Co* v. *American Credit Indemnity Co*, 53 F 818, 819 (SDNY 1893).

[130] *In re Moeser*, 27 App DC 397, 310 (1906).

[131] 160 F 467 (2nd Cir. 1908).

[132] See *State Street Bank & Trust Co* v. *Signature Financial Group, Inc.*, 149 F 3d 1368, 1376 (Fed. Cir. 1998) (noting that *Hotel Security Checking* is "the case frequently cited as establishing the business method exception to statutory subject matter"); R. Del Gallo, III, "Are 'Methods of Doing Business' Finally Out of Business as a Statutory Rejection?" (1998) 38 *Idea* 403, 405.

[133] 160 F 467 (2nd Cir. 1908).

[134] *Ibid.*, 471.

[135] *Ibid.*, 469.

[136] 1894 Comm'r Dec 36, 38 (Comm'r Pat. 1894).

[137] *Rand, McNally & Co* v. *Exchange Scrip-Boon Co*, 187 F 984, 986 (7th Cir. 1911).

tion—would not suffice to fulfill the requirement. Only physical structure exhibiting a functional relationship between the substrate and written material would enter the realm of the patentable.[138]

Numerous decisions applied this standard while denying patents on business-oriented inventions. Citing a lack of physical structure other than printed matter, the courts struck down patents claiming a method for transferring writings from manuscript form to printed publication form;[139] a system of blank cheques and stubs useful in a combined checking/savings account;[140] and a system for national co-ordination of firefighting efforts.[141] Some patents were upheld: a railway ticket consisting of a base and separable attachment was held not to "relate merely to a 'method of transacting business'", but to involve a unique physical structure.[142]

The requirement of physical instantiation is not an illogical one. It ties the relatively abstract proprietary interests created by the patent law to the corporeal things that form the traditional objects of property. The identifiable boundaries that result better enable individuals to complete transactions, form markets and determine the sorts of conduct that will be judged permissible. The stricture that processes generate embodied results also places appropriate limits upon infringement liability, for the courts may far more readily observe the market impact of manipulated objects than trace the effect of more rarefied teachings. In all these matters the patent law reflects the precepts of the copyright law, which offers protection only to works fixed in a tangible medium of expression.[143]

B Computer-Implemented Methods

The demand for physical structure proved a serviceable patent eligibility standard for most of the history of the patent system. But the rise of computer technology would sorely test whether the presence of physical structure was a useful discriminant between those processes which could be patented and those which could not. Applicants in the computer arts urged that electronic circuits and the software to command them were as industrial in character as more traditional technologies. But examiners initially cast an extremely wary eye at their applications. They recognised that much of the precedent exempting abstract

---

[138] See *In re Bernhart*, 417 F 2d 1395 (CCPA 1969); *In re Jones*, 373 F 2d 1007 (CCPA 1967); Note, "The Patentability of Printed Matter: Critique and Proposal" (1950) 18 *Geo Wash L Rev* 475.

[139] *In re Bolongaro*, 62 F 2d 1059 (CCPA 1933).

[140] *In re Sterling*, 70 F 2d 910 (CCPA 1934).

[141] *In re Patton*, 127 F 2d 324 (CCPA 1942).

[142] *Cincinnati Traction Co v. Pope*, 210 F 443 (6th Cir. 1913).

[143] 17 USC §§ 101, 102(a) (1994). See W.J. Gordon, "An Inquiry into the Merits of Copyright: The Challenges of Consistency, Consent, and Encouragement Theory" (1989) 41 *Stan L Rev* 1343, 1380–2.

ideas from the patent system would be swept away by allowing patents on computers programmed to perform newly invented mathematical algorithms.[144]

The Supreme Court entered this debate when it granted certiorari in *Gottschalk* v. *Benson* in 1972.[145] There the applicant claimed a method of converting numerals from binary-coded decimal to pure binary format. The steps of the method comprised mathematical operations that shuffled a sequence of bits in order to express appropriately a particular number. The application contained claims both reciting the method as performed by a computer, and the abstract performance of the method without regard to any particular physical means. The method had broad application in data processing tasks, ranging, in the words of the Court, from "the operation of a train to verification of drivers' licenses to researching the law books".[146]

In a cryptic opinion, the Court upheld the Patent Office's rejection of the application. The Court first recited the traditional requirement that patentability hinged upon the "[t]ransformation and reduction of an article 'to a different state or thing'".[147] Arguably, at least those claims reciting computer implementation of the numerical conversion method did involve some sort of physical conversion. Operation of the computer would not only manipulate those electrical signals representing the data, but generate electrical signals in order to instruct the computer to perform certain tasks. Yet the Court found this hardware insufficient, drawing its analysis to a close with a self-styled "nutshell":[148]

> It is conceded that one may not patent an idea. But in practical effect that would be the result of the formula for converting BCD numerals to pure binary numerals in this case. The mathematical formula involved here has no substantial practical application except in connection with a digital computer, which means that if the judgment below is affirmed, the patent would wholly pre-empt the mathematical formula and in practical effect would be a patent on the algorithm itself.

Thus the Court held that computerisation of mathematical equations could not shift them from the realm of ideas to that of industry. Internal circuitry operations were not enough to uphold even those claims reciting computer hardware, for barring the presence of an idiot savant or enormous mechanical computer to

---

[144] The bookshelves groan under the weight of numerous articles discussing the early interaction between computer technologies and the patent system, as well as the subsequent debate over the patenting of computer-related inventions. More recent publications on this topic include B.R. Yoshida, "Claiming Electronic and Software Technologies: the Effect of the Federal Circuit Decisions in Alappat, Warmerdam, and Lowry on the Claiming of Mathematical Algorithms and Data Structures" (1997) 45 *Buff L Rev* 457; S.G. Kunin, "Patentability of Computer Related Inventions in the United States Patent and Trademark Office" (1995) 77 *J Pat & Trademark Off Soc'y* 833; M.R. Peterson, "Note, Now You See It, Now You Don't: Was It a Patentable Machine or an Unpatentable 'Algorithm'? On Principle and Expediency in Current Patent Law Doctrines Relating to Computer-Implemented Inventions" (1995) 64 *Geo Wash L Rev* 90; Samuelson *et al.*, n. 87 above.

[145] 409 US 63 (1972).
[146] *Ibid.*, 68.
[147] *Ibid.*, 70.
[148] *Ibid.*, 71–2.

perform the claimed conversions rapidly, a digital computer presented the only context in which the equations had meaning. The digital computer amounted only to "nominal apparatus" that placed no meaningful limitations upon the scope of the claims.[149]

The Court of Customs and Patent Appeals had numerous opportunities to follow the lead of the Supreme Court. In *In re Maucorps*,[150] the applicant had claimed a "computing system for processing data" that determined the optimum number of sales representatives for a given organisation as well as the number of times they should visit customers over a period of time. The invention consisted of various formulae that Maucorps had derived from sales experience and implemented via software written in the Fortran programming language. The Court affirmed the rejection of the application, reasoning that the "claimed invention as a whole comprises each and every means for carrying out a solution technique for a set of equations wherein one number is computed from a set of numbers".[151]

In re Meyer[152] was to similar effect. Meyer's application described a computer-based expert system for aiding a neurologist in diagnosing patients. His claims were drafted broadly, calling for a more generalised "process for identifying locations of probable malfunction in a complex system".[153] In essence Meyer called for test data to be accumulated and conclusions reached in accordance with statistical formulae. The Court again affirmed the rejection of the application, quoting with approval the Patent Office's conclusion that the "process recited is an attempt to patent a mathematical algorithm rather than a process for producing a product".[154]

This early resistance to patents on computer-related inventions faded over time, however. By the early 1980s, Patent Office examiners found more favour in computer-related inventions, and the courts seemed more willing to uphold the issued patents.[155] While the omnipresence of computer technology and its significance to the United States economy may have carried the day, one suspects that both the Patent Office and the courts grew weary of the relentless argumentation of a bar that has scant motivation to favour restraints upon the scope of patenting. Also influential was the 1980 opinion in *Diamond* v. *Chakrabarty*,[156] a Supreme Court decision that opened the patent system to biotechnology.

That opinion involved the Patent Office rejection of Dr Ananda Chakrabarty's application claiming an artificially generated micro-organism. At the Supreme Court, chief among the arguments of the Patent Office Solicitor

---

[149] See Stern, n. 29 above.
[150] 609 F 2d 481 (CCPA 1979).
[151] *Ibid.*, 486.
[152] 688 F 2d 789 (CCPA 1982).
[153] *Ibid.*, 792.
[154] *Ibid.*, 794.
[155] See, e.g., *In re Deutsch*, 553 F 2d 689 (CCPA 1977); *In re Chatfield*, 545 F 2d 152 (CCPA 1976).
[156] 447 US 303 (1980).

was that because genetic technology could not have been foreseen at the time the patent statute was drafted, the resolution of the patentability of such inventions should be left to Congress. *En route* to reversing the Patent Office decision, the Court disagreed: "[a] rule that unanticipated inventions are without protection would conflict with the core concept of the patent law that anticipation undermines patentability".[157]

The difficulty with this reasoning is that it mixes two logical classes, that of individual technologies, with the entire domain of invention. As neatly illustrated by Bertrand Russell in his famous debate with Father Copleston, the fact that every person has a mother does not lead to the conclusion that the human race as a whole must have a mother.[158] And simply because the patent statute in part judges patentability though an anticipation standard hardly suggests that we lack other principles to govern the extent of patentable subject matter.

However apparent the weaknesses of this aspect of *Chakrabarty*, the Supreme Court leaned heavily upon its reasoning in its 1981 opinion in *Diamond* v. *Diehr*.[159] The *Diehr* applicants claimed a process for operating a rubber-moulding press with the aid of a digital computer. Their computer continuously monitored the temperature within a press and employed the well-known Arrhenius equation to calculate the amount of time required to cure rubber placed within the press. When the computer calculated that the elapsed time equalled the actual moulding time, it signalled a device to open the press.[160]

At the Patent Office, the examiner considered that the process steps that were implemented in computer software were non-statutory. The examiner further reasoned that the "remaining steps—installing rubber in the press and the subsequent closing of the process—were 'conventional and necessary to the process and cannot be the basis of patentability'".[161] The Court of Customs and Patent Appeals reversed the rejection, however. Following a grant of *certiorari*, the Supreme Court affirmed. Relying upon *Chakrabarty*, the Court explained that the applicants:[162]

> do not seek to patent a mathematical formula. Instead, they seek patent protection for a process of curing synthetic rubber. Their process admittedly employs a well-known mathematical equation, but they do not seek to pre-empt the use of that equation. Rather, they seek only to foreclose from others the use of that equation in conjunction with all of the other steps in their claimed process. These include installing rubber in a press, closing the mold, constantly determining the temperature of the mold, constantly recalculating the appropriate cure time through the use of a formula and a digital computer, and automatically opening the press at the proper time.

[157] 447 US 303, 316 (1980).
[158] See B. Russell and F.C. Copleston, "A Debate on the Existence of God" in A. Seckel (ed.), *Bertrand Russell on God and Religion* (Buffalo, NY, Prometheus Books, 1986),123, 131.
[159] 450 US 175 (1981).
[160] *Ibid.*, 177–8.
[161] *Ibid.*, 181.
[162] *Ibid.*, 187.

A number of difficulties attend the *Diehr* Court's analysis as well. The advancement offered by the *Diehr* applicants consisted of mathematical computations. The physical steps on which so much depended—reading a thermometer and signalling a press door to open—were trite. Allowing patentability to hinge upon the minimal recitation of these steps within the claims seems unfounded, for they merely stated the only valid technical context in which the mathematics would operate. They did not present meaningful limitations upon the scope of the claims. To the extent that the prohibition against patenting ideas presents sound policy, allowing applicants to avoid these limitations through artful claim drafting appears unwise.

The patent bar nonetheless proved attentive to the lessons of *Diehr*. Technologists proved increasingly adept at claiming newly formulated mathematical equations alongside some sort of physical manifestation. In response, the Court of Customs and Patent Appeals formed the two-part *Freeman-Walter-Abele* test. Initiated in 1978 by the *In re Freeman*[163] decision, the Court refined the test in the 1980 opinion in *In re Walter*.[164] Following the Supreme Court's issue of its *Diehr* decision, the Court once again modified the standard in its 1982 decision *In re Abele*.[165] As later described by the Federal Circuit:[166]

> It is first determined whether a mathematical algorithm is recited directly or indirectly in the claim. If so, it is next determined whether the claimed invention as a whole is no more than the algorithm itself; that is, whether the claim is directed to a mathematical algorithm that is not applied to or limited by physical elements or process steps. Such claims are nonstatutory. However, when the mathematical algorithm is applied in one or more steps of an otherwise statutory process claim, or one or more elements of an otherwise statutory apparatus claim, the requirements of section 101 are met.

The Federal Circuit employed the *Freeman-Walter-Abele* test both to reject[167] and to allow[168] various applications as patentable subject matter. But its decisions demonstrated an increasingly permissive tenor, and a glance through the Patent Office Gazette showed a growing number of issued patents directed towards computer-related inventions.

Emboldened by this state of affairs,[169] applicants eventually abandoned even the pretext of tying the mathematics to a traditionally industrial process such as curing rubber. Instead, the tangible thing upon which patentability was keyed was the combination of a computer and the software-driven electrical signals employed to instruct it. Because general purpose computers could be conceived

---

[163] 573 F 2d 1237 (CCPA 1978).

[164] 618 F 2d 758 (CCPA 1980).

[165] 684 F 2d 902 (CCPA 1982).

[166] *Arrhythmia Research Technology, Inc.* v. *Corazonix Corp.*, 958 F 2d 1053 (Fed. Cir. 1992).

[167] *In re Grams*, 888 F 2d 835 (Fed. Cir. 1989).

[168] *In re Iwahashi*, 888 F 2d 1370 (Fed. Cir. 1989).

[169] See *Arrhythmia Research Technology, Inc.* v. *Corazonix Corp.*, 958 F 2d 1053 (Fed. Cir. 1992); *In re Iwahashi*, 888 F 2d 1370 (Fed. Cir. 1989). But see *In re Grams*, 888 F 2d 835 (Fed. Cir. 1989).

as special purpose computers once instructed by software, virtually any fragment of software code could be viewed as statutory subject matter.[170]

Although this reasoning had been impliedly rejected in *Gottschalk*, it met with great success in the Federal Circuit's *en banc* decision in *In re Alappat*.[171] There, the Court considered a claimed apparatus useful for generating smooth and continuous lines for display on an oscilloscope. Alappat's invention completed various mathematical computations in order to convert so-called "vector list data" into "pixel illumination intensity data"; that is, it converted one set of numbers into another set of numbers.[172] The majority held that the claimed invention comprised statutory subject matter:[173]

> Although many, or arguably even all, of the means elements recited in claim 15 represent circuitry elements that perform mathematical calculations, which is essentially true of all digital electrical circuits, the claimed invention as a whole is directed to a combination of interrelated elements which combine to form a machine for converting discrete waveform data samples into anti-aliased pixel illumination intensity data to be displayed on a display means. This is not a disembodied mathematical concept which may be characterised as an "abstract idea", but rather a specific machine to produce a useful, concrete, and tangible result.

The *en banc* Court also quickly distinguished *Maucorps*[174] and *Meyer*.[175] According to the Court, "*Maucorps* dealt with a business methodology for deciding how salesmen should best handle respective customers and *Meyer* involved a 'system' for aiding a neurologist. Clearly, neither of the alleged 'inventions' in those cases falls within any § 101 category."[176]

Reconciliation of *Alappat* with *Gottschalk* appears difficult. Both inventions concerned data transformations performed by a computer using mathematical calculations. Yet, according to the Federal Circuit, the *Gottschalk* court had instead attempted to express the concept that "certain types of mathematical subject matter, standing alone, represent nothing more than *abstract ideas* until reduced to some type of practical application, and thus that subject matter is not, in and of itself, entitled to patent protection".[177] That the applicant in *Gottschalk* could have circumvented the Supreme Court's objection simply by naming one practical application for his algorithm seems quite implausible,

---

[170] This argument had met with success in *In re Bernhart*, 417 F 2d 1395, 1400 (CCPA 1969). See also *In re Prater*, 415 F 2d 1393, 1494 n. 29 (CCPA 1969).

[171] 33 F 3d 1526 (Fed. Cir. 1994). See J.A. Burtis, "Note, Towards a Rational Jurisprudence of Computer-Related Patentability in Light of *In re Alappat*" (1995) 79 *Minn L Rev* 1129; S.H.M. Kim, "*In re Alappat*: A Strict Statutory Interpretation Determining Patentable Subject Matter Relating to Computer Software?" (1995) 13 *John Marshall J Computer & Info L* 635; W.W. King, Jr, "The Soul of the Virtual Machine: *In re Alappat*" (1995) 2 *J Intell Prop L* 575.

[172] *Ibid.*, 1537–9

[173] *Ibid.*, 1544.

[174] 609 F 2d 481 (CCPA 1979).

[175] 688 F 2d 789 (CCPA 1982).

[176] 33 F 3d 1526, 1541 (Fed. Cir. 1994).

[177] *Ibid.*, 1543.

particularly since the Court took pains to catalogue some of the many uses of that algorithm in its opinion.

After *Alappat*, the long-running saga concerning the patentability of computer-related inventions seemed of little more than historical interest. Seemingly any applicant who drafted patent claims within the strictures of the vitiated physicality standard could obtain a patent on nearly any data processing technique. That the advance was found not in computer circuitry or programming techniques was besides the point; so long as the technique could be performed by a computer and was so characterised, then a patent could issue.

Given that many such techniques are only practically realisable when performed on a computer, this minimal stricture was one many applicants could live with. Yet few failed to realise that the artful claims drafting inspired by *Diehr* and *Alappat* comprised little more than a charade.[178] Although a robust physical transformation requirement was itself quite defensible, its hobbled remnant proved so provocative of contorted claims drafting that it appears scarcely worth maintaining.[179] Some jurists seemed willing to abandon the requirement of physicality in favour of a more expansive vision of patentability, as suggested by Judge Newman's view in a 1994 dissent that:[180]

> A statutory process is limited only in that it must be technologically useful. . . . All mathematical algorithms transform data, and thus serve as a process to convert initial conditions or inputs into solutions or outputs, through transformation of information. . . . The test is simply whether the mathematical formula is all that is claimed, or whether the procedures involving the specified mathematics are part of a useful process. When the latter requirement is met the subject matter is statutory.

Only four years would elapse before a view of statutory subject matter that embraced the "transformation of information" would make its way from the dissent to the majority. The occasion was the inevitable resolution of the conflict between the venerable case law on business methods and more recent developments on computer-related inventions, the Federal Circuit decision in *State Street Bank & Trust Co v. Signature Financial Group, Inc.*[181]

[178] *Ibid.*, 1564 (Archer CJ dissenting).

[179] See J.R. Thomas, "Of Text, Technique, And The Tangible: Drafting Patent Claims Around Patent Rules" (1998) 17 *John Marshall J Computer & Info L* 219.

[180] *In re Schrader*, 22 F 3d 290, 297 (Fed. Cir. 1994) (Newman J dissenting).

[181] 149 F 3d 1368 (Fed. Cir. 1998). Also of note was the District Court opinion in *Paine, Webber, Jackson & Curtis, Inc.* v. *Merrill Lynch, Pierce, Fenner & Smith, Inc.*, 564 F Supp. 1358, 1364, 1369 (D Del. 1983) (holding that Merrill Lynch's claimed "system for processing and supervising a plurality of composite subscriber [investment] accounts" comprised "statutory subject matter because the claims allegedly teach a method of operation on a computer to effectuate a business activity").

C Computer-implemented Business Methods

Signature Financial Group held the patent at suit.[182] Directed to a "Data Processing System for Hub and Spoke Financial Services Configuration", it described a data processing system for implementing an investment structure known as a "Hub and Spoke" system. This system allowed individual mutual funds ("Spokes") to pool their assets in an investment portfolio ("Hub") organised as a partnership. According to the patent, this investment regime provided the advantageous combination of economies of scale in administering investments coupled with the tax advantages of a partnership.[183]

Maintaining a proper accounting of this sophisticated financial structure proved difficult. Indeed, due to "the complexity of the calculations, a computer or equivalent device is a virtual necessity to perform the task".[184] Signature's patented system purported to allow administrators to "monitor and record the financial information flow and make all calculations necessary for maintaining a partner fund financial services configuration".[185] In addition it tracked "all the relevant data determined on a daily basis for the Hub and each Spoke, so that aggregate year end income, expenses, and capital gain or loss can be determined for accounting and for tax purposes for the Hub and, as a result, for each publicly traded Spoke".[186] Crucially, Signature's invention marked no advance in

---

[182] United States Patent No 5,193,056 (9 March 1993). The first claim of the '056 patent provided:

'1. A data processing system for managing a financial services configuration of a portfolio established as a partnership, each partner being one of a plurality of funds, comprising:

(a)   computer processor means for processing data;

(b)   storage means for storing data on a storage medium;

(c)   first means for initialising the storage medium;

(d)   second means for processing data regarding assets in the portfolio and each of the funds from a previous day and data regarding increases or decreases in each of the funds, [sic, funds'] assets and for allocating the percentage share that each fund holds in the portfolio;

(e)   third means for processing data regarding daily incremental income, expenses, and net realised gain or loss for the portfolio and for allocating such data among each fund;

(f)   fourth means for processing data regarding daily net unrealised gain or loss for the portfolio and for allocating such data among each fund; and

(g)   fifth means for processing data regarding aggregate year-end income, expenses, and capital gain or loss for the portfolio and each of the funds.'

Interestingly, Signature's claim fails to recite how the various means elements interact with each other, either functionally or structurally. The claim appears to recite a mere aggregation not in conformity with 35 USC § 112 ¶ 2 (1994): see *In re Worrest*, 201 F 2d 930, 934 (CCPA 1953) (defining an unpatentable aggregation as "a device having two or more unrelated, independent units or elements, each of which performs its function separately, uninfluenced by and indifferent to the action of the other units. There is no essential or inherent correlation, or cooperation, or coordination of elements which mutually contribute to a common purpose or result, other than mere convenience due to juxtaposition or collection of the units in a common setting").

[183] 149 F 3d 1368, 1370 (Fed. Cir. 1998).

[184] *Ibid.*, 1371.

[185] *Ibid.*

[186] *Ibid.*

computer technology or mathematical calculations. The basis for patentability was the uniqueness of the investment package Signature claimed in its patent.

Following issue of the patent, Signature entered into licensing negotiations with a competitor, State Street Bank, that ultimately proved unsuccessful. State Street then brought a declaratory judgment action against Signature, seeking the invalidity of the patent. The District Court granted summary judgment in favour of State Street under two alternative grounds.[187] First, the Court applied the *Freeman-Walter-Abele* test,[188] concluding that:[189]

> At bottom, the invention is an accounting system for a certain type of financial investment vehicle claimed as a means for performing a series of mathematical functions. Quite simply, it involves no further physical transformation or reduction than inputting numbers, calculating numbers, outputting numbers, and storing numbers. The same functions could be performed, albeit less efficiently, by an accountant armed with pencil, paper, calculator, and a filing system.

The Court then buttressed its holding by turning to "the long-established principle that business 'plans' and 'systems' are not patentable".[190] The Court judged that "patenting an accounting system necessary to carry on a certain type of business is tantamount to a patent on the business itself. Because such abstract ideas are not patentable, either as methods of doing business or as mathematical algorithms", the patent was held invalid.[191]

On appeal, the Federal Circuit reversed in a magisterial opinion. Writing for a three-judge panel, Judge Rich found the patent claimed not an abstract idea but a programmed machine that produced a "useful, concrete, and tangible result".[192] "This renders it statutory subject matter, even if the useful result is expressed in numbers, such as price, profit, percentage, cost, or loss."[193] According to the Court, "[t]he question of whether a claim encompasses statutory subject matter should not focus on which of the four categories of subject matter a claim is directed to—process, machine, manufacture, or composition of matter—but rather on the essential characteristics of the subject matter, in particular, its practical utility".[194] The Court further trumpeted that:[195]

> Today, we hold that the transformation of data, representing discrete dollar amounts, by a machine through a series of mathematical calculations into a final share price, constitutes a practical application of a mathematical algorithm, formula, or calculation, because it produces 'a useful, concrete and tangible result'—a final share price

---

[187] *State Street Bank & Trust Co v. Signature Financial Group, Inc.*, 927 F Supp. 502 (D Mass. 1996).

[188] *Ibid.*, 512–5.

[189] *Ibid.*, 515.

[190] *Ibid.*, 515–6.

[191] *Ibid.*, 516.

[192] 149 F 3d 1368, 1373 (Fed. Cir. 1998) (quoting *In re Alappat*, 33 F 3d 1526, 1544 (Fed. Cir. 1994)).

[193] *Ibid.*, 1375.

[194] *Ibid.*

[195] *Ibid.*, 1373.

momentarily fixed for recording and reporting purposes and even accepted and relied upon by regulatory authorities and in subsequent trades.

The Federal Circuit then turned to the District Court's business methods rejection, opting to "take the opportunity to lay this ill-conceived exception to rest".[196] According to Judge Rich, restrictions upon patents for methods of doing business were ill-conceived from the start and no longer the law under the 1952 Patent Act. Following issue of the *State Street* opinion, methods of doing business were to be subject only to the same patentability analysis as any other sort of process.[197]

State Street is a curious opinion on a number of fronts. First, the Court's characterisation of the patented invention as generating a "final share price" appears inaccurate. Neither the term "final share price" nor its reasonable approximation appears in any of Signature's claims, which are instead directed towards the processing of data relating to portfolio income, expenses and net gain or loss. This interpretation seems especially odd in light of an earlier opinion by Judge Rich, *In re Iwahashi*,[198] which admonished that the precedents have "held some claims statutory and other claims nonstatutory, depending entirely on what they said. We have to do the same here."[199]

The *State Street* court also squarely stated that the District Court had erred by applying the *Freeman-Walter-Abele* test. According to Judge Rich, "[a]fter *Diehr* and *Chakrabarty*, the *Freeman-Walter-Abele* test has little, if any, applicability to determining the presence of statutory subject matter".[200] As a matter of chronology this statement is plainly false: the Supreme Court issued *Chakrabarty* in 1980 and *Diehr* in 1981. The Court of Customs and Patent Appeals authored *Abele*, an opinion Judge Rich had joined, in 1982.

This aberrant reinterpretation of *Diehr* and *Chakrabarty* also does a disservice to any number of Federal Circuit opinions which applied the *Freeman-Walter-Abele* test in patent eligibility determinations.[201] It further seems to misread *Chakrabarty*. There the Court expressly stated that a "claim for an improved method of calculation, even when tied to a specific end use, is unpatentable subject matter under § 101".[202] This standard appears to provide ample basis for striking down Signature's claimed "system", which does nothing more than maintain the accounting books for a particular financial product.

As well, the Federal Circuit failed to acknowledge fully *Maucorps*[203] and *Meyer*,[204] or the manner in which those cases had been treated in *Alappat*.[205]

[196] 149 F 3d 1368, 1375 (Fed. Cir. 1998).
[197] *Ibid.*
[198] 888 F 2d 1370 (Fed. Cir. 1989).
[199] *Ibid.*, 1374.
[200] 149 F 3d 1368, 1374–5 (Fed. Cir. 1998).
[201] See, e.g., *Arrhythmia Research Technology, Inc.* v. *Corazonix Corp.*, 958 F 2d 1053 (Fed. Cir. 1992); *In re Iwahashi*, 888 F 2d 1370 (Fed. Cir. 1989); *In re Grams*, 888 F 2d 835 (Fed. Cir. 1989).
[202] 447 US 303, 315 (1980), citing *Parker* v. *Flook*, 437 US 584, 595 n. 18 (1978).
[203] 609 F 2d 481 (CCPA 1979).
[204] 688 F 2d 789 (CCPA 1982).
[205] 33 F 3d 1526, 1540–1 (Fed. Cir. 1994).

Each of those opinions rejected claims quite analogous to those of Signature Financial Group's patent. The *State Street* Court dismissed this precedent quickly, stating only that "closer scrutiny of these cases reveals that the claimed inventions in both *Maucorps* and *Meyer* were rejected as abstract ideas under the mathematical algorithm exception, not the business method exception".[206] But this distinction tells us only that the District Court's first basis for invalidating Signature's patent should have stood. It also fails to inform us why the statement of the *en banc* court in *Alappat* that "a business methodology" does not fulfill the strictures of section 101 is no longer the law.[207]

In perhaps the most telling line of the opinion, the *State Street* opinion further told us that the key inquiry concerning statutory subject matter involves "the essential characteristics of the subject matter, in particular, its practical utility".[208] This remark appears to collapse the subject matter inquiry into another patentability requisite, that of utility. The utility standard has always been a minimal one in the United States, requiring only that the invention confer a "specific benefit . . . in currently available form".[209] The difficulty with this approach is that, since the early nineteenth century, the utility standard has been understood to present a distinct, additional hurdle to patentability.[210] Not only does this dramatic reinterpretation of section 101 seem to relegate that statute's recitation of categories of patentable subject matter into little more than claim formatting protocols, but it also presents an extremely vitiated gatekeeper to the patent system.[211]

At bottom, the Federal Circuit also said vastly more than it needed to with regard to methods of doing business. The claims of the patent were not directed to methods at all, but to computer hardware programmed to perform certain calculations.[212] In fact, the Court noted that the patent application as filed originally included method claims. But the applicant had abandoned them following examiner concerns over patentable subject matter.[213] Given the absence of method claims in the patent at suit, not due to happenstance but because of their knowing deletion by the applicant, this portion of the *State Street* opinion may amount to nothing more than dicta.

---

[206] 149 F 3d 1368, 1376 (Fed. Cir. 1998).

[207] 33 F 3d 1526, 1541 (Fed. Cir. 1994).

[208] 149 F 3d 1368, 1375 (Fed. Cir. 1998).

[209] *Brenner* v. *Manson*, 383 US 519 (1966). See also *In re Brana*, 51 F 3d 1560 (Fed. Cir. 1995); A.T. Kight, "Note, Pregnant with Ambiguity: Credibility and the PTO Utility Guidelines in Light of *Brenner*" (1998) 73 *Ind L J* 997; M.L. Johnson, "*In re Brana* and the Utility Examination Guidelines: A Light at the End of the Tunnel?" (1996) 49 *Rutgers L Rev* 285.

[210] See *Lowell* v. *Lewis*, 15 F Cas. 1018 (CC Mass. 1817); *Bedford* v. *Hunt*, 3 F Cas. 37 (CC Mass. 1817).

[211] See R.P. Merges, "Commercial Success and Patent Standards: Economic Perspectives on Innovation" (1988) 76 *Calif L Rev* 803, 811–2 (noting that the utility requirement has "devolved over the years into a rather minimal obstacle to obtaining a patent").

[212] 149 F 3d 1368, 1371–2 (Fed. Cir. 1998).

[213] *Ibid.*, 1371.

Enthusiastic commentators thus may have read too much into the *State Street* opinion.[214] Still, each issue of the PTO Gazette seems to include another patented business method. As but one example of recent PTO work product, consider the following claim:[215]

> A method for remodeling an existing building, said method comprising:
> cataloging design ideas that utilise predetermined building products;
> presenting the design ideas to a client;
> allowing the client to select a design idea . . . and
> preparing a visual image . . . representing the building remodeled with the design idea selected by the client.

Wholly divorced from particular artefacts, this claim broadly appropriates an architectural services technique. Recently issued PTO Guidelines further suggest that other business, artificial intelligence and mathematical processing applications are firmly within the grasp of the patent system.[216]

Of course, it is the fate of patent offices to lead the courts on patentability standards. In some sense, *State Street* merely presents the latest in a series of cases confirming PTO practice as to the subject matter appropriate for patenting. But in many ways, *State Street* presents the most disturbing episode yet. It seems one thing for courts to place biotechnologies and computer-related inventions within the patent system, but quite another to hold that business methods may be patented. One need only recall the techniques of the Hanseatic League[217] or the theory of mercantilism[218] to realise that such methods are far older than the patent system itself. Yet only recently have we been made to understand that this sort of practical knowledge may be appropriated via the regime of patents.[219]

---

[214] See, e.g., E. Updike, "What's Next—a Patent For The 401(k)?: A Court Decision Protecting Business Methods Could Wreak Havoc from E-commerce to Banking", *Business Week* (26 October 1998); L. Buchanan, "Can You Actually Patent a Business Model? A Recent Decision from the Patent and Trademark Office Says You Can. And that isn't Good News for Entrepreneurs", *Inc* (1 November 1998); "It Was My Idea", *The Economist*, 15 August 1998, 54 (interpreting *State Street* to hold that "business models are generally patentable if they are unique—just like any other invention that is 'new and useful'").

[215] United States Patent No 5,668,736 (16 September 1997).

[216] See United States Patent and Trademark Office, *Manual of Patent Examining Procedure* (7th edn., 1998) (available at <http://www.uspto.gov/web/offices/pac/compexam/comguide.htm>).

[217] See T.H. Lloyd, *England and the German Hanse, 1157–1611: A Study of Their Trade and Commercial Diplomacy* (Cambridge, CUP, 1991); J. Schildhauer, *The Hansa: Their History and Culture* (K. Vanovitch (trans.), Leipzig, Edition Leipzig, 1985).

[218] See L. Magnusson, *Mercantilism: The Shaping of an Economic Language* (London, Routledge, 1994); L. Gomes, *Foreign Trade and the National Economy: Mercantilist and Classical Perspectives* (New York, St Martin's Press, 1987).

[219] In this regard, *State Street* Bank held particularly unsettling possibilities for inventors who maintained their business methods as trade secrets. Under the rule articulated by Judge Learned Hand in *Metallizing Engineering Co, Inc.* v. *Kenyon Bearing & Auto Parts Co, Inc.*, 153 F 2d 516 (2nd Cir. 1946), cert. denied, 328 US 840 (1946), a firm that put a business method into commercial practice for more than one year, but maintained the method as a trade secret, is barred from obtaining a patent on the invention. Moreover, third parties are free to patent the method: see *DL Auld Co* v. *Chroma Graphics Corp*, 714 F 2d 1144 (Fed. Cir. 1983). Because business method innovators may

That the dialogue of the patent law itself scarcely limits the possibilities of patenting presents a source of concern. If the only remaining restraints upon patentable subject matter are the lenient strictures of novelty or utility, then the pretensions of the patent system have expanded vastly beyond its traditional province of industrial technologies. For although the patent system is caught up with technology, it has done little to refine its sense of its own subject matter other than to say that patents properly canvas the entire waterfront of technique. In the regime of patents, technology has become not merely artificial object or industrial activity, but the entire body of human knowledge unencumbered by further qualification.

Among the more reviled PTO grants has been its 1968 patent on a method of swallowing a pill.[220] Now we need scant imagination to envisage patents on corporate ingestion of poison pills as well. With business and medical techniques firmly under wing, and patents on sports methods[221] and procedures of psychological analysis[222] trickling out of the PTO, patents appropriating almost any sort of communicable practice seem easily attainable. Claims to methods within the disciplines of sociology, political science, economics and the law appear to present only the nearest frontier for the regime of patents. Under increasingly permissive Federal Circuit case law, techniques within such far-flung disciplines as language,[223] the fine arts[224] and theology[225] appear as well to be within the realm of patentability.

We have good reason to doubt whether such innovations lie within the "useful arts", the constitutional stricture concerning patentable subject matter.[226] The sparse materials we possess regarding this term suggest that the drafters of

have opted for trade secret protection based upon the traditional rule that such methods were unpatentable, a practical effect of *State Street* may be to convert the first inventors of business methods into infringers. Congress attempted to respond to this concern by enacting the First Inventor Defense Act of 1999, Public Law No. 106–13. This statute creates a prior user right for those charged with infringing a "method of doing or conducting business." The prior user must have reduced the invention to practice one year before the effective filing date of the patent and "commercially used" that subject matter in the United States before the effective filing date.

220 United States Patent No 3,418,999 (31 December 1968).

221 See generally C.A. Kukkonen, III, "Be a Good Sport and Refrain from Using My Patented Putt: Intellectual Property Protection For Sports Related Movements" (1998) 80 *J Pat & Trademark Off Soc'y* 808.

222 United States Patent No 5,190,458 (23 March 1993) ("character assessment method").

223 See United States Patent No 4,864,503 (5 September 1989) ("[m]ethod of using a created international language as an intermediate pathway in translation between two national languages"); See also "The Wired Diaries", 7.01 *Wired* 97, 135 (January 1999) (attributing to Norman Fischer, Abbot, Green Gulch Farm Zen Center, the observation that "[t]he real technology—behind all of our other technologies—is language. It actually creates the world our consciousness lives in").

224 See United States Patent No 5,730,052 (24 March 1998) ("[m]ethod of high resolution silk screen printing"). But see *Greenewalt* v. *Stanley Co of America*, 54 F 2d 195, 196 (3rd Cir. 1931) ("We do not find authority in the law for the issuance of a patent for results dependent upon such intangible, illusory, and nonmaterial things as emotional or aesthetic reactions").

225 See United States Patent No 5,734,795 (31 March 1998) ("[s]ystem for allowing a person to experience systems of mythology").

226 See V. Chiappetta, "Patentability of Computer Software Instruction as an 'Article of Manufacture': Software as Such as the Right Stuff" (1998) 17 *John Marshall J Computer & Info L* 89, 129–34.

the US Constitution were unlikely to see every created thing as encompassed within it.[227] They undoubtedly contemplated the industrial, mechanical and manual arts of the late eighteenth century, in contrast to the seven "liberal arts" and the four "fine arts" of classical learning.[228]

D   Business Methods under the Statute of Monopolies and the European Patent Convention

Jurisdictions that continue to interpret the Statute of Monopolies perhaps have an improved perception of these issues. The drafters of the US Constitution too were aware of the English experience leading to the Statute of Monopolies,[229] an appreciation that may be lost to the current stewards of the US patent system. In a passage especially worthy of consideration following *State Street*, the Court of Customs and Patent Appeals had earlier explained that the inclusion of the patent and copyright clause in the Constitution "doubtlessly was due to the fact that those who formulated the Constitution were familiar with the long struggle over monopolies so prominent in English history, where exclusive rights to engage even in *ordinary business activities* were granted so frequently by the Crown . . .".[230]

For example, the early decision in *DA & K's Application*[231] concluded that "in order to show that an invention is a 'manner of new manufacture', it is not sufficient to produce a scheme or plan, however ingenious, even though it is put forward in a concrete shape, or is reduced to writing or diagrammatic form". The court in *Stahl & Larssons's Application*[232] also held that "however ingenious the alleged invention appeared to be, if in reality it was no more than a plan for the conduct of business in a particular way, it was not a manner of manufacture".

However, developments both in the USA and with respect to the European Patent Convention suggest that this issue may be revisited. It is well known that the EPC requires that patentable inventions be capable of industrial application and excludes both programs for computers and methods of doing business. Yet the EPO has been notoriously liberal in granting patents on computer-related

---

[227] See *Federalist 43* (Madison), in *The Federalist Papers* (C. Rossiter (ed.), New York, New American Library of New York, 1961), 271–2 ("The copyright of authors has been solemnly adjudged in Great Britain to be a right of common law. The right to useful inventions seems with equal reason to belong to the inventors. The public good fully coincides in both cases with the claims of individuals"). Madison's reference to contemporary British law hardly suggests a radical view of patentable subject matter.

[228] See R.I. Coulter, "The Field of the Statutory Useful Arts" (1952) 34 *J Pat Off Soc'y* 487, 494–6. "The seven historic 'liberal arts' were: grammar, logic (dialectic), rhetoric, arithmetic, geometry, music and astronomy. The four 'fine arts' were: painting, drawing, architecture and sculpture; to which were often added: poetry, music, dancing and drama": *ibid.*, 494.

[229] See E.C. Walterscheid, "To Promote the Progress of Useful Arts: American Patent Law and Administration, 1787–1836 (Part 2)" (1998) 80 *J Pat & Trademark Off Soc'y* 11, 26–7.

[230] *In re Shao Wen Yuan*, 188 F 2d 377, 380 (CCPA 1951) (emphasis added).

[231] (1926) 43 RPC 154, 158 *per* Sir Thomas Inskip.

[232] [1965] RPC 596, 600 *per* Lloyd-Jacob J.

inventions, so much so that the European Commission has pushed for the abolition of this portion of Article 52. Perhaps the same will happen with regard to the business methods exception, particularly where the claims drafter frames the invention within a hardware platform. While New Zealand is of course not an EPC signatory, the *Pharmac* opinion suggests that interpretations of the EPC may have influence there.

Of particular note is the controversial decision in *General-Purpose Management System/SOHEI*.[233] The lengthy claims at issue before the European Patent Office Board of Appeal there defined computer hardware, data storage files and a plurality of processing means for controlling the hardware and for storing, updating, reading and outputting the data. The patent application described the system as useful for financial and inventory management, and in particular construction management. Thus the system might, for example, track the work to be done on a particular site within the construction industry.

According to the Board, the claimed invention involved technical considerations because it involved a novel use of different files to cause the computer to perform different tasks. Moreover, the Board noted that management of construction sites was comparable to the management of traditional manufacturing processes. The claimed invention could therefore not be considered a method of doing business excluded from patentability by the European Patent Convention.

SOHEI seems to conflict with an earlier, well-known interpretation of the EPC by the English Patents Court in *Merrill Lynch*.[234] There, the Court had rejected the claimed data processing system for enabling a securities trading market. What does not accompany the *Merrill Lynch* opinion in the reporters, however, is an account of how the applicant did manage to obtain a patent from the UK Patent Office on remand by stressing the technical features of the claimed system. In any event, forum shopping at the patent acquisition stage is always a possibility in Europe, and the reasoning of the *SOHEI* Board offers ample possibilities for artful claims drafters to overcome the restrictions upon patentable subject matter within the European Patent Convention.

IV CONCLUSION

Throughout its history the patent system has demonstrated an increasing permissiveness, both in terms of creative claim formatting and the subject matter proper for patenting. *Pharmac* and *State Street* continue this trend, each acting to increase the ability of private individuals to appropriate those aspects of human endeavour previously thought to be outwith the patent system. But whether done indirectly, through the approval of the artful drafting of a patent instrument, or directly, through the express introduction of particular subject

[233] T 769/92 [1995] OJ EPO 525 (31 May 1994).
[234] *Merrill Lynch Inc's Application* [1988] RPC 1 (HC). See also *Merrill Lynch's Appliction* [1989] RPC 561 (CA).

matter into the patent system, our experience teaches us that some care should accompany the expansion of the scope of patentee power. The stewards of our patent system would do well to consider informed responses to our increasingly ambitious scope of patenting, rather than rely upon the patent bar to stage an informed debate on the appropriate vision of appropriable subject matter.

8

Patentability in Australia and New Zealand Under the Statute of Monopolies

JOHN SMILLIE

I INTRODUCTION

In the previous chapter, Professor John Thomas described recent developments in the United States which extend the ambit of patent protection in that jurisdiction. Some of those developments involve the use of innovative claim-drafting techniques to circumvent traditional constraints on patentability, or extend the practical reach of the exclusive rights conferred by patent grants. Professor Thomas also traced the American experience with computer software related inventions where direct extension of the scope of patentable subject matter has blurred the core distinction between industrial technology (the traditional concern of patents) and principles, schemes and methods of presenting information or organising businesses which have traditionally been viewed as more appropriately protected by contract, copyright or obligations of confidence. In particular, Professor Thomas draws attention to the decision of the Federal Circuit Court of Appeals in *State Street Bank & Trust Co* v. *Signature Financial Group, Inc.,*[1] where the Court's identification of the "practical utility" of the outcome achieved by the claimed invention as the essential characteristic of patentable subject matter seems to open the way to patent grants in respect of methods and practices which find application in diverse fields of activity far removed from the traditional patent province of industrial technology.

What lesson should other jurisdictions take from this recent American experience? Professor Thomas's message is a cautionary one: we should be wary of attempts to extend progressively the range of patentable subject matter. Otherwise, instead of providing necessary incentives for innovation, patent grants may serve only to block competition without attracting any compensating benefits.

Professor Thomas does suggest that jurisdictions, like Australia and New Zealand, that still define a patentable "invention" by reference to section 6 of the

[1] 149 F 3d 1368 (Fed. Cir. 1998).

English Statute of Monopolies of 1623,[2] may have a clearer perception of the proper function and limits of the patent system, and be better placed to question and assess the constant demands for extension of the scope of patentable subject matter. This chapter examines that suggestion.

II STATUTORY BACKGROUNDS COMPARED

Certainly the United States Patent Act and the Statute of Monopolies proceed from quite different foundational premises. The United States Act defines patentable subject matter very broadly as embracing "any new and useful process, machine, manufacture or composition of matter"[3] and contains no express exclusions from patentability. As interpreted by the Supreme Court, the United States legislation reflects a presumption that strong patent protection advances the overall public interest. In *Diamond* v. *Chakrabarty*,[4] the Supreme Court explained that the original Patent Act of 1793 "embodied Jefferson's philosophy that 'ingenuity should receive a liberal encouragement'",[5] and the legislative history to the 1952 re-codification indicated that "Congress intended statutory subject matter to include anything under the sun that is made by man".[6] The only categories of subject matter deemed unpatentable were "the laws of nature, physical phenomena, and abstract ideas"[7]—the building blocks of scientific investigation which must remain in the public domain freely available to all. And once the court is satisfied that the language of the Act "fairly embraces" the applicant's invention, its role is exhausted; the court has no mandate to weigh ethical, social or environmental objections to the grant of patent rights.[8]

By contrast, the Statute of Monopolies of 1623 displays a strong preference for free competition over monopoly rights. The Statute removed the King's prerogative power to dispense trading monopolies for reasons of patronage or convenience. All monopolies were declared void, except patents for inventions preserved by section 6, which provided:

> that any declaration before mentioned shall not extend to any letters-patent and grants of privilege, for the term of fourteen years or under, hereafter to be made of the sole working or making of any manner of new manufacture within this realm, to the true and first inventor and inventors of such manufactures, which others, at the time of making such letters-patent or grant, shall not use, so as also they be not contrary to

---

[2] In both Australia and New Zealand, the term "invention" is defined as "any manner of new manufacture the subject of letters patent and grant of privilege within section 6 of the Statute of Monopolies . . .": Patents Act 1990 (Cth), Sched. I; Patents Act 1953 (NZ), s. 2(1).

[3] 35 USC § 101 (1994).

[4] 447 US 303 (1980).

[5] *Ibid.*, 308.

[6] *Ibid.*, 309.

[7] *Ibid.*

[8] *Ibid.*, 315–8.

the law, nor mischievous to the state, by raising prices of commodities at home, or hurt of trade, or generally inconvenient; . . .

So section 6 of the Statute of Monopolies permitted the grant of a patent monopoly in respect of "any manner of new manufacture", provided that such grant was not contrary to the overall public interest as "mischievous to the state . . . or generally inconvenient".

Of course the United Kingdom abandoned the Statute of Monopolies in 1977 when it adopted a new Patents Act based on the European Patent Convention. In the jurisdictions which continue to apply section 6 of the Statute of Monopolies, its continuing utility and suitability as the basic touchstone of patentability remains a controversial issue. In 1984 the Australian Industrial Property Advisory Committee took the view that the concept of "manner of new manufacture" operated quite satisfactorily as a threshold test of patentability.[9] It had the advantage of "being underpinned by an extensive body of decided case law which facilitates its application in particular circumstances". At the same time, it had, over the years, "exhibited a capacity to respond to new developments". The Committee concluded that to replace this concept by an explicit statutory statement of what is and is not patentable subject matter along the lines of the English Act of 1977 "would be likely to produce far more problems, with attendant costs, than it would solve". It recommended that Australian law continue to define a patentable invention by reference to section 6 of the Statute of Monopolies without any specific legislative inclusions or exclusions, and this was reflected in the revised Patents Act of 1990.

But in New Zealand the Ministry of Commerce, in a paper published in 1992,[10] viewed the current definition of "invention" incorporating section 6 of the Statute of Monopolies as an anachronism that presents an unnecessary obstacle to progress. The Ministry expressed concern at what it considered to be the rather conservative approach to interpretation and application of the definition adopted by the Court of Appeal in *Wellcome Foundation Ltd* v. *Commissioner of Patents* (hereafter "*Wellcome*").[11] There, Cooke J observed that the expression "manner of new manufacture" has no ordinary meaning today, and the present scope of the idea it conveys "can only be ascertained by seeing how the law has evolved in the decided cases".[12] Accordingly, he concluded that in New Zealand "the history of the case law must play a more dominant role in determining patentability than it apparently does in the United States".[13] McMullin J seemed reluctant to accept any argument for extension of the scope of patentable subject matter, observing that:[14]

[9] Industrial Property Advisory Committee, *Patents, Innovation and Competition in Australia* (Canberra, IPAC, 1984), 41.
[10] Ministry of Commerce, *Reform of the Patents Act 1953. Proposed Recommendations* (Wellington, 1992).
[11] [1983] NZLR 385.
[12] *Ibid.*, 387.
[13] *Ibid.*, 393.
[14] *Ibid.*, 398.

The grant of a patent is the grant of a monopoly. In recognition of this feature the patents legislation aims to balance the desirability of encouraging and protecting technological advances against the restrictions, impediments and even abuse which may result from monopolies. A shift in emphasis which favours one interest will probably be achieved only at the expense of the other. Whether, and to what extent, any significant innovative movement is justifiable is, I think, not a matter for the Courts.

On the particular point at issue in *Wellcome*, the Court decided that it should adhere to the established English practice of refusing patents for new methods of treating human illness, and leave any change to Parliament.

The approach taken by the Court in *Wellcome* caused the Ministry of Commerce to express concern that it may prove difficult to extend the statutory definition of invention to embrace new technologies.[15] Computer software was given as an example. The Ministry therefore recommended that New Zealand follow the example of the United Kingdom Patents Act of 1977 by repealing the statutory definition of the term "invention" and leaving patentability to be determined by application of three criteria: the invention must be new, it must involve an inventive step, and it must be industrially applicable. But unlike the Untied Kingdom statute, and the European Patent Convention from which it was derived, the Ministry recommended that the New Zealand Act should contain no specific exclusions from patentability.[16] This reform would detach the meaning of "invention" from the jurisprudence associated with section 6 of the Statute of Monopolies, so that "[a]ny possibility of being restricted by previous practice would be removed".[17] In practical terms, New Zealand practice would be brought closer to the American model.

But for the intervention of Maori groups objecting to the patenting of genetic material and new life forms, the Ministry's recommended reforms would have been implemented long ago. However, since 1994 the Ministry has been engaged in a protracted course of consultation with Maori and its reform process has stalled.[18] In my view, the Maori objectors deserve a vote of thanks. The Ministry's concerns have been proved groundless: it is now clear that the present statutory definition of invention does not present an insurmountable obstacle to the patenting of new forms of technology. But at the same time, the core ideas that underlie the terms of section 6 of the Statute of Monopolies continue to provide a valuable check upon unreflective acceptance of novel or over-broad claims, and over-enthusiastic adoption of overseas developments.

[15] Ministry of Commerce, *Reform of the Patents Act 1953. Proposed Recommendations* (Wellington, 1992), 7.

[16] *Ibid.*, 9.

[17] *Ibid.*, 7. Whether this expectation would be fully realised in practice is somewhat uncertain: see *Biogen, Inc* v. *Medeva plc* [1997] RPC 1, 31–2, *per* Lord Mustill, and 41–2, *per* Lord Hoffmann.

[18] See *Patenting of Biotechnological Inventions*, A Ministry of Commerce Paper on Issues for Discussion with Maori (Wellington, 1999), and *Maori and the Patenting of Lifeform Inventions*, An Information Paper Produced by the Patenting of Life Forms Focus Group for The Ministry of Commerce (Wellington, 1999).

III THE ESSENCE OF SECTION 6 OF THE STATUTE OF MONOPOLIES

The grant of a patent monopoly represents state-supported curtailment of competition at the point where competition is likely to be most intense. This is *prima facie* undesirable. It is justified by the need to provide an economic incentive for technical innovation that will increase the range and efficiency of the goods and services available to the community, and at the same time procure early disclosure of information about advances so that competitors in the industry have a chance to survive and flourish by making improvements and variations. Since the object is to encourage the development and commercialisation of new products, patents are properly limited to technological advances, and the monopoly rights they confer must preclude competition only in proportion to the scale and utility of the advance disclosed. To the extent that patent rights extend beyond these limits, they represent dead weight costs to the economy that serve only to suppress competition and stifle progress.

The essential idea conveyed by the term "manner of new manufacture" is that intellectual conceptions become patentable only to the extent that they have become embodied in specific new technical applications that have economic value. For many years that central idea was captured in the requirement that a patentable process must result in the production or improvement of a "vendible product". That idea still finds clear expression in the High Court of Australia's explanation and elaboration of the vendible product test in *National Research Development Corporation* v. *Commissioner of Patents* (hereafter "NRDC").[19] There the High Court emphasised that a patentable process or method must produce a new end result in the form of a discernible "artificially created state of affairs",[20] and that result must have value "in the field of economic endeavour"—it must belong "to a useful art as distinct from a fine art".[21]

Further, the proviso in the last part of section 6 of the Statute of Monopolies reminds us that the patent system is a *public* instrument of economic and social policy and the rights it confers must advance overall public welfare, not undermine it. So even if an application discloses a "manner of new manufacture", a patent grant must nevertheless be withheld if it would be "mischievous to the State . . . or generally inconvenient".

It is these fundamental precepts that inform the ultimate determination of whether a claimed product or process is "a proper subject of letters patent according to the principles that have been developed for the application of s 6 of the Statute of Monopolies".[22]

---

[19] (1959) 102 CLR 252. See also [1961] RPC 134.
[20] *Ibid.*, 277.
[21] *Ibid.*, 275.
[22] *Ibid.*, 269; *Wellcome Foundation Ltd* v. *Commissioner of Patents* [1983] NZLR 385, 401 *per* Somers J.

IV THE NRDC CASE

The judgment of the High Court of Australia in the NRDC case[23] in 1959 has assumed an almost iconic status in Australia, and it has also been approved and applied in New Zealand. Certainly it resulted in a significant extension of the range of patentable methods and processes. As well as explaining and extending the core notion of a "vendible product", the High Court held that the discovery that a known substance can be used to achieve a new and useful purpose will support a valid method claim even if the proposed mode of use is neither novel nor inventive. English cases which had insisted that a "mere new use for an old thing" is never patentable, and that a valid claim must disclose "novelty in the mode of using [the old thing] as distinguished from novelty of purpose",[24] were explained as cases where the claimed use was "analogous" to the established use and therefore obvious.[25] By contrast, the NRDC specification claimed "a new process for ridding crop areas of certain kinds of weeds, not by applying chemicals the properties of which were formerly well understood so that the idea of using them for this purpose involved no inventive step, but by applying chemicals which formerly were supposed not to be useful for this kind of purpose at all".[26]

The High Court also abandoned the longstanding administrative practice of refusing patents for processes having application in the fields of horticulture and agriculture. While it might be true that in an area of human activity as old as primary production, a newly devised procedure would often turn out to be nothing more than an analogous application of an age-old technique and the claim would therefore fail for obviousness or lack of novelty, this did not justify a generalised rule that horticultural or agricultural processes can never qualify as a manner of new manufacture.[27]

The High Court's reasoning was soon approved and followed in New Zealand in Swift & Co v. Commissioner of Patents,[28] where Barrowclough CJ went on to hold that biological and physiological processes may qualify as patentable inventions.

More recently, controversy and debate about the proper scope of patentable subject matter have focused on three areas: biotechnology, computer software, and methods of treating human illness.

[23] (1959) 102 CLR 252.
[24] See T.A. Blanco White, Patents for Inventions (4th edn., London, Stevens & Co, 1974), para. 1–208.
[25] National Research Development Corporation v. Commissioner of Patents (1959) 102 CLR 252, 262–3. Of course, if it is apparent from the specification that the claimed use is one for which the known properties of the substance made it particularly suitable, the claim will lack the necessary quality of inventiveness required to qualify as a manner of new manufacture: NV Philips Gloeilampenfabrieken v. Mirabella International Pty. Ltd (1995) 183 CLR 655; Advanced Building Systems Pty. Ltd v. Ramset Fasteners (Aust.) Pty. Ltd (1998) 194 CLR 171.
[26] Ibid., 264–5.
[27] Ibid., 278–9.
[28] [1960] NZLR 775.

V BIOTECHNOLOGY AND NEW LIFE FORMS

As developed and applied in the *NRDC* and *Swift* cases, the concept of a manner of new manufacture is clearly capable of embracing new life forms, and Patent Office practice in both Australia and New Zealand has been to accept claims to living organisms and products derived from them. The Australian practice dates from the decision of the Assistant Commissioner in *Rank Hovis McDougall Ltd's Application*[29] in 1976 where a patent was granted in respect of artificial variants of a new strain of micro-organism which was useful for producing a form of edible protein. This decision was confirmed in an Office Notice published by the Australian Patent Office in 1980, which stated that applications concerning living organisms would be treated in the same way as other applications, and that no distinction would be drawn between micro-organisms and higher life forms such as plants and animals.[30] The New Zealand Intellectual Property Office follows the same practice, and patents are granted in respect of both micro-organisms and higher life forms. Section 10(7) of the New Zealand Patents Act 1953 does provide that a claim to a new substance "shall be construed as not extending to that substance when found in nature", and this precludes patents for naturally occurring micro-organisms when found in their natural state. But such organisms do become patentable once they have been "isolated" in the sense of being removed from their natural environment and modified in some way.[31]

Both Australia and New Zealand give some limited recognition to ethical concerns about genetic manipulation of human beings. Section 18(2) of the Australian Patents Act 1990 expressly provides that "human beings, and the biological processes for their generation" are not patentable inventions. The critical term "human being" is not defined in the Act and it has not yet been the subject of judicial interpretation. However, the Australian Patent Office treats it as including foetuses, embryos and fertilised eggs.[32] Whether the prohibition extends to isolated parts of human beings, and if so what parts, remains uncertain. But claims to "purified and isolated" DNA sequences encoding human proteins have been accepted as patentable inventions.[33]

The New Zealand Patents Act contains no equivalent to section 18(2) of the Australian Act. However the New Zealand Intellectual Property Office has a

---

[29] (1976) 46 AOJP 3915.

[30] "Patent Applications Concerned with Living Organisms" (1980) 50 AOJP 1162, subsequently confirmed in Practice Note No. 6 of 1991 issued in April 1991.

[31] See *Patenting of Biotechnological Inventions*, A Ministry of Commerce Paper on Issues for Discussion with Maori (Wellington, 1999), 6.

[32] *Ibid.*, 11. The APO also treats "processes beginning with fertilisation and ending with birth, which are wholly biological, and result in a human being", as excluded under this provision.

[33] *Kiren-Amgen, Inc.* v. *Board of Regents of University of Washington* (1995) 33 IPR 557, 569 (Deputy Commissioner Herald); affirmed *Genetics Institute, Inc.* v. *Kirin-Amgen, Inc. (No 3)* (1998) 41 IPR 325 (Heerey J).

practice of excluding human beings from patentability.[34] While the Office justifies this practice on the basis that a human being cannot be regarded as a "manner of new manufacture", it is probably better founded on the "generally inconvenient" public policy proviso in section 6 of the Statute of Monopolies, or section 17 of the Patents Act 1953 which gives the Commissioner a discretion to refuse an application if the use of the claimed invention would be "contrary to morality". Of course, adoption of the recommendations for reform of the Patents Act proposed by the Ministry of Commerce would remove all of these justifications for the current practice, and the Ministry concedes that a specific statutory exclusion along the lines of section 18(2) of the Australian Act would be needed to authorise it.[35] This would raise the further question whether the term "human being" should be specifically defined in the statute or, as in Australia, left to the interpretation of the Commissioner and ultimately the courts.

In New Zealand, public concern is no longer focused only on the sanctity of human life, and now extends to the ethical, environmental and health implications of genetic modification of all forms of living organisms. But it is clear that the Ministry of Commerce sees any further adjustment of Patent Office practice to reflect these wider concerns as inappropriate and undesirable. The Ministry argues that since patents confer only negative rights on patentees to prevent others from exploiting an invention, effective regulation of the development and use of biotechnological inventions cannot be achieved through patent law. Direct regulatory controls are required, and in New Zealand these are imposed by the Environmental Risk Management Authority pursuant to the Hazardous Substances and New Organisms Act 1996. As to moral and ethical issues, resolution of such questions is seen as beyond the role and competence of the Intellectual Property Office, and therefore should not be attempted.[36]

This attitude is consistent with the American view of the patent system as a morally neutral system for rewarding invention. But it is not consistent with the Statute of Monopolies. Under the Statute of Monopolies system, patents are justified only to the extent that they provide effective incentive for the development of new technologies that advance public welfare. If a particular form of invention, or the manner in which it has been developed, threatens the public welfare, the patent incentive must be withheld. The public policy proviso in section 6 of the Statute of Monopolies instructs the Commissioner and the courts in precisely these terms.

The recent European Biotechnology Directive[37] provides a useful source of guidance on these matters, and the Australian and New Zealand Patent Offices should give serious consideration to adopting some of the restrictions it imposes

---

[34] *Patenting of Biotechnological Inventions*, A Ministry of Commerce Paper on Issues for Discussion with Maori (Wellington, 1999), 6, 14.

[35] *Ibid.*, 14.

[36] *Ibid.*, 8–9 and 14.

[37] See (1998) 29 IIC 567.

on patentability of biotechnological inventions. For example, we could usefully adopt the practice of refusing patents for inventions which are based on the use of biological material of human origin unless there is clear evidence that the person from whose body the material was taken gave free and informed consent.[38] The Commissioner should also consider adopting the four classes of biotechnological inventions specifically excluded from patentability under the Directive.[39]

Of course, claims by New Zealand Maori, pursuant to the Treaty of Waitangi of 1840, to exclusive ownership and control of the genetic resources of all indigenous plants and animals[40] cannot be accommodated within the present patent legislation. Those claims can be resolved only by a political settlement, and that may take some considerable time.

VI   COMPUTER PROGRAMS

In common with most other jurisdictions, patent practice in Australia and New Zealand in relation to computer software inventions has shifted quite dramatically over the years and remains a subject of controversy. From initial positions of suspicion and hostility, both jurisdictions now take a very liberal approach to software claims.

Until the mid-1980s, the practice of the Australian Patent Office was to deny claims relating to the operation of computers.[41] Since computer programs embody algorithms, they were equated with methods of mathematical calculation, scientific theories and principles, mere schemes and plans, and other purely intellectual conceptions—subject matter that lacks the technical character and application of a "manner of manufacture". Australian examiners and hearing officers refused to follow decisions of the English Patents Appeal Tribunal under the 1949 United Kingdom legislation on which the Australian Act was based. The Tribunal had afforded software quite generous patent protection by adopting the *NRDC* approach to method claims and focusing attention on the

[38] Recital 26.
[39] Art. 6 of the Directive expressly excludes from patentability:

(1) processes for cloning human beings;
(2) processes for modifying the germ-line genetic identity of human beings;
(3) uses of human embryos for industrial or commercial purposes; and
(4) processes for modifying the genetic identity of animals which are likely to cause them suffering without any substantial medical benefit to man or animal, and also animals resulting from such processes.

[40] The WAI 262 claim before the Waitangi Tribunal asserts the right of ownership and control of the genetic resources of native plants and animals.
[41] See *British Petroleum Co Ltd's Application* (1968) 38 AOJP 1020; *Mobil Oil Corp.'s Application* (1973) 43 AOJP 1282, (1975) 45 AOJP 2323; *Telefon A/B Ericsson's Application* (1974) 44 AOJP 846, [1975] FSR 49; *Context Systems, Inc.'s Application* (1978) 48 AOJP 1093. See generally, J. Lahore, *Patents, Trade Marks & Related Rights* (Sydney, Butterworths, 1996), i, para. 12,520.

physical effect of the program when applied to the computer, rather than on the program (and the underlying algorithm) itself. So in *Burroughs Corporation (Perkins') Application*,[42] the Tribunal held that where a method of programming a computer "results in a new machine or process or an old machine giving a new and improved result, that fact should . . . be regarded as the 'product' or result of using the method. . .". Provided that "product" or result has "consequent economic importance or advantages in the field of the useful as opposed to the fine arts"[43] the method will be patentable.[44]

In the early 1980s the Australian Patent Office reviewed its practice in the light of developments in the United States. In 1986 it issued official guidelines[45] which adopted the "*Freeman* test" developed by the United States Court of Customs and Patent Appeals[46] to determine the patentability of software inventions. This test involved a two-stage inquiry: first, does the claim directly or indirectly recite a mathematical algorithm?; and, secondly, if so, does it "wholly pre-empt" the algorithm in the sense that the claim is for the algorithm itself rather than for some physical application of it? So if the claim recites application of the algorithm in a specific manner "to define structural relationships between the physical elements of the claim (in apparatus claims) or to refine or limit claim steps (in process claims)",[47] then it is likely to pass muster as disclosing patentable subject matter. But if the algorithm is merely presented as a problem and solved, and is not "applied in any manner to physical elements or process steps", the application will fail.[48] Although expressed in rather complex terms, the *Freeman* test had the same emphasis and effect as the pre-1977 English decisions, requiring claims to be limited by reference to the physical environment in which the program operates.

Then in 1991, in the first judicial consideration of the issue in Australia, the Federal Court seemed to abandon the *Freeman* test in favour of an approach founded directly on the *NRDC* case. The test for patentability identified by Burchett J in *International Business Machines Corp.* v. *Commissioner of Patents* (hereafter "*IBM*")[49] is very broad indeed—simply, whether the program, when applied in a computer, produces "a commercially useful effect". As an exclusive test, this is far too broad. It is, of course, very similar to the "practical utility" criterion applied by the United States Federal Circuit Court of Appeals in the *State*

---

[42] [1974] RPC 147, 158.

[43] *Ibid.*, 160.

[44] The *Burroughs* approach was rejected by the Australian Patent Office in *Telefon A/B Ericsson's Application* (1974) 44 AOJP 846, [1975] FSR 49; and *Context Systems Inc.'s Application* (1978) 48 AOJP 1093.

[45] Patent Office, *Guidelines for Considering the Patentability of Computer Program Related Inventions* (Canberra, Patent Office, 1986).

[46] See *In re Freeman*, 573 F 2d 1237 (CCPA 1978); *In re Walter*, 618 F 2d 758 (CCPA 1980); *In re Abele*, 684 F 2d 902 (CCPA 1982).

[47] *In re Walter*, n. 46 above, 767.

[48] As in *Re Application by Honeywell Bull, Inc.* (1991) 22 IPR 463, 468 *per* W.J. Major, Delegate.

[49] (1991) 22 IPR 417, 424.

Street Bank case,[50] and attracts the same problems. Applied literally, and without due caution, such an approach may allow claims that have the practical effect of removing from the public domain mathematical algorithms and conventional computer applications of methods of processing information and doing business.

In the *IBM* case itself, the applicant claimed a mathematical algorithm as a "method for producing a visual representation of a curve image". The Commissioner's Delegate held that since the claim was not limited to any particular physical environment or field of use, it "wholly pre-empted" the algorithm and failed the *Freeman* test. Burchett J overcame this objection by finding that the claim was limited, by necessary implication, "to the operation of computers".[51] But limiting the claim to the field of computing places no meaningful limit on its application since the algorithm has no practical application outside this broad field. Although Burchett J insisted that the program must have "a commercially useful effect", which he found in its capacity to produce an improved curve image for use in computer graphic displays,[52] the claim was not expressly limited to that particular effect or application. In practical terms, identification of *one* commercially useful effect for a mathematical algorithm in the field of computing gave a monopoly over *all* commercially useful effects.[53] While Burchett J justified his decision by reference to the *NRDC* case, he seemed to focus his attention exclusively on the High Court's explanation of the "vendible" limb of the vendible product requirement. But of course the High Court also insisted, as a separate condition of patentability, that a claimed method must produce a "product" in the sense of a discernible "artificially created state of affairs". In the case of a computer program, this will not be satisfied until it is physically applied to achieve a particular end result, and the claim must be limited to that particular application.

The subsequent decision of the Full Federal Court of Australia in *CCOM Pty. Ltd* v. *Jiejing Pty. Ltd*[54] seems to have corrected the position on this point. There the Court accepted that *NRDC* requires that a claim in respect of a computer program must be limited by reference to a particular end result which qualifies as an "artificially created state of affairs".[55]

So the "commercially useful effect" test operates as an additional requirement to limit the range of "end results" (or "products") that qualify as suitable subject matter for a patent grant. But even when applied for this more limited purpose, the test is too loose and undemanding. In fact it is difficult to envisage a claimed invention that would fail the test, since it is highly unlikely that anyone would pursue a patent application in respect of a product or process that clearly

---

[50] *State Street Bank & Trust Co* v. *Signature Financial Group, Inc.*, 149 F 3d 1368 (Fed. Cir. 1998).

[51] (1991) 22 IPR 417, 422.

[52] *Ibid.*, 424.

[53] See C. Wood, "Patents in Computer Software—Commercially Useful is Not Enough" (1998) 9 *AIPJ* 134, 139.

[54] (1994) 28 IPR 481.

[55] *Ibid.*, 514. The current guidelines applied by IP Australia reflect this position: see Wood, n. 53 above, 142.

had no commercial potential. As the recent American experience demonstrates, a standard of "commercial utility" is clearly capable of embracing orthodox computer applications of plans, financial schemes, business methods and arrangements of information that traditionally have been treated as falling outside the field of industrial technology which the grant of a patent monopoly is designed to stimulate. In the past, it has been assumed that sufficient incentive to generate material of that kind is provided by less restrictive legal rights to prevent copying and breaches of confidence.

The judgment delivered in the *NRDC* case discloses no intention to disturb the traditional understanding, the High Court emphasising that a patentable process "must be one that offers some advantage which is material, in the sense that the process belongs to a useful art as distinct from a fine art . . .—that its value to the country is in the field of economic endeavour".[56] Yet in the *IBM* case Burchett J seemed to regard his "commercially useful effect" test as capturing and subsuming the distinction drawn in *NRDC*: if the claimed invention has a commercially useful effect, its value lies in the field of economic endeavour, and it therefore belongs to a useful art.[57]

The trial judge in the *CCOM* case[58] did not accept this reasoning. It was clear that the claimed invention—a word-processing program operated in a conventional computer to permit storage and assembly of Chinese language characters—had commercial value. Nevertheless Cooper J held that the invention did not qualify as a "manner of manufacture" since it made no technical contribution in the field of computing and simply performed a linguistic mental task which "lies in the fine arts and not the useful arts".[59] However, the Full Federal Court of Australia reversed Cooper J on this point. The Full Court considered it sufficient that the artificially created state of affairs achieved by application of the program had "utility in the field of economic endeavour", and found that requirement to be satisfied on the facts of the case before them.[60] In my opinion, the trial judge got it right.

If the range of patentable subject matter is extended to embrace any kind of conventional computer software application that has commercial or economic

---

[56] (1959) 102 CLR 252, 275; and see *Burroughs Corporation (Perkins') Application* [1974] RPC 147 and accompanying text to n. 43 above. See also *Quigley Co Inc.'s Application* (1973) 43 AOJP 3375; [1977] FSR 373, where the Assistant Commissioner took the view that nothing in the *NRDC* case suggested that "a commonplace management technique such as scheduling for the better utilisation of manpower" was patentable subject matter despite the fact that it resulted in greater output from a steel plant.

[57] (1991) 22 IPR 417, 423. See A. Christie and S. Syme, "Patents for Algorithms in Australia" (1998) 20 *Sydney L Rev* 517, 526–7.

[58] (1993) 27 IPR 577 (Cooper J).

[59] *Ibid.*, 593. See also *A Couple 'A Cowboys Pty. Ltd* v. *Ward* (1995) 31 IPR 45, 58, where Commissioner's Delegate Tolhurst seemed to treat the *IBM* test as distinct and separate from the useful arts/fine arts distinction: the claimed invention "must be in the useful arts and not the fine or intellectual arts, *and* should produce something of economic value or a commercially useful effect" (emphasis added).

[60] (1994) 28 IPR 481, 514: "[i]n the present case, a relevant field of economic endeavour is the use of word processing to assemble text in Chinese language characters".

utility, the focus of attention will merely shift to questions of novelty and obviousness. But it is clear that patent examiners face serious practical difficulties in establishing the "prior art" against which the novelty of computer software inventions is to be judged, due to the wide diversity of sources of prior art in the field of computer science and the rapid pace of developments in this area.[61] So there is a real risk that patents will be granted in respect of software that displays no true innovation and simply employs established procedures and techniques.[62] Obviously, patent grants of this kind frustrate the purpose of the patent system by blocking rather than encouraging development of the industry. Practical concerns of this kind lay behind the widespread initial reluctance to grant patents for software inventions.[63]

The same concerns explain the present insistence of the European Patent Office that in order to take a software invention outside the expressly excluded category of a computer program "as such",[64] it must make a *technical* contribution to the known art. If the software addresses a technical problem, either external to the computer or relating to the functioning of the computer itself, it is patentable subject matter and the search of the prior art can be confined to the technical field in question. But if the claimed invention merely discloses an improvement in the manipulation and presentation of information, it is not patentable and there is no need to examine for novelty and inventiveness. Examples of inventions which failed this test and were held unpatentable include a data processing program for implementing an automated trading market in securities;[65] a program enabling the faster calculation of the square roots of numbers;[66] a program for automatically abstracting, storing and retrieving documents by use of a conventional computer;[67] and a Chinese language word processing program similar to that in issue in the *CCOM* case.[68]

---

[61] See Christie and Syme, n. 57 above, 531.

[62] See I. Lloyd, "Patenting Software", 1995 *Scots LT* 163, 166–7. This risk is exacerbated in New Zealand where examiners do not examine for obviousness, so that objection on that ground can only be made by a third party after an application has been accepted. See J. Terry, "Software Patents: Good or Bad?" (1995) 1 *NZIPJ* 10, 12–3, recommending a number of changes to New Zealand practice in order to reduce the risk of acceptance of over-broad claims.

[63] In the United States, see *Gottschalk* v. *Benson*, 409 US 63, 72 (1972) quoting from the *Report of the President's Commission on the Patent System* (1966): "reliable searches would not be feasible or economic because of the tremendous volume of prior art. . . . Without this search the patenting of programs would be tantamount to mere registration and the presumption of validity would be all but non-existent". In Australia, one of the reasons given by the Industrial Property Advisory Committee for not recommending "explicit extension of the field of patentability to cover software" was "the great practical difficulty . . . of conducting systematic and thorough novelty searches": *Patents, Innovation and Competition in Australia* (Canberra, 1984), 41. In the United Kingdom, the Banks Committee (Cmnd. 4407, 1970) expressed the same concerns.

[64] European Patent Convention, Art. 52(2)(c). The parallel provision of the UK Patents Act 1977 is s. 1(2)(c).

[65] *Merrill Lynch's Application* [1989] RPC 561 (CA).

[66] *Gale's Application* [1991] RPC 305 (CA).

[67] *IBM/Document Abstracting and Retrieving* [1990] EPOR 98 (Technical Board of the EPO).

[68] *Re the Computer Generation of Chinese Characters* [1993] FSR 315 (German Federal Supreme Court).

As Cooper J correctly appreciated in *CCOM*,[69] the European distinction expresses the same concept and addresses the same concern as that drawn in the *NRDC* case between the useful and the fine arts. And ultimately, of course, the term "manner of new manufacture", shorn of unnecessary embellishment, reminds us that patent monopolies should be reserved for technical advances in areas of industrial rather than intellectual activity.

In New Zealand, the Patent Office refused to accept software related claims until 1993. Then, in *Clarks Limited's Application*,[70] Commissioner Burton allowed an application in respect of a method of programming a computer to produce a range of shoe patterns. But, at the same time, the Commissioner was critical of the Australian *IBM* decision and expressed strong reservations about the patentability of software inventions, emphasising that his decision was based on the principle that an applicant is entitled to the benefit of any doubt. Those doubts were substantially removed two years later by the decision of Commissioner Popplewell, in *Hughes Aircraft Company's Application*,[71] to accept an application in respect of a computer-controlled method for determining *en route* airspace conflict alert status for aircraft. However, the implications of the decision are not altogether clear, since the Commissioner gave two alternative justifications for his ruling. First, he endorsed and applied the test advanced by Burchett J in the *IBM* case, finding the required "commercially useful effect" in an "improvement in air traffic control and, ultimately, the prevention of mid-air collisions". However, the Commissioner also justified his decision on a narrower basis by reference to the criteria set out by the English Patents Appeal Tribunal in the *Burroughs* case.[72] These require a claim to be clearly directed to the physical application of the program to achieve a particular new and improved result that offers "advantages in the field of the useful as opposed to the fine arts". I favour the narrower justification for the decision.

VII METHODS OF TREATING HUMAN ILLNESS

A Methods of Treatment Generally

The issue that is presently attracting most attention in Australia and New Zealand is the status and scope of the longstanding rule that denies patent protection to methods of medical treatment. Of course product patents can be obtained in respect of apparatus designed for use in treating medical conditions, and for new compounds and compositions for treating human illness. But claims to new surgical techniques and new processes for treating the human body by using known substances were, until recently, held unpatentable.

---

[69] (1993) 27 IPR 577.
[70] Unreported, 30 June 1993. Noted [1993] 9 EIPR 217.
[71] Unreported, 3 May 1995. Noted [1995] 7 EIPR 203.
[72] [1974] RPC 147.

The legal justification for this rule has shifted over the years. At first, it was explained on the basis that a process for treating the human body did not qualify as a "manner of new manufacture" because it did not result in the production of a vendible article of commerce.[73] But in the *NRDC* case the High Court of Australia explained the concept of a vendible product in terms sufficiently broad to cover methods of medical treatment and cast doubt upon the traditional justification for their exclusion. Nevertheless, the Court itself seemed to assume that methods and processes for treating the human body would remain unpatentable, offering as a possible explanation the suggestion that "the whole subject is conceived as essentially non-economic".[74] That explanation was rejected by the High Court in *Joos* v. *Commissioner of Patents*,[75] where Barwick CJ observed that good methods of surgery promoted the national economic interest by assisting the rehabilitation of workers, and this was sufficient to satisfy the "economic element of an invention". While the High Court was prepared to accept (without finally deciding) that methods of treatment remained outside the range of patentable subject matter, Barwick CJ preferred to explain this result in terms of the public policy proviso to section 6 of the Statute of Monopolies. But the High Court saw no reason to extend the exclusion beyond methods of curing or preventing human disease, and since the application before the Court related to a method of "cosmetic" treatment for improving the strength and elasticity of human hair and nails, it fell outside the exclusion and was allowed to proceed.

The decision in *Joos* prompted the Australian Patent Office to change its practice. The Office interpreted Barwick CJ's judgment as casting sufficient doubt on the validity of the traditional rule that in future no objection should be taken to claims for methods of treatment, medical or otherwise, of the human body.[76]

In New Zealand, the Patent Office adhered to the traditional practice and refused claims for methods of medical treatment. This was challenged in *Wellcome Foundation Ltd* v. *Commissioner of Patents*,[77] where Wellcome appealed from a decision of the Assistant Commissioner refusing an application relating to a method of treating an illness with a drug previously used for treating another medical condition. The trial judge, Davison CJ, allowed the appeal. Applying the *NRDC* case, which he described as "a landmark decision in patent law",[78] the Chief Justice held that the claimed method qualified as "a manner of

---

[73] See *Re C & W's Application* (1914) 31 RPC 235; *Maeder* v. *Busch* (1938) 59 CLR 684, 706, *per* Dixon CJ (obiter); *Maeder* v. *"Ronda" Ladies Hairdressing Salon* [1943] NZLR 122 (NZCA).

[74] (1959) 102 CLR 252, 275.

[75] (1972) 126 CLR 611, 618.

[76] The change was noted and explained by the Acting Assistant Commissioner, Mr R.W. Brown, in his decision in *Upjohn's Application* (1979) 49 AOJP 382 (noted in Lahore, n. 41 above, at para. 12,350) and was later incorporated in the *Australian Patent Examiner's Manual* (Canberra, Patent Office, 1984), para. 35.80.

[77] [1979] 2 NZLR 591 (Davison CJ); [1983] NZLR 385 (NZCA).

[78] [1979] 2 NZLR 591, 611.

new manufacture", and there were no policy reasons to withhold a grant. Davison CJ saw no good reason to distinguish between product patents for new drugs and medical apparatus, and new methods of treating illness with existing substances. Research directed at discovering new properties and new uses for existing drugs was just as valuable and deserving of a patent incentive as research into the development of new pharmaceutical compounds.

But the Court of Appeal reversed the decision of the Chief Justice and unanimously reaffirmed the rule that a method of treating human disease or illness is not a patentable invention. The Court endorsed the approach taken in the *NRDC* case, and accepted that a method of using a known substance for a new purpose was a "manner of new manufacture". However, the Court invoked the proviso to section 6 of the Statute of Monopolies, holding that the application should be rejected on public policy grounds as "generally inconvenient". The Court relied on both economic and ethical arguments in support of this conclusion. The economic argument, as explained by Cooke J,[79] was that the ability of drug companies to secure product patents for new compounds already provides an incentive for pharmaceutical research, and the additional benefits derived from providing a further patent incentive to develop new therapeutic uses for known drugs may be outweighed by the increased costs to consumers consequent upon effective extension of the patent term. The Court also relied on the ethical argument that medical professionals should not be inhibited by fear of patent infringement from using any means at their disposal to treat human illness, Cooke J quoting an Israeli judge:[80]

> We are confronted here with saving human life or alleviating human suffering and one should take great care lest a restriction on the freedom of action of those who treat, caused by patents, should affect human life or health.

The New Zealand Court of Appeal seems to have been unaware that the Australian Patent Office had already changed its practice in favour of accepting claims to methods of medical treatment.[81]

But the Australian practice has since come under challenge and its present legal status is uncertain. The first challenge was successfully overcome in *Anaesthetic Supplies Pty. Ltd* v. *Rescare Ltd*,[82] where a majority of the Full Federal Court held that a method for treating a chronic sleep disorder was a patentable invention. The New Zealand *Wellcome* case featured prominently: Lockhart J, delivering the leading majority judgment, endorsed and relied upon the reasoning of Davison CJ; while the dissenting judge, Sheppard J, invoked the Court of Appeal's decision in support of his conclusion that patent grants for methods of treating human disease should be denied as "generally inconve-

---

[79] [1983] NZLR 385, 391–2.

[80] *Ibid.*, 388, quoting Kahn J in *Wellcome Foundation Ltd* v. *Plantex Ltd* [1974] RPC 514, 539.

[81] Somers J observed that "no case of a grant of such a patent has been found in England, New Zealand or Australia . . .": *ibid.*, 404.

[82] (1994) 28 IPR 383.

nient". But since the patent was held invalid on other grounds, the views expressed on this issue in *Rescare* were technically obiter dicta, and when the point was raised before a single judge of the Federal Court in *Bristol-Myers Squibb Co* v. *F.H. Faulding & Co Ltd*,[83] Heerey J felt free to adopt the view preferred by the dissenting judge in *Rescare* and the New Zealand Court of Appeal in *Wellcome*. Consequently, he held that patents claiming a method of administering the known drug taxol in the treatment of cancer were "generally inconvenient" in terms of section 6 of the Statute of Monopolies and therefore invalid. However, the Patents Office (now IP Australia) has declined to follow this ruling. In a recent decision, the Commissioner's Delegate treated Heerey J's comments as obiter, and preferred to follow the view of the majority in *Rescare*.[84] Clearly there is a sharp division of judicial opinion on this issue within the Federal Court.[85] But until the legal position is finally settled, it seems that IP Australia will adhere to its current practice of accepting all methods of medical treatment as patentable subject matter.

In Australia, the merits of a rule barring methods of medical treatment from patentability have been debated on a general "all-or-nothing" basis. But in New Zealand, faced with the clear decision of the Court of Appeal in *Wellcome*, attention has been directed at confining the ambit of the exclusionary rule as narrowly as possible,[86] and devising ways of avoiding its application. In particular, drug companies sought to persuade the Commissioner to accept the "Swiss" form of claim devised in Europe to take claims for second therapeutic uses of known pharmaceutical drugs outside the express exclusion of methods of treatment under the European Patent Convention and the national laws of the Member States.

B "Swiss"-type Claims in New Zealand

The Swiss-type claim recites the use of a known compound in the manufacture of a known medicament for a newly discovered therapeutic use.[87] As a matter of substance, the subject matter of a Swiss claim clearly falls within the

---

[83] (1998) 41 IPR 467.

[84] *Re Application 657686 by Synaptic Pharmaceutical Corporation*, 9 September 1998, noted in Lahore, n. 41 above, Bulletin No 99, April 1999, 11–12.

[85] The issue was raised most recently in *Aktiebolaget Hassle* v. *Alphapharm Pty. Ltd* (1999) 44 IPR 593, 636, but Lehane J found it unnecessary to decide the point.

[86] An Office Practice Note issued on 26 March 1996 ((1996) 85 NZPOJ 249) reversed the emphasis of the rule, stating: "[c]laims to methods for the treatment of humans are allowable *except* where the treatment identified relates to surgery or to the treatment or prevention of disease". Claims to methods of cosmetic treatment were allowed in *Joseph H. Handelman's Application* No 213805, 23 February 1993, and the Note indicates that claims to methods of contraceptive treatment and methods of diagnosis of illness in humans would be allowed. A further Practice Note issued in October 1998 allows claims "to the treatment of conditions that do not cause suffering or which might be matters of choice".

[87] Claims in this form were first approved in a practice statement issued by the Swiss Federal Intellectual Property Office in 1984 ([1984] OJ EPO 581).

Wellcome exclusion of methods of treatment, and in 1990 the New Zealand Commissioner of Patents disallowed such a claim on that ground.[88] But in January 1997 the Commissioner changed his mind, issuing a Practice Note which stated that in future Swiss claims would not be rejected by patent examiners. The legal validity of this ruling was immediately challenged by the government agency responsible for deciding whether and to what extent pharmaceutical products qualify for subsidy in the administration of the national health services. In *Pharmaceutical Management Agency Ltd* v. *Commissioner of Patents* (hereafter "*Pharmac*"),[89] Gallen J upheld the validity of the Commissioner's ruling, holding that claims in the Swiss form are "legitimate in principle" and do not conflict with the *Wellcome* decision. The judge emphasised that the actual decision in *Wellcome* related only to claims to a method of medical treatment. Because the Swiss claim is drafted in the form of a claim to a method of manufacturing a drug it does not formally, on its face, infringe the *Wellcome* ban on methods of treatment.

The great attraction of the Swiss claim lies in its ability to distinguish industrial uses of second pharmaceutical indications from purely therapeutic uses. Infringement is established only by unauthorised manufacture of the drug with a view to its being used for its new specified therapeutic effect. Since the Swiss-type claim does not extend to or inhibit the actual therapeutic administration of the compound to a patient in the course of medical treatment, the ethical concerns about denying health professionals the right to use available means of treating human illness have no application.[90]

Nor was Gallen J persuaded by the economic argument against patentability advanced by Cooke J in *Wellcome*. He accepted that allowing patents for new therapeutic uses of known drugs may result in increased costs to Pharmac and therefore to the New Zealand public as a whole. But his Honour was also satisfied, on the basis of evidence tendered by drug companies in support of the Commissioner's ruling, that "the protection of a patent may be necessary to not only encourage, but justify the expenditure of very significant sums of money, to develop products which may in the end be of very considerable benefit to the community . . .".[91] In the end, Gallen J held that the opposing arguments as to overall "public utility" were "equally supportable" and therefore cancelled each other out.[92]

However, the legal reasoning employed by Gallen J to justify his decision in the *Pharmac* case is not altogether convincing. The problem with Swiss-type

---

[88] *Re Massachusetts Institute of Technology*, Application No 199328, 17 September 1990.

[89] [1999] RPC 752. See further section IX below.

[90] *Ibid.*, 762.

[91] *Ibid.*, 756. In the case of some of the products for which second use protection was being claimed, the drugs had not proceeded to commercial production during the term of the product patent so that the initial costs of research and development in relation to the "first use" had not been recovered. Further, expert evidence indicated that the average development cost of an approved second use was between 40 and 50% of the first use development cost.

[92] *Ibid.*

claims is that they suffer from an inherent lack of novelty. Since both the active pharmaceutical compound and the manufactured medicament are known, the only novelty disclosed by a Swiss claim lies in the newly discovered use of the drug for treating a particular human illness. But since the exclusionary rule upheld in *Wellcome* deems that use to be unpatentable subject matter, it cannot be relied on to establish novelty. For this reason the English Patents Court accepted that a Swiss claim would not be patentable under the 1949 United Kingdom statute on which the present New Zealand Act is based.[93] The Enlarged Board of Appeal of the European Patent Office overcame this obstacle by employing a strained interpretation of Article 54(5) of the European Patent Convention which provides an exception to the express exclusion from patentability of methods of medical treatment, and is mirrored in section 2(6) of the United Kingdom Patents Act 1977. The natural meaning of this provision is that the *first* therapeutic use of a known substance or composition in an excluded method of medical treatment will be considered novel and will support a claim to the substance limited by reference to that use. But, in *Re Eisai Co Ltd*[94] the Board extended the literal meaning of this provision "by analogy" to confer novelty on second and subsequent therapeutic uses, and despite serious misgivings the English Patents Court finally accepted this interpretation.[95]

In *Pharmac*, Gallen J recognised that since the New Zealand Patents Act contains no equivalent to Article 54(5) of the European Patent Convention, there was no *statutory* foundation for the "novelty by analogy" argument available to him.[96] However, he proceeded to "fill the gap" by interpreting the *Wellcome* case as permitting the grant of a patent in New Zealand for a *first* therapeutic use of a known substance previously used outside the field of medical treatment.[97] In my view, this interpretation of *Wellcome* is wrong. While a pharmaceutical composition containing a known active compound prepared for therapeutic use may attract a limited purpose product patent, the novelty of such a "composition" claim must be found in the formulation of the product; not the use thereof. Despite one loose obiter statement by Cooke J,[98] it seems clear that all members of the Court accepted that a new therapeutic use (whether first or subsequent) of a known substance would not support a patent.

Pharmac immediately lodged an appeal against the decision of Gallen J and sought to prevent the Commissioner acting on the judgment until the Court of Appeal delivered a final ruling on the matter. Pharmac obtained from Gallen J a curious order in the form of a declaration that the Commissioner "ought not to grant Swiss type patents before determination" of Pharmac's appeal.[99]

[93] *John Wyeth & Brother Ltd's Application* [1985] RPC 545, 562–3.
[94] [1985] OJ EPO 64.
[95] *John Wyeth & Brother Ltd's Application* [1985] RPC 545, 567.
[96] [1999] RPC 752, 772.
[97] *Ibid.*, 762 and 772.
[98] [1983] NZLR 385, 388 (line 15).
[99] *Pharmaceutical Management Agency Ltd* v. *Commissioner of Patents*, Oral Order of Gallen J, 12 February 1999. See further section IX below.

So what alternatives are open to the New Zealand Court of Appeal when it reviews Gallen J's decision? First, it could reaffirm the position taken in *Wellcome* and strike down the Swiss-type claim as being in substance no more than a claim to a new method of treatment. That would be unfortunate. Most jurisdictions allow claims in some form or other for second therapeutic indications of known drugs, and full legislative review of the New Zealand Patents Act may still be some time away.

At the other extreme, a Full Court of five judges could overrule *Wellcome* and remove the ban on patenting methods of medical treatment. This would bring New Zealand law into conformity with the current practice of IP Australia, and would also be consistent with the Ministry of Commerce's proposals for reform. In my view, this response would also be unwise because it would allow patent grants in respect of "pure" methods of treatment involving medical procedures and surgical techniques unrelated to pharmaceutical drugs or apparatus. The ethical objection to patentability has considerable force in respect of pure method claims and many jurisdictions exclude them. At the same time, arguments based on the need to provide economic incentives to devise and disclose new methods seem unconvincing in an environment where professionals find their rewards in peer recognition and follow an ethic of free information sharing.[100] The New Zealand Ministry of Commerce recognised that medical professionals and laypersons should be protected from liability for infringing method of treatment patents,[101] but this would require enactment of a special statutory defence to infringement along the lines of the recent amendment to the United States Patent Act,[102] and may contravene the TRIPS Agreement.[103] Further, in the absence of clear statutory provision for indirect or contributory infringement,[104] ordinary method patents are difficult to enforce against manufacturers and suppliers.[105]

---

[100] See generally P. Culbert, "Patents on Methods of Medical Treatment: Where Should the Balance Lie?" (1996) 2 *NZIPJ* 136; P. Loughlan, "Of Patents and Patients: New Monopolies in Medical Methods" (1995) 6 *AIPJ* 5.

[101] Ministry of Commerce, *Reform of the Patents Act 1953. Proposed Recommendations* (Wellington, 1992), 47 (para. 6.2.1).

[102] 35 USC § 287(c) (1994).

[103] Art. 28(1)(b). Such a defence could hardly be viewed as a "limited exception" within Art. 30.

[104] The New Zealand Patents Act 1953 makes no express provision for contributory infringement. S. 117 of the Australian Patents Act 1990 was apparently intended to impose indirect liability on suppliers, but it has been interpreted very narrowly so as to defeat this purpose: *Rescare Ltd* v. *Anaesthetic Supplies Pty. Ltd* (1992) 25 IPR 119, 153–5 (Gummow J), aff'd. *Anaesthetic Supplies Pty. Ltd* v. *Rescare Ltd* (1994) 28 IPR 383, 405 (Full Fed Ct); *Bristol-Myers Squibb Co* v. *F.H. Faulding & Co Ltd* (1998) 41 IPR 467, 487–8 (Heerey J). See generally A. Monotti, "Contributory Infringement of a Process Patent under the Patents Act 1990: Does it Exist after *Rescare*?" (1995) 6 *AIPJ* 217.

[105] The scope of common law liability in tort for inciting or procuring an infringement by the end user remains uncertain. In particular, it is unclear whether merely supplying a product with instructions to use it in a way that will infringe the plaintiff's process patent attracts tort liability: see *Bristol-Myers Squibb Co* v. *F.H. Faulding & Co Ltd* (1998) 41 IPR 467, 488–9 (Heerey J); *Ramset*

Thirdly, the Court of Appeal could simply affirm the decision of Gallen J with a minimum of explanation. It is true that the Swiss claim, framed as a method of manufacture, is a bare fiction. Nevertheless, it achieves a sensible result. The Swiss-type claim gives effective protection against rival drug manufacturers without restricting therapeutic use in the course of medical treatment, and without any need for corrective legislative intervention.

Finally, the Court of Appeal could address itself directly to the substance of the matter. The Court could approve a simple use claim in the form "the use of compound X in combating disease Y", but expressly limit the exclusive exploitation rights conferred by the patent to the industrial acts of manufacture, sale or importation for the purpose of the protected use. This approach involves recognition that a use claim in this form embraces two quite distinct aspects: the industrial aspect of manufacture and sale which is properly the subject of a patent monopoly; and the therapeutic aspect of administration of the compound which must remain unrestricted on public policy grounds. If necessary, the applicant can be required, as a condition of the grant, to disclaim expressly any rights in respect of the therapeutic act of administering the drug.[106] There are precedents for this type of approach. It was adopted by the German Federal Court of Justice in the early 1980s,[107] and in Canada the Patent Appeal Board and the Federal Court of Appeal have upheld use claims in respect of second therapeutic indications on the understanding that they cover "industrial activities" but do not extend to the actual administration of the products for medical purposes.[108] The English Patents Court[109] and the Enlarged Board of Appeal of the European Patent Office[110] both rejected this direct solution on the ground that since the use claim inherently embraced the therapeutic act it could not be reconciled with the clear terms of the statutory provisions that expressly excluded methods of therapy. But the New Zealand Court of Appeal is not subject to any such statutory constraint. In New Zealand, the rule excluding

---

Fasteners (Aust.) Pty. Ltd v. *Advanced Building Systems Pty. Ltd* (1999) 44 IPR 481, 494–507 (Full Fed. Ct.); and see generally J. McKeough and A. Stewart, *Intellectual Property in Australia* (2nd edn., Sydney, Butterworths, 1997), 324–6. However, the Full Federal Court has held that a supplier may contravene s. 52 of the Trade Practices Act 1974 (misleading or deceptive conduct in trade) by failing to warn its customers that use of the product in accordance with the instructions would expose them to liability for patent infringement: *Ramset Fasteners, ibid.*, 510–1. The New Zealand equivalent of s. 52 of the Trade Practices Act is s. 9 of the Fair Trading Act 1986.

[106] *Joseph H. Handelman's Application* No 213805 (23 February 1993) provides a useful precedent. A New Zealand patent was granted for a method of retarding the growth of human hair on condition that the applicant limited the claim to cosmetic treatment and expressly disclaimed therapeutic treatment of medical conditions such as female hirsutism.

[107] See *Hydropyridine* [1984] OJ EPO 26.

[108] *Re Application for Patent of Wayne State University* (1988) 22 CPR (3d) 407, 410–1 (Patent Appeal Board and Commissioner of Patents); *Merck & Co* v. *Apotex, Inc* (1995) 60 CPR (3d) 356, 384 (Fed. CA). See also T. Orlhac, "How to Draft Use Claims in the Pharmaceutical Field or Overcoming a Dichotomy of Interpretation" (1994) 11 *CIPR* 185.

[109] *John Wyeth & Brother Ltd's Application* [1985] RPC 545.

[110] *Re Eisai Co Ltd* [1985] OJ EPO 64.

methods of medical treatment from patentability is a purely judicial creation, representing the *Wellcome* court's assessment of where the balance of public policy lay in 1983. The Court of Appeal is perfectly free to reassess that balance and adjust the scope of the rule accordingly.

VIII CONCLUSION

The current Australian and New Zealand definition of a patentable invention as a "manner of new manufacture the subject of letters patent and grant of privilege within section 6 of the Statute of Monopolies" is not an anachronism that presents an inconvenient obstacle to rational development of our patent laws. In fact, it has proved to be a flexible vehicle quite capable of accommodating new technologies within its ambit. At the same time, the spirit that underlies and informs the Statute of Monopolies and the body of jurisprudence associated with it provide valuable reference points for any consideration of novel claims. In my view, the present definition should be retained.

IX POSTSCRIPT: *PHARMAC* IN THE COURT OF APPEAL

The decision of the New Zealand Court of Appeal in the *Pharmac* case[111] was handed down when this chapter was in proof form. In a single judgment delivered by Gault J, a full bench of five judges upheld the decision of Gallen J and confirmed that patent claims in the Swiss form are valid in New Zealand. Since composition claims for formulations directed at therapeutic uses of known compounds achieve the same practical result as the limited purpose product claims permitted by Article 54(5) of the European Patent Convention, New Zealand law and practice was viewed as being "little different from that provided for in the EPC".[112] While the Court of Appeal did recognise a difference about where "novelty is perceived to reside"[113] (in the case of a composition, novelty is found in the formulation as opposed to the use), this distinction was dismissed as more apparent than real. Once it was accepted that in reality the novelty of a pharmaceutical composition lies in the newly discovered therapeutic use, the reasoning of the Enlarged Board of Appeal in the *Eisai* case[114] was fully applicable and the further step of accepting Swiss claims to second and subsequent pharmaceutical uses could be taken "by analogy".

However, the Court of Appeal was not content merely to supplement the reasoning of Gallen J in this way, and went far further than was necessary to jus-

---

[111] *Pharmaceutical Management Agency Ltd* v. *The Commissioner of Patents*, (2000) 46 IPR 655.
[112] *Ibid.*, 670.
[113] *Ibid.*
[114] *Re Eisai Co Ltd* [1985] OJ EPO 64.

tify the result. The Court expressed "doubt" whether the public policy proviso in the last part of section 6 of the Statute of Monopolies, which requires that a patent must be withheld if the grant would be "generally inconvenient", has been incorporated in the statutory definition of "invention" provided by section 2(1) of the Patents Act 1953. In light of this "doubt", the Court concluded that there was no longer any firm legal basis for denying that a new method of medical treatment qualifies as an "invention". To the extent that the *Wellcome* decision suggested otherwise, it was disapproved.[115] Consequently, the evidence tendered by the parties on the general economic and social utility of granting patents for second pharmaceutical indications could be disregarded as irrelevant; the exclusion from patentability of methods of medical treatment could be justified only on moral grounds by reference to section 17(1) of the Patents Act 1953.

The Court then emphasised that once it is accepted that a claim discloses a new invention, the TRIPS Agreement obliges New Zealand to make patent protection available and New Zealand law and practice should, if at all possible, be construed or modified so as to give that result. While Article 27(3) of the TRIPS Agreement permits the exclusion of methods of medical treatment, its "rationale" is merely "that there should be no interference with the medical practitioner's diagnosis and treatment of patients . . .".[116] In light of this, the Court concluded:[117]

> perhaps the logical approach would be to permit claims to extend to the method of treatment using the compound or composition but to require from the patentee a disclaimer of any right to sue the practitioner.

However, the Court found no need to take that further step, because the same practical result could be achieved by allowing claims in the Swiss form while maintaining the *Wellcome* ban on claims for methods of medical treatment.

While the Court of Appeal's observations on the scope of the definition of "invention" are strictly obiter dicta, no doubt the Commissioner will now proceed on the basis that a "manner of new manufacture" cannot be denied the status of an "invention" on grounds of public policy. But in fact there is no sound basis for the Court's suggestion that the statutory definition of invention may not include the public policy proviso in the final part of section 6 of the Statute of Monopolies. It runs contrary to previous judicial understanding[118] and to the

---

[115] *Pharmaceutical Management Agency Ltd* v. *The Commissioner of Patents*, (2000) 46 IPR 655, 664.

[116] *Ibid.*, 672.

[117] *Ibid.*

[118] See, e.g., *Rolls-Royce Ltd's Application* [1963] RPC 251, 255; *Hiller's Application* [1969] RPC 267, 268, 269; *L'Oréal's Application* [1970] RPC 564, 571; *Organon Laboratories' Application* [1970] RPC 574, 579; *Joos* v. *Commissioner of Patents* (1972) 126 CLR 611, 623; *Eli Lilly & Co's Application* [1975] RPC 438, 444–5; *Wellcome Foundation Ltd* v. *Commissioner of Patents* [1983] NZLR 385, 391–2, 404; *Anaesthetic Supplies Pty. Ltd* v. *Rescare Ltd* (1994) 28 IPR 383, 401, 413, 421, 423; *Advanced Building Systems Pty. Ltd* v. *Ramset Fasteners (Aust.) Pty. Ltd* (1998) 194 CLR 171, 190; *Bristol-Myers Squibb Co* v. *F.H. Faulding & Co Ltd* (1998) 41 IPR 467, 479–81.

plain meaning of the definition itself. The only authority cited by the Court is T.A. Blanco White who, in the fourth edition of his *Patents for Inventions,* suggested that the words of the public policy proviso "do not, strictly, govern the phrase 'manner of new manufactures' which is all that the present [statutory definition] takes over from the old section 6"; and that the fact that the area of the proviso had been "worked over by other sections of the present Act" created a "presumption that Parliament intended to supersede it".[119] The Court of Appeal found "some support for this view" in the fact that the New Zealand Patents Act of 1953 made express provision in section 17(1)(b) for the Commissioner to refuse an application if it appeared to him "[t]hat the use of the invention in respect of which the application is made would be contrary to law or morality".[120]

This reasoning simply does not hold up. The terms of the statutory definition make it clear that a "manner of new manufacture" qualifies as an "invention" only if it would be "the subject of letters patent and grant of privilege within section 6 of the Statute of Monopolies": the latter phrase qualifies "manner of new manufacture" and incorporates all the requirements laid down in section 6 for the grant of letters patent. And since section 17(1)(b) of the Patents Act 1953 did not cover the whole field of the public policy proviso,[121] its inclusion provides no basis for an inference that Parliament intended to supersede the proviso in its entirety. In fact, in the very year that Blanco White's fourth edition was published, a full bench of the English Patents Appeal Tribunal held that the definition of invention "must, as a matter of construction, import also the proviso at the end of section 6", emphasising that "[t]he proviso at the end of the section can no more be ignored than can the earlier part of the section".[122] That may explain why the paragraph on the "generally inconvenient" proviso was omitted from the fifth edition of Blanco White's text.[123]

So while the actual decision in the *Pharmac* case is perfectly sensible, the Court of Appeal's wider reasoning is both wrong and undesirable. In my view, the current New Zealand (and Australian) definition of the term "invention" requires the Commissioner and the courts to consider the implications for the overall public welfare before granting patent monopolies in respect of new and controversial types of subject matter.

---

[119] T.A. Blanco White, *Patents for Inventions* (4th edn., London, Stevens & Co, 1974), para. 1–212.

[120] This provision followed s. 10(1)(b) of the Patents Act 1949 (UK). S. 3 of the Patents Amendment Act 1994 (NZ) substituted a new s. 17(1) of the principal Act which confined the Commissioner's power to refuse an application to cases where the use of the invention would be contrary to morality.

[121] The power conferred by s. 17(1)(b) was limited to cases where the *use* of the claimed invention would be contrary to law or morality, whereas the proviso in s. 6 embraces the full range of economic, social, environmental and ethical objections, whether to the use of the claimed invention or to the grant of monopoly rights in respect of it.

[122] *Eli Lilly & Co's Application* [1975] RPC 438, 444, 445 (Graham and Whitford JJ).

[123] T.A. Blanco White, *Patents for Inventions* (5th edn., London, Stevens & Co, 1983). Ordinarily, one would have expected that para. to follow para. 4–911 of the 5th edn.

9

The Protection of Designs

THE HON SIR NICHOLAS PUMFREY

I INTRODUCTION

Designs and their protection is a large subject. Those industries which are inherently technologically less innovative, but which produce products whose attractiveness to the consumer is based upon both appearance and other aspects of design which, though important, are not intrinsically deserving of patent protection, are concerned to protect the skill and labour expended upon industrial design. In this chapter, I propose to give a survey of the various treaty and convention provisions relating to designs; to indicate in outline how the law of the United Kingdom has sought to accord protection to industrial designs; and to discuss the success of the attempts which have been made. Finally, I shall discuss the most recent phase: Directive 98/71/EC on the Legal Protection of Designs, and the Amended Proposal for a Council Regulation on Community Design. The views which I express are personal.

II TREATY PROVISIONS

As ever, the starting point is the Paris Convention. Article 5*quinquies* of the Convention provides that industrial designs shall be protected in all the countries of the Union. Article 5B provides that the protection of industrial designs shall not, under any circumstances, be subjected to any forfeiture, either by reason of failure to work or by reason of the importation of articles corresponding to those which are protected. As will become clearer if the development of national laws is examined, one of the increasingly common features of design protection is the concept of reciprocity: a state extends protection to the nationals of other states to the extent only that those other states extend a corresponding protection to its nationals.[1] This development results in anomalies which are worthy of further investigation.[2] But the Paris Convention required protection for industrial designs. No particular form of protection is mandated.

---

[1] See, in particular, the UK provisions in relation to "unregistered" design right, discussed below, and in relation to semiconductor topography protection.

[2] See, e.g., the decision in *Mackie Designs, Inc.* v. *Behringer Specialised Studio Equipment (UK) Ltd* [1999] RPC 717.

Many states have used copyright to provide a measure of protection for industrial designs. The Berne Convention accordingly contains two relevant principal provisions. Article 2(7) provides that it shall be a matter for legislation in the countries of the Union to determine the extent of the application of their laws to works of applied art and industrial designs and models, as well as the conditions under which such works, designs and models shall be protected. Works protected in the country of origin solely as designs and models shall be entitled in another country of the Union only to such special protection as is granted in that country to designs and models. However, if no such special protection is granted in that country, such works shall be protected as artistic works. Article 7(4) provides for a minimum period of 25 years from the making of the work as the minimum period of protection for a work of applied art which is being protected as an artistic work.

It is generally realised that, as technology has advanced, particular problems for existing forms of protection have been thrown up. Sometimes it seems that the problems have been more imagined than real (as, for example, in the case of computer programs), but a number of *ad hoc* alterations to international obligations have been made to accommodate these developments. In the field of designs, a measure of importance and of considerable legal interest was the introduction of a special form of protection for semiconductor chip topographies. The impulse for this form of protection appears to have been the impossibility of protecting under existing US designs or copyright law the layout of an integrated circuit, and, possibly, the electronic circuit of which it is an embodiment. In the US the result was the Semiconductor Chip Protection Act of 1984. The protection of chip mask design was expressly conferred by this statute on a reciprocal basis, and in response the European Council issued a directive (87/54/EEC) to Member States concerning the legal protection of topographies of semiconductor products. While the Washington Treaty was concluded on this subject in 1989 it required a period of protection of eight years only and failed. It has effectively been supplanted and extended by the TRIPS Agreement which has adopted its formulation of the basis of protection.

TRIPS is the last international agreement to which I must turn. It is a controversial document, but so far as designs are concerned I need only look at Articles 25 and 26, which impose an obligation on the members of the World Trade Organisation to provide for the protection of independently created industrial designs that are new or original, a concept in respect of which members are granted a margin of appreciation. The TRIPS Agreement provides that members may provide that designs are not new or original if they do not significantly differ from known designs or combinations of known design features, and are equally permitted to exclude from protection designs dictated essentially by technical or functional considerations.

The protection required by TRIPS extends only to making, selling, or importing articles bearing or embodying a design which is a copy or substantially a copy of the protected design, and the minimum duration of protection is at least ten years. Moreover, members are given a wide discretion in respect of exceptions to protection: limited exceptions are permitted provided that they do not unreasonably conflict with the normal exploitation of protected industrial designs and do not unreasonably prejudice the legitimate interests of the owner of the protected design, taking account of the legitimate interests of the parties.

While TRIPS deals with the huge field of industrial design in two Articles, the topographies of integrated circuits require four Articles, 35–38. These Articles contain the modifications to the provisions of the Washington Treaty to which I have referred.

III PROTECTION OF DESIGNS IN THE UNITED KINGDOM

It is notorious that the law of the United Kingdom relating to the protection of industrial design has for many years lacked coherence. Until the beginning of the 1960s, it was generally safe for a practitioner to advise that absent any relevant patent or registered design, it was not objectionable to copy a rival's product, provided that the copying did not go so far as to make what were called "capricious additions" which might have some impact in an action for passing-off. Before 1911, there was no risk that copyright protection might have some impact in this area. Registered designs were introduced piecemeal. The first statute clearly relating to designs was, I understand,[3] a statute of 27 Geo. III, relating to printing on linens, cottons, calicoes and muslins, the principles of which were carried over to designs applied to fabrics of wool, silk and hair by 2 Vict. c. 13. The protection was in the nature of a copyright and there was no requirement for registration. It bears, therefore, some resemblance to the modern "unregistered" design right. In 1839 the Designs Act extended protection to three classes of design:

(1) for the pattern or print to be either worked into or worked on, or printed on or painted on, any article of manufacture, being a tissue or textile fabric, except lace;
(2) for the modelling, or the casting, or the embossment, or the chasing, or the engraving, or for any other kind of impression or ornament, on any article of manufacture, not being a tissue or textile fabric;
(3) for the shape or configuration of any article of manufacture.

These three categories of design clearly suggest a distinction between surface decoration ("pattern or ornament") on the one hand, and overall three-dimensional design ("shape or configuration") on the other. This is not the place to go through the history of the development of design protection in detail over the

---

[3] This discussion is taken with grateful thanks from P. Prescott, H. Laddie and M. Vitoria, *The Modern Law of Copyright* (2nd edn., London, Butterworths, 1995), chap. 29, which is an excellent discussion of the way in which, down to 1956, it was sought to keep design and copyright protection distinct.

ensuing decades, but I should pick the story up again briefly in 1911. In the Copyright Act of that year, overlap between designs and copyright legislation is avoided by section 22(1), which provides that the Act shall not apply to designs capable of being registered under the Patents and Designs Act 1907, except designs, which, though capable of being so registered, are not used or intended to be used as models or patterns to be multiplied by any industrial process. This provision, if given a broad construction, is capable of working injustice, and the courts tended to construe it narrowly in consequence. It also perpetuated an unsatisfactory drafting technique, which is to deal with the two forms of protection by saying that the scope of one is to determine the scope of the other, thus requiring two statutes to be construed.

In 1949, the Registered Designs Act gave us what is to all intents and purposes our modern law of registered designs. It has been amended by the Copyright, Designs and Patents Act 1988 in significant, but not fundamental, respects. The Copyright Act 1956 attempted, in section 10, to perpetuate the same division between the respective spheres of registered design protection and copyright protection as had been achieved by section 22 of the Act of 1911. The idea was that if a design was registered, it was not an infringement of any relevant copyright to do anything which was an infringement of the design registration or (after expiry) would have been an infringement if the registration had not expired. If the design had not been registered, the scope of copyright protection was modified in the same way as would have occurred had the design been registered. The policy was therefore to get designers to register. But that was thought to be unfair, and so a short statute, the Design Copyright Act 1968, was passed, which provided that copyright protection would cease in relation to registered and registrable designs only after the expiry of the 15-year period during which the design could or had been registered. Two more or less simultaneous legal developments were also important. In *Dorling* v. *Honnor Marine Ltd*,[4] the Court of Appeal construed section 10 of the 1956 Act so that it did not relate to designs which were inherently unregistrable because they did not satisfy the definition of a design in the 1949 Act (that is, features of shape, configuration pattern or ornament which appeal to and are judged solely by the eye). Thus, utterly functional designs with no "eye appeal" suddenly became entitled to full artistic copyright. At the same time, in the case concerned with electrical terminals, *Amp Incorporated* v. *Utilux Pty. Ltd*,[5] the House of Lords made it clear that the scope of the words "which appeal to and are judged solely by the eye" was far narrower than had previously been supposed. The combined effect of these decisions was greatly to expand the field of designs entitled to full copyright protection, and the result was a great increase in litigation, fuelled in part by the highly anomalous provisions of the 1956 Act relating to damages.

---

[4] [1965] Ch 1.
[5] [1972] RPC 103.

IV DEVELOPMENT OF THE MODERN LAW IN THE UNITED KINGDOM

The essentially disproportionate and unsatisfactory consequences of extending full artistic copyright protection to designs led to endless anomalies and attempts at judicial resistance. Thus, designs which had never been drawn first on paper might lose protection altogether, although there was sometimes a model (and so a sculpture) to help.[6] An *ad hoc* exception for spare parts had to be constructed by the House of Lords in the teeth of the clear statutory provision, a decision which is still under critical examination.[7] It is not surprising, therefore, that a new start was taken in the Copyright, Designs and Patents Act 1988. What was done was to introduce a new form of protection which is now the cornerstone of protection for industrial designs in the United Kingdom.

A "Unregistered" Design Right

Design right is a copyright. Design right is a limited monopoly, available to protect the maker of a design against copyists. In that respect, it is of more limited scope than a design registration, but it may be that in the normal commercial context this is of little significance, since it is unusual to find an infringer of a registered design who arrived at his design in ignorance.

For the purposes of Part III of the 1988 Act, which is concerned with design right, "design" is defined in section 213 as follows:

(2) In this Part "design" means the design of any aspect of the shape or configuration (whether internal or external) of the whole or part of an article.

(3) Design right does not subsist in—

(a) a method or principle of construction,
(b) features of shape or configuration of any article which—

(i) enable the article to be connected to, or placed in, around or against, another article so that either article may perform its function, or
(ii) are dependent upon the appearance of another article of which the article is intended by its designer to form an integral part, or

(c) surface decoration.

(4) A design is not "original" for the purposes of this Part if it is commonplace in the design field in question at the time of its creation.

---

[6] *J. & S. Davis (Holdings) Ltd* v. *Wright Health Group Ltd* [1988] RPC 403 (dental impression trays, not saved by models), but compare *Wham-O Manufacturing Ltd* v. *Lincoln Industries Ltd* [1985] RPC 127 (frisbee saved by model).

[7] *British Leyland Motor Corp.* v. *Armstrong Patents Ltd* [1986] AC 577 (HL), criticised and distinguished in *Canon Kabushiki Kaisha* v. *Green Cartridge Co. (Hong Kong) Ltd* [1997] AC 728 (PC).

There is a parallel here with the definition of a registrable design in section 1 of the Registered Designs Act 1949:

(1) In this Act "design" means features of shape, configuration, pattern or ornament applied to an article by any industrial process, being features which in the finished article appeal to and are judged by the eye, but does not include—

(a) a method or principle of construction, or
(b) features of shape or configuration of an article which—

(i) are dictated solely by the function which the article has to perform, or
(ii) are dependent upon the appearance of another article of which the article is intended by the author of the design to form an integral part.

...

(3) A design shall not be registered in respect of an article if the appearance of the article is not material, that is, if aesthetic considerations are not normally taken into account to a material extent by persons acquiring or using articles of that description, and would not be so taken into account if the design were to be applied to the article.

The interrelationship with copyright is prescribed by s 51 of the 1988 Act:

(1) It is not an infringement of any copyright in a design document or model recording or embodying a design for anything other than an artistic work or a typeface to make an article to the design.
(2) Nor is it an infringement of the copyright to issue to the public or include in a film, broadcast or cable programme service, anything the making of which was, by virtue of subsection (1), not an infringement of that copyright.
(3) In this section—

"design" means the design of any aspect of the shape or configuration (whether internal or external) of the whole or part of an article, other than surface decoration; and
"design document" means any record of a design, whether in the form of a drawing, a written description, a photograph, data stored in a computer or otherwise.

I shall leave aside designs for artistic works which are probably a limited class of designs (maquettes, preliminary sketches and the like) and concentrate for the purposes of this chapter on the design of industrial articles. The problem with functional designs is brought to an end. A corresponding problem, that of designs which are deprived of design right by reason of the exceptions to protection contained in section 213(3)(a), (b) and (c) of the 1988 Act, produced above, is avoided by exempting from copyright protection all designs, whether entitled to design right or not. Duration is a maximum of 15 years from first recording or first making. Infringement is copying the design so as to produce articles exactly or substantially to the design in question. Design right possesses a number of interesting features.

(i) *"the whole or part of an article"*

This provision has caused a number of practical difficulties. Since there is no requirement that a design have "eye appeal" for design right to subsist, there is the potential for the protection of small functional features of designs. A proprietor of a design suing an alleged copyist will wish to rely upon as many individual "aspects" of the design of his article as possible. There is no check on this, save to the extent that individual aspects of the design are either commonplace, or lack originality, or fall within the "must fit" or "must match" exceptions. It does not take a very strong imagination to see that this provision has a distinct potential for abuse. It also has the potential for very long trials in which many individual aspects of the design of a given article are examined. It is possible to take procedural steps to limit the scope of allegations of design right infringement, but the scope of the protection is remarkably broad. For example, a manufacturer makes a range of plastic disposable contact lenses. Each lens has been held to be a distinct design, albeit not entitled to protection for other reasons.[8]

(ii) *"commonplace"*

"Commonplace" means ordinary and undistinguished. It suggests that which is trite, trivial, common-or-garden or of the type which would excite no peculiar attention in the relevant art.[9] The restriction on the scope of design right which is introduced by the use of this word is potentially far-reaching. It marks the clearest departure from the scope of the protection which was available when protection of designs was by way of copyright law. Because the only qualification for copyright protection is that the work should possess originality,[10] pretty well anything was entitled to protection. This is not now the case.

It is too soon to predict with confidence whether design right will be effective to protect designs which are both ordinary and difficult and expensive to make. The *Aspect* case[11] provides a suggestive example. The lens designs in question were largely generated by the use of a computer program, which was itself based upon optical principles which would be known to an undergraduate but which required, nonetheless, a considerable amount of skill to write from first principles. Certain choices of features to be incorporated in the lenses had to be made, and judgement had to be exercised in the running of the program, which produced as output the dimensions of the steel mould tools which would be used to mould the plastic moulds in which the lenses themselves would be cast. The designs were intricate, but there was nothing special about them and so they were disentitled to protection. It is clear that the amount of skill and labour

---

[8] *Ocular Sciences Ltd* v. *Aspect Vision Care Ltd* [1997] RPC 289, 429.
[9] *Ibid.*
[10] That is, originality in the "copyright sense", which means originating with the author.
[11] *Ocular Sciences Ltd* v. *Aspect Vision Care Ltd* [1997] RPC 289.

which goes into the making of a design is not at all a sure guide to its protectability: on the contrary, it seems to me to be largely irrelevant.

(iii) "must fit" and "must match"

Features of the article satisfying the provisions of paragraphs (b)(i) and (b)(ii) of section 213 of the 1988 Act, produced above, are not designs within the definition. They are thus disregarded for all purposes. These provisions have received a wide interpretation. In *Aspect*,[12] the word "article" was construed to include a human eye. The word is not limited, therefore, to manufactured articles. The exceptions are important since, between them, they remove protection for the designs of spare parts, and prevent design right from affecting competition in any market where there is no design freedom either for functional or for æsthetic reasons. Although there is a decision to the contrary,[13] it seems to me that the exclusions apply to the "interface features" of the different parts of a single article: any other construction threatens to provide protection for spare parts. It is to be noted that the "must fit" exception is limited to those features of the article which are required so that "either article may perform its function", a restriction which did not affect back surface radius of the contact lens.

The "must match" exception is now present in the law of registered designs as well. It too is concerned with æsthetic (or at least eye-appeal) features of articles as opposed to features required only for functional reasons. Logically, the exceptions from both forms of protection are the same because the underlying policy must necessarily extend across the whole field of protections of designs.

B Reciprocity

A design will qualify for design right protection if either the designer, his employer or the person who commissioned the design is a qualifying person, or the first marketing provisions of the Act are complied with. In essence, the designer must be a citizen of the EEC or habitually resident there, or his employer must either be an EEC resident, or incorporated there, or have a place of business in the EEC at which a substantial business is carried on.[14] So, no Pacific Rim company and no US company will, for the most part, be entitled to design right. This approach is not that which is taken by the UK in respect of any other intellectual property, with the exception of semiconductor chip topography protection. Many of the ideas underlying design right originate from this source, including the idea of the commonplace design. The protection for chips was reciprocal, no doubt because the US protection for chip topogra-

---

[12] *Ocular Sciences Ltd* v. *Aspect Vision Care Ltd* [1997] RPC 289.

[13] *Baby Dan AS* v. *Brevi SRL* [1999] FSR 377.

[14] This is not comprehensive. It identifies the important qualifying grounds, really to show who is left out.

phies was itself reciprocal. I have some doubt whether reciprocal protection is appropriate in a field which is so fundamental, and to which it seems to me that the Paris Convention so clearly applies.

C Design Right Generally

So far as I am aware, nobody else has anything like design right. It is somewhat cumbersome, but I believe it has a number of attractive features. It has been suggested that while the government retains the requirement for reciprocity, it will never be a model which others will consider,[15] and I have some sympathy with this view. Its existence at all is another manifestation of the deep reluctance in the UK to trust unfair competition laws to protect products against copying (or "slavish imitation"). The problem which it presents will become more acute when registered design law is harmonised across the European Community, and followed by a Community Registered Design, since the proposed Community Design is probably of wider scope than the existing registered design and overlaps to some extent with design right.

D Registered Designs

Registered design protection is more familiar. The UK version of the registered design is a true monopoly. Protection is independent of proof copying, the law in relation to fraudulent imitation having been left behind in 1949. Most of the 1949 Act was substituted with a new version by the 1988 Act. The result of the amendment to the definition of "design" for the purposes of the 1949 Act is impossible to relate to the definition of design for the purposes of design right.

(i) "Article"

One starts with the well-known requirement that the design consists of features of shape, configuration, pattern or ornament applied to an article. "Article" is defined as any article of manufacture, and includes any part of an article which is made and sold separately.[16] There are two problems. Is it possible to have a partial design (e.g., a design which relates to an elevation of the article, which is all that is ever seen in use)? And how far is it possible to register a design for only part of an article (a part which is capable of being made and sold separately)? The answers to these questions are quite unclear.

The House of Lords has recently refused registration for motor car door panels on the ground that, although they were made and sold separately, they were

---

[15] W.R. Cornish, *Intellectual Property* (4th edn., London, Sweet & Maxwell, 1999), 5–11.
[16] Copyright, Designs and Patents Act 1988, s. 44(1).

still not articles.[17] The House held that the statute distinguished in the definition between "on the one hand, an item designed for incorporation, whether as a spare part or as an original component, in a particular article or range of articles made by the manufacturer of the component, and on the other an item designed for general use, albeit perhaps aimed principally at use with the manufacturer's own artefacts".[18] A suggested test is far too wide: "to qualify under section 44(1) a spare part has to have an independent life as an article of commerce and not merely an adjunct of some larger article of which it forms part".[19]

It is far from clear why the House of Lords was worried about spare parts at all: their exclusion is the function of the "must match" exception. But in the present context, observe the enormous departure from the unregistered design right, which will attach not only to these articles but to every part of them. Thus, even articles which in point of fact are sold separately, and in respect of which there has, since conception of the design, been an obvious possibility of separate sale, have been excluded.

(ii) "Appeal to and are judged solely by the eye"

There are two provisions which relate to eye appeal: these words of the definition, and the provisions of section 1(3) of the Registered Designs Act 1949 which, while not affecting the definition of design, exclude articles whose æsthetics are irrelevant to users and purchasers of articles of this description in general and of the design in question in particular. This is a very clumsy double test, difficult to apply and requiring, it seems, expert evidence in every case in which the article is not of a sort with which the tribunal is familiar. Since *Amp Incorporated* v. *Utilux Pty. Ltd*,[20] the law is that the words of the definition requiring eye-appeal are to be read together with the functional limitation ("dictated solely by the function the article has to perform") with the effect of excluding primarily functional designs. The only case in which the new provision of section 1(3) might (not would) have operated to produce a different result is *Gardex Ltd* v. *Sorata Ltd*,[21] in which a design for the *underside* of a shower tray was upheld, notwithstanding *Amp Incorporated* v. *Utilux Pty. Ltd.* Again, there is a serious inconsistency with design right, which, I suggest, cannot be justified merely on the basis either that the term of the design right is shorter (a maximum of 15 years against 25 for a registered design) or that the registered design confers a monopoly.

---

[17] *Ford Motor Co. Ltd's Design Application* [1995] RPC 167.
[18] *Ibid.*, 178 *per* Lord Mustill.
[19] *Ibid.*, 179 *per* Lord Mustill.
[20] [1972] RPC 103.
[21] [1986] RPC 623.

(iii) What is a "Design"?

In some ways, the most surprising development in the law of registered designs comes in the decision of the Privy Council in *Interlego AG v. Tyco Industries, Inc.*,[22] another case in which the real problem was caused by the interaction of registered design and copyright protection for manufactured articles. Again, the court was looking for ways to deprive the plaintiff of copyright protection. In the result, the court held the whole of the designs of the bricks, including those features which had no eye appeal and were dictated by the interlocking function which the bricks had to perform, were part of the design. This is not readily explicable when infringement comes to be considered, and it is contrary to much authority. The problem is that the correct construction was not argued. The result is to reduce the scope of design protection, by incorporating irrelevant features into that which forms the design.

V THE FUTURE: COMMUNITY LEGISLATION

There are two instruments of importance: the Design Directive 98/71/EC, and a draft Regulation on Community Design.

A Design Directive 98/71/EC

The Design Directive is an unusual document in that it is a harmonisation directive which is admittedly transitional[23] in respect of designs for spare parts, as to which no agreement could be reached.

(i) The Definition of "Design"

We start with yet another definition of design. The definition for the purposes of the Directive is "the appearance of the whole or a part of a product resulting from the features of, in particular, the lines, contours, colours, shape, texture and/or materials of the product itself and/or its ornamentation". "Product" is defined as any industrial or handcraft item, including *inter alia* parts intended to be assembled into a complex product, packaging, get-up, graphic symbols and typographic typefaces, but excluding computer programs. A "complex product" is a product composed of multiple components which can be replaced, permitting dis-assembly and re-assembly of the product.

It is by the way to criticise these definitions as obscure. The present definitions are obscure, as well. The difference is between familiar and unfamiliar obscurity.

---

[22] [1988] RPC 343.
[23] See Recital 16.

It is clear, however, that the definition cuts straight across the division estab-lished by the Copyright, Designs and Patents Act 1988 between registered designs and design right. A design includes the appearance of part of a product. Moreover, it includes a new visual effect produced by the use of new materials.

The definition of "product" is most interesting. It represents a major alter-ation to the scheme of the Registered Designs Act 1949. There is no requirement that the product be produced by an industrial process; and there is no require-ment that that part of the product be made and sold separately. There is no exclusion of articles of a primarily literary or artistic character, and even type-faces are included (no doubt someone will wish to argue that some electronic typefaces, which are properly viewed as programs, will be outside the defini-tion). The reference to get-up is surprising, since it seems to cover for example surface decoration of a box (for breakfast cereal, for example).

(ii) The Scope of Protection

A design shall be protected by a design right "to the extent that it is new and has individual character". There is an additional requirement for designs for articles forming a component part of a complex product: it shall be considered to be new and have individual character if the component part remains visible during normal use of the complex product, and to the extent that the visible features of the component themselves possess novelty and individual character.

The requirement of novelty is straightforward. "A design shall be considered new if no identical design has been made available to the public before [the pri-ority date,] . . . Designs shall be deemed to be identical if their features differ only in immaterial details." This, it seems to me, sweeps away the whole of the law on novelty of designs. It will be recalled that under the 1949 Act, although a design was registered for a particular article, its novelty was destroyed if applied to any article. Now it is clear that the design cannot be considered divorced from the article, and an old tea-pot decorated with an old wallpaper pattern may well be novel, although obviously there is scope for the contrary argument.

The requirement for "individual character" has an echo of "commonplace". The definition is curious:

1. A design shall be considered to have individual character if the overall impres-sion it produces on the informed user differs from the overall impression produced on such a user by any design which has been made available to the public before the [pri-ority date].

2. In assessing individual character, the degree of freedom of the designer in devel-oping the design shall be taken into consideration.

The sting is in the tail. Some guidance on its meaning can be obtained from the recitals, in particular Recital 13, which states that the assessment of whether a design has individual character should be based on whether the overall impression produced on an informed user viewing the design clearly differs from that produced by the existing design corpus, taking into consideration the nature of the product to which the design is applied or in which it is incorporated, and in particular the industrial sector to which it belongs and the degree of freedom of the designer in developing the design. One can regret that the word "clearly" did not find its way into the actual provisions of the Directive, but the recital provides some sort of pointer. Nonetheless, I can see that this provision is potentially productive of a great deal of dispute, which will have to be resolved by references to the Court of Justice.

(iii) Matters Excluded from Protection

The Directive provides in Article 7 a quite remarkably narrow exception from protection:

> 1. A design right shall not subsist in features of appearance of a produce which are solely dictated by its technical function.
> 2. A design right shall not subsist in features of appearance of a produce which must necessarily be reproduced in their exact form and dimensions in order to permit the product in which the design is incorporated or to which it is applied to be mechanically connected to or placed in, around or against another product so that either product may perform its function.
> 3. Notwithstanding paragraph 2, a design right shall, under the conditions set out in Articles 4 [Novelty] and 5 [Individual character] subsist in a design serving the purpose of allowing multiple assembly or connection of mutually interchangeable products within a modular system.

As to 1, we will have to fight *Amp Incorporated* v. *Utilux Pty. Ltd*[24] again, this time not merely in the House of Lords, but in the European Court of Justice as well. The wording invites the same discussion. Oddly, the corresponding Recital 14 is more generous in its terms, and seems to think that matters excluded from protection do not form part of the design:

> Whereas technological innovation should not be hampered by granting design protection to features dictated solely by a technical function; whereas it is understood that this does not entail that a design must have an æsthetic quality; whereas, likewise, the interoperability of products of different makes should not be hindered by extending protection to the design of mechanical fittings; whereas features of a design which are excluded from protection for these reasons should not be taken into consideration for the purpose of assessing whether other features of the design fulfil the requirements of protection.

However generous the recital, Article 7(2) is hopelessly narrow. It has been suggested that it would not apply to a plug and socket: I think there is a real risk that this is right. I am afraid that I have to say that time alone will tell.

---

[24] [1972] RPC 103.

(iv) Repair

This turned out to be too difficult a problem for the Community legislature. Article 14 is as follows:

> Until such time as amendments to this Directive are adopted on a proposal from the Commission in accordance with the provisions of Article 18, member States shall maintain in force their existing legal provisions relating to the use of the design of a component part used for the purpose of the repair a a complex product so as to restore its original appearance and shall introduce changes to those provisions only if the purpose is to liberalise the market for such parts.

This is called the "freeze plus" compromise. The idea is that consultation will continue for three years, and the Directive will then be amended. The same coyness has overtaken the draft Regulation, which I shall now discuss briefly.

B The Proposal for a Council Regulation on Community Design

The draft Regulation is analogous to the Regulation in respect of the Community trade mark, which has introduced a new granting authority (the Office for the Harmonisation of the Internal Market, or OHIM) and a new right, the Community trade mark. The idea is that the same will be done with designs, but the problems over repair rights mean that the present proposal does not provide for the registration of designs for parts of complex products, and thus does not need a repair provision (or so it is thought). A small unregistered design right is introduced. The definition of design is the same; it has to have been published; duration is three years from publication; and protection is against copying the design protected "in bad faith". The registered design right tracks the Directive, subject to the complex product point to which I have referred.

The design Regulation represents a further step in the creation of Europe-wide registered intellectual property rights. There is presently an informal proposal to deal with the Community patent by analogous means, rather than wait for the Community Patent Convention to come into force.

VI CONCLUSION

I do not think that it can be maintained that the UK law relating to the protection of designs for manufactured articles is in a satisfactory state. It shows too many scars from previous encounters with the requirements of industry. The unregistered design right, which is poorly integrated with registered design protection, could have been a way forward and indeed corrects many of the faults of the artistic copyright-based law which preceded it. But it is too wide in scope, and is undoubtedly open to abuse. Registered designs law suffers from too much legal exposition, and too much modification to meet particular circumstances. To a large extent, I cannot help feeling that an opportunity was lost with the 1988 Act to make industrial design protection more coherent. The new provisions envisaged by the European Directive will come into effect: these represent yet another attempt to catch that most elusive legal creature, the satisfactory regime for the protection of industrial designs.

10

Industrial Property in a Globalised Environment: Issues of Jurisdiction and Choice of Law

JOHN N. ADAMS

I INTRODUCTION: SO WHAT'S NEW?

A What is Globalisation?

Even if we accept that the phenomenon of "globalisation" exists, so far as *industrial* property is concerned, I do not believe that very much has changed in recent years. However, as I will explain, there are worrying developments on the horizon.

As a first step, it may be helpful to decide what we mean by "globalisation". A definition would be useful in this connection: unfortunately, there does not seem to be one. Some economists think the modern world is changing in fundamental ways which can be grouped under the banner "globalisation", but there are sceptics. As one leading authority observes:[1]

> Although the notion of a *globalised* world has become pervasive there are strong opponents who argue, in effect, that globalisation is a mirage. . . . The world economy, it is argued, was actually more open and more integrated in the half century prior to World War One (1870–1913). . . .

It is clearly the case that whatever changes are occurring at present around the world are not affecting all areas equally, a fact which has bedevilled the uniform development of electronic substitutes for paper, such as bills of lading in international sales of basic commodities.[2] Thus, a term preferred by many economists is "internationalisation".

---

[1] See P. Dicken, *Global Shift: Transforming the World Economy* (3rd edn., London, Paul Chapman Publishing Ltd, 1998), 3.

[2] Attempts to transfer the documents used in international sales transactions to electronic form go back many years, but have been impeded by the fact that in many countries producing basic commodities, even the electricity supply is unreliable. The WIPO initiative of giving poorer countries computer equipment, so that they could access patent and other data, foundered on the same problem.

If by "internationalisation" we mean that goods the subject of industrial property rights[3] ("IPRs") are traded around the world, that is nothing new, though the volume of such trade has no doubt grown, and the mechanisms which facilitate it have improved *so far as the individual consumer is concerned.* The development of sales through the Internet is an aspect of this. As a recent World Trade Organisation report puts it:[4]

> These modern technologies [computer, telecommunications and information techno-logy] are being combined, especially thought the Internet, to link millions of people in every corner of the world. Communications are increasingly unburdened from the constraints of geography and time. Information spreads more widely and more rapidly than ever before. Deals are struck, transactions completed, and decisions taken in a time-frame that would have seemed inconceivable a few years ago.
>
> [W]ith the Internet all elements of a commercial transaction can be conducted on an interactive basis with one or many people, unconstrained by time and space, in a mul-timedia environment with sound, image and text transmission, and at relatively low (and still declining) costs.

But, is this a change in quantity or kind? I would argue merely the former. The major change is the facility with which *ordinary members of the public* can, in principle, order goods from other countries through the Internet.[5] They have been able to do the same thing by mail order for years, of course, and it is just becoming a lot easier, at least for those with credit cards.[6] There is nothing much new to be said about this. Nor is there anything new about deciding *where* and *when* contracts are formed by electronic means.[7] In principle, the contract is formed at the point in time, and place, at which the message of acceptance is received (not sent).[8] In the absence of a choice of law clause, the applicable law is generally that of the seller's place of business.[9] The sale of goods warranties concerning title (for example, the seller's warranty that he has the right to sell without infringing industrial property rights) and quality will similarly be deter-mined according to the seller's law, rather than the buyer's.[10]

[3] For present purposes, IPRs include patents, designs (registered and unregistered), industrial copyright and trade marks (registered and unregistered). Trade secrets are sometimes included in this category, but the better view is that they should not be because they are not property: see A. Coleman, *The Legal Protection of Trade Secrets* (London, Sweet & Maxwell, 1992), chap. 3.8.

[4] *Electronic Commerce and the Role of the* WTO (Geneva, WTO Publications, 1998), 1 and 5.

[5] However, the scale of this trade outside the USA is still minute: see Report of the House of Commons Trade and Industry Committee, Electronic Commerce (15 July 1999, HC 648), xi.

[6] Mail order sales *far* exceed Internet sales at present. A reason for this is that a large part of mail order trading involves credit, whilst Internet sales require credit cards. A large part of the target audience for mail order sales does not have credit cards, and at present there does not appear to be a satisfactory mechanism for setting up credit transactions through the Internet.

[7] *Entores* v. *Miles Far Eastern Corporation* [1955] 2 QB 327; *Brinkibon* v. *Salig Stahl und Stahlwarenhandelsgesellschaft mbH*[1983] 2 AC 34.

[8] Unlike contracts effected by post: see *Adams* v. *Lindsell* (1818) 1 B & Ald 681.

[9] *Benaim & Co* v. *Debono* [1924] AC 144; *Compangnie Tunisienne de Navigation SA* v. *Compagnie d'Armement Maritime SA* [1971] AC 572.

[10] *Sumner Permain* v. *Webb* [1922] 1 KB 55; *Teheran-Europe Co* v. *S.T. Belton (Tractors) Ltd* [1968] 2 QB 545. Though, as noted below, the extent to which case law which developed in relation to sales between merchants will still be relevant in the consumer context must be questioned. In

The important effect of any significant growth in international *consumer* sales which may take place could be that it will result in a change in consumer expectations, and the rules set out above as to applicable law, which were developed in relation to merchant sales, may not be appropriate to consumer sales.

What is certainly novel, according to the European Commission,[11] is the internationalisation of research and technology. This seems to encompass three main types of activities:[12]

(a) International exploitation of technology produced on a national basis, which includes exports, granting of licences and patents, and foreign manufacturing of innovations generated in the home country, carried out by profit-seeking organisations and individuals.

(b) International techno-scientific collaboration between partners in more than one country for the development of know-how and innovations, whereby each partner retains its own institutional identity and ownership remains unaltered. Actors here are enterprises as well as other research performing institutions (for example, universities, public R & D institutes).

(c) International generation of innovations carried out by multinational enterprises, which develop R & D strategies to create innovations across borders by building up research networks. R & D and innovation activities which are carried out simultaneously in the home and host country, the acquisition of foreign R & D and the establishment of new R & D units in the host countries are all means to this end research and technology.

The internationalisation of research and technology is growing, and it may be supposed that as a consequence so also is the international generation of innovation.[13] This development is still characterised by "triadisation" involving the United States of America, the Member States of the European Union (plus Switzerland) and Japan. The involvement of countries from South East Asia is still small, though increasing.[14] The feature common to all three kinds of activity is that the relations will be covered by *contract*. The allocation of jurisdiction and choice of law will be, or at least should be, governed by the terms of the contract.

practice, in the case of Internet sales, there is almost certain to be a choice of law clause imposed as part of the seller's terms of business. There will be a question whether such a clause can override the mandatory provisions of the law of one of the contracting parties, e.g. the Unfair Contract Terms Act 1977 in the case of a UK buyer, but this issue again is not new. The exclusion of international supply contracts in s. 26 of the 1977 Act only applies between business buyers and sellers. Accordingly. the issue will fall to be determined under the principles laid down in *The Hollandia* [1983] 1 AC 565. If, for example, the prohibition in s. 6 of the 1977 Act of the exclusion of the Sale of Goods Act 1979 warranties as to quality contained in ss. 13–15 of the latter Act were held to be mandatory, then the attempt to rely on the choice of law clause to effect an exclusion of liability would be ineffective.

[11] European Commission DGXII, ETAN Report, *Internationalisation of Research and Technology: Trends, Issues and Implications for S & T Policies in Europe* (Brussels, European Commission, 1998).

[12] *Ibid.*

[13] *Ibid.*, especially at fig. 1.

[14] *Ibid.*

Whilst, therefore, developments can be identified which may have implications for the development of choice of law and jurisdiction in relation to the law of contract, none of these seem to have implications in this regard in relation to IPRs.

B   Where is the Challenge in Relation to IPRs?

I believe that the greatest challenges presented by the Internet and other new technologies are not in relation to the world industrial property system, which is long established, and long used to dealing with the fact that goods cross frontiers in greater or lesser quantity. Rather, *the Internet is an aspect of (and contributor to) a change in outlook*. People increasingly *think* internationally (a consequence of the fact that electronic communication of all kinds is cheap and easy). The relevance of this for present purposes is that people increasingly know about differences between jurisdictions and, as a result, the phenomenon of "forum shopping" is growing.[15] Europe, by the allocation of jurisdiction between the various Member States of the Brussels and Lugano Conventions, effectively ushered in what was virtually a "free for all".[16] I will explain the technicalities of how this has occurred in due course. But to give a few examples of what can be done, if you are afraid of being sued for infringement of a patent, file for a declaration of non-infringement in one of the slower jurisdictions (the longest Italian patent suit has been going on for 30 years!); if you need to sue on a dodgy patent, sue in Germany where the state courts cannot adjudicate on validity, and the Federal courts, which can declare patents invalid, are reluctant to stay actions. As we will see, within Convention countries the court first seised of the action has jurisdiction. As Laddie J said in *Sepracor, Inc.* v. *Hoechst Marion Roussel Ltd*,[17] "[a] less sensible system could not have been dreamt up by Kafka". It does not meet the legitimate needs of patent holders and potential infringers within European Patent Convention countries, and simply proliferates pre-emptive litigation.[18]

It is timely to examine this, because the Hague Conference on Private International Law has just produced a preliminary draft of a Convention on International Jurisdiction and the Effects of Foreign Judgments in Civil and Commercial Matters,[19] which, if eventually implemented in its present form, will replicate the problems to which the Brussels and Lugano Conventions have led. I propose to approach my critique of the draft Convention in three stages: first, by considering some basic common law rules governing jurisdiction; sec-

---

[15] I can support this assertion only by anecdotal evidence based on what has been told to me by some senior members of the industrial property departments of multi-national companies.

[16] As explained below, the situation is now a little better than it was a year or two ago, but there are still major problems.

[17] [1999] FSR 746, 752.

[18] *Ibid.*

[19] The text commented on in this chap. is that of June 1999.

ondly, by considering the extent to which these are overridden by the Brussels and Lugano Conventions; and, thirdly, by considering the preliminary draft of the Convention itself.

In principle, there is a clear divide between rules allocating jurisdiction, and rules deciding what law the court with jurisdiction should apply. In reality, there is not such a clear-cut divide. However, it is useful as a starting point.

II SOME OF THE KEY RULES GOVERNING THE JURISDICTION OF THE COURTS OF ENGLAND AND WALES

A The Common Law

(i) The Moçambique Rule

In *British South Africa Co* v. *Companhia de Moçambique*, Lord Herschell said:[20]

> common law personal actions being transitory may be brought in any place where the defendant can be found; . . . real actions must be brought in the *forum rei sitae*.

This rule is one of public policy founded on comity, whereby the English courts would refuse to adjudicate upon claims of title to foreign land founded on an alleged invasion of the proprietary rights attached to it, and to award damages founded on that adjudication.[21]

This rule was subsequently held to apply to actions relating to infringements of copyright, trade marks and patents, by analogy.[22] This was not merely based on the fact that these rights are equivalent to immovables, but was founded on similar considerations of public policy. In *Plastus Kreativ AB* v. *Minnesota Mining and Manufacturing*, Aldous J said:[23]

> although patent actions appear on their face to be disputes between two parties, in reality they also concern the public. A finding of infringement is a finding that a monopoly granted by the state is to be enforced.[24] The result is invariably that the public have to pay higher prices than if the monopoly did not exist. . . . One only has to imagine a decision of this Court that the German public should pay to a British company substantial sums of money to realise the difficulties that might arise. . . . I believe it is at least convenient that infringement, like validity, is decided in the state in which it arises.

---

[20] [1893] AC 602, 623.

[21] *Ibid.*, 625.

[22] See *Tyburn Productions Ltd* v. *Conan Doyle* [1990] RPC 185.

[23] [1995] RPC 438, 447. See also *Coin Controls Ltd* v. *Suzo International (UK) Ltd* [1997] FSR 660, 670.

[24] Economists would disagree that a patent is *per se* a monopoly: it may or may not be depending on the demand for the goods embodying it and the level of consumer substitutability.

So, the *Moçambique* rule is (or at least was, until, as we shall see below, modified by the Brussels and Lugano Conventions) a fundamental barrier to the courts of England and Wales assuming jurisdiction over infringements of foreign IPRs, and in principle, for the same reasons, an obstacle to other jurisdictions doing likewise.[25]

The next problem is the so-called "double actionability" rule: the rule in *Phillips* v. *Eyre*.[26]

(ii) The Double Actionability Rule

Under the double actionability rule, an action done in a foreign country is a tort, and actionable as such, in England only if it is both (a) actionable as a tort according to English law, or in other words was an act, which, if done in England, would be a tort; and (b) actionable according to the law of the foreign country where it was done.[27] The rule is not strictly a test of jurisdiction, but a choice of law rule providing, in effect, that actions on foreign torts were brought in English courts under English law.[28]

In *Def Lepp Music* v. *Stuart-Brown*,[29] the double actionability rule was held to apply to prevent an action in England for infringement of a foreign copyright. Such an action would, in any event, have been barred by the *Moçambique* rule, but the decision was based on the double actionability rule. The actual decision in *Def Lepp* may well still be supportable, as the claim in question was for infringement of UK copyright by acts wholly committed abroad. It is clear from both the then applicable Copyright Act,[30] and its successor, the Copyright,

---

[25] Although the territoriality principle has authority in other jurisdictions as being applicable to statutory industrial property rights (see, e.g., *Potter* v. *The Broken Hill Pty. Co Ltd* (1906) 3 CLR 479; *Norbert Steinhardt and Son Ltd* v. *Meth* (1961) 105 CLR 440), it is not without its critics. See G. Cheshire and P. North, *Private International Law* (12th edn., London, Butterworths, 1992), 263, criticising *Tyburn Productions Ltd* v. *Conan Doyle* [1990] RPC 185, in which Vinelott J expressed the view that there was no difference between copyright, patent and trade mark rights, suggesting that the *Moçambique* case was decided on the issue of whether or not an English court could give an *effective judgment*, not on a procedural distinction between local and transitory actions. Moreover, in European Patent Convention countries, the law of patents is supposed to be harmonised, and certainly the Jenard Report stated in relation to Art. 16(4) of the Brussels and Lugano Conventions (discussed below) that actions for infringements of patents are governed by the general rules of the Conventions, and this should similarly apply to declarations of non-infringement. To this extent, the approach taken by Aldous J in *Plastus Kreativ AB* v. *Minnesota Mining and Manufacturing* [1995] RPC 438 may be criticised, though, having regard to the way the case was pleaded, the decision itself was probably right (see also for a similar point, discussion below of *Def Lepp Music* v. *Stuart Brown* [1986] RPC 273).

[26] (1870) LR 6 QB 1. In Scotland, an equivalent rule was laid down in *McElroy* v. *McAllister*, 1949 SC 110.

[27] *Dicey and Morris on the Conflict of Laws* (12th edn., London, Stevens, 1993), Rule 203.

[28] See *Def Lepp Music* v. *Stuart Brown* [1986] RPC 273, 276, *per* Browne-Wilkinson V-C, and the exhaustive analysis of the rule by the Canadian Supreme Court in *Tolofson* v. *Jensen* [1994] 3 SCR 1022. In the latter case, the Court opted for the application of the *lex loci delicti*. See also E. Bragiel, "A Funny thing Happened on the Way to the Forum—Actionability in the UK of Infringements of Intellectual Property Rights Committed Abroad" [1999] 2 *IPQ* 135.

[29] [1986] RPC 273.

[30] Copyright Act 1956 (UK), s. 5(2).

Designs and Patents Act of 1988, that acts committed abroad do not infringe UK copyright.[31] The double actionability rule was subjected to criticism in *Boys* v. *Chaplin*.[32] However, it was unclear following that case to what extent the rule survived, because extracting a *ratio* from it was exceedingly difficult.[33] Following the recommendations of the English and Scottish Law Commissions,[34] section 10 of the Private Law (Miscellaneous Provisions) Act 1995 abolished the rule. The abolition has the effect that the rule is no longer a bar to actions for the infringement of such industrial property and similar rights as are not considered local. Thus, the rule is abolished in relation to passing off, and other common law torts. This would, theoretically, have the result that an action for the commission by the defendant of one of the more exotic forms of unfair competition (such as misappropriation of the claimant's (or plaintiff's) market achievement where there is no likelihood of confusion[35]) could be brought in the English courts,[36] even though English common law does not recognise a tort of this nature.[37] However, in the Committee stage of the Bill in the House of Lords, Lord Wilberforce observed in relation to clause 9, which introduces Part III of the Act containing the choice of law rules for tort:[38]

> [The forum] has to decide under English law whether this is a tort or whether it is not a tort. I put my cards absolutely on the table, because I attach importance to it being possible under this section to say that English law does not recognise this claim—privacy, adultery, unfair competition whatever it is—as a tort. Many witnesses have said that is the purpose of Clause 9(1).

There is also section 14(3)(a). This provides:

> (3) ... nothing in this Part—
>   (a) authorises the application of the law of a country outside the forum as the applicable law for determining issues arising in any claim in so far as to do so—
>   (i) would conflict with principles of public policy. . . .

In short, having regard to the above, I think it is highly unlikely that the courts of England and Wales *would* entertain an action in unfair competition in such cases, although in a sense that might appear to be reintroducing the double actionability rule "through the back door", as it were. However, as we will see,

---

[31] Copyright, Designs and Patents Act 1988, s. 16(1).

[32] [1971] AC 356.

[33] See Report of the English and Scottish Law Commissions 1990 No 193 para. 2.3

[34] *Ibid.*

[35] As in *Cadbury Schweppes Pty. Ltd* v. *Pub Squash Co Pty. Ltd* [1981] RPC 429 (PC).

[36] Before the 1995 Act, passing off actions could be brought in respect of passing off abroad provided the act would amount to passing off in England and Wales and would amount to passing off in the country concerned: *Walker* v. *Ost* [1970] RPC 489. The same conclusion was reached by the Scottish courts: see *James Burroughs Distillers plc* v. *Speymount Whisky Distributors Ltd* 1989 SLT 561.

[37] See *Cadbury Schweppes Pty. Ltd* v. *Pub Squash Co Pty. Ltd* [1981] RPC 429.

[38] Now Private Law (Miscellaneous Provisions) Act 1995, s. 9(1) and (2). See House of Lords Committee, Paper 36, Part II Official Report of the Committee on the Bill col. 11.

so far as Member States of the Brussels and Lugano Conventions are concerned, Lord Wilberforce's reservations seem to be overridden.

B The Brussels and Lugano Conventions

These Conventions are principally intended to allocate jurisdiction between the courts of the signatory states. They have the effect of overriding both the *Moçambique* and (formerly) the double actionability rules.[39] However, with regard to registered rights such as patents, and registered designs and trade marks, as we will see, the position is not so very different from before. The principal relevant provisions of these Conventions for present purposes are the following.

(i) The Basic Rule

The basic rule on choice of jurisdiction, if these Conventions apply, is set out in Article 2. The claimant[40] *must* sue the defendant in the courts of the defendant's domicile[41] and no other court, *unless* one of the exceptions set out in the Conventions apply. The important ones for present purposes are set out below.

(ii) Provisional Measures

Article 24 provides:[42]

> Application may be made to the courts of a Contracting State for such provisional, including protective, measures, as may be available under the law of that State, even if, under this Convention, the courts of another Contracting State have jurisdiction as to the substance of the matter.

The Dutch High Court in Rotterdam adopted an especially enterprising approach based on this provision. It would grant pan-European injunctions in respect of the infringement of registered rights in other member states. It has, however, now pulled back from this.[43]

---

[39] *Pearce* v. *Ove Arup Partnership Ltd* [1997] Ch 293; upheld on this point by the Court of Appeal [1999] 1 All ER 769.

[40] The term for "plaintiff" introduced by the Civil Procedure Rules for England and Wales.

[41] Under Art. 52, domicile is determined by the internal law of the Contracting State whose courts are seised of the matter. Art. 53 provides that in the case of companies, the seat of a company shall be treated as its domicile. However, in order to determine that seat, the court shall apply its rules of private international law.

[42] On the interpretation of this provision, see the Opinion of Mayras A-G in *Denilauler* v. *Couchet Frèrer* [1980] ECR 1553; *Reichert* v. *Dresdner Bank* [1992] ECR I–2149.

[43] See cases cited below at nn. 57 and 58.

(iii) Lis Pendens—*Related Actions*

Article 21 is important. This provides:

> When proceedings involving the same cause of action and between the same parties are brought in courts of different Contracting States, any court other than the court first seised shall of its own motion decline jurisdiction in favour of that court.

It is this Article which gives rise to the possibility of effectively stopping a likely infringement action by filing for a declaration of non-infringement in jurisdictions known for their slow procedures (the "Italian torpedo").

(iv) *Actions in Tort, Delict and Quasi-delict*

Article 5(3) provides an exception to the general rule laid down in Article 2 that the defendant is to be sued in the courts of the Contracting State in which he or she is domiciled. In matters relating to tort, delict or quasi-delict, the defendant may be sued in the courts of the place where the harmful event occurred.

Thus, where the claim is in tort, as it is in the case of patent infringement or the infringement of other IPRs, the plaintiff can choose either the courts of the defendant's domicile *or* the courts of the place where "the harmful event occurred". In *Handelskwekerij G.J. Bier BV and Stichting Reinwater* v. *Mines de Potasse d'Alsace SA*,[44] the European Court of Justice ruled that the expression "place where the harmful event occurred" in Article 5(3) must be interpreted in such a way as to acknowledge that the plaintiff has an option to commence proceedings either at the place where the causative event giving rise to the damage occurred[45] *or* in the jurisdiction where the damage occurred. Under the former alternative, the plaintiff will be able to choose the jurisdiction where the defendant's factory is, *even though there is no subsisting patent there*. Under the latter alternative, the plaintiff will additionally be able to choose the courts of countries where the infringing goods are circulating if there is a patent in such countries. Because in the modern commercial world products tend to be traded throughout the Member States of the Convention (and indeed the rest of the world), this rule assumes considerable importance. However, where jurisdiction is based merely on the fact that the goods are circulating in the jurisdiction, a court can rule only on the harm, i.e. the damage, occurring within its jurisdiction.[46] Where jurisdiction is founded on the fact that the jurisdiction is the place where the event giving rise to the harm occurred, it seems that the court

---

[44] [1977] 1 CMLR 284.

[45] The first plaintiffs in this case were nursery gardeners in Holland. The defendants were alleged to have discharged more than 10,000 tonnes of chlorides into the Rhine each day in Alsace, thereby increasing the salinity of the water reaching Holland, which caused damage to the plaintiffs' seed beds.

[46] *Shevill* v. *Presse Alliance SA* [1995] All ER (EC) 289.

can award damages for *all* the harm caused by the infringement, if the factory in question is the sole relevant source of infringing goods.[47]

The upshot of this is curious. A person can be sued in a country where he has done no wrong, and on the basis of a law which is foreign to the courts of that country. So, if I make goods in a country where there is no patent, and these circulate in a country where there is one, I can be sued in the former country, and have to pay for *all* damage caused by the infringement.[48] This seems absurd, but it is consistent with the wording of the Convention. The reservations expressed by Lord Wilberforce in relation to the 1995 Act have no application in this regard, because the Convention is overriding.

(v) Exclusive Jurisdiction in Proceedings Concerned with Registration of Validity

Under Articles 16(4) and 19,[49] in actions concerning the registration or validity of registered intellectual property rights,[50] only the national courts of the Contracting State where the registration has taken place, or been applied for, have jurisdiction. However, at least so far as the European Court of Justice is concerned, it appears that these provisions are to be construed restrictively and do not apply to infringement or issues concerning ownership.[51]

Where infringement proceedings are first brought in the state of the defendant's domicile, and validity is then challenged in another state, this could result in irreconcilable judgments for the purposes of Article 27(3),[52] and thus non-recognition under that Article. Although Article 27 does not specifically contemplate the court first seised staying its proceedings, since the object of this provision, and of Article 21, is to prevent irreconcilable judgments arising in different states, it is suggested that the court first seised should use its inherent powers to stay the infringement action, unless the challenge to validity appears to be a mere delaying tactic, or some other good reason exists for not staying the proceeding.[53]

It can be said that the position regarding actions for the infringement of patents, and registered designs and trade marks, where the issue of validity of

---

[47] *Shevill* v. *Presse Alliance SA* [1995] All ER (EC) 289.

[48] *Ibid.*

[49] Art. 19 provides: "[w]here a court of a Contracting State is seised of a claim which is principally concerned with a matter over which the courts of another Contracting State have exclusive jurisdiction by virtue of Article 16, it shall decide of its own motion that it has no jurisdiction".

[50] Or principally concerning such rights: see Art. 19.

[51] *Duijnstee* v. *Goderbauer* [1983] ECR 3663, [1985] 1 CMLR 220. As noted above, this is consistent with the view expressed in the Jenard Report.

[52] Art. 27 provides: "[a] judgment shall not be recognised: . . . (3) if the judgment is irreconcilable with a judgment given in a dispute between the same parties in the State in which recognition is sought . . ."

[53] The Dutch Court of Appeal has held that an injunction should not be granted where there is a serious, not negligible, chance that the patent will be revoked or cancelled: *recFSH*, 3 February 1994, noted in [1994] EIPR 243.

the right sued upon is put in issue (presumably this must be done *bona fide*)[54] is, in effect, not much different from what it was before the Brussels Convention. This is the result of *Coin Controls Ltd* v. *Suzo International UK*[55] and *Fort Dodge Animal Health Ltd* v. *Akzo Nobel NV*.[56] Under the *Moçambique* rule, as explained above, the courts will decline jurisdiction where the rights concerned are registered in another jurisdiction. Where that other jurisdiction is a Contracting State, they must decline jurisdiction because of Article 16(4).

The Dutch courts, which previously had not followed *Coin Controls*, seem as a result of *Akzo Nobel* v. *Webster*[57] and *Expandable Grafts Partnership* v. *Boston Scientific*[58] to have reached much the same position with regard to this issue as the English courts.

There is currently, I believe, no reference to the European Court of Justice to settle matters, as *Fort Dodge* is not proceeding.

To summarise: where the infringement of registered rights is the issue, Article 16(4) is an obstacle where there is a challenge to validity of rights registered in another Member State. Where non-member states are concerned, the *Moçambique* rule remains an obstacle. On the other hand, where what is alleged is infringement of copyright or other unregistered rights, or common law rights, the English courts may exercise jurisdiction, even where these rights are conferred by other Member States.

III THE DRAFT CONVENTION ON INTERNATIONAL JURISDICTION AND THE EFFECTS OF FOREIGN JUDGMENTS IN CIVIL AND COMMERCIAL MATTERS

The present preliminary draft emerged from the Hague Conference on Private International Law in June 1999. The grounds of jurisdiction are set out in Chapter II. Article 3 provides:

Subject to the provisions of this Convention, a defendant may be sued
—in the case of a natural person, in the courts of the [Contracting State] [place] where that person is habitually resident;
—in any other case, in the courts of the [Contracting State] [place]—
a) where it has its statutory seat,
b) under whose law it was incorporated or formed,
c) where it has its central administration, or
d) where it has its principal place of business.

Although there are differences of detail, this provision provides a similar starting point to Article 2 of the Brussels and Lugano Conventions.

---

[54] The German courts have had to confront this issue, because validity has to be tried at a Federal level, whilst infringement is tried in the Land courts.
[55] [1997] FSR 660.
[56] [1998] FSR 222. See also *Boston Scientific* v. *Cordis*, unreported, 18 November 1997.
[57] District Court of the Hague, 23 December 1997.
[58] Dutch Court of Appeal, 23 April 1998.

Article 10 is the next which concerns us. This provides that:

1 The plaintiff may bring an action in tort or delict in the courts of the Contracting State

a) in which the act or omission that caused injury occurred; or

b) in which the injury arose, unless the defendant establishes that the [defendant] [person claimed to be responsible] could not reasonably have foreseen that the act or omission could result in an injury of the same nature in that State.

2 The plaintiff may also bring an action in accordance with paragraph 1 when the act or omission, or the injury is threatened.

3 If an action is brought in the courts of a Contracting State only on the basis that the injury arose or is threatened there, those courts shall have jurisdiction only in respect of the injury that occurred or may occur in that State, unless the [plaintiff] [injured party] has its habitual residence or seat in that State.

It will be appreciated that although there are differences in detail which might be an improvement on Article 5(3) of the Brussels and Lugano Conventions, fundamentally it seems likely to give rise to the same sort of difficulties we encountered in respect of Article 5(3) in relation to the infringement of industrial property rights, and in particular the absurdity pointed out above. Moreover, it is likely to open wide the door to "forum shopping". This is further promoted by Article 14 which deals with the important question of provisional or protective measures:

1 A court having jurisdiction under Articles 3 to 13 to determine the merits of the case has jurisdiction to order any provisional or protective measures.

2 A court of the place where property is located has jurisdiction to order provisional or protective measures in respect of that property.

3 A court of a Contracting State not having jurisdiction under paragraphs 1 or 2 may order provisional or protective measures, provided that

(a) their enforcement is limited to the territory of that State, and

(b) their [sole] purpose is to protect on an interim basis a claim on the merits which is pending or to be brought by the requesting party.

Since goods move around, Article 14(2) appears to enable the owner of an industrial property right to instigate proceedings for provisional relief in any court of a jurisdiction where its right exists which is likely to give a favourable result. If jurisdictions can be found which adopt the same bullish approach formerly adopted by the Dutch courts (and the need for jurisdictions to attract lucrative legal business is likely to offer strong temptations to go down this route!), the door will be opened to global injunctions, perhaps granted on fairly dubious grounds.

In the new draft there is an equivalent of Article 16(4) of the Brussels and Lugano Conventions. Article 13(4) provides:

In proceedings which have as their object the registration, validity or nullity of patents, trade marks, designs or other similar rights required to be deposited or registered, the courts of the Contracting State in which the deposit or registration has been applied for, has taken place or, under the terms of an international convention, is deemed to have taken place, have exclusive jurisdiction.

This presumably is to be given a similar restrictive interpretation to that given by the European Court of Justice in the case discussed above.

Finally, there is the provision dealing with *lis pendens*. Article 23 provides:

1 When the same parties are engaged in proceedings in courts of different Contracting States and when such proceedings are based on the same causes of action [and requests for relief], the court second seised shall suspend the proceedings if the court first seised has jurisdiction and is expected to render a decision capable of being recognized [under this Convention] in the State of the court second seised [, unless the latter has exclusive jurisdiction under Article 4 or 13].

2 The court second seised shall decline jurisdiction as soon as it is presented with a decision rendered by the court first seised that complies with the requirements for recognition or enforcement [under this Convention].

[3 Upon application of a party, the court second seised may continue to hear the case if the plaintiff in the court first seised has failed to take the necessary steps to bring the proceedings to a decision on the merits or if that court has not rendered a decision on the merits within a reasonable time.]

[4 The provisions of the preceding paragraphs apply to the court second seised in a Contracting State even in a case where the jurisdiction of that court is based on the national law of that State under the provisions of Article 19.]

[5 For the purpose of this Article, a court shall be deemed to be seised -

  a) when the document instituting the proceedings or an equivalent document is lodged with the court, or
  b) if such document has to be served before being lodged with the court, when it is received by the authority responsible for service or served on the defendant.

[As the case may be, the universal time is applicable.]]

[6 This article shall not apply if—

  a) in the action in the court first seised the plaintiff seeks a determination that it has no obligation to the defendant, or]
  b) [the court first seised] [either court], on application by a party, determines that the court second seised is clearly more appropriate to resolve the dispute taking into account the requirements of Article 24,[59] the procedural status of the proceedings in the court first seised and any ruling that court has issued in response to a request to decline jurisdiction.]

Now the addition of the words "within a reasonable time" in Article 23(3) is an improvement over the wording of Article 21 of the Brussels and Lugano Conventions, but how in practice is this going to work? Clearly, under the provision as now drafted, it is envisaged that the defendant will be able to apply to a second court when it becomes evident that the first court has been deliberately

[59] Which deals with exceptional circumstances for declining jurisdiction, such as inconvenience to the parties in view of their habitual residence or seat.

selected as a delaying tactic, or where the plaintiff has been permitted to drag its feet, but the defendant could have lost much valuable time before it is able to assemble evidence to present to a second court on these matters under Article 23(3), and assembly of this evidence may, in the nature of things (because procedures differ so greatly from jurisdiction to jurisdiction), be quite difficult. The *lis pendens* provision still gives plaintiffs a considerable incentive to choose slow jurisdictions to file for declarations of non-infringement.

IV CONCLUSION

I hope I have said enough about the problems to which the Brussels and Lugano Conventions have given rise in relation to the infringement of industrial property rights to suggest that the way in which work on the Convention on International Jurisdiction and the Effects of Foreign Judgments in Civil and Commercial Matters is proceeding should give rise to concern. To those who may welcome a free market in litigation, I would give an additional warning: the playing field is not level. Traditionally, in common law litigation most of the costs are borne by the parties themselves; by contrast, in civil law countries a large part of the costs are borne by the state, including in patent actions the considerable costs of expert witnesses.[60]

Some people have suggested that the only real solution for Europe is a European Court or courts to deal with industrial property disputes. Perhaps this is the solution which needs to be looked at globally.

---

[60] See J. Adams and J. Thomas, *Patent Litigation: A Comparative Study* (European Patent Office, 1995).

Part 3

Competition and Market Regulation

Increasingly, scholars and policy-makers are looking beyond the traditional confines of intellectual property law for checks and balances to the expansion of intellectual property rights. The two final Chapters in this collection exemplify this trend. Susy Frankel considers the scope of intellectual property rights in the light of principles of the law of unfair competition. The Chapter by Ian Eagles concerns the relationship between intellectual property rights and competition law. Both Chapters suggest that thinking beyond the traditional heuristic structures that underlie intellectual property law may be necessary if intellectual property is to continue to serve the public good.

11

*Unfair Competiton Law—"Over Protection Stifles the Very Creative Force it is Supposed to Nurture"**

SUSY FRANKEL

I INTRODUCTION

The term "unfair competition" means different things in different jurisdictions. It also sparks different conclusions in different disciplines. The legal perspective of what amounts to unfair competition differs from that of the economist or business person. From a legal perspective unfair competition may mean a doctrine of law. In the continental legal systems of Europe there is a recognised independent doctrine of unfair competition. This doctrine is said to derive from the natural rights orientation of continental legal systems.[1] In the Anglo-Australasian jurisdictions there is no independent unfair competition doctrine,[2] but notions of unfair competition may be found in specific areas of law, particularly those of consumer protection and intellectual property.

In New Zealand the cornerstone of consumer protection legislation is section 9 of the Fair Trading Act 1986, which provides:

> No person shall, in trade, engage in conduct which is misleading or deceptive or that is likely to mislead or deceive.

The conduct section 9 prohibits not only protects consumers, but also protects traders from certain types of unfair competition.[3] This chapter is, however,

---

* The quotation is from *White* v. *Samsung Electronics America, Inc.*, 989 F 2d 1512, 1513 (9th Cir. 1993).

[1] W.J. Derenberg, "The Influence of the French Code on the Modern Law of Unfair Competition" (1955) 5 *Am J of Comp L* 1.

[2] A. Terry, "Unfair Competition and the Misappropriation of a Competitor's Trade Values" (1988) 51 *MLR* 296; M. Blakeney, "The Demise of Unfair Competition in Australia" (1985) 59 *ALJ* 366; W.L. Morison, "Unfair Competition at Common Law" (1953) 2 *UWA Ann L Rev* 34.

[3] S. 9 is often used as a cause of action between rival traders. See, e.g., *Levi Strauss & Co* v. *Kimbyr Investments Ltd* [1994] 1 NZLR 332 and *Bonz Group (Pty.) Ltd* v. *Cooke* [1994] 3 NZLR 216 (HC) and (1996) 7 TCLR 206 (CA).

primarily concerned with the notions of unfair competition in intellectual property law.[4]

Unfair competition may also describe legal, but, in the eyes of some, morally bad behaviour. In New Zealand "unfair competition" is more often than not used in this descriptive sense. For example, the Court of Appeal recently used the term in the same name case *Neumegen* v. *Neumegen*.[5] Although dissenting as to the result, Thomas J said:[6]

> As Lord Scarman has observed in another context when asserting that competition must remain free, a person does no wrong by entering a market created by another and then competing with its creator. To do so is not *unfair competition*.

His Honour also stated[7]:

> it is to be accepted that s 9 [of the Fair Trading Act 1986] falls to be interpreted and applied in a competitive environment and is to be construed and applied in a manner which is consistent with the object of promoting competition. *Unfair competition* would not be condoned, but where there is nothing adverse or unfair to the relevant group of consumers, the Courts should not hesitate before intervening under s 9.

The descriptive use of the term has given hope to optimistic litigants whose cases fall short of any recognised intellectual property or related right to argue that they have protection under the "law of" or "tort of" unfair competition.

Deane J, in giving the leading judgment of the High Court of Australia in *Moorgate Tobacco Co Ltd* v. *Philip Morris Ltd (No. 2)*,[8] provided a useful summary of the meanings of "unfair competition":[9]

> The phrase "unfair competition" has been used in judgments and in learned writings in at least three distinct ways, namely, (i) as a synonym for passing off; (ii) as a generic name to cover the range of equitable and legal causes of action available to protect a trader against the unlawful trading activities of a competitor; and (iii) to describe what is claimed to be a new and general cause of action which protects a trader against damage caused either by "unfair competition" generally or, more particularly, by the "misappropriation" of knowledge or information in which he has a "quasi proprietary" right.

The concept of unfair competition as a synonym for passing off is discussed below. The High Court of Australia rejected the idea that unfair competition

---

[4] It is noted that in New Zealand s. 9 of the Fair Trading Act 1986 is often pleaded as a cause of action in conjunction with intellectual property rights: trade mark infringement, passing-off or copyright. One early High Court decision held that a finding of a breach of s. 9 was too much of a "branding" in the circumstances. This was overturned on appeal (see *Wineworths* v. *Comité Interprofessionel du Vin de Champagne* [1992] 2 NZLR 327, 333). Otherwise, findings of the courts under s. 9, when pleaded alongside intellectual property causes of action, are usually in accordance with the findings relating to the intellectual property causes of action. (See, e.g., *Levi Strauss & Co* v. *Kimbyr Investments Ltd* [1994] 1 NZLR 332, 381–3.)

[5] [1998] 3 NZLR 310.

[6] *Ibid.*, 329 (emphasis added).

[7] *Ibid.*, 323 (emphasis added).

[8] (1984) 3 IPR 545.

[9] *Ibid.*, 562.

could sensibly be used as a generic term to describe a range of equitable and legal causes of action[10] on the grounds that it implied an underlying unity of principle.[11] As regards the concept of a separate cause of action known as unfair competition, there is no separate doctrine of unfair competition in the United Kingdom, Australia or New Zealand.[12]

In recent times advocates of an independent unfair competition right have continued to press for it under a variety of titles, such as the "tort of misappropriation" or "unjust enrichment".[13] Whatever name is used, the function of an unfair competition right is to plug the perceived gaps in intellectual property and competition law. On the other hand, those gaps, if indeed they are gaps, may fulfil a useful function. They allow a form of competition which may appear to be a bit sneaky, or even to be very cheeky, but which falls short of a legal wrong. Not all competition need be legally sanctioned. It is a fundamental tenet of our legal system that what is not prohibited may be done. It is not the place of intellectual property law or competition law to sanitise all aspects of competition.

Furthermore, a separate law of unfair competition has the potential to undermine the structure of intellectual property. Intellectual property is traditionally divided into three broad areas: copyright and designs, trade marks and passing off, and patents.[14] There are other related rights, such as breach of confidence and modern statutory protections like plant variety rights[15] and circuit layout designs.[16] This division may be inappropriate in a technological world.[17] Nonetheless, this division arguably has at least three valuable functions:

(a) preserving the balance between protecting the rights of creators and owners of intellectual property and encouraging creativity and innovation; and

---

[10] The "range of equitable and legal causes of action" could include copyright, designs, trade marks, patents, passing off, breach of the Fair Trading Act 1986, defamation, injurious falsehood/deceit, interference with contractual relations, unlawful interference, breach of confidence, conspiracy and intimidation.

[11] *Moorgate Tobacco Co Ltd* v. *Philip Morris Ltd (No. 2)* (1984) 3 IPR 545. To use the term "unfair competition" to cover all of these causes of action is misleading because it is "liable to imply that there exists a unity of underlying principle between different actions when, in truth, there is none" (at 86, *per* Deane J).

[12] See n. 2 above.

[13] For a proposal for a general principle of liability to cover all situations of reaping without sowing, see S. Ricketson, "Reaping Without Sowing: Unfair Competition and Intellectual Property Rights in Anglo-Australian Law" (1984) 7 *UNSWLJ* 1 (special issue). For a discussion of the use of unjust enrichment as a general principle in relation to unfair competition, see B. Fitzgerald and L. Gamertsfelder, "Protecting Informational Products (including Databases) through Unjust Enrichment Law: An Australian Perspective" [1998] *EIPR* 244.

[14] For New Zealand, see Copyright Act 1994, Designs Act 1953, Trade Marks Act 1953 and Patents Act 1953.

[15] See Plant Variety Rights Act 1987 (NZ).

[16] See Layout Designs Act 1994 (NZ).

[17] E.g., is there any sense in both copyright and patent law protecting computer programs?

(b) assisting competition; and

(c) connecting intellectual property rights to notions of property.[18]

This chapter considers what we mean by competition. It then considers the various ways in which the concept of unfair competition emerges in conjunction with intellectual property rights. I conclude that there is not and should not be a separate law of unfair competition in New Zealand.

II WHAT IS COMPETITION?

Advocates of the free market philosophy which dominated Western economic policy during the last two decades of the twentieth century might say that "competition" is a cornerstone of that philosophy. It is the prime belief of capitalism that competition is efficacious. The rationale offered is that firms competing leads to lower prices, cheaper means of production and industrial innovation. This competition in turn benefits society as a whole. As the "patron saint" of capitalism, Adam Smith, observed in *The Wealth of Nations*:[19]

> It is not from the benevolence of the butcher, the brewer or the baker that we expect our dinner, but from their regard to their own interest.

However, despite this view that competition is itself a good thing, the way in which competition is conducted can be harmful. As Adam Smith further observed:[20]

> People of the same trade seldom meet together, even for merriment and diversion, but the conversation ends in a conspiracy against the public, or in some contrivance to raise prices.

Firms, rather than competing fiercely, can end up agreeing to eliminate competition among them. This is arguably to society's detriment. It is not just that sort of agreement that Smith found odious. He also railed against giant monopolies that crushed their opposition and kept prices to the public high. Indeed, much of the thrust of *The Wealth of Nations* is against "the mean rapacity, the monopolising spirit of merchants and manufacturers, who neither are, nor ought to be the rulers of mankind".[21] This diatribe was against mer-

---

[18] Copyright works, patents and trade marks are property rights. S. 14(1) of the Copyright Act 1994 (NZ) states that "copyright is a property right". This status as property is useful. E.g., it means property remedies are available if the rights are infringed. Pickering suggests that calling trade marks property "is more useful as a conclusion than an analytical starting point": C.D.G. Pickering, *Trade Marks in Theory and Practice* (Oxford, Hart Publishing, 1998), 154. It is beyond the scope of this chap. to consider the issue of what it means to categorise intellectual property as property. Suffice it to say that a general unfair competition right is unlikely to be easily categorised as a single property right.

[19] A. Smith, *An Inquiry into the Nature and Causes of the Wealth of Nations* (E. Cannan (ed.), New York, Random House, 1937), 369.

[20] *Ibid.*, 374.

[21] *Ibid.*, 382.

cantilism, but it can easily be translated into one against monopolists and monopolisation.

Accordingly, there must be rules for competition if consumers are to reap any benefits from it. Competition law in New Zealand, Australia, the European Union and the United States includes rules to prevent competing firms from agreeing on prices and thereby allowing giant or not so giant monopolies from exploiting their power against actual or would be competitors.[22] This seems to be the end of the matter. Competition is good for society, but it can be subverted. Accordingly competition law provides rules by which competition is to be conducted. If a firm or firms breach these rules competition law provides sanctions. If this is so, is there any need for a so-called doctrine of unfair competition?

However, quite what is meant by the concept of competition has never been agreed upon, and there is still debate over the relationship between intellectual property and competition.[23] While "competition" is a word that is relatively easily defined, "competition law" is a term which raises much disagreement over its meaning. Does it, for example, mean the state of perfect competition so beloved by neoclassical economists? Such an ideal state involves numerous competing firms which have numerous customers all of whom have perfect information. These firms sell standardised products, and entry to and exit from the market is quick and easy. This ideal view of competition is unworkable and unrealistic. A playground of perfect competition is a theoretical state. Of necessity, firms have economies of scale and scope, which militate against the structure of numerous firms in every market. There are barriers to newcomers to a market and not all consumers have perfect information.

There is much philosophical debate over the meaning of competition. The neoclassicists, known as the "Chicago School", argue that competition equates with efficiency.[24] That is, the whole aim of competition is to lower prices for consumers. On the other side are those who do not deny the efficiency of lower prices, but argue that competition has other goals. Intellectual property plays an awkward role in this debate. Neoclassicists regard intellectual property and competition law as complementary, since both are aimed at encouraging industry, innovation and competition. The counter-argument is more ambivalent. It recognises intellectual property as vital for fostering innovation, but considers that it can lead to firms gaining substantial market power. This gain of power may be through a statutorily created monopoly, such as a patent, or by the creation of a statutory barrier to entry, such as needing a licence from a patent owner. The ink spilled on this issue might fill Lake Baikal. However, one of the

---

[22] New Zealand: Commerce Act 1986, Part II; Australia: Trade Practices Act 1974, Part IV; Europe: Arts. 81 and 82 EC (ex Arts. 85–86); United States of America: Sherman Act 1890, ss. 1–2.

[23] W. Pengilley. "Antitrust Law v. Intellectual Property Law: Where is the Interface?" (1989) 5 *Canterbury L Rev* 103.

[24] For a standard exposition of the Chicago School, see R. Bork, *The Antitrust Paradox: A Policy At War With Itself* (2nd edn., New York, The Free Press, 1993); R. Posner, "The Chicago School of Antitrust Analysis" (1979) 127 *U of Penn L Rev* 925.

contributions the neoclassicists have made in the context of competition law is to alert us to the danger of free riding. Free riding can occur when one firm advertises a product and another firm takes advantage of the advertising campaign.[25] Free riding may also occur where one firm offers pre- or post-sale services and another firm which does not provide those services takes advantage of their availability.[26] Competition law restraints, such as exclusive dealing or resale price maintenance, are now justified on the ground of avoidance of free riding.[27]

It is this concept, the avoidance of free riding, which is targeted by the supporters of a separate law of unfair competition to sit alongside, or even to operate instead of, intellectual property rights. If a firm takes a free ride, it is reaping without sowing. It is arguably engaging in unfair competition.

Competition law by its very nature addresses the issue of what amounts to legally acceptable or unacceptable competition. Intellectual property law also provides protection to prevent certain types of unfair competition.

III   EXISTING INTELLECTUAL PROPERTY AND RELATED RIGHTS

A Passing Off and Unfair Competition

A significant factor behind the impetus for a separate legal doctrine to prevent unfair competition is the inadequacies of the doctrine of passing off.

A plaintiff can invoke passing off to prevent certain types of unfair competition. Classic passing off is said to protect a trader from having other traders pass off their goods as if they are the goods of the first trader.[28] This form of passing off has been extended to provide a cause of action for other types of misrepresentation and damage, on the basis that passing off protects the goodwill of a business.[29] The other recognised types of damage include dilution of a trader's goodwill and damage to a trader's reputation.[30] All these forms of passing off require some sort of misrepresentation. Accordingly, free riding on or the

---

[25] L. Telser, "Why Should Manufacturers Want Fair Trade?" (1960) 3 *J Law & Econ* 86; R. Posner, "The Rule of Reason and the Economic Approach: Reflections on the *Sylvania* Decision" (1997) 45 *U of Chic L Rev* 1.

[26] *Ibid.*

[27] For exclusive dealing, see *Fisher & Paykel Ltd* v. *Commerce Commission* [1991] 1 NZLR 569 (HC). For retail price maintenance, see Telser, n. 25 above.

[28] *Reddaway* v. *Banham* [1896] AC 199 (HL). Lord Herschell (at 209) quoted Lord Kingsdown in *The Leather Cloth Company* v. *The American Cloth Company* (1865) 11 HLC 523, 538, 11 ER 1435, 1442: "[t]he fundamental rule is that one man has no right to put off his goods for sale as the goods of a rival trader, and he cannot therefore . . . be allowed to use names, marks, letters, or other indicia, by which he may induce purchasers to believe that the goods which he is selling are the manufacture of another person".

[29] *Erven Warnink BV* v. *J. Townend & Sons (Hull) Ltd* [1979] AC 731; adopted in New Zealand (*Wineworths Group Ltd* v. *Comité Interprofessionel du Vin de Champagne* [1992] 2 NZLR 327) and in Australia (*McWilliams Wines Pty. Ltd* v. *McDonald's System of Australia Pty. Ltd* (1980) 33 ALR 394.

[30] *Taylor Bros. Ltd* v. *Taylors Group Ltd* [1988] 2 NZLR 1, 22.

appropriation of goodwill, without a misrepresentation, will not amount to passing off. The Privy Council refused to extend passing off to cover the situation where the defendant was free-riding on the plaintiff's advertising campaign because the public was not deceived.[31] In reaching their decision, their Lordships stated:[32]

> But competition must remain free; and competition is safeguarded by the necessity for the plaintiff to prove that he has built up an "intangible property right" in the advertised descriptions of his product, or, in other words, that he has succeeded by such methods in giving his product a distinctive character accepted by the market. A defendant, however, does no wrong by entering a market created by another and there competing with its creator. The line may be difficult to draw; but, unless it is drawn competition will be stifled.

In Australia, the Federal Court has extended the law of passing off to character merchandising or image filching of fictional characters and real persons.[33] This extension provides a plaintiff with a cause of action to prevent others from misappropriating its image. This is so even if the image filching does not amount to an actual misrepresentation or quantifiable damage, other than the lost opportunity of charging a licensing fee.[34]

New Zealand has not yet stretched passing off in this way. To date, the leading case of *Tot Toys Ltd* v. *Mitchell*[35] expresses serious reluctance to do so. The first reason for this reluctance is that the essence of passing off is deception and, therefore, a passing off action must involve an actual misrepresentation.[36] Secondly, the tortious basis of passing off requires damage or a real likelihood of damage. The loss of opportunity to charge a licensing fee was not considered adequate proof of damage in *Tot Toys Ltd*. Fisher J regarded such an argument as circular. The right to charge a fee is the very question at issue in the image filching type of case.[37] As *Tot Toys Ltd* was a High Court decision and the Court of Appeal has not considered the issue of further extending passing off in the field of character merchandising, it is arguable that the position has yet to be conclusively determined in New Zealand. However, what is settled is that passing off is limited to protecting traders from only certain types of unfair competition. In particular, in New Zealand, it does not protect against free riding, unless there is an actual misrepresentation.[38] In Australia, it incorporates misappropriation of reputation without deception.[39]

---

[31] *Cadbury Schweppes Pty. Ltd* v. *Pub Squash Co Pty. Ltd* [1981] RPC 429 (PC).
[32] *Ibid.*, 218.
[33] *Hogan* v. *Koala Dundee Pty. Ltd* (1988) 83 ALR 187.
[34] *Ibid.*
[35] [1993] 1 NZLR 325.
[36] *Ibid.*, 361–2.
[37] *Ibid.*, 363.
[38] The law is similar in the United Kingdom. A merchandising right was deliberately not included in the Copyright Designs and Patents Act 1988. See also *Mirage Studios* v. *Counter-Feat Clothing Co Ltd* [1991] FSR 145.
[39] *Hogan* v. *Koala Dundee Pty. Ltd* (1988) 83 ALR 187.

In the United States, individual state laws include torts of misappropriation and of publicity rights.[40] The publicity right is used to protect the ability to "merchandise" a famous personality. The law gives protection greater than that available under passing off. There has been some judicial opposition to extending the right too far.[41] In *White* v. *Samsung Electronics America, Inc.*,[42] Vanna White objected to the use of a robot dressed in a wig, gown and jewelry reminiscent of [her] hair and dress, posed next to a "Wheel of Fortune"-like game board, with the caption "Longest Running Game Show 2012 AD". White was entitled to prevent this use of [her] image under Californian law. The dissenting judgment warned against preventing such use of an image:[43]

> Saddam Hussein wants to keep advertisers from using his picture in unflattering contexts. Clint Eastwood doesn't want tabloids to write about him. Rudolf Valentino's heirs want to control his film biography. The Girl Scouts don't want their image soiled by association with certain activities. George Lucas wants to keep Strategic Defense Initiatives fans from calling it "Star Wars". Pepsico doesn't want singers to use the word "Pepsi" in their songs. Guy Lombardo wants an exclusive property right to ads that show big bands playing on New Year's Eve. Uri Geller thinks he should be paid for ads showing psychics bending metal through telekinesis. . . .
>
> Something very dangerous is going on here. Private property, including intellectual property, is essential to our way of life. It provides an incentive for investment and innovation; it stimulates the flourishing of our culture; it protects the moral entitlements of people to the fruits of their labors. But reducing too much to private property can be bad medicine. Private land, for instance is far more useful if separated from other private land by public streets, roads and highways. Public parks, utility rights-of-way and sewers reduce the amount of land in private hands, but vastly enhances the value of the property that remains.
>
> So too it is with intellectual property. Overprotecting intellectual property is as harmful as under protecting it. Creativity is impossible without a rich public domain. Nothing today, likely nothing since we tamed fire, is genuinely new. Culture like science and technology grows by accretion, each new creator building on the works of those who came before. Over protection stifles the very creative force it is supposed to nurture.

In *Tot Toys Ltd*,[44] the main reason for not extending passing off to most character merchandising situations was the absence of a misrepresentation or independent actionable damage. The dangers of over-protection provide an additional argument against extending passing off to any form of misappropriation in relation to either real or fictional characters.[45] Over-protection can have the effect of lessening competition.

[40] R.P. Merges, P.S. Menell, M.A. Lemley and T.M. Jorde, *Intellectual Property in the New Technological Age* (New York, Aspen Law & Business,1997), 738.

[41] *Cadbury Schweppes Pty. Ltd* v. *Pub Squash Co Pty. Ltd* [1981] RPC 429, 491–2.

[42] *White* v. *Samsung Electronics America, Inc*, 989 F 2d 1512 (9th Cir. 1993).

[43] *Ibid.*, 1513 *per* Kozinski J, joined by O'Scannlain and Kleinfeld JJ.

[44] [1993] 1 NZLR 325.

[45] It is arguable that there is a greater need for an extension of the law to protect real persons from image filching. Fictional characters have protection by way of other intellectual property rights such

B Registered Trade Marks and Unfair Competition

Trade marks law has expanded to allow the registration of shapes, sounds, smells and anything which functions as a trade mark and is capable of being graphically represented.[46] This development is recognition of the expanding nature of what businesses use in a trade mark sense. Commentators have argued that because of the liberalisation of trade mark law, passing off may be freed to pursue the ambition of becoming a tort of unfair competition.[47] However, the liberalisation of one area of intellectual property rights does not, on its own, provide sufficient reason to liberalise another area in a different way.

The primary function of a trade mark is as a badge of origin.[48] Therefore, the initial development of registered trade marks was justified as protecting the consumer from confusion as to source.[49] Another function of trade marks, which was recognised relatively early, is that a mark may indicate a particular quality of goods or services.[50] For example, "Rolex" has come to mean high quality watches and "Armani" suits are fashionable high quality suits.

As well as protecting consumers from confusion, a registered trade mark also protects the trade mark proprietor's interests. Trade mark law originally gave the proprietor the right to prevent the use of its mark on goods identical to the proprietor's goods.[51] As the use of marks developed, the right extended to prevent the use of an identical mark on similar goods and also the use of a confusingly similar mark on identical or similar goods.[52] Arguably, proprietor protection has become the main objective of trade mark protection.[53] These developments are a clear recognition that such uses would amount to unfair competition.

Trade marks law has also developed to include the ability of a proprietor of a famous mark to register defensive trade marks.[54] This is where a proprietor may register a mark in a class of goods, in which it does not trade, in order to prevent others from using the mark in that category. This benefit also protects a

---

as copyright. See *Tot Toys Ltd* v. *Mitchell, ibid; Mirage Studios* v. *Counter-Feat Clothing Co Ltd* [1991] FSR 145; and *Childrens Television Workshop, Inc.* v. *Woolworths (NSW) Ltd* [1981] RPC 187.

[46] S. 2 of the Trade Marks Act 1953 (NZ) provides: "'[t]rade mark' means . . . any sign or combination of signs, capable of being represented graphically and capable of distinguishing the goods or services of one person from those of another person . . . 'Sign' includes a device, brand, heading, label, ticket, name, signature, word, letter, numeral, colour, or any combination thereof."

[47] Pickering, n. 18 above, 33.

[48] *Levi Strauss & Co* v. *Kimbyr Investments Ltd* [1994] 1 NZLR 332, 347–8; Pickering, n. 18 above, 43.

[49] *Re Powells Trade-mark* [1893] 2 Ch 388.

[50] F.T. Schechter, "The Rationale Basis of Trade Mark Protection" (1927) 40 *Harv L Rev* 813.

[51] Now embodied in s. 8(1A)(a) of the Trade Marks Act 1953 (NZ).

[52] Now embodied in s. 8(1A)(b) and (c) of the Trade Marks Act 1953 (NZ).

[53] Pickering, n. 18 above, chap. 4.

[54] Trade Marks Act 1953 (NZ), s. 36.

proprietor from potential unfair competition.[55] This sort of proprietor protection has been described as being to "compensate for the absence of a general unfair competition law".[56] In fact, it is recognition of the concept of unfair competition within the existing framework of intellectual property law.

Trade marks law has also evolved to prevent free-riding in advertising where a trade mark is used. In *Irving's Yeast-Vite Ltd* v. *Horsenail*,[57] the defendant marketed its yeast tablet product with a label stating "Yeast tablets a substitute for 'Yeast-Vite'". The plaintiff was the registered proprietor of "Yeast-Vite". The plaintiff was not successful in bringing a trade mark infringement action as the defendant had not used the mark to indicate the origin of the goods. There was unlikely to be any consumer confusion because the defendant had quite clearly distinguished its product from the plaintiff's.[58] As a result, Parliament amended the law in the United Kingdom and the same amendment was subsequently adopted in New Zealand.[59] The purpose of the amendment was to make the "the exploitation of goodwill", exemplified by *Yeast-Vite*, a trade mark infringement.

In New Zealand, the first case in this area was *Villa Maria Wines Ltd* v. *Montana Wines Ltd*[60] Villa Maria had included three of Montana's trade marks in its advertisements. It did not make any disparaging comments about Montana's goods. However, the Court of Appeal held its motive was "to promote its wines by equating their quality with those of a better known competitor whose products have an established reputation and thereby enlarge its share of the market".[61] Villa Maria was taking a free ride on Montana's goodwill. Montana established that its trade marks had been infringed, but did not succeed overall because Villa Maria successfully relied on the relevant statutory defence.[62] The defence applied because the use complained of did not indicate a connection in the course of trade between Villa Maria and Montana. Therefore the use would not cause confusion or deception, and thus there was no infringement.

In 1994, the New Zealand legislation was amended.[63] The effect of the amendment was that the defence will now only apply where the defendant has

---

[55] New Zealand trade mark law does not provide a cause of action equivalent to the dilution of a trade mark doctrine in the United States. For a general discussion, see T. Martino, *Trade Mark Dilution* (Oxford, Oxford University Press, 1996) and K L Port, "The 'Unnatural' Expansion of Trade Mark Rights: Is a Federal Dilution Statute Necessary?" (1995) 85 *The Trademark Rep* 525.

[56] Pickering, n. 18 above, 33.

[57] (1934) 51 RPC 110.

[58] *Villa Maria Wines Ltd* v. *Montana Wines Ltd* [1984] 2 NZLR 422, 427.

[59] The change to English law was made as a result of the *Report of the Departmental Committee on the Law & Practice Relating to Trade Marks* (Goschen Committee), Cmd. 4568 (HMSO, London, 1934): see Trade Marks (Amendment) Act 1937 (UK) (consolidated into the Trade Marks Act 1938), adopted by Patents, Designs and Trade Marks Amendment Act 1939 (NZ) (consolidated into the Trade Marks Act 1953, s. 8(1)(b)).

[60] [1984] 2 NZLR 422.

[61] *Ibid.*, 424 *per* Somers J, giving the judgment of the Court.

[62] Trade Marks Act 1953 (NZ), s. 9(2) (pre-1994 amendment).

[63] Trade Marks Amendment Act 1994, s. 4, repealing and replacing Trade Marks Act 1953, s. 9(2).

used either (a) an identical mark in relation to similar goods, or (b) a similar mark in relation to identical or similar goods. Most comparative advertising involves the use of an identical mark in relation to identical goods. After the 1994 amendment, this is not caught by the defence. As a result, the defence available in *Villa Maria* was not available to the defendant in *PC Direct Ltd* v. *Best Buy Ltd*.[64] The defendant had compared its product extensively to the plaintiff's product and had used the plaintiff's trade mark "PC Direct" in order to make its comparisons. Thus, it had infringed the plaintiff's trade mark by using an identical mark in relation to identical goods. The defence was not available because the 1994 amendments made it inapplicable to the situation where an identical trade mark was used in relation to identical goods. This result accords with the literal interpretation of the legislation. However, if this is so it is difficult to see what function the amended statutory defence could ever have. In order to establish an infringement relying on either the use of (a) an identical mark in relation to similar goods, or (b) a similar mark in relation to identical or similar goods, the use must be likely to deceive or confuse.[65] In order to rely on the defence the use must not be likely to deceive or confuse.[66]

It cannot have been Parliament's intention to enact a section, in excess of 100 words long, which can have no practical effect. The reasoning of the Court in *PC Direct* does not address the apparent redundancy of the defence in question. Even though PC Direct established the cause of action of trade mark infringement, an interlocutory injunction was not granted.[67] Elias J, as she then was, held that the effect of preventing the comparative advertising, even though it amounted to a trade mark infringement, was an "extraordinary fetter on freedom of expression".[68] The effect of *PC Direct* is that comparative advertising involving a trade mark may be an infringement, but the court may not give an injunction as a remedy. This may be contrary to the legislative intent which extended the trade mark law to protect a trader from unfair competition by way of comparative advertising using trade marks. Elias J's refusal to grant an injunction expresses the view that this strand of unfair competition law has gone too far. Protection of trade marks is one thing, but it should not be done at the cost of freedom of speech.[69]

---

[64] [1997] 2 NZLR 723.

[65] Trade Marks Act 1953 (NZ), s. 8(1A)(b) and (c).

[66] Trade Marks Act 1953 (NZ), s. 9(2) (post-1994 amendment).

[67] [1997] 2 NZLR 723, 733.

[68] *Ibid.*, 726. The law in the United Kingdom is different. There, s. 10(6) of the Trade Marks Act 1994 provides: " [n]othing in the preceding provisions in this section shall be construed as preventing the use of a registered trade mark by any person for the purpose of identifying goods or services as those of the proprietor or licensee. But any such use otherwise than in accordance with honest practices in industrial or commercial matters shall be treated as infringing the registered trade mark if the use without due cause takes unfair advantage of, or is detrimental to, the distinctive character or repute of the trade mark." See also *PC Direct Ltd* v. *Best Buy Ltd, ibid.*, 730.

[69] See also *White* v. *Samsung Electronics America, Inc.*, 989 F 2d 1512 (9th Cir. 1993).

C Copyright and Unfair Competition

Modern copyright law scarcely resembles early copyright law. Early copyright law was created to hinder competition. The first copyright statute was the Statute of Anne of 1709, which was enacted to prevent competition in the printing business. The Statute's preamble provided:

> An Act for the encouragement of learning, by vesting the copies of printed books in the authors or purchasers of such copies.

The Statute of Anne was enacted after substantial lobbying by the Stationers' Company. A royal charter established the Stationers' Company in 1557. The charter gave it a monopoly over printing in England. This monopoly lasted for the next 150 years.[70] The Stationers' Company issued exclusive licences to its members to print and publish. This had an effect which resembles today's exclusive right of copyright owners to control the copying of their works, but was clearly a way of controlling competition. A leading copyright text describes the Stationers' Company as "a cartel of booksellers, and mainly London booksellers at that".[71] It was a form of guild, which had a monopoly on printing.

When the Stationers' Company lost its printing privileges in the late seventeenth century, its members lobbied for control over the copying of printed works on its register and this led to the Statute of Anne. The statute provided a 14-year right for owners of books to control the publishing of those books.[72]

It is often said that one of the purposes of copyright is to encourage creativity and innovation.[73] Copyright purports to balance the protection of innovation and creativity against the needs for creators or owners of works to reap a reasonable return for their skill, judgement, labour or investment.[74] This balance of policies includes elements of protecting creators or owners of copyright works from unfair competition.

Copyright law allows certain works to be used in certain ways without infringing copyright. In the United States, this is called fair use of a work.[75] In

---

[70] A Star Chamber Declaration of 1586 limited the number of Master Printers in England to 25.

[71] H. Laddie, P. Prescott and M. Vitoria, *The Modern Law of Copyright and Designs* (2nd edn, London, Butterworths, 1995), 20.

[72] Members of the Stationers' Company also claimed there was a common law copyright which existed after the statutory right expired. This argument over the vestiges of common law copyright lingered for some time. *Donaldson* v. *Beckett* (1774) 4 Burr 2048, 98 ER 257, held that the statutory right replaced any common law rights. The English Copyright Act 1911 made it clear that common law copyright did not survive that statute.

[73] G. Hammond, "The Legal Protection of Ideas" (1991) 29 *Osgoode Hall LJ* 93; D. Vaver "Intellectual Property Today: Of Myths and Paradoxes" (1990) 69 *Can Bar Rev* 98.

[74] A creator of a copyright work will have to invest sufficient skill, judgement or labour in order for the work to be original and thus qualify for copyright protection: see *Ladbroke (Football) Ltd* v. *William Hill Ltd* [1964] 1 All ER 465 and, generally, W.R. Cornish, *Intellectual Property: Patents, Copyright, Trade Marks and Allied Rights* (4th edn., London, Sweet & Maxwell, 1999), para. 10–04.

[75] Copyright Act 1976, 17 USC § 107.

New Zealand, the Copyright Act 1994 accommodates the concept of fair use by way of specified permitted uses.[76] Such permitted uses are condoned internationally, as long as they do not interfere with the copyright owner's normal exploitation of the work.[77] The function of permitted uses is to strike a balance between the exclusive rights of the copyright owner and the ability for others to make use of existing copyright works to create new copyright works.

Another way of describing this balancing act is that copyright is a mechanism for preventing certain types of unfair competition, but fair competition is legitimate and therefore excuses what would otherwise be an infringement of copyright. In this context, "unfair competition" means competition that conflicts with the normal exploitation of the work.

Copyright law embodies the concept known as the "idea/expression dichotomy".[78] Broadly explained, this dichotomy is that copyright protects the expression of a work, but not the idea behind that work. The dividing line between idea and expression is difficult to draw with precision,[79] but the rationale behind the divide is clear. If copyright protected more than the expression it would be unfair to users of copyright works and other creators of copyright works. It would have the effect of stifling new works and thus potential competition.[80]

From time to time, courts have interpreted certain aspects of copyright law in ways to prevent copyright from being used as a mechanism to hinder competition. An example is the "spare parts exception" in the United Kingdom. This was established[81] in *British Leyland Motor Corp.* v. *Armstrong Patents Ltd*[82] There, the House of Lords held that it was not an infringement of copyright in certain design drawings if the defendant made spare parts for the plaintiff's cars. Their Lordships said that the right to repair overrode the plaintiff's copyright. If the copyright had precedence, this would allow the plaintiff to derogate from grant of sale. It was held that the plaintiff could not be allowed to derogate from its grant in this way.[83] The "spare parts exception" has not been accepted in New Zealand[84] or Australia.[85]

---

[76] Copyright Act 1994 (NZ), ss 40–7. Recent English case law indicates the possible widening of this approach: see *Pro Sieben Media AG* v. *Carlton UK Television Ltd* [1999] 1 WLR 604.

[77] Art. 9(2) of the Berne Convention on Literary and Artistic Works (Paris, 1971), adopted by Art. 9 of the Trade Related Intellectual Property Rights Agreement (World Trade Organisation). TRIPS came into force on 1 January 1995.

[78] *Feist Publications, Inc.* v. *Rural Telephone Service Co*, 499 US 340 (1991). For a critical discussion of the "idea/expression fallacy", see Laddie, Prescott and Vitoria, n.71 above, 61.

[79] *Nichols* v. *Universal Pictures Corp.*, 45 F 2d 119 (2nd Cir. 1930).

[80] See, e.g., *Ravenscroft* v. *Herbert* [1980] RPC 193 and *Elanco* v. *Mandops* [1980] RPC 213.

[81] It has been suggested that it was "invented" by the House of Lords acting as legislators: Laddie, Prescott and Vitoria, n. 71 above, 1337.

[82] [1986] AC 577 (HL).

[83] *Ibid.*, 641.

[84] *Dennison Manufacturing Co* v. *Alfred Holt & Co Ltd* (1987) 10 IPR 612; *Mono Pumps (New Zealand) Ltd* v. *Karinya Industries* (1986) 7 IPR 25.

[85] *Warman* v. *Envirotech* (1986) 6 IPR 578.

D Patents and Unfair Competition

Patents protect inventions. To obtain a patent, the invention must be novel.[86] A grant of a patent represents a contract between the inventor and the state. In return for a monopoly of a limited term to use the invention, the information about the invention is made publicly available.[87] The policy behind patent protection is to provide reward and consequent encouragement for inventors to invent. In addition, patent protection provides the possibility of financial returns to those who invest in research and development.[88]

The relatively strong monopoly provided by a patent is perhaps anti-competitive. Public knowledge of the invention and a general right to use it when the patent expires is supposed to lessen the anti-competitive effect.[89]

What amounts to an invention has in part increased as technology grows. This widening of patentable inventions has both competitive and anti-competitive elements. On the one hand, the ability to register "Swiss claim" patents allows a greater number of patents in relation to the same known substance.[90] On the other hand, it potentially increases the duration for which a known pharmaceutical substance can be subject to patent monopoly.[91]

E Other Intellectual Property Rights and Unfair Competition

There are other intellectual property rights which merit brief consideration.

(i) Breach of Confidence and Trade Secrets

Breach of confidence is an action which prevents the unauthorised disclosure of confidential information. A plaintiff may bring an action against a person with whom it has a contractual relationship. A plaintiff can also bring an action against a person who is bound to confidentiality by the operation of equity rather than contract.[92] The use of confidential information by a trade competitor amounts to unfair competition. Therefore, the law provides a remedy to prevent breaches of confidence from allowing, amongst other things, unfair competition.

---

[86] For a general discussion, see Cornish, n. 74 above, para. 5–03.

[87] This may be compared to trade secrets, where the information is kept secret in order that it not be exploited by others.

[88] Cornish, n. 74 above, paras. 3–36–3–39.

[89] For a critical discussion, see Vaver, n. 73 above, 114–24.

[90] "Swiss claim" patents are registrable in New Zealand: see *Pharmaceutical Management Agency Ltd* v. *The Commissioner of Patents and Others*, (2000) 46 IPR 655.

[91] The writer expresses no view on the issue of "Swiss claim" patents.

[92] For a general discussion, see F. Gurry, *Breach of Confidence* (Oxford, OUP, 1984) and *Coco* v. *A.N. Clark (Engineers) Ltd* [1969] RPC 41.

(ii) Registered Design Rights

The registered designs system is little used in New Zealand, primarily because many industrial designs can receive copyright protection. In theory the registered design system protects:[93]

> Features of shape, configuration, pattern, or ornament applied to an article by any industrial process or means, being features which in the finished article appeal to and are judged solely by the eye; but does not include a method or principle of construction or features of shape or configuration which are dictated solely by the function which the article to be made in that shape or configuration has to perform.

(iii) Layout Designs

The Layout Designs Act 1994 protects the layout design of integrated circuits. These terms are defined in section 2 of that Act as follows:

> "Integrated circuit" means a circuit, in its final or an intermediate form, in which the elements, at least one of which is an active element, and some or all of the interconnections are integrally formed in or on a piece of material and that is intended to perform an electronic function; and
>
> "Layout design" means the three-dimensional disposition, however expressed, of the elements, at least one of which is an active element, and of some or all of the interconnections, of an integrated circuit; and includes such a three-dimensional disposition prepared for an integrated circuit intended for manufacture.

The owner of the layout has the exclusive rights to copy the layout design, to make an integrated circuit in accordance with the layout design, and to exploit commercially the layout design in New Zealand.[94]

(iv) Plant Variety Rights

Plant variety rights grant exclusive rights to the sale and reproduction of a plant variety. Variety is defined in the Plant Variety Rights Act 1987 as follows:[95]

> "Variety" means a cultivar, or cultivated variety, of a plant, and includes any clone, hybrid, stock, or line, of a plant; but does not include a botanical variety of a plant.

IV THE "GAPS" IN EXISTING INTELLECTUAL PROPERTY RIGHTS

Part of the reason for the pursuit of a separate law of unfair competition is the perceived gaps in the protection afforded by the existing structure of intellectual property law. What are those gaps? It is not easy to predict all scenarios where

---

[93] Designs Act 1953 (NZ), s. 2.
[94] Layout Designs Act 1994 (NZ), s. 13.
[95] Plant Variety Rights Act 1987, s. 2.

protection may not exist under the present intellectual property law regime. "While the present law of intellectual property leaves relatively few gaps, there is still no general principle of liability applicable to all situations in which a trader misappropriates the intangible results of his competitor's skill and labour".[96] The apparent "gaps" are most closely related to passing off.

Passing off protects a trader from certain types of unfair competition. As discussed above, the actions which fall just outside the ambit of passing off are misappropriation of reputation or of a publicity right. In New Zealand, character merchandising of a fictional character, which does not involve a misrepresentation, is outside the ambit of passing off. If a person's image, or their name, is used to make a false endorsement of a product there may well be protection in New Zealand under the Fair Trading Act[97] or passing off.[98] However, anything short of a false endorsement is not actionable.

Fisher J has considered that perhaps there ought to be greater protection in this area for real persons.[99] If, for the sake of argument, this is accepted, the answer is not necessarily a general unfair competition right. A broad right against unfair competition is going too far. It has the potential to capture a range of commercial activities, which arguably, for the benefit of competition, should not be prevented. In the United States, where there is a right to prevent misappropriation of reputation, powerful arguments have emerged about the dangers of extending the right.[100]

Two broad approaches have emerged in favour of an unfair competition right. One is that it be substituted for all existing intellectual property rights, and the other is that it exist alongside presently recognised intellectual property rights.

Ricketson has outlined a general principle to prevent reaping without sowing in place of existing intellectual property rights.[101] He provides extensive guidance on the application of the broad principle. However, the acceptance of such a principle requires the belief that all "reapers" who do not do any, or much, sowing need to be prevented from reaping on the basis of unfair competition. This is not always so. For example, it is difficult to see that there is any benefit for competition in preventing the use of a girl scout image in an advertisement for contraception.[102] *Feist Publications, Inc.* v. *Rural Telephone Services Co*[103] provides another example. There the Supreme Court of the United States held that there was no copyright in Rural's white pages of its telephone directories, because there was no originality of selection or arrangement. Thus, Feist was free

---

[96] Ricketson, n. 13 above, 30.

[97] Fair Trading Act 1986 (NZ), s. 9. See also *Talmax Pty. Ltd* v. *Telstra Corporation* (1996) 36 IPR 46, decided under s. 52 of the Australian Trade Practices Act 1974.

[98] *Tot Toys Ltd* v. *Mitchell* [1993] 1 NZLR 325, 365.

[99] *Ibid.*, 363–4.

[100] *White* v. *Samsung Electronics America, Inc.*, 989 F 2d 1512 (9th Cir. 1993).

[101] Ricketson, n. 13 above.

[102] *Girl Scouts* v. *Personality Posters Mfg*, 304 F Supp. 1228 (SDNY 1969); see also *White* v. *Samsung Electronics America, Inc.*, 989 F 2d 1512, 1513 (9th Cir. 1993).

[103] 499 US 340 (1991).

to use Rural's individual directories to compile a combined directory. Commentators have argued that justice was not done in this case.[104] Arguably, however, justice was done. Why should Rural have been able to prevent others from using an alphabetical listing of purely factual information, particularly for such a useful purpose? Rural provided its directories to its subscribers without charge. It did not lose any revenue from Feist's activities. It derived revenue from its services, and its yellow page directories, which Feist did not make use of.

I believe that it is better to develop the individual intellectual property rights to accommodate forms of unfair competition which conflict with the general principles of those doctrines, rather than to develop a separate unfair competition law, even if this strategy involves stretching the present law.[105] Behind each head of intellectual property law various elements which prevent unfair competition can be identified, but there is no "unity of principle" beyond the fact that the law recognises certain types of competition as unfair. In *Moorgate Tobacco Co Ltd* v. *Philip Morris Ltd (No. 2)*, Deane J explained the rejection of a general cause of action for unfair competition in the following terms:[106]

> The rejection of a general cause of action for "unfair competition" involves no more than a recognition of the fact that the existence of such an action is inconsistent with the established limits of the traditional and statutory causes of action which are available to a trader in respect of damage caused or threatened by a competitor. Those limits, which define the boundary between the area of legal or equitable restraint and protection and the area of untrammeled competition, increasingly reflect what the responsible Parliament or Parliaments have determined to be the appropriate balance between competing claims and policies. Neither legal principle nor social utility requires or warrants the obliteration of that boundary by the importation of a cause of action whose main characteristic is the scope it allows, under high-sounding generalisations, for judicial indulgence or idiosyncratic notions of what is fair in the market place.

Fitzgerald and Gamertsfelder have criticised this approach on the basis that the decision was "prior to the (re)emergence of Australian unjust enrichment law in the late 1980s".[107] The authors argue that the principles of unjust enrichment can be used to justify an independent unfair competition action.[108] This approach, particularly in New Zealand, can be questioned. Unjust enrichment cannot be described as a separate cause of action.[109] At most it is a common theme running through several different causes of action.[110] In addition, the use of unjust enrichment in this way assumes the existence of a property right. Such an assumption should not easily be made. The arguments against a general cause of action for unfair competition alongside existing intellectual property are not overcome by dressing up the doctrine in the disguise of unjust enrichment.

---

104 Fitzgerald and Gamertsfelder, n. 13 above.

105 This can be seen as a fault with existing intellectual property law: see Ricketson, n. 13 above, 31.

106 (1984) 3 IPR 545, 566.

107 Fitzgerald and Gamertsfelder, n. 13 above, 247.

108 The focus of their thesis is on "informational products including databases".

109 *Rod Milner Motors Ltd* v. *The Attorney General* [1999] 2 NZLR 568, 576.

110 For a general discussion, see P. Birks, *An Introduction to the Law of Restitution* (rev'd edn, Oxford, Clarendon Press, 1989).

There is a common theme of the prevention of unfair competition throughout intellectual property law, but it is not a consistent theme, nor is it the only theme. The principle of preventing unfair competition is intertwined with other principles. To single out unfair competition, and elevate it above those other principles, distorts the other aims of intellectual property law, in particular, the fostering of innovation and creativity through copyright and patent law.

Furthermore, to elevate the common, but differently manifested, theme of the prevention of unfair competition to a separate cause of action potentially means that the action becomes wide-sweeping in an anti-competitive way. For example, making use of what already exists should not easily be termed "unfair" or "reaping without sowing".

The folly of a separate doctrine of unfair competition is comparable to the concept of inequality of bargaining power which was once thought to exist in contract law. In search of a common theme linking the ability to set aside a contract for duress, undue influence or unconscionable bargain, Lord Denning MR extracted a principle of inequality of bargaining power.[111] The synthesising of the doctrines into a common principle had an enormous appeal. It seemed to simplify the law and make it predictable and easy to follow. However, this common principle was soon discovered not to be the formidable principle as was first thought.[112] Inequality of bargaining power was a factor in many cases, but to elevate it to the main principle ultimately distorted the law.

There is no clear benefit in creating one general law to accommodate several existing doctrines, since such a general law will inevitably end up creating its own many exceptions. In addition, the other extensive types of intellectual property rights already protect creators of copyright works, designs, patents, plant varieties and layout designs from misappropriation of their works. And a trade mark owner has the benefit of a system which prevents a wide range of misuses of its trade marks.

V   CONCLUSION

The traditional paradigm of separate types of intellectual property rights serves many useful functions. It provides a framework which allows closely competing creations and products to co-exist. To turn the law upside down and to create a general law of unfair competition risks losing this great benefit. This is not to deny that aspects of intellectual property law are less than perfect[113] and that the law may need refinement and overhauling from time to time. Nonetheless, a generalised action does not solve the problems. Rather, it creates a new monster.

---

[111] *Lloyds Bank Ltd* v. *Bundy* [1975] QB 326, 329 (CA).

[112] *National Westminster Bank Ltd* v. *Morgan* [1985] AC 686 (HL).

[113] E.g., one problem is that a plaintiff may have any number of intellectual property rights in relation to the same subject matter. These rights may give different protection for different lengths of time.

12

Intellectual Property and Competition Policy: The Case for Neutrality

IAN EAGLES

I INTRODUCTION

As the pace of legal specialisation quickens it is sometimes difficult for those locked inside the law's increasingly introspective sub-disciplines to see across the doctrinal walls which separate them from each other. Viewed from the inside, the life of the intellectual property lawyer may well seem to be increasingly given over to frantic attempts to plug endlessly proliferating holes in the protective legal dykes erected against the rising tides of theft and misappropriation threatening to overwhelm them. Viewed from the outside (the usual vantage point of the competition lawyer) the history of intellectual property[1] in the last century is apt to be seen as one of continuing and accelerating expansion both within, and across, jurisdictions. Judges and legislators leapfrog over each other to create new rights and push ever outwards the limits of those which already exist. Occasional judicial laggards quickly find themselves statutorily overtaken at the urging of the large and well funded army of intellectual property lobbyists conjured into being by the market's discovery that these shadowy intangibles have become the mainsprings of investment and profit in any modern economy worthy of the name. New digital technologies are used to spur this process on, most commonly by waving doomsday scenarios at worried law reformers and politicians, terrifying them with images of massed fleets of digital pirates ever ready to spirit away the creative outputs of others to shadowy cybersanctuaries beyond the forensic reach of plaintiffs. Alternatively, and somewhat contradictorily, these very same technologies are used to bypass

---

[1] "Intellectual property" is used in this chapter to embrace both true proprietary rights and such arguably non-proprietary obligations as passing off and breach of confidence. For similar reasons the terms "rights holder" and "rights owner", although in theory conceptually distinct, are used interchangeably. Such usage should not be taken as acceptance that all these rights are, or must become, property rights in any meaningful sense of that much abused term. Indeed, it is the increasing "propertisation" of what were formerly liability rules which makes it difficult for courts to adjust stakeholder interests in accordance with competition values. The problem is likely to be worse in jurisdictions in which courts take the view that new property rights are not just creatures of statute, but can be judicially crafted out of what were always historically regarded as mere obligations. Once created, property rights are hard to roll back.

intellectual property rights altogether by setting up private systems of regulation whenever an expanded right does not meet the expectations of the right owner.[2]

The globalisation of intellectual property markets both drives, and is driven by, this expansionist push.[3] The culmination of this process is that new transnational intellectual property bible, the TRIPS Agreement.[4] TRIPS serves the expansionist cause both by oiling the increasingly creaky mechanisms for trans-jurisdictional enforcement laid down in previous conventions and treaties and by providing a negotiating platform from which protectionist intellectual property regimes may, in the name of harmonisation, be beamed outwards to become supranational standards in which competition values play little or no part and from which it is increasingly difficult for individual jurisdictions to retreat without being painted as treaty breakers by their fellow signatories.[5] Before we allow this kind of intellectual property imperialism the automatic credence it has come to expect we should perhaps pause to ask ourselves what is the likely effect of rights owners' increasingly assertive claims on the effective operation of those free and open markets in whose name such claims are so often made. It is also pertinent to enquire whether and how such assertiveness can be made to mesh with the competition principles now enacted into law in most Organisation for Economic Co-operation and Development countries. It is these issues with which this chapter is concerned.

II RATIONALES AND LIMITS: A LAW AND ECONOMICS OVERVIEW

Most legal precepts can be given an economic rationale, and intellectual property and competition law are no exceptions. In neither case does economics rule supreme. Both sub-disciplines recognise, to differing degrees it is true, that there

---

[2] J.H. Reichman and J.A. Franklin, "Privately Legislated Intellectual Property Rights" (1999) 147 *U of Penn L Rev* 875; M. Gimbel, "Some Thoughts on the Implications of Trusted Systems for Intellectual Property Law" (1998) 50 *Stan L Rev* 197.

[3] One should not underestimate the forces of economic jingoism at work here. Intellectual property is increasingly sold to national governments both as bestower of victory in future trade wars and (somewhat contradictorily) the ultimate economic deterrent which will so diffuse technological progress and innovation across all of the world's economies that such wars will become unthinkable and pointless. For a description of this process at work in the United States, see R.W. Kastenmeier and D. Beier, "International Trade and Intellectual Property; Promise, Risk and Reality" (1989) 22 *Vand J Transnat L* 285.

[4] Agreement on Trade-Related Aspects of Intellectual Property Rights including Trade in Counterfeit Goods 1993, reprinted in *The Results of the Uruguay Round of Multilateral Trade Negotiations—The Legal Texts* (Secretariat edn., GATT, 1994).

[5] Witness the United States' finger-wagging response to the removal of parallel importing restrictions in Singapore and New Zealand. See E.S.Y. Goh-Low, "Parallel Imports of Copyright Goods in Singapore: The Role of Government and Public Policy" (1997) 13 *J of World Trade L* 164, and A. Van Melle, "Parallel Importing in New Zealand: Historical Origins, Recent Developments and Future Directions" [1999] *EIPR* 63. Direct assaults of this kind on rights owners' remedies are more easily portrayed as TRIPS backsliding, than as subjecting those remedies to competition scrutiny, something which after all is expressly permitted in Art. 8.2 of TRIPS.

are other values important to the legal system which they must also internalise,[6] and each of them distorts the economics (in different ways) by forcing it into unsympathetically constructed black letter boxes. Nor is it simply, or even most importantly, a clash between law and economics. The *nexus* between intellectual property and competition policy is also the collision point between seemingly competing economic theories. In the resolution of this apparent conflict lies not only the key to understanding why competition analysts and intellectual property lawyers so often talk past each other, but also a useful device for nudging that dialogue back on track. However restricted its vocabulary, economics is the only conceptual language which intellectual property and competition law share. Resort to it cannot be avoided.

A Identifying the Stakeholders

Economic analysis does not take place in a human void. It seeks to explain and predict the actions of various market players, all of whom are assumed to be driven by a self-interest which is both conscious and rational.[7] Who are these economic actors and how are their actions likely to be affected by the existence and enforcement of intellectual property rights? Four basic groups may be identified.

(i) Holders of Intellectual Property Rights

Much of the early law and economics analysis focuses on the incentive to create or invent and points to an identifiable individual author or inventor who must be bribed into innovation or creativity with some form of legal protection against imitation or misappropriation. That focus has now shifted: first, to team-based collective creativity and the financial processes which drive it and, secondly, to the corporate and commercial channels through which creative outputs are promoted and distributed. These shifts in emphasis are sometimes

---

[6] In the case of intellectual property, the most important of these is freedom of expression. Like more utilitarian analyses, this also points in two directions: an author's natural rights to appropriate her own words (see W.J. Gordon, "A Property Right in Self-Expression: Equality and Individualism in the Natural Law of Intellectual Property" (1993) 102 *Yale L J* 1533) and a potential infringer's equally natural right to adapt and modify those words in the name of artistic or political freedom (see S.L. Burr, "Artistic Parody: A Theoretical Construct" (1996) 14 *Cardozo Arts & Ent L J* 65). Commentators and courts sometimes *segue* from economics to natural rights whenever arguments based on the former falter: see J. Waldron, "From Authors to Copiers: Individual Rights and Social Values in Intellectual Property" (1993) 68 *Chicago-Kent L Rev* 841, 851, 855. See also C. Rose, "The Comedy of the Commons: Custom, Commerce and Inherently Public Property" (1986) 53 *U of Chic L Rev* 771, 778. While non-economic values are greatly obscured in most competition regimes, they continue to exist: see n. 67 below.

[7] That this sometimes offers a less than complete explanation for human behaviour is conceded. It is a concession rarely given overt expression in Anglo-American intellectual property law, where *homo economicus* tends to reign supreme. An exception may be those recent imports from the civilian world collectively known as moral rights. Even here economic arguments sometimes intrude: see H. Hansmann and M. Santilli, "Authors and Artists Moral Rights" (1997) 26 *J Leg Stud* 95.

obscured by economists' use of homely and traditional images of individualised endeavour when modelling corporate behaviour. This should not be allowed to disguise the stark commercial reality that individual innovators and creators, even where they are the first owners of intellectual property rights, seldom retain those rights for any length of time. Nor in most cases do they have the personal or monetary resources to set up and oversee the licensing systems through which their outputs find their market.

(ii) Competitors and Rivals

Rivals of the right holder do not figure largely in traditional attempts to justify intellectual property rights. This is not surprising. From the perspective of the right holder, competitors are no more than potential infringers. Competition policy, by contrast, has a focus which is as much external as internal, one which treats intellectual property owners much as it would treat any other incumbent fending off actual or potential rivals.[8] This external focus, while a useful corrective to intellectual property's often inward-looking perspective, can sometimes slide into the dangerous fallacy that the aim of competition policy is to protect competitors.

(iii) Users and Consumers

Markets for creative or innovative products or processes could not exist at all without customers. Consumers and users nonetheless get short shrift on both sides of the competition law/intellectual property divide. From the rights holders' point of view, they are simply the grateful (and hopefully price insensitive) recipients of the creative bounty of others.[9] Competition analysis, on the other hand, tends to conflate the interests of consumers and producers. Indeed, some theorists are at pains to deny the interests of consumers any special place in regulatory policy, as we shall see.

(iv) Other Markets, Other Players

So far we have proceeded as if the debate about the economic role of intellectual property rights was a simple struggle for ascendancy in particular markets for

---

[8] Labels have more than their usual resonance in such exchanges. "Infringer" connotes thief, while "competitor" radiates rugged free market virtue. The suggestivity of labels for impressionable judges and legislators can be seen by reversing them so that "intellectual property owner" becomes "privileged monopolist", and "infringer" becomes "innovative new entrant". See Waldron, n. 6 above, 841–2; P. Drahos, *A Philosophy of Intellectual Property* (Brookfield, Vt, Dartmouth, 1996), 213.

[9] Even where consumer interests are factored into the equation, they often depend on non-empirical, highly impressionistic assumptions about consumer behaviour. For a critique of this kind of logical leap, see C.D.G. Pickering, *Trade Marks in Theory and Practice* (Oxford, Hart Publishing, 1998).

the particular goods and services covered by the right in question. Such an analysis is both incomplete and misleading. Competition problems may surface in upstream or downstream markets, sometimes far removed from those in which the intellectual property right visibly operates. Nor is it always right-owners who are responsible for creating the net increase in social value associated with a particular right. A properly inclusive economic analysis would recognise the contributions of:

(a) the owners of the technology through which the protected work or product is disseminated;

(b) the creative predecessors on whose effort the inventor or author builds (not all such predecessors will themselves be protected by intellectual property rights); and

(c) wealth creators in society as a whole, that is anyone who contributes to the consumer surplus which makes purchase of the protected work or process possible.[10]

The difficulty with this way of proceeding is that the more widely the economic net is cast the more fuzzily imprecise is the analysis. On the other hand, if policy-makers ignore these dispersed stakeholders entirely, they run the risk of unfairly tipping the balance of argument in the direction of right-holders by leaving qualitatively important (if not always easily quantified) factors out of the equation.

B The Economics of Intellectual Property

Almost all economists agree that intellectual property rights increase price and reduce consumer choice, at least in the short term.[11] If they did not do these things, they would not work. They are tolerated only because they produce external long-term efficiencies which are supposed to cancel out their short term effects.

Economic analysis of the role of creativity and innovation in the market place usually starts with the following propositions:

(a) Creativity and innovation are, in the great majority of instances, positive contributors to net social wealth.

(b) Appropriate rewards must therefore be devised for innovators and creators.

(c) These rewards must be protected against third party capture or destruction, by enforceable rules. Each legal rule requires independent economic verification.[12]

---

[10] G.S. Lunney, "Re-examining Copyright's Incentives Access Paradigm" (1996) 49 *Vand L Rev* 483.

[11] W.M. Landes and R.A. Posner, "An Economic Analysis of Copyright Law" (1989) 18 *J Legal Stud* 325, 333.

[12] The legal rule need not apply *ex post facto*. It could operate *ex ante* in the form of bounties, salaries or research funds, in which case it would be protected by the ordinary law of theft and fraud.

None of these propositions presupposes the existence of a general property right in intangibles. Nor as a matter of legal fact do all legal protections for innovation or creativity take this form. Property is one answer; regulated privilege might be another;[13] liability rules a third. Property is, however, the incentive system to which most economists will instinctively turn first, if only because its apparently non-situational rules greatly assist the process of model building. This is not to say that intellectual property rights do not have their detractors amongst economists. They are, however, vastly outnumbered by defenders. Again, the nature of both attack and defence has varied over time. There has been a subtle shift from justifying (or attacking) the existence of particular rights to an approach which applauds (or condemns) their expansion. It is important to separate these arguments.

(i)   The Economics of Rights Justification

Intellectual property is now such a long established and durable part of the legal landscape that it is easy to forget the considerable weight of serious economic commentary which once sought to demonstrate that it was or was not a good thing.[14] This was usually done by constructing empirically undernourished models of what the world would look like without it and inviting us to cheer or boo the resulting almost wholly hypothetical construct.[15]

That these learned contests have faded from sight does not mean that the defenders of intellectual property always had the best of the argument. Their opponents sometimes made telling points: inventors and innovators, they said, may be driven to invest and innovate without any direct economic spur, and that if any incentives are indeed needed, they might be more effectively provided by grants to individuals, or tax policies designed to direct corporate funding towards research and development and away from other forms of expenditure.[16] While these arguments may now seem both dated and intuitively wrong, this owes more to ideological fashion than rational demolition.[17] Intellectual property rights won the war because they were too firmly entrenched to be dis-

[13] See Drahos, n. 8 above.

[14] Some commentators took the agnostic stance that intellectual property did neither observable good nor observable harm: see, e.g., A.C. Pigou, *The Economics of Welfare* (4th edn., London, Macmillan & Co, 1952).

[15] For one of the few economists prepared to own up to the empirical underfeeding, see G.L. Priest, "What Economists Can Tell Lawyers About Intellectual Property: Comment on Cheung" (1986) 8 *Res L and Econ* 19.

[16] Some went further by raising the intriguing possibility that patents, for example, might actively divert research into what is patentable and away from other areas: see A. Plant, "An Economic Theory of Patents" [1934] *Economica* 3. On the general issue of over-production of information in response to legal protections, see E.F. Fame and A.B. Laffer, "Information and Capital Markets" (1971) 44 *J Bus* 289.

[17] That elusive phenomenon in the economic analysis of legal institutions and structures known as "path dependence": see M.J. Roe, "Chaos and Evolution in Law and Economics" (1996) 109 *Harv L Rev* 641. On this view, a world of limited (or no) intellectual property represents yet another "path not taken".

lodged, not because the economic case for them was watertight. The reality was that both sides spent most of their time tilting at windmills because neither could convincingly isolate a control group of the intellectual property deprived in a world otherwise full of the stuff.[18]

That the debate continues to be of more than historical interest is due not to the conflicting, but largely unverifiable, positive arguments advanced by each side, but to the emergence of a set of negatives on which they largely agreed. These were:

(a) Intellectual property rights are not always the only, or even the most effective, way of fostering innovation and creativity.[19]

(b) Rules which encourage innovation and creativity also inhibit, at least temporarily, their dissemination and use.[20]

(c) The match between incentive and right is never perfect. Fixed rules about what is protected and the nature and duration of protection means that some innovative or creative activities will be over rewarded while others will be undervalued. Property based rules are more likely to produce this result than liability rules.[21]

(d) Intellectual property should be minimalist in its aspirations. Even if it is not always possible to deliver the precise quantity of protection required to

---

[18] This is not to say that such empirical studies are not sometimes attempted. See, e.g., C.T. Taylor and Z.A. Silberston, *The Economic Impact of the Patent System* (Cambridge, CUP, 1973). Nor do such studies always point unequivocally in the direction of more and stronger intellectual property protection. Comparative studies using countries with underdeveloped or under-enforced intellectual property rights as a control group occasionally conclude that there is a negative correlation between the robustness of an economy's intellectual property regime and early economic take off: see A.S. Oddi, "The International Patent System and Third World Development: Reality or Myth?" [1987] *Duke L J* 831. Empirical studies which avoid the big question, "are IP rights justified?", in pursuit of smaller objectives, such as the appropriate duration or subject matter of particular rights, seem to produce more immediately usable results. See *Report on Vehicle and Recreational Marine Craft Repair and Insurance Industries* (Industry Commission, Australia, 1994), 123. Another potentially fruitful area for empirical investigation seems to lie in cross-border studies of the economic effect of variations in substantive intellectual property law across jurisdictions: see S. Erickson, "Patent Law and New Product Development: Does Priority Claim Basis Make a Difference?" (1999) 36 *Am Bus LJ* 327. To be effective, such studies would have to focus on clear points of difference (duration, priority rights). They can thus be easily outflanked by the global push to harmonise the content of intellectual property across jurisdictions.

[19] Even writers who are, on balance, supportive of intellectual property as a prime driver of research and development, acknowledge that in the case of basic scientific research, state or charitable funding may be more effective. See, e.g., K. Arrow, "Economic Welfare and the Allocation of Resources for Inventors" in *The Rate and Direction of Inventive Activity: Economic and Social Factors* (A Report of the National Bureau of Economic Research, Princeton, NJ, 1962), 609; R.R. Nelson, "The Simple Economics of Basic Scientific Research" (1959) 67 *J Pol Econ* 297. Other commentators see intellectual property in general, and patents in particular, as a driver of innovation only in certain atypical industries (such as pharmaceuticals and chemicals), while in the rest of the economy they are largely irrelevant: see F.M. Scherer, "Antitrust Efficiency and Progress" (1987) 62 *NYU L Rev* 998, 1013.

[20] F.H. Easterbrook, "Insider Trading, Secret Agents, Evidentiary Privileges and the Production of Information" [1987] *Sup Ct Rev* 309.

[21] Liability rules are more easily adjusted to fit extraneous social factors: see F.A. Rowley, "Dynamic Copyright Law Its Problems and a Possible Solution" (1998) 12 *Harv J L Tech* 481.

trigger the optimal amount of innovation or creativity, this is, and should remain, its objective. Such an objective is better served by rights which are deliberately limited in scope to achieve the social aims in pursuit of which the rights were instituted in the first place. On this analysis, more is not better even if sometimes unavoidable within the context of a uniformly applicable system of rules.[22]

This essentially negative consensus, concerning what were seen at the time as a fairly stable set of rights serving limited social ends, was destined to have a very short life, undone both by the massive expansion in the set of legal constructs we call intellectual property, and by a direct shift in the thinking of some economists which saw them give those constructs a much more central and dynamic role in the economy.[23] Other economists continued to resist the expansionist wave or even sought to push it back within what they saw as economically defensible borders.

(ii)   The Economics of Rights Expansion

Intellectual property, precisely because it is disconnected from any *res,* will often have fuzzier boundaries than interests in land or physical objects. This fuzziness is what leads infringers to chance their arm. It is also what gives intellectual property rights a rubber-like expandability in the race to head off those self-same infringers. If pushed too far, such expansion will drive otherwise substitutable products or processes out of the market. But how far is too far? Can economics set rational and defensible limits to this process? Unfortunately, it is on precisely these issues that the implicit economic consensus breaks down into a cacophony of competing voices.

(a)   Cheering on the Expansion

The expansion of intellectual property over the last two decades has not been without its law and economics acolytes. These fall into two main groups: the neoclassicists and the "new institutionalists".[24] While each group has its own conceptual slant on the role of intellectual property in the economy, their points of agreement far outweigh their differences. Both dismiss the "incentive to cre-

---

[22] S. Breyer, "The Uneasy Case for Copyright: A Study of Copyright in Books, Photocopies and Computer Programs" (1970) 84 *Harv L Rev* 281, 322. Professor Breyer's views are all the more interesting because they are based on some rare (if in this case, necessarily limited) empirical fact finding.

[23] Repeating the earlier experience, it is the former which seems to have driven the latter in most instances.

[24] I accept that affixing labels to various schools of economic thought can, on occasion, distort the viewpoints of individual writers by exaggerating differences between, and minimising the sometimes subtle distinctions within, the "schools" so described. (For a judicial chiding on this score, see *Fisher & Paykel Ltd* v. *Commerce Commission* [1990] 2 NZLR 731, 761). It is also unfair to those such as Professor Gordon, who demonstrate a refreshing ability to move on from the sometimes dogmatic stances taken in their earlier writing to a more nuanced explanation of market phenomena. (cf sources cited in nn. 25 and 26 below). A general survey of the kind embarked on here, however, has to paint with a broad brush if it is to paint at all.

ate" approach as primitive reductionism,[25] based on "highly dubious and decidedly non-empirical assumptions about real life bargains".[26] What they share is a belief that intellectual property is best viewed as a pricing mechanism designed to ensure that creative or innovative products and services end up in the hands of those who value them most (this being both groups' optimal measure of social gain).[27] To this end they support, wherever possible, broad property-based rights with strictly limited defences,[28] rights which are designed to capture the full value of every potential market niche for as many uses of the creative output as possible.

If the abiding fear of incentive theorists is the uncreated work or invention, what keeps neoclassicists awake at night is the nightmare of the undervalued output. For them, intellectual property is no more than a metering device for measuring the worth of all the potential uses a work or invention might have. Their focus is not so much on the activities of the creator or innovator, but on those who invest in getting the fruits of creativity and innovation to market, or who distribute, develop and promote those fruits once there.[29] The monopoly rents which attend any intellectual property right are not there primarily as a creativity carrot, but rather as a channel of communication through which consumers can signal their preferences in advance, thus enabling creators, innovators and their financial backers to bend their efforts to producing the kind of product or service that consumers most want.[30] Crucial to this thesis is the notion that all the potential threads by which a work or invention may be exploited should start off in a single pair of hands (not necessarily, or even desirably, those of the author or inventor). For neoclassicists, the virtue of concentrated ownership is that it requires those who wish to build on or embellish the protected invention or work to deal with its first owner, rather than utilising

---

[25] W.J. Gordon, "An Inquiry Into the Merits of Copyright: The Challenges of Consistency, Consent and Encouragement Theory" (1989) 41 *Stan L Rev* 1343, 1435; R.P. Merges and R.R. Nelson, "On the Complex Economics of Patent Scope" (1990) 90 *Colum L Rev* 839, 842.

[26] W.J. Gordon, "On Owning Information: Intellectual Property and the Restitutionary Impulse" [1992] *Virg L Rev* 149,184. As was stated earlier, building large theories on a small empirical base is a vice shared by most of the law and economics writers, neoclassicists included. Postulating likely consumer responses to hypothetically "broad" or "narrow" intellectual property rights, as Professor Gordon does, is not to my (admittedly untrained) eye noticeably more scientific.

[27] P. Goldstein, *Copyright's Highway: From Gutenberg to the Celestial Jukebox* (New York, Hill and Wang, 1994), 236. Digital technology greatly assists this process: first, by identifying all potential users and tracking their use; and secondly, by subdividing these uses into separately chargeable preferences. See A.M. Froomkin, "Flood Control on the Information Ocean: Living with Anonymity, Digital Cash and Distributed Data Bases" (1996) 15 *J L and Com* 395, 450ff.

[28] For commentators such as Goldstein, n. 27 above, 224, infringement rules which allow copying for socially worthy causes are a deplorable distribution of wealth from owners to users. The same hostility to distributive outcomes also surfaces in competition law (see text accompanying n. 71 below).

[29] E. Kitch, "The Nature and Function of the Patent System" [1977] *J L and Econ* 265.

[30] One beneficial side effect of this in the copyright arena is thought to be the conscious production of works which are particularly well suited to the development of derivative spin offs, for example, books which are easily turned into films or cartoon characters particularly suited to becoming toys. See Goldstein, n. 27 above.

their own free-standing rights to capture the full value of the improvement or embellishment. This belief is in no way diminished by the need for subsequent subdivision and dispersal of that ownership, something which neoclassicists fully accept (and indeed praise). For them, it is the starting point rather than the final destination which is important. In this world, the first owner is to be regarded as being as much a manager of the intellectual resource as its creator.[31]

None of this is contested by the new institutionalists. While they may differ from their colleagues on some fundamental conceptual issues,[32] these differences surface in the intellectual property debate at one point only: the importance and effect of transaction costs in organising markets. Neoclassicists treat transaction costs as occasional, easily avoided and essentially minor bumps on the high road to economic efficiency. New institutionalists regard those same costs as major potholes, with the urge to avoid them as a central factor in business decision-making. Where a neoclassicist would reluctantly admit that there will be cases in which transaction costs might be high enough to require the abandonment of property in favour of liability rules,[33] new institutionalists preach that, even in these circumstances, a judicial and legislative preference for property over obligation forces market players to devise new and creative ways of minimising or even eliminating transaction costs.[34] Businesses, they say, must learn to negotiate their way around market failure rather than rely on the courts to repair that failure by inventing new torts or extending old ones. It is this viewpoint which makes new institutionalists particularly receptive to attempts to extend intellectual property through restrictive licensing arrangements[35] or technology "lock ins", and to applaud the horizontal aggregation of copyright through collection agencies.

None of this should be allowed to obscure the broad commonalities between these two schools of thought. If neoclacissists and new institutionalists were

[31] Kitch, n. 29 above, describes patentees as "co-ordinators of the investment of others" whose job it is to dissuade those others from duplicating research or hoarding information. Professor Gordon initially applied the same logic to copyright, describing the owner's role as being to "facilitate or organise post-creation dissemination of the work": see W. Gordon, "Asymmetric Market Failure and the Prisoner's Dilemma in Intellectual Property" (1992) 17 *U Dayton L Rev* 853, 855. She was later to resile somewhat from this view: see Gordon, n. 26 above. See also K. Edward, "The Nature and Function of the Patent System" [1977] *J L and Econ* 265.

[32] New institutionalists tend to eschew the formal model-building of the neoclassicists, having little faith in the latter's emphasis on price rather than structure and process. New institutionalists are also more prepared to concede that markets do not always behave rationally, at least in the short term: see D.C. North, *Institutions, Institutional Change and Economic Performance* (Cambridge and New York, CUP, 1990). For a good, non-technical, summary of the differences between these two schools, see N.W. Netanel, "Copyright and a Democratic Civil Society" (1996) 106 *Yale L J* 254.

[33] R.A. Posner, *Economic Analysis of Law* (4th edn., Boston, Mass., Little Brown, 1992), 51; G. Calabresi and A.D. Melamed, "Property Rules, Liability Rules and Inalienability: One View of the Cathedral" (1972) 85 *Harv L Rev* 1089, 1106.

[34] E. Krier and S.J. Schwab, "Property Rules and Liability Rules: The Cathedral in Another Light" (1995) 70 *NYU L Rev* 440, 464.

[35] The new institutionalists' enthusiasm for contractual extension of intellectual property rights should not be read as a general preference for contract over property. They remain zealous supporters of broadly-based property rights as an initial launching pad for later contractual enhancement.

each asked to paint a picture of their ideal intellectual property right, there would be a clear familial resemblance in the resulting portraits: minimal prohibitions on protectable subject matter; limited public interest defences; and clear first-comer priority over developmental or derivative users. Both portraits would be framed by clear property rights, rather than the indeterminate case by case balancing which characterises much of the law of obligations (contract apart).

(b) Worried Bystanders and Prophets of Doom

Not all economic theory points in an expansionist direction. Rational arguments can be, and are, advanced for the contrary viewpoint that all is not roses in the intellectual property garden. Beyond their shared doubts, however, these groups have little in common. Some are, in essence, restatements of the incentive theory,[36] holding that any protection over and above that required to induce new works and inventions creates a deadweight loss to society as a whole and that the aim is not to maximise the amount of innovation produced but to determine the point at which such gains are marginal. The only limitation which these reborn incentivists will accept is the administrative savings conferred by the need for uniform rules. Pragmatism drives them to agree sadly that the case by case fine-tuning, which pure theory seems to require in order to give each author or inventor only that precise dose of protection which will propel them to the word processor or laboratory bench, would in practice lead to astronomical transaction costs both for the legal system and individual litigants.[37]

At the other end of the conceptual spectrum are those digital anarchists who believe that the Internet is its own instigator of authorship and innovation, needing little or no legislative or judicial boost in the form of enhanced intellectual property rights.[38] In this property-less cybertopia, everyone will, in the words of one of their number, "be free to play in the fields of the word".[39] Ironically perhaps, the digital anarchists share one thing with neoclassicists, the notion that all content is equal. In their case, however, it leads not to an

---

[36] More often than not these restatements are judicial rather than academic: see, e.g., *Sony Corp. of America* v. *Universal City Studios, Inc.*, 464 US 417, 429 (1984); *Harper and Row, Publishers, Inc.* v. *Nation Enterprises*, 471 US 539, 546 (1985). Restatements of the incentive theory tend to be tinged with regret that both legislative enhancement and judicial exegesis have escaped its bounds without describing any clear way back such as might be provided by competition policy: see S.E. Sterk, "Rhetoric and Reality in Copyright Law" (1996) 94 *Mich L Rev* 1205. This is perhaps just as well. Their competition analysis tends to be over-simplified and one-dimensional, all too easily equating statutory monopoly with market power.

[37] The same point is sometimes made in relation to the "rule of reason" analysis in competition cases, although in a properly working competition regime such cases would be rare exceptions to a competitively functioning market rather than a ubiquitous norm.

[38] The more exuberant of these anarchists sometimes follow their own internal logic to its ultimate destination: the abolition of copyright. See T.G. Palmer, "Intellectual Property: A Non Posnerian Law and Economics Approach" (1989) 12 *Hamline L Rev* 261.

[39] D. Lange, "At Play in the Fields of the Word: Copyright and the Construction of Authorship in the Post Literate Millennium" (1992) 55 *Law and Contemp Prob* 139, 151. Digital anarchism concentrates its attention on copyright. It has little to say about other forms of intellectual property.

equality of over protection, but to a conviction that the proliferation of unstructured communication on the Internet needs no legal protection at all to conjure it into existence. This is no doubt true, but the digital anarchists' failure to distinguish between ephemeral cyberchat and works requiring sustained intellectual effort or large financial investment, diminishes their case. Electronic dissemination tells us nothing new about authorial or investor incentives for the latter type of work.[40] More interesting than these increasingly marginalised groups (at least from a competition policy viewpoint) are the perspectives offered by three other strains of law and economics thinking: public choice analysis; game theory; and investment displacement.

Public choice theory (or at least its law and economics manifestation) seeks to demonstrate that legal rules and structures are more likely to reflect the interests of small and well-organised lobby groups than those of wider but less cohesive economic interests.[41] Translated into an intellectual property context, this means:

(a) Large diffuse groups of users and consumers seldom have their interests reflected in the content of intellectual property statutes; and
(b) Where it is necessary to reconcile the interests of well-organised groups such as authors, inventors and investors, the easiest way is to expand the scope of the intellectual property right in question so that everyone gets something, even if the slices of that something are anything but equal.[42]

Whatever its empirical foundation, public choice theory certainly has an intuitive question-raising resonance when applied to efforts at intellectual property law reform in particular jurisdictions.[43]

Game theory has to date only been used to deal intellectual property the most glancing of blows. Its central tenet is the idea that negotiating parties will inevitably, and often successfully, seek to keep from their opponents how each of them values a particular legal entitlement. Such poker playing, game theorists say, can inhibit efficient market exchanges. The best legal antidote for such gaming is deliberately to create uncertainty by dividing ownership between potential stakeholders, so that no-one quite knows who is seller and who is buyer, an ambiguity trap from which full disclosure affords the only effective

---

[40] This is not to say that copyright can or should operate in exactly the same way in the digital and hard copy worlds.

[41] This follows from the more general public choice principle that all collective activity confers benefits on those outside the collectivity, and the larger and more diffuse the collectivity the greater the external benefits conferred: see M. Olson, *The Logic of Collective Action* (Cambridge, Mass., Harvard UP, 1971).

[42] J.D. Litman describes this process at work during the legislative gestation of the 1976 Copyright Act in the United States in "Copyright Legislation and Technological Change" (1989) 68 *Oregon L Rev* 275, 317. As she puts it, "the Bill that emerged . . . enlarged the copyright pie and divided its pieces . . . so that no leftovers remained". A similar statutory largesse seems to have been distributed (albeit much more hurriedly) by the New Zealand legislature when enacting the Copyright Act 1994. The loser in each case was the public domain.

[43] See text accompanying nn. 138 and 139 below.

exit.[44] An alternative to "stretched" ownership is to prefer obligation (with its inbuilt uncertainty) over property.[45] Applications of this logic to the case of intellectual property are rare,[46] but they seem to indicate a preference for allocating different aspects of protectable subject matter to different stakeholders, each such aspect to be narrowly defined. Game theorists also (here reversing the neoclassicists' logic) favour liability rules and broadly based infringement defences precisely for the delicious uncertainty they create.

It is, however, investment displacement analysis which offers the most sustained and directly applicable critique of expanded intellectual property regimes. On this theory, the costs of over-protection lie not so much in the increased cost to consumers and users, but in the resources sucked out of the rest of the economy into the ring-fenced safety of the protected work or invention.[47] Some of the diverted resources may otherwise have gone into (although this is not necessary to the theory) alternative forms of creativity and innovation. (This last point is particularly true of derivative or developmental uses of the over-protected work or innovation.)

(iii) Adjusting the Argument to the Right

So far it has been assumed that the economic arguments operate evenly across all forms of intellectual property. This is not so. Different rights have different rationales and the legal forms in which they are cast, as well as reflecting the economic analysis, also feed back into that analysis in ways both obvious and subtle. These differences become more important when individual rights (or dealings in them) are subjected to competition scrutiny.[48]

(a) Legal Form

The intellectual property pie can be sliced in various ways using different legal devices to separate the pieces. The most obvious (and in competition terms, the least significant) is to distinguish between statutory and judge-made rules.[49]

---

[44] I. Ayres and E. Talley, "Solomonic Bargaining: Dividing a Legal Entitlement to Facilitate Coasean Trade" (1995) 104 *Yale L J* 1027.

[45] *Ibid.*, 1039. For a strongly critical response to this particular use of game theory, see L. Kaplow and S. Shavell, "Do Liability Rules Facilitate Bargaining?: A Reply to Ayres and Talley" (1995) 104 *Yale L J* 221. Kaplow and Shavell are prepared to concede some credence to the efficiency enhancing aspects of "divided ownership". It is the obligationist preference which arouses their ire.

[46] For one such application, in this case to copyright, see Netanel, n. 32 above, 334.

[47] W.F. Baxter, "Legal Restrictions on the Exploitation of the Patent Monopoly: An Economic Analysis" (1966) 76 *Yale L J* 267: R.M. Hurt and R.M. Schuhman, "The Economic Rationale of Copyright" (1966) 56 *Am Ec Rev* 421, 430: Lunney, n. 10 above.

[48] The aim of the exercise is not to demonstrate that particular rights are *per se* virtuous or vicious in competition terms, but rather to indicate the starting point for the case by case analysis which seeks to assess the purpose and effect of particular dealings in relation to particular intellectual property rights in particular markets, the normal methodology of competition analysis.

[49] This is also the line which shows least consistency across jurisdictions. In North America, trade secrets have received considerable legislative attention, while in Australia, New Zealand and the United Kingdom, trade secrets law largely remains an offshoot of the equitable obligation of confidence.

Statutory rights can be further subdivided into those which depend on prior disclosure through a system of state registration and/or grant (e.g., patents, registered trade marks and designs), and those (such as copyright and layout designs) which are self-constituting, coming into existence at the moment of creation or fixation. It is more useful (and arguably more principled) to try to draw a line between obligation and property.[50] On one side lies the classic trinity of patent, copyright and registered trade marks and their more recent *sui generis* attendants, plant variety protection and some forms of design right. On the other is that penumbra of liability rules which surrounds, sustains and extends these property rights: fair trading, passing off, unfair competition and breach of confidence. While this line largely corresponds with the statutory/common law divide, the fit is not perfect.[51] Nor is the barrier impermeable. Commentators are constantly urging that a particular right be pushed across the property/obligation line.[52] Very occasionally, the rare judicial activist will oblige.

(b) Fitting the Rationale to the Rule

In order to decide whether intellectual property over-protects in a competition sense, it is necessary to isolate precisely what it is that a particular rule seeks to protect in the first place. At considerable risk of oversimplification, it is possible to identify three quite distinct economic objectives at work here and classify the legal rules accordingly.

First, some rules foster innovation and creativity. It is these rules on which economists have lavished most attention and with which, up to this point, this chapter has been largely concerned. Copyright and patent are the two traditional prototypes. To them may now be added *sui generis* rights protecting layout designs for integrated circuits, plant varieties and novel but non-functional designs. While these rules have the common objective of encouraging various forms of innovative and creative endeavour, they proceed towards that end by

---

[50] I concede that it is possible to argue that this line, too, is meaningless, and that property rights are simply Hohfeldian bundles of obligations of greater or lesser onerousness and that intellectual property rights, precisely because they deal with intangibles, provide more than usually appropriate *rostra* from which to shout that this particular jurisprudential emperor has no clothes. Nevertheless, the label "property" does have consequences for any "bundle" so described, especially in the competition/intellectual property debate. Its theoretical dissection I am content to leave to others more skilled in the art. "Property" has considerable rhetorical advantages when waved at judges and legislators in the expansionist cause, and it is on these that I wish to focus.

[51] Some liability rules, such as those relating to fair trading, are statutory. Nor is it conceptually impossible for judge-made liability rules to become fully fledged property rights, or so neoclassicist writers like to tell judges. (Few judges are yet to be convinced in any jurisdiction.) While a judge-created intellectual property right might seem odd, it is no odder than judge-created property in general. (Most property rights in common law systems are precisely that.)

[52] Usually the flow is from obligation to property (see text accompanying n. 21 above). Occasionally, writers urge judicial and legislative traffic in the opposite direction: see Gordon, n. 26 above, 214 and 262. Statutes do get in the way here, as even Professor Gordon concedes. Only judge-made rules can effectively be de-propertised, absent a shift in legislators' perceptions and priorities.

two quite distinct means. Some (patents, plant varieties and registrable designs) create true legal (but not necessarily economic) monopolies which outlaw parallel creativity or invention. Potentially infringing processes, shapes or products do not cease to become so because they have been independently arrived at. By contrast, copyright and layout designs law forbids only imitative uses of the protected work, not independent creativity as such.[53] While this instrumental distinction between the patent and copyright families is important, it is not, as some commentators would have it, determinative in a competition sense. The existence or absence of a *legal* monopoly tells us nothing useful about market power associated with particular intellectual property rights.[54]

Second, there are reputation-based rules. These are rules which restrict attempts by the right-holder's rivals to confuse or mislead consumers as to the origin of goods, or suggest a commercial connection with the right-holder which does not exist. Trade mark law, the most developed of these rules, has never rested on an incentive justification.[55] Its objective has always been the preservation of the mark owner's goodwill by restricting rival traders' ability to attach themselves to the business reputation represented by the mark. Similar objectives are served (if somewhat more loosely) by the tort of passing off and its legislative counterparts in various jurisdictions.[56] Unlike patent and copyright law, reputation-based rules do not place restrictions on the *kinds* of goods or services a competitor may produce or supply, but rather only about what a competitor may *say* about what is produced or supplied. It is therefore sometimes suggested that such rules pose no competition problems, or even that they actively assist competition by facilitating the product recognition and differentiation on which that competition must depend.[57] This is, in a limited sense, true, if we confine our attention to traders *inside* a given market. It underestimates, however, the potential for reputation-based rules to inhibit entry to existing markets or the creation of new ones. (Such inhibitions may be economic, or in the case of parallel importing restrictions, legal.)

Thirdly, there are fair dealing rules. This apparently disparate group includes rules designed to protect information because it is secret[58] and/or

---

[53] The force of the distinction is somewhat weakened by copyright's evidentiary equation that access plus substantial similarity equals a presumption of copying.

[54] See text accompanying nn. 164–168 below.

[55] Pickering, n. 9 above, 97.

[56] E.g., the Fair Trading Act 1986 (NZ), s 9, and the Trade Practices Act 1974 (Cth), s 52. The Lanham Act in the United States, while it casts a much wider net, also serves this function, at least in part. The various torts relating to misappropriation of commercially valuable personality in the United States and Canada can probably be counted as reputational rules even though their pedigree owes as much to privacy as to the more traditional economic torts: see J. Kahn, "The Origins of the Tort of Appropriation of Identity Reconsidered" [1996] *Legal Theory* 301.

[57] Posner, n. 33 above, 5.

[58] In most American States and some Canadian provinces, trade secrets law protects information which is secret and likely to disadvantage the holder if it is disclosed or used without authority. Such

valuable.[59] While they seem to lack any coherent unifying principle across juris-dictions,[60] they could be said broadly to embody notions of fair dealing or com-mercial morality, principles too vague and formless to put up much opposition to attempts to use or extend these rules in anti-competitive ways.

(c) Internal Competition Controls

Even the most zealous intellectual property proponent accepts that not every working of the human brain can be commodified. All intellectual property rights have always had some inbuilt restraints intended to limit their scope and potential application. Some are limited in time. Others, while potentially immortal, can be lost through disclosure, inaction or inappropriate use. In addi-tion to temporal limitations, each set of rights has a core concept which restricts the subject matter to which the right may be applied. Patents and copyright were not originally designed to protect ideas as such. Reputation rights were not intended to be cut loose from the reputations they were created to defend. In this prelapsarian world, facts were thought to be free and mere information was only protected in the service of some notion of fair dealing (however inarticu-late) or because of the original form in which it was expressed. It was also thought important that the boundaries between the various forms of intellectual property be preserved so that core concepts did not bleed into each other in ways which defeated each right's distinctive purpose. Copyright was not to be used to confer patent-like protection on functional aspects of works without the patent penalties of disclosure and registration. Know-how had to be kept secret or be constrained by patent claims and specifications. Courts and legislators were content to leave the shape and get-up of goods to be protected by copyright or registered design law, rather than have them become reputational indicators in

laws usually require that the information relates to some kind of business context, even if it does not have a tradeable value in itself. In the majority of Commonwealth jurisdictions, however, such information is protected by the ordinary equitable action for breach of confidence, irrespective of commercial content or context.

[59] Such information may be (and usually is) public. It is protected because of the money and effort which has gone into collecting, arranging or storing it. In the United States, such rules are repre-sented by the various "unsowing reaper" torts tracing their ancestry to the Supreme Court decision in *International News Serv. v. Associated Press*, 248 US 215 (1918). In the European Union's com-mon law jurisdictions (the United Kingdom and Ireland), there are new *sui generis* rights protecting databases in which there has been substantial investment: see Copyright and Rights in Databases Regulations 1997 (UK).

[60] One candidate for such a principle is restitutionary analysis based on concepts of unjust enrich-ment: see A. Gronow, "Restitution for Breach of Confidence" (1996) 10 *IPJ* 222; B.F. Fitzgerald and L. Gamertsfelder, "Protecting Informational Products Including Databases Through Unjust Enrichment Law: An Australian Perspective" [1998] *EIPR* 244. While academic comment abounds on matters restitutionary, it is seldom overtly referred to in judicial decisions protecting valuable or sensitive information. This is perhaps understandable. Restitution theorists divide themselves into a variety of fiercely antagonistic sects. It is also a pity. As Professor Gordon has shown, restitution-ary theory can be made to mesh more readily with competition analysis than more generalised explanations based on fairness or commercial morality. (Indeed, she would subsume all of these rules into a single tort which, significantly enough, she calls "malcompetitive copying".) See Gordon, n. 26 above, 211ff. For a critique of Professor Gordon's approach, see Sterk, n. 36 above.

themselves. Judges were generally at pains to preserve these distinctions when-ever it was obvious they were under threat (this last was not always the case). Nor did legislators generally disturb this happy state of affairs. Intellectual property statutes remained discrete and internally self-referencing. There were few consolidations or codifications drawing rights together.[61]

None of the internal controls described here has any avowedly pro-competitive purpose. Indeed, most of them long predate the idea that intellec-tual property rights serve any economic function. They can, however, be given an economic rationale after the event and most have been. Ideas are not pro-tected, it is said, because in many cases no particular incentive is needed to pro-duce them,[62] or because of the massive deadweight loss which occurs when ideas are withdrawn from the public domain.[63] Investment and effort are not pro-tected as such, since this will often reward careless business decisions, discour-age proper assessment of risk[64] and pointlessly redistribute income from users to owners.[65] Whatever the validity of these *ex post facto* justifications, there is no doubt that the informal controls described above do limit, however crudely and blindly, rights owners' ability to act in anti-competitive ways. Their removal or erosion must therefore give any competition regulator cause for con-cern, even if (or perhaps especially because) the impact of that removal or erosion on the competition process cannot be precisely predicted.

C The Economics of Competition Policy

Competition law is more directly informed by economics on a day to day basis than intellectual property has ever been or is likely to be. While it may not quite yet deserve the epithet "economic law" bestowed on it by some judges and com-mentators,[66] input from the dismal science is much more a constant and visible part of the forensic process than is the case with most other areas of legal study. Economics is here something more than a usually inaccessible sub-stratum to be occasionally mined for Dworkinian principles. It directly guides the decisions of judges and regulators in individual cases (hence the ongoing presence of econo-mists as witnesses or even deciders of fact). This forced (and often initially resisted) economics education has led to a certain *hubris* among competition lawyers when confronted with intellectual property issues, a belief that only

---

[61] Indeed for most of their history, these rules were not seen by courts in common law jurisdic-tions as forming part of any wider whole. Even today, the subject heading "intellectual property", while useful to those who have to teach it, does not betoken any large number of unifying principles. The unity is more apparent to economists than lawyers.

[62] Landes and Posner, n. 11 above.

[63] *Ibid.*, 347. See also Lunney, n. 10 above, 517.

[64] Gordon, n. 26 above, 170.

[65] *Ibid.*

[66] M. Brunt, "Antitrust in the Courts: The Role of Economics and of Economists", paper pre-sented at Fordham Corporate Law Institute Conference on International Antitrust Law and Policy, 23 October 1998.

they have the key to the hard choices cupboard, one which will enable them unerringly to strike the appropriate balance between under- and over-protection. The truth is both less flattering and more interesting. To see why, we need to focus directly on the economic concepts most frequently used in competition analysis and ask what light these might shed on potentially anti-competitive uses of intellectual property and related legal rights.

(i) Competition as a Process

Like intellectual property law, competition law has as one[67] of its ultimate goals the pursuit of economic efficiency. Also like intellectual property, it does not (in most jurisdictions, most of the time) approach that goal directly, but instead uses a surrogate, in this case the preservation and enhancement of the competitive process which is usually (if not always) assumed to produce efficient results.[68] In this way of looking at things, it is the competition dynamic which matters, not the interests of competitors or consumers as such.[69] Applying the same logic to intellectual property means that the erosion of the public domain or the use of the right to lock out the right-holder's rivals is not in itself the problem to be addressed. It is the effect of these things on the functioning of particular markets[70] which may properly be said to raise competition concerns. Stakeholders, be they consumers, rights-holders or competitors, have no presumptive rights in this process.

(ii) Dollar Blindness Versus Consumer Protection

One tenet of neoclassical economics which has found a limited acceptance among competition regulators and judges is that competition policy has no distributive role. By this, they mean that a dollar in the hands of a producer is as good as the dollar in the hands of a consumer, and that it is not the business of

---

[67] Efficiency has not always been, and is not now, its only goal. Antitrust law in the United States has populist rather than economic roots, to which it periodically tries to return: see E.M. Fox and L.A. Sullivan, "Antitrust-Retrospective and Prospective: Where are we Coming From? Where are we Going?" (1987) *NYU L Rev* 936. Similarly, in the European Union competition policy has been heavily influenced by interventionist values which are as much political as economic: see G. Amato, *Antitrust and the Bounds of Power: The Dilemma of Liberal Democracy in the History of the Market* (Oxford, Hart Publishing, 1997). Even in jurisdictions such as New Zealand and Australia, whose competition law, at least as developed through the cases, generally eschews non-economic interests, some small room, however residual, is left for values other than efficiency.

[68] Most jurisdictions allow prosecutorial or administrative discretion to deflect competition objectives in the interests of efficiency in those few cases where the two are not congruent.

[69] Where they figure it is once again as surrogates. Impact on consumers and competitors is sometimes assumed to tell us something, if only presumptively, about the competitive process.

[70] The plural is deliberate. The market in question may not be the one in which the subject matter of the intellectual property is exploited. The effect on an upstream, downstream or collateral market may be crucial to the outcome of a case, as in *Image Technical Services, Inc v. Eastman Kodak Co*, 125 F 3d 1195 (9th Cir. 1997).

this branch of the law to alter that balance.[71] This needs to be contrasted with other viewpoints[72] which explicitly[73] or implicitly prefer the interests of consumers over those of other stakeholders. This is why, for neoclassicists, the potential of intellectual property to raise prices and restrict access is a matter of supreme indifference, whereas for their opponents it is an outcome to be regretted and, as far as possible, minimised. These differences would quickly move from the realm of pure theory to forensic centre stage once intellectual property was unequivocally subject to competition rules.

(iii) The Three Efficiencies

If economic efficiency is indeed the core concept of competition law, it is a remarkably elusive one, both in theoretical and empirical terms. In the broadest sense, it simply means achieving more or better outputs with the same or cheaper inputs across the economy as a whole.[74] A definition so wide, while it might attract universal approbation, is unlikely to be immediately useful, especially in the cut and thrust of antitrust litigation. Economists have therefore sought to put analytical flesh on these bare definitional bones by positing three types of economic efficiency: allocative, productive and innovative.

Allocative efficiency exists where goods and services find their way to those consumers who value them most, as evidenced by a willingness to pay more or forego other forms of consumption. Innovative efficiency is achieved when new products and technologies are spread throughout the economy in wealth-creating ways.[75] Productive efficiency is found whenever goods and services are made available using the most cost effective inputs and processes available under current technology. While each of the trinity has its own sect of economic believers, courts and competition regulators wisely refuse to give any particular form of efficiency automatic primacy. Of the three, only allocative and innovative efficiency can easily be brought to bear on intellectual property problems, and even these two do not unerringly point in a single direction.

Innovative efficiency is loved by all, but measured by few. For neoclassicists, innovative efficiency and technological progress are best assured by marshalling capital and encouraging it to invest in innovation.[76] Broad intellectual property

---

[71] Such views have received judicial endorsement in some jurisdictions: see, e.g., *New Zealand Co-operative Dairy Co Ltd* v. *Commerce Commission* [1992] 1 NZLR 601, 634; *Fisher & Paykel Ltd* v. *Commerce Commission* [1990] 2 NZLR 731, 767.

[72] See, e.g., D.F. Greer, *Efficiency and Competition: Alternative, Complementary or Conflicting Objectives* (NZIER Research Monograph No 47), 11.

[73] Most schemes for directly regulating utilities and networks expressly give primacy to the interests of consumers.

[74] Professor Brodley defines efficiency as events or decisions that increase "the total value of economically measurable assets in society": see J.F. Brodley, "The Economic Goals of Antitrust: Efficiency, Welfare and Technological Progress" (1987) 62 *NYU L Rev* 1020, 1025.

[75] *Ibid.*

[76] J.A. Schumpeter, *Capitalism, Socialism and Democracy* (London, Allen & Unwin, 1947), 83, 89.

rights do this, by pulling investment into as many derivative niches as a particular intellectual property right will stand. They are therefore to be applauded
rather than feared or decried.[77]

Investment displacers, on the other hand, see over-broad rights as both
allocatively inefficient in themselves, and as discouraging innovative efficiency
in some situations (most notably in relation to transformative use). If lay readers detect a certain circularity in these arguments, they are right. It is precisely
this circularity which causes efficiency arguments to be marginalised in most
competition law regimes, revered as an objective, but seldom determinative, in
particular cases.[78]

(iv) Barriers to Entry and Potential Competition

Competition policy has latterly been concerned less with rivalrous behaviour
within markets at any given moment in time, and more with the ease with which
markets may be entered or left by potential competitors offering the same products or services or close substitutes for them. This too, is a contested subject
within industrial economics.[79] It concerns us here only in so far as intellectual
property rights can be said to deter entry or exit.

(a) The Weak Case for Intellectual Property as a Barrier to Entry

Attempts are sometimes made to argue that the costs of defeating or bypassing
an intellectual property right are deterrents to entry by competitors. Such costs
include litigation expenses, research and development of alternative products or
processes[80] and the money expended to fight the branding implications of a

---

[77] Allocative efficiency has a muscular clarity which makes it hugely attractive to neoclacssicists.
The clarity of the model, indeed its very quantifiability, conceals the usual empirical hole.
Deadweight loss is enticingly easy to represent by graphs. This does not necessarily make it easier
to isolate and measure in the real world.

[78] The forensic usefulness of efficiency arguments is much diminished by the difficulty of measuring it *ex ante* as litigation requires: see Brodley, n. 74 above, 1028. It is more useful (and more
used) in jurisdictions which have set up administratively constructed safe harbours whereby potential antitrust infringers may avoid government initiated litigation or in some cases relieve themselves
of the risk of private suits as well. See US Department of Justice/Federal Trade Commission,
Antitrust Guidelines for the Licensing of Intellectual Property, 6 April 1995, §4.2. See also
Commerce Act 1986 (NZ), s. 3A. Such two-step screening systems still suffer from the defect that
they are seldom reviewed post-authorisation or approval, even in jurisdictions where this is legally
possible.

[79] Here the core debate is between the "categorisers", who insist that the only barriers which
count are those of the same type or kind which the incumbent whose anti-competitive potential is
feared did not have to face itself (see, e.g., H. Demsetz, "Barriers to Entry" (1982) 72 *Am Econ Rev*
47), and the "quantifiers", who are content simply to estimate the height of the barriers (see, e.g.,
J. Bain, *Barriers to New Competition* (Cambridge, Mass., Harvard UP, 1956)). Categorisers also
tend to believe that barriers to entry cannot be constructed by market players themselves, but must
lie in legal or economic facts beyond their immediate control (see R. Bork, *The Antitrust Paradox:
A Policy at War With Itself* (New York, Basic Books, 1978), 240, 259). Quantifiers more readily
accept the notion that barriers to entry may be behavioural.

[80] See sources cited in n. 79 above.

trade mark or other reputational right.[81] These are barriers to entry only in so far as (i) they represent sunk costs, that is, they cannot be recovered on exit from the market;[82] (ii) they bring no collateral advantage beyond bypassing the intellectual property right; and (iii) they are quantifiably high enough to deter entry[83] or qualitatively different from the costs already borne by the incumbent.[84]

Only rarely will the costs of bypassing or contesting the right qualify on all three fronts. Most would-be entrants would spend something on product differentiation or research and development even if the incumbent held no intellectual property rights, and some such expenditure would be recoverable on exit from the market. Even litigation costs are a problematic barrier, since it cannot be assumed that competition with the incumbent necessarily means contesting the right. Potential competitors may be able to compete using non-infringing products or processes.[85] The structural uncertainties associated with vague rules are perhaps more plausibly described as entry barriers. (They certainly increase the right holder's opportunities for gaming.[86])

(b) The Strong Case for Intellectual Property as a Barrier to Entry

Intellectual property is much more convincingly described as a barrier to entry not when it raises potential infringers' costs *per se*, but when it raises them to levels which are quantitatively high enough or qualitatively different enough to cause real problems in real cases. This is most likely to occur when the right in question (or its exercise) has the effect of (i) inhibiting the creation of new markets by limiting derivative or developmental use of protected products or processes, or (ii) facilitating market segmentation by erecting geographic obstacles to product movement (parallel importing restrictions act in this way, as do some forms of licence or assignment), or (iii) permitting rights holders to use the power conferred by the rights to deter entry into markets not covered by the rights or requiring would-be entrants to enter all markets simultaneously or not at all.

(v) Defining Markets and Delimiting Rights

Competition is assessed within markets, not across whole industries or economies. Markets are the controlling framework within which most

---

[81] E.H. Chamberlin, *The Theory of Monopolistic Competition* (8th edn., Cambridge, Mass., Harvard UP, 1962), 62. D.M. McClure summarises these viewpoints in "Trademarks and Unfair Competition: A Critical History of Legal Thought" (1979) 69 *The Trademark Rep* 309, 331. Arguments treating trade marks as barriers to entry too easily slide into arguments that *all* nonfactual advertising is anti-competitive. N. Parr and M. Hughes, "The Relevance of Consumer Brands and Advertising in Competition Inquiries" [1993] *ECLR* 157, 158; N.S. Economides, "The Economics of Trade Marks" (1988) 18 *The Trademark Rep* 523, 535.

[82] Costs which can be recovered in full pose no threat to would be entrants.

[83] As quantifiers require: see n. 79 above.

[84] As the categorisers would prefer: *ibid.*

[85] To assume otherwise in every case is to embrace the twin fallacies that (i) rights define markets and (ii) legal monopolies confer market power. See text accompanying n. 165 below.

[86] See sources cited in n. 79 above.

competition regimes operate.[87] Markets are defined in terms both of products (which term here includes services and intangibles) and of geography. Product markets are groupings of outputs and inputs which are substitutable for each other in the eyes of consumers and producers. Such markets are said to have a demand side (who will buy at what price?) and a supply side (who can produce at what cost in money or resources?). Geographic markets, on the other hand, are bounded by those invisible lines across which it is not economic (or in some cases legally possible) to trade competing products. Sometimes the lines become visible in the form of national borders, an artificial and purely legal limit which ignores the realities of free trade.[88] All of this bears a superficial resemblance to the ways in which boundaries of intellectual property rights are set by limitations on subject matter, territorial licences and the principle of national protection. However, there is one important distinction: delimiting rights is a question of law, defining markets is an issue of fact. The two may correspond in a given case, but that is purely coincidental. There is no law of nature which says that this has to be so, and in the great majority of cases it will not be. Failure to make this fundamental distinction adds a great deal of unnecessary heat to the debate about the proper interface between intellectual property and competition law.[89]

(vi) From Theory to Rule

While competition law may be more dependent on economic theory than most areas of law, it nevertheless has to translate that theory into legal rules and processes. It uses three quite discrete techniques for this purpose:

---

[87] "Market" is as much the creation of lawyers as economists. It is the language of the statute which makes market definition so crucial in competition legislation. Economists tend to use the term as an analytical tool in much more open-ended discussions concerning market power, usually as a surrogate for measuring the demand curve facing individual market players. For them, it is a means rather than a legislatively mandated end.

[88] Most competition regimes set the outer limits of the market at national boundaries while allowing some extra-territorial reach for external factors affecting nationally defined markets. For an uncommon recognition of the realities of cross-border markets (in goods, if not services) without surrender of sovereignty, see Commerce Act 1986 (NZ) s. 36A; Trade Practices Act (Cth) 1974, s. 46A. Even here, it is still the *combined* national boundaries, not trading realities, which set the outer limits of the market.

[89] Further confusion is occasionally introduced by postulating the existence of an "innovation market" consisting of research and development in goods or processes which do not yet exist or to improve existing goods or processes: see *Anti Trust Guidelines for the Licensing of Intellectual Property*, issued by the US Department of Justice and the Federal Trade Commission, 6 April 1995, §3.2.3. The *Guidelines* are set out in [1995] 7 *EIPR Supp* 3. Such markets cause competition problems only when the practice complained of inhibits research and development by competitors, *and* it can be demonstrated that the research and development in question would be likely to affect competition in downstream or collateral markets, something that is seldom easy to prove *ex ante* for litigation purposes. It is usually easier to analyse and understand innovation as a source of *potential* competition in existing markets than to treat it as a market on its own: see W.K. Tom and J.A. Newberg, "Anti Trust and Intellectual Property: From Separate Spheres to Unified Field" (1997) 66 *Anti Trust L J* 167, 223.

(a) Rule of reason or case by case analysis in which the economics is confined only by broadly framed prohibitions expressed in terms of actual or intended economic outcomes.

(b) *Per se* rules which assume particular economic outcomes from various types of prohibited activity. (Horizontal cartels and various forms of price fixing are the usual candidates for such treatment).

(c) Discretionary safe harbours which provide refuges against some forms of liability, and which are usually applied by administrative or prosecutorial agencies under minimal statutory guidance but stiffened by agency-issued guidelines and block exemptions.[90]

The mechanisms by which economic analysis is fed into this system vary from jurisdiction to jurisdiction, sometimes entering as expert testimony, on other occasions by providing for economists to be included among the deciders of fact. The application of these techniques is further tempered by two other devices: express exclusion from liability in the competition statute itself, and a liberal use of evidentiary presumptions by judges faced with disharmonious economics.

When individual jurisdictions come to apply these techniques and processes to intellectual property matters, their approaches vary much more widely than one would expect, given that the policy issues facing them are much the same. The United States and the European Union carefully keep open the prospect that intellectual property cases will be subject to the full rigours of rule of reason analysis. (The prospect recedes somewhat given the actuality of safe harbours, alternative forms of regulation and judicial assumptions about the role and vulnerability of intellectual property rights in general.) New Zealand and Australia, by contrast, proceed by way of statutory exemptions *for* particular rights *against* particular forms of trade practices liability. The former approach at least preserves the possibility that intellectual property dealings (and non-dealings) can and will reach the courtroom, so that the issue with which this chapter is concerned may be subjected to judicial scrutiny and find at least partial resolution within the boundaries set by the facts of a particular case. Statutory exemption prevents any such scrutiny for the matters so exempted, leaving re-examination to the political perceptions of governments and the vagaries of the legislative timetable.

Cutting across all these methodologies is a further distinction, one which seems to owe more to habit and history than conscious economic analysis. This is the fundamental divide in all competition regimes, between unilateral and multilateral conduct. While this distinction is starting to bend under the assaults

---

[90] The discretionary element is sometimes more apparent than real. Guidelines can assume a distinctly legislative cast and European competition law's block exemptions are promulgated through what, in common law terms, would be subordinate (but not delegated) legislation. Despite these various forms of legal subordination, it has to be said that few competition regulators in any jurisdiction seem to be much troubled by thoughts of reviewability or fettered discretion when issuing guidelines.

of such concepts as oligopolistic dominance[91] and deemed (but in fact unshared) collective purpose,[92] it remains important, especially as regards intellectual property. This is because collusion visibly seeks to *extend* intellectual property rights, while unilateral abuses of power seem on their face to do no more than enforce the right itself, a confusion which has surfaced in more than one competition case in more than one jurisdiction[93] and which sometimes dominates the commentary in unhelpful ways.[94]

D The Implicit Social Bargain

One way of looking at the interaction between competition law and intellectual property is to view it as a loose and largely unexpressed social bargain, one in which intellectual property arrangements would be free from external competition scrutiny on anything but an occasional basis, provided that individual rights stayed roughly within their traditional bounds and their internal controls remained intact. Acceptance of this bargain also meant accepting that, while traditional boundaries and controls provided a less than perfect fit in individual cases, this lamentable (from a competition perspective) fact was in general outweighed by the savings in transaction costs conferred by a uniformly applicable rule. Even in this unrealistically static universe, however, it was made clear that attempts to *extend* the rights, whether by contract or though more informal arrangements, would be resisted where adverse competition effects could be demonstrated.

The implicit bargain may not have always lived up to economic realities, but it did at least provide a fixed *datum* against which negative competition outcomes could be measured and, hopefully, monitored. The bargain had only one foot in economics, however. The arguments for upholding it were essentially pragmatic. Even this pragmatism was soon to be undone when the *datum* point began to shift (largely before accurate and comprehensive empirical measurement could be undertaken).

III   THE BARGAIN UNRAVELS

Rights owners have used two techniques to unravel the implicit social bargain. One is to dismantle intellectual property's own internal competition constraints

---

[91] *Tetra Pak International* v. *European Commission* [1992] 4 CMLR 726; [1997] 4 CMLR 726. For a discussion of oligopolistic dominance, see M.A. Berkahn, *Are Oligoppolies Anti-Comptitive? Competition Law and Concentrated Markets*, Massey University College of Business, Discussion Paper 182, August 1998.

[92] See, e.g., *Port Nelson Ltd* v. *Commerce Commission* [1996] 3 NZLR 554.

[93] See text accompanying n. 184 below.

[94] See text accompanying n. 183 below.

case by case. The other is for rights-holders collectively to lobby legislatures for ever-increasing doses of protection.

A The Collapse of Internal Controls

As we saw in the preceding section, each intellectual property right has evolved its own set of internal controls which, perhaps inadvertently but nevertheless effectively, limit the anti-competitive uses to which the right can be put. Many of these internal constraints (some of them never very conceptually robust to begin with) are now collapsing. This collapse is due partly to a judicial reluctance to apply them rigorously in the face of plaintiffs' claims that this will leave valuable new forms of technology or entertainment unprotected, and partly to an observable (and in some contexts, unexceptionable, not to say praiseworthy) search for unifying principles which cut across the categories into which intellectual property rights have traditionally been subdivided. While neither process is inherently dangerous from a competition perspective, they can easily become so, given that such a perspective is largely unrepresented in the great majority of actions for infringement or breach.

(i) The Erosion of Core Concepts

As was described earlier, all forms of intellectual property have a core concept which confines potentially protectable subject matter within socially (and more latterly, economically) defensible bounds. These concepts are becoming increasingly anæmic. While this happened in different ways to different degrees in different jurisdictions, some broad trends are discernible beneath the mass of parochial detail.

(a) Towards the Protectible Idea

Patent and copyright are edging ever closer to protecting ideas as such. Should they reach that point, the shift in market power thus conferred would be enormous. John Thomas has vividly described for us the conceptual drift which has allowed process patents in the United States to become almost entirely disconnected from any anchor in the physical world.[95] Copyright law is equally in danger of losing its idea/expression core under the twin pressures of digitalisation and the industrial use of works. Granted that the idea/expression dichotomy has not always been evenly applied across the whole field of copyright activity, and has sometimes operated at too high a level of abstraction to be immediately useful in hard cases,[96] its abandonment without any obvious replacement in

---

[95] J.R. Thomas, chap. 7 of this volume.
[96] It has always been more of a desired outcome than a workable rule. See comments of Learned Hand J in *Peter Pan Fabrics, Inc.* v. *Martin Weiner Corp.*, 274 F 2d 487, 489 (2nd Cir. 1960) and those of Pritchard J in *Plix Products Ltd* v. *Frank M. Winstone (Merchants) Ltd* (1984) 3 IPR 390, 419.

sight[97] (or indeed any sign that it is actively being sought) is particularly worrying from a competition perspective because of the flow-on effect on other important distinctions traditionally used to keep copyright within bounds. The further one moves away from protectable expression, the closer one comes to protecting collections of facts or functional aspects of products (witness the often successful attempts by copyright holders to expand digitally the scope of protected subject matter to include non-literal elements of computer programs which arguably owe as much to function or idea as form, the so-called "look and feel" test).[98] The problem is compounded in jurisdictions where the originality threshold is low. Even a mundane idea may have a large number of potential expressions or applications. Market power over all such applications confers rewards which are vastly disproportionate to the cost of creating them in the first place, with a corresponding deadweight loss to society as a whole.

(b) Cutting the Link between Signifier and Reputation

An increasing trend in respect of reputational rights is to loosen, and in some cases cut, the connection between particular types of commercial activities and the mark, name or character (real or fictional) through which those activities impinge on the consuming public. If taken far enough, this process can result in the signifier becoming a protected (and hence commodifiable) interest in its own right. The process most commonly occurs when a worst case scenario is converted into a prophylactic rule. Courts deem a business connection to exist in the minds of consumers by attributing to them a familiarity with licensing practices which is inherently unlikely and empirically unsupported in the case before them.[99] Consumer reactions are judged not by across the board tests of reasonableness, but by concentrating on the likely reactions of the numerically insignificant, the marginally afflicted and the congenitally imperceptive.[100] Trade marks have to be protected against feared dilution, even when the use in question is connected with products or services completely unrelated to those of the mark owner.[101] Honest traders lose their rights to use their own names on

[97] One interesting replacement suggested by Lunney is a test explicitly based on market power analysis, one which would overtly distinguish between pro- and anti-competitive copying: see n. 10 above, 561 and 601. However attractive this idea might be to a competition lawyer, there is no sign of it catching on in any jurisdiction. Similar views were expressed in S. Abrahamsom, "Making Sense of the Copyright Merger Doctrine" (1998) 45 *UCLA L Rev* 1125.

[98] *Whelan Associates, Inc.* v. *Jaslow Dental Laboratory*, 797 F 2d 1222 (3rd Cir. 1986) and *Autodesk* v. *Dyson* (1992) 173 CLR 330 are generally acknowledged as representing the high water mark of this trend.

[99] See *Children's Television Workshop, Inc.* v. *Woolworths (NSW) Ltd* [1981] RPC 187; *Hogan* v. *Koala Dundee Pty. Ltd* (1988) 83 ALR 187; *Pacific Dunlop Ltd* v. *Hogan* (1989) 14 IPR 398; *Mirage Studios* v. *Counter-feat Clothing Co Ltd* [1991] FSR 145.

[100] This is a seemingly inevitable consequence when broadly drafted consumer protection statutes are captured by intellectual property lawyers: see I. Eagles, "Of Firms, Families and Fair Trading" [1998] *NZLJ* 241.

[101] See the European Trade Marks Directive, Art. 5(2), 40/94/ EEC OJ and the Trade Mark Dilution Act 1995, 15 USC § 1125 (c). For a study of developments under the latter legislation, see L.J. Oswald, "Tarnishment and Blurring under the Federal Trade Mark Dilution Act 1995" (1999) 36 *Am J Bus L* 255.

the remote chance that potential customers of same name rivals may be deceived or misled.[102] In few of these cases is the impact on competition addressed, much less weighed.[103] All have the potential to affect not only what competitors may say about their own product, but also what they may say about the right owner's product. (Restrictions on comparative advertising are a case in point here.)[104]

(c) Effort and Investment Protected *per se*

All legal systems have some difficulty devising principled rules to protect information which is not secret, but on whose collection, retrieval or storage money or effort has been expended. Fair dealing and commercial morality are such vague and unsatisfactory principles that they can easily slip out of sight altogether, leaving courts and legislators to be seduced by three attractive but dangerous fallacies: (i) that mere possession of information entitles the possessor to protection;[105] (ii) that investment in information creates rights in the investor;[106] and (iii) that value equals property, i.e. because information is valuable, the possessor must in some sense "own" it. These conceptual slippages are aided by two of the law's more runaway metaphors: that one should not reap where one has not sown, and that attempts to do so must be prevented as "free riding" on the efforts of the sower. Like most examples of soundbite law, these propositions have a glib facility which conceals their intellectual impoverishment.[107] As Professor Gordon has pointed out, some free riding is an essential part of every capitalist economy. The trick is to work out how much and what kind.[108] Most technological and creative advances depend on there being gleaners and replanters, as well as first sowers. The real point at issue is to determine everyone's appropriate share of present and future crops. Different jurisdictions have taken different roads to this particular principleless hell. In the United States, it is misappropriation torts based on notions of "quasi-property"[109] or vulgarisations of unjust enrichment theory.[110] In Commonwealth jurisdictions,

---

[102] *Neumegen v. Neumegen* [1998] 3 NZLR 310.

[103] For a rare example of such analysis see the dissenting opinion of Thomas J, *ibid.*

[104] See *Villa Maria Wines Ltd* v. *Montana Wines Ltd* [1984] 2 NZLR 422; cf *PC Direct Ltd* v. *Best Buy Ltd* [1997] 2 NZLR 723. Attitudes of US courts are far less restrictive: see *Smith* v. *Chanel, Inc*, 402 F 2d 562 (9th Cir. 1968). The United Kingdom Trade Marks Act 1994, s. 10(6), attempts to strike a balance between these two positions. As to the European position on comparative advertising generally, see E. McCormick, "The Future of Comparative Advertising" [1998] *EIPR* 241.

[105] What is sometimes called the status quo or "what I have I hold" theory: see Gordon, n. 26 above, 170 and 194.

[106] For a succinct demolition of the "investment equals legally guaranteed reward" formula, see Waldron, n. 6 above, 854.

[107] Such metaphors can lead even economists astray. See, e.g., D.G. Lichtman's use of research and development costs to establish the baseline for intellectual property protection in "The Economics of Innovation: Protecting Unpatentable Goods" (1997) 81 *Minn L Rev* 693.

[108] Gordon, n. 26 above, 248 and 279.

[109] This was the original conceptual umbrella under which the US Supreme Court sought to bring its decision in *International News Serv.* v. *Associated Press*, 248 US 215 (1918).

[110] This seems to be part of a trans-jurisdictional trend towards a greater willingness to explore the "enrichment" side of the restitution question while neglecting the much harder "unjust" issue, at least in those cases where the enrichment occurs via the acquisition or use of information. A

something similar occurs when so-called "sweat" tests in copyright law drive originality thresholds to new depths.[111] From here, it is but a short step to *sui generis* protection of databases, a step already taken in the European Union.[112] If one steps back and looks at this from a competition point of view, what we have is the extraordinary spectacle of governments which loudly proclaim their opposition to picking winners doing precisely that when it comes to information intensive industries. In economic terms, this is state-directed investment, no more, and no less. This is one area where investment displacement theory scarcely needs to prove its case.

(ii) Shifting Copyright's Internal Markers

Not only are the boundaries between rights becoming blurred, but there has also been a subtle conceptual shift within them, most notably in relation to copyright.[113] This internal shift, while gradual, has nevertheless markedly altered the balance between copyright stakeholders. More importantly for our purposes, it has the potential to distort the competitive process as the rights owners twist and turn to avoid these sudden potholes on a legal road which they had previously assumed to be safely marked. The progress of this internal shift can only be traced in broadest outline here. (It is well documented elsewhere.) Three separate processes are at work.

(a) Forcing New Protections into Existing Categories

Faced with the digital revolution, many judges responded by slotting protection for computer programs (in source code, if not always object code form) and compilations of computer programs into the existing hard copy category of lit-

---

principled restitutionary analysis balances the interests of plaintiff and defendant according to some pre-existing calculus depending on the defendant's state of mind and the vulnerability of the plaintiff. That calculus should also, as Professor Gordon points out, make room for the wider public interest, one factor in which should be the preservation of competitive markets: n. 26 above, 215, 220 and 227. It should also take into account that creating a cause of action can involve greater transaction and enforcement costs than denying one: *ibid*. Restitutionary theory also poses another problem in this context. To the extent that it is dependent on corrective justice, "restoring" already recognised legal interests, it has an obvious circularity when used to determine whether such rules or interests exist in the first place: see Sterk, n. 36 above.

[111] See, e.g., *Waterlow Directories* v. *Reed Information* (1990) 20 IPR 493.

[112] The final step was arguably unnecessary in the United Kingdom given the general prevalence in UK cases of the sweat test: *ibid*. This posed a dilemma for the United Kingdom when enacting database protection, a dilemma solved by the conceptual legerdemain of importing the higher civilian creativity threshold when protection is sought for these works under copyright law (a move resisted for other works) and removing it entirely under the *sui generis* limb.

[113] Copyright is more susceptible to internal shifts because, while its external structure is statutory, much of its internal framework is judge-made. Shifting the markers within registration-based rights requires legislative action and public debate. When legislative change does come to copyright, it usually takes the form of adding to, or tinkering with, the exhaustive statutory lists of protected subject matter. Because common law copyright regimes lack the civilian's overarching (and limiting) concept of *œuvre d'esprit*, courts cannot easily control these legislative accretions in any principled way even if they should wish to.

erary work.[114] Pleased with the trend, copyright owners lost little time lobbying legislators to set these changes in statutory concrete. Thus, we have a voraciously open-jawed definition of "compilation", capable of swallowing whole other categories of work, demolishing half a century of carefully crafted case law as it feeds.[115]

(b) First Comers Trump Derivative Authors

Innovation and creativity do not exist in a vacuum.[116] Not only do most innovators and creators build on the work of others, but the pursuit of efficiency goals requires that they continue to be able to do so. The law must therefore configure the right balance between protecting first comers, and encouraging transformative or improving uses of their work by others. While the problem is not confined to copyright,[117] it is there that it is at its most acute. In part, this is due to the extension of tests for infringement described below.[118] A more important factor, however, is the concept of the derivative work or adaptation. Never very easy to square with the idea/expression dichotomy, it now seems to have broken out of the square entirely. Originally introduced to deal with the problem of simple translations, the test for derivative work is now wide enough in some jurisdictions, most notably the United States, to confer on copyright owners something approaching a veto on the use of particular characters (or worse, the fictional world they inhabit).[119] A similar logic is sometimes used when it is sought to persuade courts to give the first teller of a fictionalised account of real events a pre-emptive claim over further fictionalisation of those events.[120] Again, while courts have generally been vigilant to prevent authors from capturing whole *genre* in the case of traditional literary works, they have been much less charitable to the derivative user in some parts of the popular music

---

[114] *IBM* v. *Computer Imports Ltd* [1989] 2 NZLR 385.

[115] L. Longdin, "Computerised Compilations: A Cautionary Tale from New Zealand" (1997) 5 *IJITL* 249, 264–8.

[116] Ironically, the closer the creator or innovator comes to that vacuum, the less likely she is to have legal protection because what she does is more likely to be characterised as an unprotectable idea.

[117] In patent law, the problem is sometimes reversed so that it is the second comer who is unfairly advantaged. The purer the research, the less likely it is to be patentable: see M.S. Hart, "Getting Back to Basics: Reinventing Patent Law for Economic Efficiency" (1994) 8 *IPJ* 217, 231.

[118] See text accompanying n. 124 below.

[119] The so-called prequel or sequel problem: *Titan Sports, Inc.* v. *Turner Broadcasting Systems,* 981 F Supp. 65, 69 (D Conn. 1997); *New Line Cinema* v. *Berthlesman Music Group, Inc.,* 693 F Supp. 1517 (SDNY 1988); *Warner Bros., Inc.* v. *American Broadcasting, Inc.,* 720 F 2d 231, 235 (2nd Cir. 1983); *Burroughs* v. *Metro Goldwyn Mayer,* 519 F Supp. 389, 391 (SDNY 1981). In most Commonwealth jurisdictions, the courts have generally stopped short of conferring copyright protection on characters as such, generally preferring to proceed by way of passing off or its statutory equivalent (for which a showing of misrepresentation or harm to goodwill would generally be necessary). See, e.g., *Shaw Bros. (Hong Kong) Ltd* v. *Golden Harvest (HK) Ltd* [1972] RPC 559, 563. This was once also the approach of American courts: see *Warner Bros. Pictures, Inc.* v. *Columbia Broadcasting System,* 216 F 2d 945, 950 (9th Cir. 1954).

[120] See, e.g., *Hoehling* v. *Universal City Studios,* 618 F 2d 972 (3rd Cir. 1980); *Miller* v. *Universal City Studios,* 650 F 2d 1365 (5th Cir. 1981).

industry.[121] While economists differ on the likely anti-competitive effects of such developments,[122] the problem is similar enough to the familiar competition law issue of leverage across markets to raise some warning flags.[123]

(c) Widening the Infringement Net

In its infancy, copyright law was concerned with near literal copying. The infringement net has been cast much more widely since those innocent days, giving rise to such expansive tests as "look and feel" or "substantial similarity". The point here is not that such interpretations are inherently anti-competitive, but that they are capable of raising barriers to entry through the uncertainty they create. The problem is compounded when they are supplemented by evidentiary presumptions,[124] or combined with allegations of subconscious[125] or indirect copying.[126] One should not underestimate the deterrent effect on the forensically under-funded but potentially innovative competitor. At the very least, they increase the right owner's opportunity for gaming.[127]

---

[121] For an excellent transnational analysis of the phenomenon, see A. van Melle, "Facing the Music: Liability for Musical Plagiarism in Contemporary Popular Music" [1997] *NZIPJ* 160. The problem may have been compounded by the recent reception of moral rights in common law jurisdictions: see P. Tackaberry, "Look What They have Done to my Song Ma: The Songwriter's Moral Right of Integrity in Canada and the United States" (1989) 10 *EIPR* 356.

[122] Neo-classicists are relatively relaxed about restrictions on transformative use of prior works: see W.J. Gordon, "On the Economics of Fair Use: Systemic Versus Case by Case Responses to Market Failure" (1997) 8 *J and Inf Sc* 1620, 1628; P Goldstein, *Copyright* (2nd edn., Boston, Mass., Little Brown, 1996) § 5–79; Landes and Posner, n. 11 above, 328 and 354. Their opponents, however, for a variety of reasons, all advocate either cutting back on the adaptation right or eliminating it altogether: see Lunney, n. 10 above, 650; Sterk, n. 36 above, 1207.

[123] Anything that inhibits the emergence of whole new markets or products is worrying from an allocative and innovative efficiency perspective: Lunney, n. 10 above, 520. It was precisely such "whole market" pre-emption which prompted the European Court of Justice to prohibit it in *Radio Telefis Eirean and Independent Television Publications* v. *European Commission and Magill* [1995] 4 CMLR 718. Much will depend on how the markets in question are defined: see B.W. Teyerman, "The Economic Rationale for Copyright Protection for Published Books: A Reply to Professor Breyer" (1971) 18 *UCLA L Rev* 1100, 1110.

[124] There has been a certain logical slippage in these presumptions. Thus, "substantial similarity" plus proof of access equals presumed copying (*L B Plastics Ltd* v. *Swish Products Ltd* [1979] RPC 551, 619) can become the faintly circular "substantial similarity presumes access and therefore copying" (*Francis Day and Hunter Ltd* v. *Bron* [1963] Ch 587, 612). The probative goalposts can be shifted even further if the court accepts possible, rather than actual, access as its starting point: *ibid.*, 614. For a similar process at work in the United States jurisprudence, see *Nelson* v. *PRN Productions Ltd*, 873 F 2d 1141, 1142 (8th Cir. 1989); *Gaste* v. *Kaiserman*, 863 F 2d 1061, 1067 (2nd Cir. 1988).

[125] See *Abkco Music, Inc.* v. *Harrison's Music Ltd*, 722 F 2d 988, 997 (2nd Cir. 1983); *EMI Music Publishing Ltd* v. *Papathanassiou* [1993] EMLR 306.

[126] The furthest extension of the concept of indirect copying is perhaps represented by those cases where the link between the plaintiff's work and the infringing copy is provided by a mere description: see *Plix Products Ltd* v. *Frank M. Winstone (Merchants) Ltd* [1986] FSR 608 and *House of Spring Gardens Ltd* v. *Point Blank Ltd* [1983] FSR 213.

[127] Copyright statutes lack the "bluffing" liability provisions of their patent counterparts: see, e.g., Patents Act 1953 (NZ), s. 24.

B External Boundaries Move Outwards

Not content with the slow (and not always predictable) unfolding of precedent to achieve shifts in the internal paradigm, rights owners have sought to push out the boundaries of legal protection more directly, enlisting for the purpose an eclectic but highly successful mix of defensive technology, legislative change, international diplomacy, and the law of contract.

(i) Pushing at the Time/Space Envelope

For reasons which would come as no surprise to public choice theorists, intellectual property owners have been highly effective at the lobbying game. Among their more notable victories has been their ability to secure the extension not only of the life of the right but also its geographical reach.

(a) Extending the Term of the Right

The temporal boundaries of intellectual property rights tend to remain fixed for long periods of time. (This is why more than the usual limited amount of empirical research can be done on them.) When they move, however, they move in large leaps. The primary patent term is now 20 years in most jurisdictions. The duration of copyright has been extended by a quarter of a century in Europe and the United States, and this without having to make any concessions on the continued use of the author's life as the other boundary peg, a usage which is beginning to look exceedingly quaint in economic terms given that the great majority of authors retain copyright for only the briefest of periods.[128] It looks even more quaint when one remembers that much copyrightable output is now the result of team or group efforts, in which the ascription of individual authorship is either impossible or confessedly artificial and arbitrary. The existence of fixed terms of protection across large and differentiated classes of economic activity have always been the Achilles heel of intellectual property's claims to promote innovative efficiency.[129] The likelihood of a single, arbitrarily selected, term delivering optimal protection in all circumstances is seldom seriously advanced.[130] Equally arbitrary extensions to such terms are no easier to justify.[131]

---

[128] This strange form of family protection has long passed its economic "use by" date. It is retained largely out of legislative habit, or perhaps a wish to conciliate those civil law jurisdictions which are accustomed to regarding an authors non-economic (i.e. "moral") rights as immortal.

[129] I. Eagles, *Intellectual Property and the Commerce Act* (Centre for Commercial Law and Applied Legal Search, Monash University, 1987), 17.

[130] Some neoclassicists, it is true, seek to solve the "one term can't fit all situations" conundrum by suggesting (in an unlikely convergence with the civilians) that fixed terms should in principle be abolished so that intellectual property becomes as open-ended in duration as any other form of property: see Landes and Posner, n. 11 above, 361; R.E. Meiners and R.J. Staaf, "Patents, Copyrights and Trademarks: Property or Monopoly" (1990) 13 *Harv J L and Pub Pol* 911, 924. Neoclassicists in general tend to favour longer terms because this fits best with their overall preference for encouraging the production of works with as many potential valued uses as possible. The

(b) Towards the Inexhaustible Right

Intangibles may be the subject matter of intellectual property law, but it has always been heavily dependent on dealings in tangibles to set the parameters of infringement. For most of its history, it was the *sale* of pirated copies which rights owners sought to stamp out. With this, however, went a recognition that purchasers too had rights, and that in general they should be free to sell on copies which had been legitimately acquired. In some jurisdictions, this was explicitly stated as an "exhaustion of rights" rule. In others, it had to be inferred from the manner in which infringement was defined in the statute in question. Whatever their name and provenance, such rules operated as real constraints on the power of rights-holders to subdivide markets horizontally or segment them vertically.[132] These constraints are, however, being increasingly bypassed.

First the freeing up of international trade has given new force to parallel importing restrictions long dormant within individual countries' intellectual property regimes. In a protectionist world, such restrictions were of only marginal significance in competition terms because of the existence of much higher and more effective barriers to entry in the form of tariffs and import controls. Once the latter fell, however, the former took on a much more prominent role. Private regulation could now replace state action, with anti-competitive possibilities which rights owners and their licensees were quick to recognise and sometimes act upon. The trend has been only marginally dented by isolated examples of legislative reversal in jurisdictions such as New Zealand or Singapore[133] (and, to a lesser extent, Australia[134]). Indeed, jurisdictions which

longer the period the more time the owner has to explore what those uses might be and find customers for them.

[131] Writers such as Professor Gordon, while they acknowledge that the term of protection properly varies across the three traditional intellectual property families (i.e. trade marks, copyright and patents), so that the duration of the protection is inversely proportional to the potential market power conferred by each type of right, do not apply this insight *within* each family. For an attempt to do so in patent law, see Hart, n. 117 above, 225.

[132] Neither horizontal nor vertical constraints need be anti-competitive in themselves. They can become so if they: (i) fall foul of the *per se* prohibitions in particular competition regimes; or (ii) are used as a mechanism for furthering anti-competitive dealings; or (iii) enable those with power in one market to leverage that power into other markets.

[133] To date such reversals apply only to copyright law. The restrictive possibilities of trade mark law, although less generous to licensees, continue to be able to be exploited. It can also be argued that such reversals are the antithesis of a coherent competition policy because they focus on consequences not causes and price rather than efficiency. Not every exercise of a power to restrict imports has anti-competitive results. Nor should we assume that there can never be legitimate business reasons for resisting parallel imports, where, for example, identical trade marks mask a difference in quality or function, or the entry barrier acts as a surrogate for effective cross-border checks on piracy (assuming that the ineffectiveness of border controls in a particular jurisdiction can be demonstrated as a matter of fact).

[134] Australia has chosen to remove parallel importing restrictions only in relation to particular markets, notably books and musical compact discs: see A. Fels, "Repeal of Parallel Importation Restrictions: A Step Forward for Copyright in Australia and New Zealand", paper presented at the

do go down this road may find themselves facing retaliatory action from those countries which consider themselves advantaged by parallel importing restrictions, action against which the World Trade Organisation would be powerless to provide a remedy.[135] Nor are rights owners and licensees likely to remain passive in the face of repeal. Anecdotal evidence suggests that much legal ingenuity is being expended on replacing statutory barriers with contractual ones, a response which, if it occurs, competition authorities should be free to meet.[136]

Secondly, exhaustion of rights makes sense only when the intellectual property right in question is embodied in a physical object, property in which at some stage passes out of the hands of the right-holder.[137] As the focus of copyright and database protection moves away from hard copy sales to rights to view, display or further transmit, exhaustion of rights becomes less and less relevant. While this trend is not new, the digitalisation of much that was formally held only in hard copy has greatly speeded up the process. All of this greatly enhances the ability of copyright owners to impose potentially anti-competitive conditions on both initial access to, and subsequent use of, the protected material. A parallel development can be seen at work in patent law, as applicants recast their claims from product to process, thus side-stepping the exhaustion rules which have always applied to the former.[138]

(c) Exporting Over-protection

The globalisation of markets in general, and intellectual property markets in particular, has exacerbated the growing imbalance between intellectual property protection and competition values. Jurisdictions which view themselves as important exporters of intellectual property not unnaturally wish to see their own strong (and expanding) intellectual property regimes as the model to which all jurisdictions should move as quickly as possible. Equally natural is the wish of rights-holders to structure their activities in ways which attract the protection of these stronger regimes. That both are increasingly able to have their wish is due to two factors. The first stems from the expansionist bias built into the process of negotiating international conventions. When the negotiating parties come up against a fundamental conceptual clash, the easiest exit from deadlock is to ensure that no jurisdiction loses a protection to which its rights-owners have become accustomed. Harmonisation in this scheme of things almost

---

12th Annual IPANZ Conference, 29 August 1998. For a critical appraisal of this approach, see van Melle, n. 121 above.

[135] Exhaustion of rights issues are placed outside the scope of TRIPS by Art. 6 of that document.

[136] See text accompanying n. 147 below.

[137] The intellectual property need not, and usually will not, pass with the title to the physical object. We are dealing with two property rights here, not one: *Pacific Film Laboratories Pty. Ltd* v. *FCT* (1970) 121 CLR 154; *Barson Computers (NZ) Ltd* v. *John Gilbert and Co Ltd* (1984) 4 IPR 533; *WGN Continental Broadcasting Co* v. *United Video Co*, 693 F 2d 622 (7th Cir. 1982); *United States* v. *Goss*, 803 F 2d 638 (11th Cir. 1986); *Rockford Map Publishing Co* v. *Directory Service of Colorado*, 768 F 2d 145 (7th Cir. 1985).

[138] See J.R. Thomas, chap. 7 of this volume.

always means harmonisation up, not harmonisation down, thus projecting onto the international stage the distortions endemic in domestic intellectual property law reform. The second factor, facilitating the export of over-protectionist intellectual property regimes, is the one described by Graeme Austin elsewhere in this volume:[139] the emergence of choice of law rules which erode the territoriality principle which had hitherto prevailed in transnational intellectual property litigation.

Competition law has been much less successful in leaping borders.[140] Conflicts of law rules in all jurisdictions treat it as part of public law, even when it is sought to be enforced through private litigation.[141] There can thus be no escape from the *lex fori*. Even when it is sought to give the latter some extraterritorial reach,[142] it is easily fended off by evidential "shield" laws in the jurisdictions in which the anti-competitive conduct is said to have occurred. Nor have efforts to harmonise the *content* of competition law borne much fruit. Governments have generally been content to focus on the trade-distorting aspects of various forms of economic regulation. Within this minimalist framework, states are free to construct their competition regimes largely as they please,[143] even engaging in regulatory races to the bottom if they perceive that this gives them an advantage in securing inward investment. Such cross-border unity as exists tends to come from the direct input of economists into the legal process. (There is a thriving international trade in expert witnesses.)

(ii) Taking the contractual road to expansion.

Contract and intellectual property law have always lived in symbiosis. Contract is the normal mechanism through which rights-owners exploit their rights, usually by subdividing them among different market players or different fields of activity. As well as allocating existing rights in this way, contract can also be used to create new ones. While this could give rise to competition concerns, the problem was partly contained, in common law jurisdictions at any rate, by the

---

[139] G.W. Austin, chap. 5 of this volume.

[140] Indeed the most successful competition export is the export cartel itself. These are exempt from competition scrutiny in most jurisdictions, subject to notification of the relevant competition agency: see Trade Practices Act 1974 (Cth), s. 51(2)(g); Commerce Act 1986 (NZ), s. 44(1)(g). The United States legislation exempts voluntary export activity under a patchwork of provisions: see 15 USC §§61–65; §§4001–21; §6a.

[141] Parties can sometimes avoid particular jurisdictions through suitably drafted arbitration clauses. This gives them no choice as to the applicable law. See *Mitsubishi Motors Corp.* v. *Soler Chrysler-Plymouth, Inc.*, 473 US 614 (1985).

[142] Either by projecting the boundaries of the market across borders or through extending the provisions of the competition statute to conduct, which, although external to the jurisdiction, affects competition or markets within it, e.g. Commerce Act 1986 (NZ), s. 4(1). See also *United States* v. *Aluminum Corp. of America*, 148 F 2d 416, 443 (2nd Cir. 1954).

[143] Art. 8(2) of TRIPS allows signatories to take steps to prevent abuse of intellectual property rights having adverse effects "on competition in the relevant market". The Art. goes on to list "exclusive grant back conditions, no challenge clauses and coercive package" licensing by way of illustration.

rules relating to privity and consent. Rights-owners have increasingly sought to bypass these limitations through restrictive conditions imposed on the mass of consumers through such devices as the "shrink-wrap" or "click-wrap" licence, and then persuade courts to enforce their greatly expanded rights as ordinary contracts. Some judges in some jurisdictions have been open to persuasion.[144] Others have baulked at what they see as private legislation under the thinnest of consensual veneers.[145] When confronted with such judicial roadblocks, rights-owners have typically responded with attempts to persuade legislators to dismantle them in ways which do considerable violence to both generally accepted contract principles and intellectual property's own internal balance.[146] Should such attempts be successful, rights-owners would be able (at least within the statute's sphere of operation)[147] to:

(a) confer copyright-like protection on ideas and pure facts; or
(b) negate any defences to infringement which might be contained in particular intellectual property statutes; or
(c) re-impose parallel importing restrictions even where repealed by statute or negated by judicial ruling.

These are not outcomes which competition regulators can afford to regard with equanimity.

IV CONSTRUCTING THE INTERFACE

Thus far I have been concerned to show that intellectual property rights pose dangers for the competitive process and that these dangers are increasing. This does not demonstrate, nor is it intended to demonstrate, that such dangers will be realised every time an intellectual property right crops up in a business dealing or relationship. It is my contention that intellectual property rights are neither presumptively bad in competition terms nor presumptively good. Even

---

[144] *ProCD, Inc* v. *Zeidenberg*, 86 F 3d 1447 (7th Cir. 1996).

[145] *Step Saver Systems* v. *Wyse Technology*, 939 F 2d 91, 98 (3rd Cir. 1991); *Vault Corp.* v. *Quaid Software Ltd*, 847 F 2d 255, 270 (5th Cir. 1988); *Morgan Laboratories, Inc.* v. *Micro Data Base Systems, Inc.*, 41 USPQ 2d 1850 (ND Cal. 1997).

[146] Witness current proposals in the United States to insert a new Art. 2B into the Uniform Commercial Code which would: (i) turn some sales into licenses by legislative fiat; (ii) make restrictive licence terms enforceable even if imposed *after* the licence transaction is completed; and (iii) allow licensors effectively to choose both forum and applicable law. While Art. 2B has been trenchantly criticised in the literature (see D. Nimmer, E. Brown and G.N. Frischling, "The Metamorphosis of Contract into Expand" (1999) 87 *Calif L Rev* 17; M.A. Lemley, "Beyond Pre-emption: The Law and Policy of Intellectual Property Licensing" (1999) 87 *Calif L Rev* 111), it also has its defenders (J.R. Wolfson, "Contract and Copyright are Not at War: A Reply to the Metamorphosis of Contract into Expand" (1999) 87 *Calif L Rev* 79). The American debate is complicated by the constitutional issue of whether State initiatives are pre-empted by Federal copyright law.

[147] The proposed Art. 2B would apply to all "licenses" (as newly defined) of information, as well as software leases and access contracts. Most transactions involving copyright and trade secrets would be caught, as would any trade mark or patent dealings associated with the deemed licence.

the process of rights expansion described in section III of this chapter does not automatically lead to anti-competitive outcomes. What it does do is increase the opportunities for bringing about such outcomes. The case made thus far is for competition scrutiny of intellectual property dealings, not for their outlawry. In this section, we are concerned with the form such scrutiny might take, and the procedural and conceptual obstacles to its effectiveness.

A Empiricism versus Formalism

Most economists, whatever their stripe, are uncomfortable with rules which presume particular economic outcomes from particular forms of commercial activity.[148] Their natural preference is therefore for rule of reason over *per se* approaches to determining competition liability. Only when the transaction costs attached to such an inquiry rise to too high a level and the statistical probabilities all seem to point in a single direction can they be persuaded to accept normative prescription as a substitute.[149] Rules of reason tend to lose their empirical lustre, however, when economists are asked to fit contentious theories to elusive facts for the purposes of competition proceedings with limited time for empirical enquiry and before the key events have actually occurred. When confronted with squabbling economists, lawyers and judges instinctively look for a black letter tie-breaker to resolve the stand off. Their natural preference is thus for a purely formalist solution.

Formalists and empiricists have few conceptual meeting points. Not only do they see different cures for the tension between intellectual property and competition law, but they are also apt to see very different diseases.

B Deconstructing the Caricatures

One of the difficulties facing those who wish to see a *rapprochement* between intellectual property lawyers and competition analysts is that the two groups defend their territory with arguments which, as often as not, miss the real point at issue, and which paint pictures of each other's intentions which would border on parody if they were not sincerely held. Before any meaningful dialogue can take place we must first deconstruct these mutual misperceptions.

---

[148] It is perhaps unkind to point out that public choice theory explains this preference perfectly well. Rule of reason cases provide opportunities for economists to strut their stuff. Bright line rules lock them out of the courtroom.

[149] Even here, their preferences will be dictated by their assumptions about how the economy operates in general. Neo-classicists tend to favour *per se* legality to solve the transaction costs problem, their opponents drift more naturally in the direction of presumptive illegality.

(i) Common Goals Preclude Conflict

Some commentators and regulators seek to defuse the potential conflict between intellectual property and competition law by emphasising the economic objectives that they have in common. Both, it is said, share the larger policy objective of maximising wealth and minimising costs[150] and both applaud allocative and innovative efficiencies when they find them.[151] However warm the glow of intellectual amity that these supposedly common goals provide, they are simply at too high a level of abstraction to be of much practical assistance in deciding hard cases. They can also fuel a positively Panglossian complacency in which these two branches of law sit happily on their separate mountain tops, with no need to communicate, much less interact. This in turn leads to the dangerous assumption that competition policy-makers must and will bless every expansionist step that intellectual property chooses to take. What this defective feel-good logic obscures is that, while intellectual property and competition law may share common ends, they pursue these ends through radically different means[152] and according to radically different time frames. Competition law regulates the market now to protect the competitive process for the future. Intellectual property distorts competition in the short term to enhance efficiency in the long term. Even Dr Pangloss would be hard pressed to see these as congruent methodologies. In one case, the law must strike the right balance between under- and overprotection. In the other, the fine line which has to be walked is the one between over- and under-regulation.

(ii) Sacrosanct Property versus Regulated Privilege

Neoclassicists, as we have seen, are strongly of the view that markets are best ordered through robust property rights and freely negotiated contracts. From this they derive three subsidiary propositions:

(a) An unprotected intangible will never realise its full social value.
(b) All valuable intangibles should be commodified in the form of property rights.
(c) Once created, such property rights should not be appropriated or their value diminished through state action.[153]

---

[150] W.S. Bowman, *Patent and Anti Trust Law A Legal and Economic Appraisal* (Chicago, Ill., Univ of Chicago Press, 1973), 25. See also *US Intellectual Property Licensing Guidelines*, n. 89 above, §1.

[151] Brodley, n. 74 above, 1027. See also *Atari Games Corp v. Nintendo*, 897 F 2d 1572, 1576 (Fed. Cir. 1990).

[152] M.A. O'Rourke, "Striking a Delicate Balance: Intellectual Property, Anti Trust, Contract and Standardisation in the Computer Industry" (1998) 12 *Harv J L and Tech* 1, 31.

[153] Some fudging of economic utilitarianism and natural rights theory is apt to occur at this point.

Such views are deeply satisfying to intellectual property owners. From their perspective, the state having created the property right[154] with one hand, it should not be permitted to take it back with the other.[155] Interference with their rights in the guise of regulating competition is just such an unauthorised taking. Worse, it is a redistribution of value in favour of competitors and consumers.[156] All of these arguments can be stood on their head:

(a) Creators, innovators and investors are not the only stakeholders to be considered when legal protection is sought for intangibles. Their interests must be balanced against those of users, competitors and the wider public interest.

(b) Such balancing need not take the form of property rights mitigated by narrow infringement defences. Liability rules can do the job just as well.[157] There will even be occasions where "no right" is the appropriate solution.

(c) What we call intellectual property is really a form of shorthand for a state-granted monopoly[158] and it is entirely appropriate that the state should regulate that monopoly once granted.[159] Redistributive outcomes are not presumptively bad (whether such redistribution results from regulation or internal balancing is not germane to the argument). Competition law is a relatively mild form of regulation which may have an occasion to be supplemented by compulsory licensing regimes if rights owners' interests become too strongly entrenched.

---

[154] The fact that the right is the product of willed legislative choice is thought to strengthen the argument. In point of fact, the source of the right tells us nothing useful. All property rights are a form of state action. See Calabresi and Melamed, n. 33 above, 1092.

[155] F.H. Easterbrook, "Intellectual Property is Still Property" (1990) 13 *Harv J L and Pub Pol* 108, 109; E. Maackay, "Economic Incentives in Markets for Information and Innovation" (1990) 13 *Harv J L and Pub Pol* 867, 907.

[156] It is this redistributive function which makes neo-classicists particularly hostile to compulsory licensing and compels them to defend rights-owners' refusals to deal. In a sense, the neoclassicist approach looks backwards as well as forwards. The US Supreme Court took a similar property-based stance in the early years of anti-trust enforcement, albeit that stance was intuitive rather than underpinned by economics. See, e.g., *E. Bement and Sons* v. *National Harrow Corp*, 186 US 70 (1902).

[157] Another way of looking at this is to conclude that what we call property is simply a particular matrix of liability rules. Property and obligation on this view are both about relationships between parties, not the nexus between party and thing. The argument is particularly attractive where the artificiality of the *res* is incontestable, as it clearly is with intellectual property rights. On this view of the matter, the property label states a conclusion about how rights are to be treated, not a way of categorising rights in the first place.

[158] Palmer, n. 38 above. This leads some writers to deny that "property" has anything other than rhetorical uses. Drahos, for example, would prefer the instrumental nature of intellectual property to be made more visible in statutory terminology, preferring terms such as "duty bearing privilege" to "property": see n. 8 above, 223. While his is probably a lost cause, the language of property should not be allowed to blind us to competitive realities in particular cases. All too often "property" is treated as a species of magical incantation at the utterance of which we are all supposed to suspend our critical faculties.

[159] Indeed, some would say that there is already increasing state regulation (in the positive sense) in the form of criminalised infringement and border protection measures.

These are not debates in which we have to take sides. One can accept that property rights and freedom of contract are important props for any market economy, while still maintaining that there are circumstances where they may need to be set aside to prevent competitive markets from self destructing. Regulation, by definition, is an interference with the market and regulation which left property rights and contracts untouched would not work. Arguments to the contrary are really arguments about whether we should have competition law at all. They do not explain why, once a competition regime is in place, it should fall unequally on different kinds of property. They also too easily assume that to regulate a right, however minimally, is to deprive it of all social utility.

Conversely, one can accept that property is a debatable construct without insisting that it constantly be debated. From a competition perspective, the solidity or otherwise of the line between property and obligation is supremely unimportant. Both are equally grist to the regulator's mill.[160] Again, to call something a monopoly does not automatically mean that it is ripe for regulation. Economic theory accepts that even a 100 per cent market share will confer no market power if entry barriers are low and exit costless. Indeed, the term "monopoly" is just as conceptually cloudy as property. As will be argued below, legal and economic monopolies are not the same thing. One deals with *facts,* the other with *rights*. To equate the two would draw a wholly artificial line between those intellectual property rights (such as patents) which are true monopolies[161] and others (such as trade marks)[162] which are not. It would also create a contestable but conceptually barren no man's land for those rights (most notably copyright) whose monopoly status is unclear.[163] This is why most competition regimes make no mention of monopoly in defining competition thresholds, and those that do[164] use it as a term of art signifying a degree of market power capable of raising competition concerns. Used in this way it is just as much a form of legal shorthand as "property".

Not only are "property" and "monopoly" contested concepts, but they tell us nothing useful about the competitive process. As one American commentator puts it, "[t]he choice is not between some market power and no market power",[165] but rather how much market power requires regulatory intervention

---

[160] The only difference is that since it is theoretically easier to keep the internal balance with a liability rule, the competition regulator may have less reason to intervene in the first place.

[161] J.T. McCarthy, "Intellectual Property and Trade Practices Policy: Co-existence or Conflict? The American Experience" [1985] *ABLR* 198, 205; Hart, n. 117 above, 245.

[162] Hart, n. 117 above, 202. See also B.W. Pattishall, "Trade Marks and the Monopoly Phobia" (1952) 50 *Mich L Rev* 967.

[163] See text accompanying n. 53 above.

[164] In the United States, §2 of the Sherman Act (15 USC §1) prohibits monopolisation or attempts to monopolise any part of interstate or foreign trade. S. 7 of the Clayton Act (15 USC §18) proscribes acquisitions of stock or assets where the effect of such acquisition "may be", *inter alia,* to "create a monopoly in particular industries or regions".

[165] Lunney, n. 10 above, 518. See also E.W. Kitch, "Patents: Monopolies or Property Rights" (1986) 8 *Research L and Econ* 31, 33; and Eagles, n. 129 above, 12 ff.

and what form that intervention should take. "Property" versus "monopoly" sets up a wholly false polarity. We should ignore it.

(iii) Rights Always Coincide with Markets

This particular fallacy generates more heat and less light than most. Both sides in the intellectual property/competition law debate resort to it with equal enthusiasm. The fallacy lies in assuming that the boundaries of a given intellectual property right also define the boundaries of the market in which that right is said to operate for competition purposes. This will be the case only in those infrequent situations in which the product or service protected by the right has no close substitutes on either the demand or the supply side. Very rarely will courts in competition cases find right and market to be co-extensive.[166] Plaintiffs' attempts to urge such findings on the court will more often than not founder on the substitutability point.[167] No doubt the right-holder hopes for market power, but in the nature of things hope and economic reality will seldom coincide. Why then is the fallacious reasoning persisted in? Rights owners find it useful because it enables them to argue that legislatures, by the mere act defining the right, have impliedly sanctioned all those activities which can be made to fall within the legal definition even if those activities are avowedly anti-competitive in purpose or demonstrably anti-competitive as to consequences.[168] Plaintiffs in competition cases, on the other hand, seek to conflate right and market for precisely the opposite reason: a narrowly defined market exaggerates the effect of any anti-competitive misconduct alleged.

Both arguments are equally flawed. They are given a superficial credence because of the commonly made assumption that a legal monopoly must confer an economic monopoly. In fact, the two concepts have nothing in common. One is normative, laying down what users and rivals *may do*; the other is explicatory, describing what those rivals and competitors *are likely to do* when confronted with a right owner who seeks to charge more or give less. Who wins this particular economic tug of war will depend on cross-elasticities of supply and demand, not the exact location of any intellectual property right's parameters.

(iv) Extending the Right versus Extending the Wrong

Another fruitful source of mutual misunderstanding is to be found in assumptions made about the economic effects to be attributed to attempts by intellec-

---

[166] *Digidyne Corp* v. *Data General Corp,* 734 F 2d 1336 (9th Cir. 1984).

[167] See *True Tone Ltd* v. *Festival Records Retail Marketing Ltd* [1988] 2 NZLR 354; *Abbot Laboratories* v. *Brennan,* 952 F 2d 1346, 1354 (Fed. Cir. 1991); *Broederbund Software, Inc* v. *Computermate Products Aust Pty Ltd* (1992) ATPR 41–155.

[168] See *Image Technical Services, Inc* v. *Eastman Kodak Co,* 125 F 3d 1195, 1216 (9th Cir. 1997). Sometimes such arguments are bolstered by statutory provisions expressly excluding acts done under specific (as distinct from general) legislative authority from the ambit of a particular jurisdiction's competition law. See Commerce Act 1986 (NZ), s. 43.

tual property owners to *extend* the advantages conferred by the right beyond its formal legal boundaries, either overtly by contractual means or, less visibly, through the economic muscle the right is thought to provide. From these conflicting assumptions flow very different perceptions as to how competition law should treat the attempted expansion. Two related, but opposing, fallacies are at work here.

(a) Accept the Right, Accept its Use

It is sometimes argued on behalf of rights-holders that by bestowing an intellectual property right in the first place the legal system must be presumed to have intended to cast a similar cloak of legitimacy over decisions to deal (or not to deal) in the bundle of rights thus bestowed. For rights-owners, the attractions of such an approach are obvious. Not only would *actual* licences or assignments of rights be protected from competition scrutiny, however restrictive their terms, but owners would also be free to stand pat on their rights by *refusing* to license or assign to actual or potential competitors. To understand why such claims are overstated we need to appreciate that we are really dealing with two arguments wrapped into one. The first is economic, basing itself on a factual prognosis of the efficiency outcomes supposedly attributable either to intellectual property in general or to particular licensing[169] practices (usually those which have attracted the attention of competition authorities). The second argument is really a species of legal formalism which insists that it is neither possible nor desirable to separate (whether for competition purposes or otherwise) direct use by the right-owner from authorised application of the right by others. The first argument supports a wider claim for immunity than the second.

The broad claim for immunity. This claim involves two logical leaps, one deductive, the other inductive. The deductive leap starts with the unexceptionable view that legal monopolies do not always confer market power,[170] but inflates that into the empirically under-nourished proposition that they can *never* do so. Intellectual property licences, it is therefore reasoned, cannot extend what does not exist in the first place.[171] The argument collapses once we accept that intellectual property rights, whether or not they *create* market power, are certainly designed to *sustain* such power and sometimes (but not always) succeed in doing so. Restrictive licences and refusals can be used to lever

---

[169] For ease of discussion, the terms "licence" and "licensing" are used here to include all forms of consensual use of the intellectual property right by persons other than the right owner, including outright transfer or assignment of the whole or part of the right.

[170] See text accompanying n. 166 above.

[171] A less sophisticated version of this argument is one which simply asserts that (i) because intellectual property licensing in general facilitates the effective exploitation of intellectual property, the health of a particular industry (or economy) can be measured by the total amount of such activity taking place, and (ii) any drop in the number of licences and assignments amounts to a net social loss. (See, e.g., submissions made by Toyota Australia, Telstra and the Australian Copyright Council to the National Competition Council of Australia, *Review of Sections 51(2) and 51(3) of the Trade Practices Act 1974: Final Report*, 164, 190. (hereafter "*NCC Final Report*"))

whatever market power exists into markets other than that in which the right itself operates. Whether such attempts are likely to succeed in a given case is a perfectly fitting subject for competition inquiry.

It is the inductive leap which is both more interesting and more influential. It rests on isolated case studies of particular vertical constraints (tying, exclusive dealing and pricing restrictions) which are said to demonstrate (let us assume for the moment correctly)[172] that these practices can be allocatively efficient in particular circumstances and may therefore have pro-competitive outcomes in the cases described. The validity of these studies does not depend on the examined practice being part of an intellectual property licence, although many are.[173] Exactly the same issues can arise in respect of any contract for scarce physical inputs or an incumbent's attempts to control access to bottlenecks and gateways in network industries. Similarly when franchisors seek to protect aspects of the franchised image, some of which lie outside the scope of intellectual property protection and others within, it makes no particular sense to subject each aspect to different competition treatment.

To the extent that such studies are soundly based they can act as a useful corrective to the erroneous assumption discussed below that such practices have no redeeming features at all. It is when some neoclassical scholars seek to bless all vertical constraints because of their sheer verticalness[174] that their analysis threatens to come unstuck. Only when an apparently vertical arrangement disguises a horizontal cartel among licensors or licensees do neoclassicists see any cause for competition concern[175] (a concern tempered by their equally strongly held belief that all cartels eventually self destruct because of the inbuilt incentive for participants to cheat).[176] In all other cases, they presume vertical constraints to be competitively benign. Few courts or competition regulators, even when broadly sympathetic to the neoclassicist viewpoint, have been prepared to follow them this far.[177] For the purposes of this chapter, it is unnecessary to come to any conclusion about the validity of the empirical base on which this particular argument rests. Extrapolation from isolated findings that this or that practice does not produce anti-competitive outcomes on the facts of a particular case to a rule of *per se* legality or presumptive harmlessness is no more fruitful than

---

[172] The methodologies on which these studies are based are contested by some economists. See L.A. Sullivan, "The Justice Department Guidelines on Mergers and Vertical Constraints" (1985) 16 *Antitrust L and Econ Rev* 11; W.S. Comanor "Vertical Arrangements and Anti Trust Analysis" (1987) 62 *NYU L Rev* 1153.

[173] See Bowman, n. 150 above, 53ff.

[174] Bork, n. 79 above, 280 ff; R. Posner, "The Next Stop in the Anti-Trust Treatment of Restricted Distribution: Per Se Legality" (1981) 48 *U Chic L Rev* 6, 22.

[175] F.H. Easterbrook, "The Limits of Anti Trust" (1984) 63 *Tex L Rev* 1.

[176] A. Alchian and W. Allen, *Exchange and Production: Competition Co-ordination and Control* (3rd edn., Belmont, Cal., Wadsworth Publishing Co, 1983), 169 ff.

[177] *Fisher & Paykel Ltd* v. *Commerce Commission* [1990] 2 NZLR 731 is often interpreted as bestowing the court's blessing on all vertical arrangements. A careful reading of the case, however, supports no such general conclusion. See also the decision of the majority in *Eastman Kodak Co* v. *Image Services*, 504 US 451 (1992).

similar extrapolation in the direction of *per se* illegality. Again, even if one were inclined to accompany the neo-classicists in their inductive leap from trend to rule the appropriate response would not be a permissive regime for intellectual property arrangements alone but an adjustment of the competition rule across the board. It does not make a case for stand alone intellectual property immunity.

The narrow claim for intellectual property immunity. The broad claim for immunity is unconstrained by any necessary connection with the scope of the intellectual property right. Indeed, because the connection with intellectual property is purely accidental, the broad claim will protect even those practices which seek to *add* to the protections conferred. Not so with the narrow claim, which rests on the purely formal reasoning that what the right owner can do, it may license others to do. The corollary is that the licence may stretch only as far as the limits of the right and no further. Attempts to secure collateral or additional advantages outside the four walls of the intellectual property statute[178] are left exposed to the chilly blasts of potential (but not automatic) competition liability.

Viewed in this way the narrow claim is simply a normative restatement of the "what the state confers it should not diminish" fallacy discussed earlier. Particular licensing practices are not assessed according to their actual or potential effect on the competitive process, but rather on whether they lie within the scope of whatever it is that the state has granted to the right holder. The narrow claim is thus heavily dependant on judicial attitudes to interpreting the content of what has been granted.[179] A literal or restrictive interpretation will cut down the immunity accordingly. A liberal or purposive interpretation, while on the face of it beneficial to rights holders, can easily be (and in some jurisdictions is) stood on its head with "abuse of rights arguments",[180] which examine the rights owners' actions according to broadly based tests of legislative intent. While all this might seem calculated to make the narrow claim to immunity less immediately useful to rights holders than broad economics based claims, this is not always so. Precisely because the narrow claim elevates legal form over economic substance, it can be used to justify masterful inactivity by rights-owners in the form of refusals to license or deal. It also encourages rights owners to disguise the effect of a particular licensing practice by inserting appropriate forms of linguistic camouflage into their licensing agreements. The narrow claim is sometimes called the "scope of grant" approach, a deceptively simple title which masks the complexities within.

---

[178] While non-statutory rights could in theory be subsumed within the narrow claim, they seldom are. The issue is most commonly approached as one of legislative coherence and consistency.

[179] Where the narrow claim for immunity is itself enshrined in statute, as in some jurisdictions it is, these interpretative outcomes will be reversed. See text accompanying n. 221 below.

[180] See text accompanying n. 206 below.

The two faces of formalism. There are two ways of applying the scope of grant principle. The first asks on behalf of the licensee, "if the licence didn't exist, would I need the licensor's permission to do what this clause or arrangement is trying to prevent me from doing?". This we may call the *but for* test. Alternatively, the test could be turned round so that our notional licensee is made to ask, "is the licensor trying to make me do something that the licensor has no power to compel others to do?" This could be called the "*why me*" test. A "but for" test catches only negative stipulations. The "why me" test encompasses both obligations to do and obligations to desist from doing. This can matter when the provision sought to be exempted is a "best endeavour" clause, i.e. one in which the licensee undertakes to do its best to pursue some possibly anti-competitive objective stipulated by the licensor.[181]

Obligations placed on the licensor. It is all too easy to assume that it is only licensors who can have market power. This is not so. Licensees too can act anti-competitively, especially when they combine. In such cases they will seek to impose restrictive terms on the licensor. In other situations, they will seek to deter new entrants by persuading the licensor to raise entry barriers in some way (usually by restricting the issue of new licences or issuing them on discriminatory terms). Neither the "but for" nor the "why me" test deals with this kind of thing. From a policy point of view, it should not matter whether the licensor is an instigator, ignorant dupe or willing accomplice in this anti-competitive game.[182]

Refusals to license. Those who advocate a purely formal approach to the immunity question would see rights owners as being perfectly entitled to refuse their competitors access to the technology or products covered by the rights. Indeed, they would say, an intellectual property right carries with it no inherent obligation to exploit the right at all except to the extent that statute expressly commands otherwise.[183] An empirical approach would see things rather differently. Empiricists would acknowledge the possibility (although they would disagree about the likelihood) that rights holders might, in cases of limited substitutability and high barriers to entry, possess sufficient market power to raise competition questions about their refusal to allow access to the product or service in question. Neoclassicists might opine that such cases would be rare,[184] but they would have no empirical reason to believe that the line between action and inaction would be the factual case breaker.

---

[181] Eagles, n. 129 above, 30.

[182] *Ibid.*

[183] For examples of such express prohibitions, see text accompanying n. 199 below.

[184] Generally speaking, neoclassicists are blasé about most forms of unilateral action by supposedly dominant firms unless they involve output restrictions of some kind. See the dissenting judgment of Easterbrook J in *Fishman* v. *Estate of Wirtz*, 807 F 2d 520, 566 ff (7th Cir. 1986).

Horizontal and vertical arrangements. Most schools of economic thought would also agree that collusion between actual or potential competitors poses special dangers for the competitive process.[185] For them it is the effect of the arrangement which should count, not its formal terms.[186] (Even neo-classicists are prepared to concede that an apparently vertical arrangement may be used to facilitate or disguise a horizontal price fixing or output reducing cartel.)[187] An economic analysis would never be constrained by the parties' characterisation of an agreement as either horizontal or vertical.

Formalists, on the other hand, would deliberately close their eyes to such considerations. For example, they would characterise cross-licences between competitors as two parallel vertical arrangements, each of which is entirely within the scope of the parent right. They would similarly see collective enforcement of individual copyrights through collecting societies as a multiplicity of vertical arrangements, each one of which would pass a "but for" test on its own.

Power within and across markets. An empirically based analysis accepts that power in one market can be levered into other markets. It makes no difference to this analysis whether the "lever" is an intellectual property right or some other form of commercial advantage. Nor does it matter how many pairs of hands are needed to operate the lever. The alleged possessor of market power may act alone or with (or through) others. An empiricist can even envisage the possibility that lack of close substitutes for the good or service protected by the right may require compulsory licensing of the good or service itself. There is nothing significant, much less sacrosanct about the boundaries of the right. To a formalist all of these things matter very much indeed. Intellectual property rights confer power only within the markets for the good or service protected by the right, but within that market the exercise of that power is not to be questioned.

(b) Extending Rights is Presumptively Bad for Competition

The flip side (if not quite its mirror image) of the "love my right, love my licence" approach is the equally suspect attitude which for a long time prevailed among judges[188] and antitrust regulators in the United States, that extending rights was both bad for the competitive process and without any legitimating business purpose. So strongly entrenched did this viewpoint become that

---

[185] Even though there might be considerably less agreement on whether it should be banned outright as a result. (Some neoclassicists would subject even horizontal dealings to a rule of reason analysis.) Neoclassicsts tend to focus on loss of economic efficiency through cartelisation of outputs and raised prices. They are also sceptical about the long-term durability of cartels, as we have seen.

[186] *US Guidelines*, n. 89 above, § 3.1.

[187] Such cartels are as often between licensees as licensors.

[188] See, e.g., *International Salt Company* v. *United States*, 332 US 392 (1947) (patent tie-in); *Siegel* v. *Chicken Delight*, 448 F 2d, 43 (9th Cir. 1971) (trade mark tie-in); *United States* v. *Line Material Corp*, 333 US 287 (1948) (cross-licence of patents); *United States* v. *Arnold Schwinn and Co*, 388 US 365 (1967) (exclusive territories).

intellectual property owners who stepped even the shortest distance outside the
bounds of their right were either held presumptively liable under antitrust law
or found to have rendered their right unenforceable under an interpretation of
the intellectual property statute which was both purposive and restrictive. (The
misuse of right doctrine is discussed below.) Both methodologies were manifestations of the erroneous conflation of legal and economic monopoly criticised
earlier.[189] Extending the former was thought automatically to extend the latter.[190] Whatever its origins, the doctrine came to be used to impose *per se* liability for some licensing practices and reverse the onus of proof for others. The
high water mark of the presumed illegality approach was the formulation of a
black list of putatively unlawful intellectual property licensing practices issued
by the Anti Trust Division of the US Department of Justice and its sister regulator, The Federal Trade Commission, a list jocularly known by its framers as the
Nine No No's.[191]

Fortunately for the intellectual coherence of United States antitrust law, this
prescriptive approach was first eroded by the courts,[192] then abandoned by the
regulator.[193] Unfortunately, the Nine No No's lasted long enough to sear themselves into the collective memory of rights owners. They now use them to
frighten legislators (and sometimes themselves) with the terrifying prospect that
these bad old ways may some day return from the dead unless warned off by
statutory exemptions, even in jurisdictions where the Nine No No's never held
sway.[194] Once again, this is to shift the debate sideways. All competition
regimes contain some *per se* rules, whether statutory, judge-made or the product of administrative discretion. Disputes there may be as to which types of business behaviour are heinous enough to forego any inquiry into anti-competitive
effect or purpose, but these are disputes about the shape of the competition
regime as a whole, not just as it relates to intellectual property. The only point
of importance to be made here is that if a particular jurisdiction does think it
necessary to enact special provisions relating to intellectual property then it is
important such provisions should march in step with that regime's *per se* rules
whatever these may be.

---

[189]   *Motion Picture Patents Co* v. *Universal Films*, 243 US 502 (1917).
[190]   *Siegel* v. *Chicken Delight*, 448 F 2d 43, 56 (9th Cir. 1971).
[191]   The list of purportedly deviant practices reads: (i) royalties not reasonably related to sales of
the protected products or service; (ii) restraints on licensees' activities outside the scope of the right
(tie-outs); (iii) requiring the licensee to purchase unpatented materials from the licensor (tie-ins); (iv)
mandatory package licensing; (v) requiring the licensee to assign to the patentee other patents that
might be issued to the licensee after the licensing arrangement was in place; (vi) licensee veto power
over grants of further licences; (vii) restraints on sales of unpatented products made with a patented
process; (viii) post-sale restraint on resale; and (ix) setting minimum prices on resale of the patent
products. Not all of the Nine No No's were accurate reflections of prior case law.
[192]   *Continental TV, Inc.* v. *GTE Sylvania*, 433 US 36 (1977); *Broadcast Music, Inc.* v. *Columbia
Broadcasting System*, 441 US 1 (1979).
[193]   *US Guidelines*, n. 89 above.
[194]   For some examples, see the *NCC Final Report*, n. 171 above, 241.

(v) Delicate Flower versus Voracious Monster

Very few intellectual property lawyers would recognise their discipline in the expansionist juggernaut depicted in the introduction to this chapter. They are much more likely to see it as a species of delicate, shade-dwelling pot plant which will wilt and die if taken out into the full sunlight of competition litigation. *This* property is different from other property, they say. Creative and innovative outputs are simply more vulnerable to misappropriation by competitors than more mundane physical assets. This is because the costs of creativity and innovation will always be far higher than the costs of imitation and copying. It is the law's role, these defenders assert, artificially to inflate the cost of the latter activities by restricting free riding in any form, and it is both irrational and artificial for the legal system simultaneously to pursue the goal of driving those costs down through the competitive process.[195] Seen from this skewed vantage point, the expansionist push of intellectual property law reflects weakness, not strength.

These arguments are open to objection on several fronts. The first is empirical. Vulnerability cannot be assumed in every case. It must be demonstrated. Such studies as do exist suggest that technological leads are not as easily lost as one might expect, even when unprotected by patents.[196]

The second objection is that even if intellectual property is vulnerable it is not uniquely so. Urban views and extraction rights (for example, as in fishing or hunting quotas) can be just as casually taken or destroyed and yet are not generally thought to be candidates for immunity from competition scrutiny. The same seems to apply to accounting systems or marketing methods which in many jurisdictions do not even have the advantage of intellectual property protection in the first place.

The third objection to the vulnerability thesis is that (once again) it conflates legal protection and market power, by equating zero immunity with full liability. In most situations, this will not be the case, as we have seen.[197]

The fourth objection is that it is not the role of the law to guarantee anyone a particular return on investment in the form of super or monopoly profits. The

---

[195] It is sometimes sought to give this particular argument an air of economic sophistication by expressing it in terms of marginal cost. Marginal costs of production are those costs attributable to making one more copy of the protected article after the first article has been made. Intellectual property, it is said, exists precisely to allow rights owners to charge prices above marginal costs. See the submissions of the Australian Copyright Council and Telstra to the Australian National Competition Council, NCC *Final Report*, n. 171 above, 161–2.

[196] E.W. Kitch, "The Law and Economics of Rights in Valuable Information" (1980) 9 *J Leg Stud* 683, 711 ff.

[197] The marginal cost argument also falls at this particular hurdle. Effective competition may require prices close to marginal cost when dealing with some products (usually tangibles). In other cases (particularly those involving network effects), competition law can accommodate pricing above marginal cost. The latter is not an objective of the competitive process, simply a by-product: submission of A. Van Melle to NCC *Final Report*, n. 171 above, 163.

role of the law is to protect the right from everything except anti-competitive use and then let the market decide the return.

C Competing Methodologies: A Trans-jurisdictional Overview

Most of the world's competition regimes acknowledge the existence of intellectual property in some way or other, even if only to reiterate that it requires no special treatment. Some do more than this, erecting statutory sanctuaries of greater or lesser completeness or directing rights owners to the shelter of discretionary safe harbours. Very occasionally a practice involving intellectual property will face direct legislative proscription. More usually, the disliked practice will be invisibly subsumed within a wider *per se* rule of general application which is then denied whatever immunity the regime in question sees fit to bestow.

What follows is an evaluation in general terms of the effectiveness of these methodologies in reconciling the conflicting objectives of intellectual property and competition law. It is not a jurisdiction by jurisdiction account of the finer details of individual interfaces.

(i) Mini Regulation Within the Intellectual Property Statute

Some intellectual property statutes overtly seek to incorporate competition values. In other cases, the statute will set up a regulatory scheme for some types of collective enforcement of the right which by implication involves some kind of competition assessment. These mechanisms usually predate the advent of competition law in the jurisdiction in question, and are often ineffective even within their own limited (and usually unstated) objectives.

(a) Compulsory Licensing Provisions

Despite a world-wide trend against compulsory licences,[198] these can still be obtained under patent[199] and design[200] laws of various countries where the right owner refuses to license at all, or will only license on unreasonable terms. Usually the applicant has to show that the design or patent is not being worked within the jurisdiction, or the market is being supplied from outside the country on unreasonable terms. The licences generally are subject to an array of onerous conditions which make them deeply unattractive to recipients.[201]

---

[198] TRIPS, Art. 31, restricts the granting of compulsory licences in various ways. Applications for such licences must be (i) considered individually and (ii) preceded by attempts to negotiate a voluntary licence, (iii) reviewable when market circumstances change, and (iv) subject to appropriate remuneration for the licensor.

[199] Patents Act 1977 (UK), s. 48; Patents Act 1953 (NZ), s. 46. See also Plant Varieties Act 1973 (NZ), s. 23.

[200] Registered Designs Act 1949 (UK), s. 10; Designs Act 1953 (NZ), s. 14.

[201] Eagles, n. 129 above, 59.

(b) Collective Licensing Schemes under Copyright Law

Copyright licences and licences of performers' rights are not uncommonly administered by collecting agencies on behalf of dispersed groups of rights holders. In jurisdictions such as the United Kingdom and New Zealand, such schemes are subject to confirmation and variation by a specialist tribunal at the behest of actual or would-be licensees.[202] The tests applied by such bodies are those of reasonableness and non-discrimination and they tend to focus on the interests of stakeholders represented before them rather than on the impact of those stakeholders' actions on the competitive process itself. Whether and to what extent this form of mini-regulation is subject to ordinary competition law is seldom made clear.

(c) Avoidance of Particular Tie-ins

Patent legislation in some jurisdictions allows the courts to strike down clauses in patent licences which seek to compel licensees to obtain spare parts, machinery or raw materials from the licensor or its nominee in respect of activities not covered by the patent.[203] These provisions have been restrictively interpreted and operate only by way of a defence to infringement.[204] They cannot be invoked by competitors.[205]

(ii) Abuse of Rights Doctrine

In the United States, a separate, but in some senses parallel, body of jurisprudence has grown up alongside the antitrust laws. This is the doctrine known as copyright or patent misuse. It is a much criticised principle of wide application and uncertain provenance,[206] which allows courts to refuse to enforce licensing arrangements which are thought to undermine the purpose for which the intellectual property statute in question was enacted.

The abuse of rights approach used in patent cases has generally tracked that adopted in antitrust proceedings,[207] but with something of a time lag. Indeed, misuse of patent doctrine is said by some to be yesterday's antitrust law, one with an alarming (to right owners at least) resemblance to the Nine No No's.[208] Courts have sometimes allowed the defence to succeed, whether or not there is any proof that the patent confers market power.[209] Nor have they always insisted on a

---

[202] Copyright, Designs and Patents Act 1988 (UK), Pt I, Ch 8; Copyright Act 1994 (NZ), ss. 205–224.

[203] Patents Act 1977 (UK), s. 44, Patents Act 1953 (NZ), s. 66.

[204] See *Tool Metal* v. *Tungsten Electric* (1955) 72 RPC 209, 218.

[205] Eagles, n. 129 above.

[206] It seems to have originated as a remedial "clean hands" bar to injunctive relief.

[207] *Senza Gel Corp.* v. *Seiffhart*, 803 F 2d 661, 670, at n. 14 (Fed. Cir. 1986).

[208] M.A. Lemley, "The Economic Irrationality of the Patent Misuse Doctrine" (1990) 78 *Calif L Rev* 1599.

[209] *Noll* v. *O.M. Scott and Sons*, 467 F 2d 295, 301 (6th Cir. 1972); *Berlenbach* v. *Anderson Thompson Ski Co*, 329 F 2d 782, 784 (9th Cir. 1964); *Transition Elec. Corp.* v. *Hughes Aircraft Corp.*,

showing of harm to the competitive process.[210] More importantly, patent misuse is an all or nothing defence which is incapable of adjusting the offending clause to ensure competitively neutral outcomes. The doctrine has been likened to a court-run scheme of royalty free licences for infringers.[211]

In copyright misuse cases, the nexus with antitrust principles is more nebulous (or at least has become so in recent years),[212] being chiefly concerned with attempts to expand copyright beyond its core concepts by converting it into a patent-like monopoly.[213] Copyright misuse tends to blend into wider copyright doctrines such as fair dealing or the idea/expression dichotomy. For whatever reason, defendants seem less likely to be successful in copyright abuse cases than in patent cases. Despite this low hit rate, the doctrine is still sufficiently alarming to send a frisson of fear through copyright owners.[214]

Commonwealth courts have been much slower to invoke abuse of rights theories, at least in cases involving intellectual property. In these jurisdictions, its use appears to be confined to two limited situations. The first involves mostly unsuccessful attempts to invoke the so-called spare parts rule enunciated by the House of Lords in *British Leyland Motor Corp.* v. *Armstrong Patents Ltd.*[215] The second concerns isolated refusal to protect business confidences where potential breaches of competition law are said to be involved. The former has been outflanked, at least on its United Kingdom home ground, partly because of the detour provided by the Treaty of Rome[216] and partly due to the construction of a statutory bypass.[217] Even in its heyday, the Law Lords' decision found few emulators in other Commonwealth courts,[218] or indeed any application outside

---

487 F Supp. 885, 892 (USDC, Mass., 1980). Cf *Mallinckrodt, Inc.* v. *Medipart, Inc.*, 976 F 2d 700, 708 (Fed. Cir. 1992).

[210] *Senza Gel Corp* v. *Seiffhart*, 803 F 2d 661, 670, at n. 14 (Fed. Cir. 1986). But see *Braun Medical, Inc.* v. *Abbott Laboratories*, 124 F 3d 1419, 1426 (Fed. Cir. 1997). Proof of market power is now legislatively mandated in tying cases: 35 USC § 271(d)(5).

[211] Lemley, n. 208 above, 1618.

[212] M.A. Lemley, "Beyond Pre-emption: The Law and Policy of Intellectual Property Licensing" (1999) 87 *Calif L Rev* 113, 153.

[213] *DSC Communications* v. *DGI Technologies*, 81 F 3d 597, 601 (5th Cir. 1996).

[214] D McGowan, "Regulating Competition in the Information Age: Computer Software as An Essential Facility under the Sherman Act" (1996) 18 *Hastings Comm and Ent L J* 771.

[215] [1986] AC 577. In essence, the rule held that retail purchasers of copyright articles could not be denied access to spare parts for the purpose of effecting adequate repairs. Purchasers also had a right to adequate, competitively priced, repair services. Prior authority for the rule was meagre, the Law Lords relying heavily on a perceived analogy with the "derogation from grant" principle in real property law. For a discussion of the origins and possible applications of the doctrine, see Eagles, n. 129 above, 21 ff.

[216] See *Volvo* v. *Veng* [1988] ECR 621. The *Volvo* case involved a refusal to license a competitor to produce car body panels. Since it was a clear case of leverage across markets it sits rather uneasily with the later decision of the European Court in *Radio Telefis Eirean and Independent Television Publications* v. *European Commission and Magill* [1995] 4 CMLR 718.

[217] The intricate provision for unregistered design rights in the Copyright, Designs and Patents Act 1988 (UK), and the removal of copyright protection for most industrial designs, leave little room for the application of the spare parts rule.

[218] See *Mono Pumps (New Zealand) Ltd* v. *Karinya Industries* (1986) 7 IPR 25; and *Dennison Manufacturing Co* v. *Alfred Holt & Co Ltd* (1987) 10 IPR 612.

the narrow field of indirect copyright protection for mass produced articles.[219]

The general public interest defence to breach of confidence might seem at first sight a more promising form of competition control. Certainly it has been applied in cases where the confidence sought to be protected involved alleged breaches of competition statutes,[220] but its limits are otherwise unclear. It may apply only to intentional breaches, for example, and in some cases appears to operate as an element of the cause of action rather than as a defence.

Whatever their future in particular jurisdictions, abuse of rights doctrines are an undesirable development. The benefits they confer on one group of stakeholders (potential infringers) seem out of proportion to any proven harm to the competitive process. The existence of two sets of related, but on key issues divergent, rules on the American pattern is not reassuring. Judges who are called on to deal with this particular side wind in the course of ordinary infringement proceedings will be doing so without the procedural and evidentary aids more usual in full-blown competition litigation. In particular, the opportunity for input from economists would appear to be limited, at least in jurisdictions outside the United States. Adjectival issues apart, the chief difficulty with the abuse of rights approach is conceptual. It is nothing more than the "right equals market" fallacy writ large.

(iii) Bright Line Exemption Under the Competition Statute

In some Commonwealth jurisdictions, legislatures have been reluctant to leave the development of the competition law/intellectual property interface wholly for judges and regulators to construct. Their response has instead been to enact a very broad exemption for intellectual property in the competition statute and then to temper that exemption by excluding particular kinds of breaches or particular activities from its protective umbrella. This has been the favoured approach in New Zealand, Australia and, to a more limited extent, Canada. In most cases, these provisions were introduced without any great public debate about their scope or intended purpose. They are now coming under greater scrutiny.

While it is dangerous to generalise, these statutory exemptions do all seem to present a similar set of conceptual ailments, even where their provisions differ in detail.

(a) Legislated Formalism

None of these bright line rules requires any kind of market analysis. All use the boundaries of the right to map out the activities which are to be exempt using

---

[219] The spare parts rule never applied to "true" monopolies such as patents and registered designs. In such cases, buyers had to fall back on attempts to persuade the court that there was an implied licence to effect repairs: see *Solar Thompson Engineering Co* v. *Barton* [1997] RPC 537. Such attempts were easily rebuffed by exclusionary notices.

[220] *Initial Services Ltd* v. *Putterill* [1968] 1 QB 396; *Allied Mills Industrial* v. *TPC* (1981) 34 ALR 105.

some variant of the "scope of grant" principle. The New Zealand provision is the most clearly, but also the most restrictively, worded, a "but for" test enacted into law.[221] Its Australian counterpart is more ambiguous, requiring only that the dealings specified[222] as exempt should "relate" to the subject matter protected by the right, a connection so imprecise[223] as to defy interpretation. Such authority as there is appears to have settled on the middle ground of "why me".[224] (A similar position appears to obtain under the Canadian legislation.)[225]

(b) Unprotected Rights

The exemptions apply only to rights which are both proprietary[226] and wholly creatures of statute.[227] This appears to represent a conscious choice,[228] no doubt reflecting the view that a "scope of grant" approach requires clear boundaries. This may be an overly optimistic assumption. (It is not immediately obvious for example that the boundaries of copyright are more tightly drawn than those of passing off or breach of confidence.)[229]

(c) Excluded Acts

Not every potential breach of the competition statute is protected by these exemptions. Sometimes this is expressly indicated. On other occasions, it has to be inferred from the statutory language used to link right and protected activity.

Price Restrictions. Acts which contravene the competition statute's *per se* prohibitions against resale price maintenance are expressly placed beyond the reach

---

[221] S. 45(1) of the Commerce Act 1986 (NZ) provides that most (but not all) of the Act's operative provisions shall not apply:
"(a) To the entering into of a contract or arrangement or arriving at an understanding in so far as it contains a provision authorising any act that would otherwise be prohibited by reason of the existence of a statutory intellectual property right; or
(b) To any act done to give effect to a provision of a contract, arrangement, or understanding referred to in paragraph (a) of this subsection."

[222] The exemption applies to both licences and assignments (including the assignment of the right to apply for registration in the case of patents or registered designs): see Trade Practices Act 1974 (Cth), s. 51(3).

[223] It is somewhat surprising in that the NCC should have deliberately chosen to retain "relate to" as its legislative lynch pin. Almost any other form of words would be capable of shedding more light on the subject: see NCC *Final Report*, n. 171 above, 216.

[224] *Transfield Pty Ltd* v. *Arlo International Ltd* (1980) 144 CLR 83.

[225] Competition Act, RSC 1985 c C–34, s. 79(5).

[226] These do not protect those aspects of intellectual property which are sustained only by fair trading and consumer protection statutes.

[227] The New Zealand exemption applies to patents, registered designs, trade marks, copyright, layout designs and plant varieties: see Commerce Act, s. 45(2). The omission from the Australian statute of plant breeders' rights and service marks seems to be a historical accident rather than a deliberate policy choice: see Trade Practices Act 1974, s. 51(3). The NCC has recommended that both be included: NCC *Final Report*, n. 171 above, 11.

[228] Prior to its amendment in 1990, the New Zealand provision, thanks largely to some whimsical punctuation, arguably protected unregistered trade marks as well: see Eagles, n. 129 above, 37 ff.

[229] The New Zealand statute may protect breach of confidence through the back door: see Commerce Act 1986, s. 7(2) and discussion in Eagles, n. 129 above, 40.

of the Australian and New Zealand exemptions. The statutes are silent on the effect of other forms of price restriction. They thus appear to exempt even arrangements between competitors, provided these are formally within the scope of the parent right. (This may not have been an intended result in either jurisdiction. It appears to be wholly attributable to the drafting oddity in the Australian and New Zealand legislation which *deems* horizontal price fixing to be anti-competitive for the purposes of the legislation's general prohibition against anti-competitive dealings, rather than constituting it as a separate head of liability.)[230]

Form and substance. These bright line exemptions do not distinguish between horizontal or vertical arrangements. Both are protected. Conversely, the exemptions may (and in the New Zealand case certainly do) differentiate between positive and negative stipulations. These distinctions serve no policy purpose. They are simply drafting lapses. Immunity is made to depend on the form of the arrangement. The court cannot go behind it to get at its substance.[231]

Unilateral exercises of market power and accumulation of rights. Here the jurisdictions diverge markedly. The New Zealand statute provides somewhat obscurely that rights owners do not attract liability under its use of a dominant position rule "by reason only" of seeking to enforce one of the exempt rights. Whether this protection is substantive or evidentiary is not clear.[232] The Australian Act is silent on the point, leaving one to infer that misuse of market power is not exempt.[233] Gathering rights or licences into the hands of a single owner, on the other hand, is subject to full regulatory scrutiny in both jurisdictions under ordinary business acquisition rules. Once again, if a policy point is being made here it is not easy to discern what it might be.

(iv) Guidelines and Safe Harbours

Jurisdictions which exempt by statute do not usually see a need to supplement that exemption through the use of explanatory briefings.[234] Among common law countries, only the United States uses this particular methodology to

---

[230] Commerce Act 1986 (NZ), s. 30; Trade Practices Act 1974 (Cth), s. 45A.

[231] Eagles, n. 129 above, 42.

[232] Commerce Act 1986 (NZ), ss 36(2) and 36A(2). I have argued elsewhere that s. 36(2) merely prevents the court from drawing an adverse inference from the mere fact of enforcement or threatened enforcement. Liability under s. 36(1) would still attach if there were direct evidence of a prohibited purpose: see Eagles, n. 129 above, 51 ff. For a strongly argued contrary view, see D.C. Calhoun and B.W.F. Brown, "New Zealand: Interface Between Misuse of a Document Position and the Exercise of IP Rights" [1990] *EIPR* 437.

[233] One could still mount a "scope of right" argument here, i.e., that exercising one's intellectual property rights did not amount to "taking advantage" of whatever market power the right conferred in terms of s. 46 of the Trade Practices Act 1994 (Cth).

[234] This may be mistaken. Given that the exemptions cover only part of the field, there is arguably room for guidance in relation to non-exempt matters.

construct a significant part of the interface in the form of intellectual property specific guidelines. While the result is a useful pointer to changes in approach within the regulatory agencies concerned one would be hard put to see in the current US *Guidelines* anything like a comprehensive safe harbour along the lines of the European Union's block exemption.[235] In setting up their safety zones, the US regulators make no real attempt to speak to rights owners *qua* owners.[236] The *Guidelines*-indicated danger zones on the other hand, while intellectual property specific, add little to pre-existing case law.[237] While all this is harmless enough, some of the attitudes revealed in the *Guidelines* are more worrying. Of particular concern are statements that intellectual property licensing is "generally" pro-competitive, and that intellectual property rights are especially "vulnerable to misappropriation", propositions left hanging in an empirical vacuum. They are also hard to square with the *Guidelines'* overall insistence that intellectual property and other forms of property should be treated equally for competition purposes, an objective which would perhaps be better served by administrative rulings of a more general application.

V CONCLUSION: THE CASE FOR NEUTRALITY

Two themes emerge from this chapter. The first is that intellectual property is not some static body of rules whose accommodation with competition law is to be achieved through some once and for all black letter fix. From the point of view of those whose task it is to set the parameters of competition policy, intellectual property is a constantly moving target, one with which they themselves have to move if intellectual property lawyers are not constantly to set the terms

---

[235] Technology Transfer Block Exemption 1996 No 240/96. The block exemption proceeds by way of a white list of permitted practices, a black list of definitely non-exempt (but not necessarily unlawful) practices, and a grey list of practices whose presence in an agreement does not defeat its exemption on other grounds. The White List (Art. 1) includes exclusive licences and territorial restrictions associated with technology transfer that are limited to the life of the intellectual property (or 10 years in the case of pure know-how agreements). The Grey List (Art. 2) includes obligations to keep know-how secret, not to grant sublicences, to terminate agreements where licensees challenge the validity of the licensor's intellectual property rights, and to use best endeavours to manufacture and market the licensed product. The Black List (Art. 3) includes restrictions on the selling prices of licensed products (resale price maintenance), restrictions on the quantities to be made or sold, bans on competing technologies, customer restrictions between competing manufacturers, obligations to grant-back improvements, and territorial restrictions for a duration longer than as provided under the White List. The effect of all this is not as clear-cut as it seems. The benefit of the exemption may be withdrawn if the activity in question is shown to be anti-competitive in fact (Art. 7). The regulator (DG IV) also warns that it will apply American-style market share tests in deciding on such withdrawals. The block exemption does not apply to breaches of Art. 82 EC (ex Art. 86) misuse of a dominant purpose provision. The provisions of the block exemption are picked up by the Competition Act 1998 (UK).

[236] The zones are defined by participants market share or the number of competitors.

[237] The practices listed as being likely to lead to agency action are: licensors seeking to fix minimum resale prices, market sharing agreements, agreements to reduce output, some collective boycotts.

of the debate. For regulators and legislators, this requires that the competition voice be heard whenever rights owners seek a statutory boost to their rights. Competition values have to be part of the process of intellectual property law reform. Judges, too, need to be aware that not every unprotected interest needs protecting and that economic analysis has much to say that is useful when plaintiffs urge them to extend old rights or create new ones. Both are issues for the longer term.

The second theme is more immediate. It is that from a competition perspective there is nothing unique about intellectual property. It is simply one mechanism among many which may be used to sustain or deflect market power and should be treated as such. If there is a case to be made for directing investment to this particular form of property, and away from other forms of economic activity, competition law is not the appropriate mechanism for effecting that redistribution. In this limited sense, investment displacement theorists have got it right. Bright line exemptions and abuse of rights rules bring nothing useful to this debate. At best, their efficacy depends on assumptions about the cost of compliance which are as yet unsupported. At worst, they threaten to derail the debate entirely by reducing it to a forensic free for all in which plaintiff and defendants tussle for wholly undeserved advantages. They are better avoided.

ADDENDUM

Intellectual property minders in the United States have suffered a mild legislative rebuff since this chapter went to proof. Proposals to insert a new Article 2B in the Uniform Commercial Code will not now proceed. Rights-owners must instead content themselves with stand-alone initiatives contained in the Uniform Computer Information Transactions Act 1999 (UCITA) now wending its way through State legislatures. The retreat is, however, more tactical than strategic, more about methodology than outcomes. UCITA would still elide sale and license by conferring copyright-like protection on digitally accessed facts while simultaneously bypassing long standing defences to copyright infringement. The contractual road to expansion is only marginally less trafficked as a result.

Index